Exploring the APPALACHIAN TRAIL™

THE SERIES

HIKES IN THE SOUTHERN APPALACHIANS

Georgia ◆ North Carolina ◆ Tennessee

HIKES IN THE VIRGINIAS

Virginia ◆ West Virginia

HIKES IN THE MID-ATLANTIC STATES

Maryland ◆ Pennsylvania ◆ New Jersey ◆ New York

HIKES IN SOUTHERN NEW ENGLAND

Connecticut ◆ Massachusetts ◆ Vermont

HIKES IN NORTHERN NEW ENGLAND

New Hampshire ◆ Maine

Exploring the APPALACHIAN TRAIL

HIKES in NORTHERN NEW ENGLAND

New Hampshire Maine

MICHAEL KODAS

MARK CONDON, GLENN SCHERER, ANDREW WEEGAR

STACKPOLE BOOKS

Mechanicsburg, Pennsylvania

A Word of Caution
Readers are advised that trail conditions and locations change frequently due to both natural factors (e.g., erosion) and legal factors (e.g., National Park Service real estate acquisitions). Information in this volume was as accurate as the authors could make it at the time of printing. However, readers should check with their local Appalachian Trail hiking clubs (see "Useful Information") for updated information. Readers are also advised that hiking involves some risk of accident and exposure to potentially harmful weather, animals, or impure water. Precautions are advised here under "Hiking: The Basics," and the reader uses this guide at his or her own risk. The publisher assumes no liability.

Exploring the Appalachian Trail™ Series Concept: David Emblidge
Series Editor: David Emblidge
Volume Editors: Katherine Ness, David Emblidge
Assistant Editor: Marcy Ross
Book design and cover design: Walter Schwarz, of Figaro, Inc.
Page make-up: Creative Services, Stackpole Books
Cartography: Peter Jensen, of OpenSpace (trail drawing) and trail profiles using Maptech's TopoScout® CD-ROMs
Cover photograph: White Mts., N.H., by Henry Lafleur
Page viii: photograph by David Emblidge
Page xii: photograph of Springer Mt. AT plaque (southern terminus) by Doris Gove
Interior photographs: See credits with each image.

Library of Congress Cataloging-in-Publication Data

Hikes in northern New England / Michael Kodas [et al.].—1st ed.
a. cm.– (Exploring the Appalachian Trail)
ISBN 0-8117-2667-3
1. Hiking—New Hampshire—Guidebooks. 2. Hiking—Maine—Guidebooks. 3. Hiking—Appalachian Trail—Guidebooks. 4. New Hampshire—Guidebooks. 5. Maine—Guidebooks.
2. Appalachian Trail—Guidebooks. I. Kodas, Michael. II. Series.
GV199.42.N4H55 1999
917.404'43—dc21 97—50084
CIP

Printed in the United States
10 9 8 7 6 5 4 3 2 1

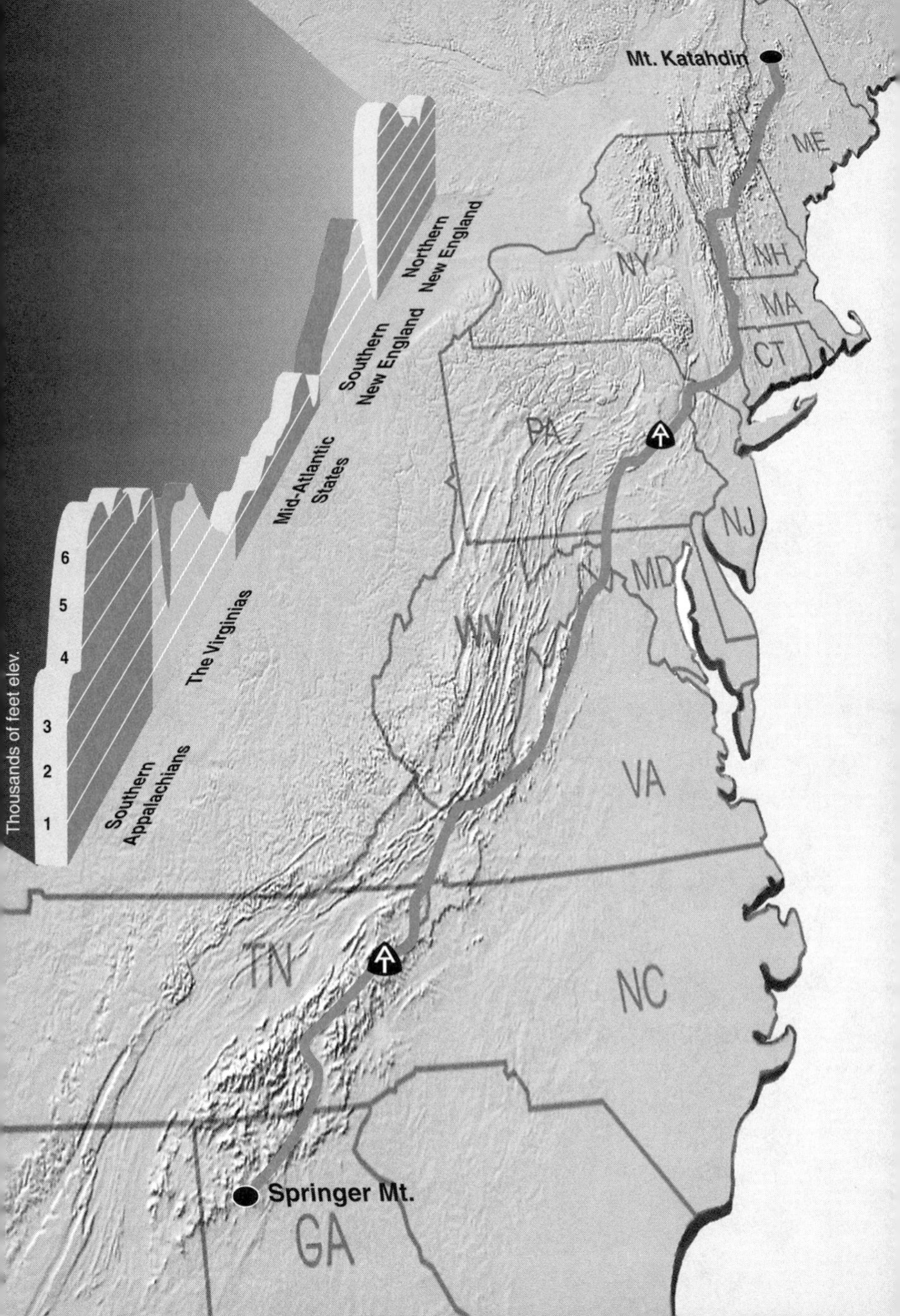

Mt. Katahdin
ME
VT
NH
NY
MA
CT
PA
NJ
MD
VA
TN
NC
Springer Mt.
GA
Thousands of feet elev.
6
5
4
3
2
1
Northern New England
Southern New England
Mid-Atlantic States
The Virginias
Southern Appalachians

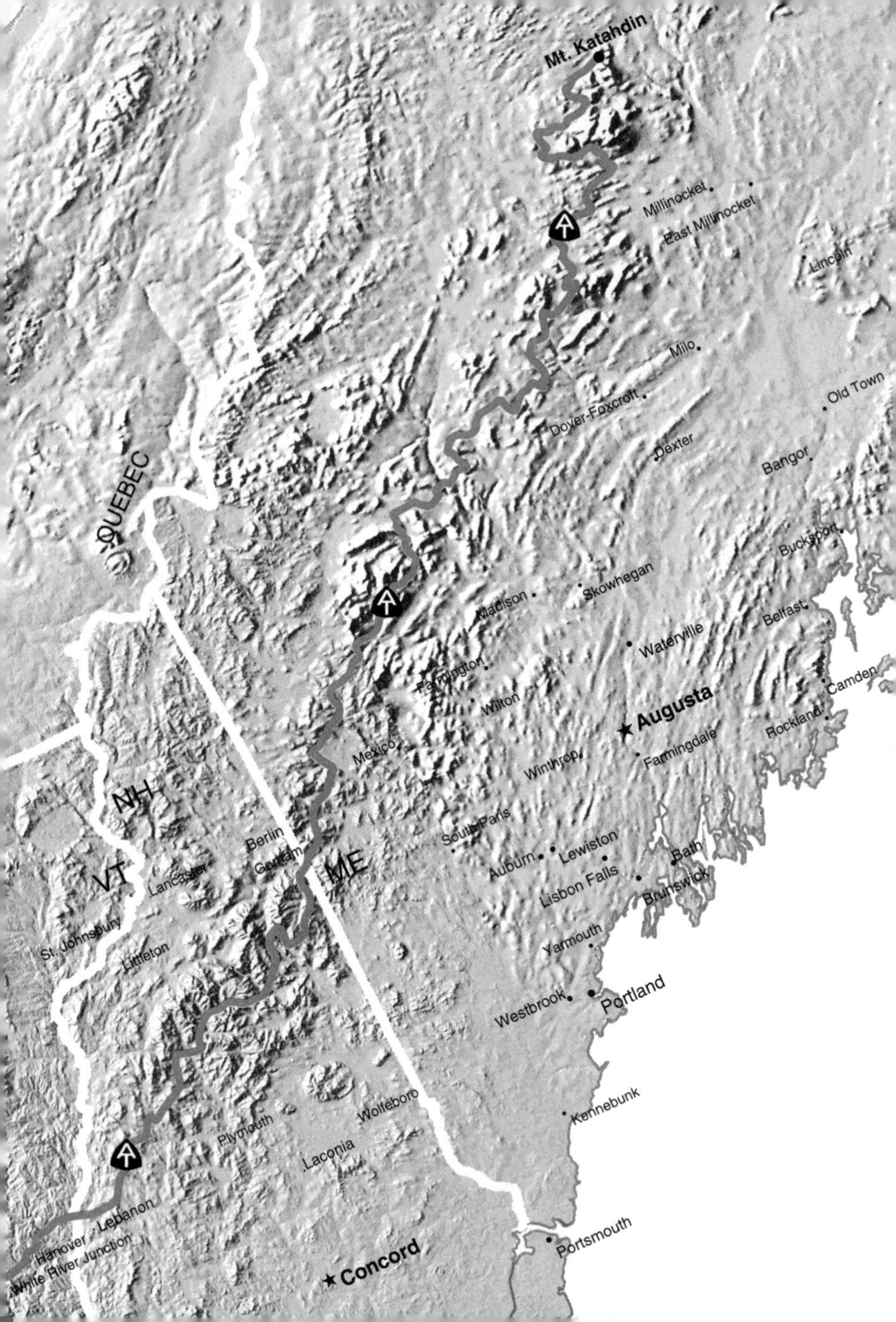

Mt. Katahdin
Millinocket
East Millinocket
Lincoln
Milo
Dover-Foxcroft
Old Town
Dexter
Bangor
QUEBEC
Bucksport
Skowhegan
Madison
Belfast
Waterville
Farmington
Wilton
Camden
Augusta
Rockland
Mexico
Winthrop
Farmingdale
NH
South Paris
Berlin
Gorham
Auburn
Lewiston
Bath
VT
Lancaster
ME
Lisbon Falls
Brunswick
St. Johnsbury
Littleton
Yarmouth
Westbrook
Portland
Kennebunk
Wolfeboro
Plymouth
Laconia
Lebanon
Hanover
White River Junction
Portsmouth
Concord

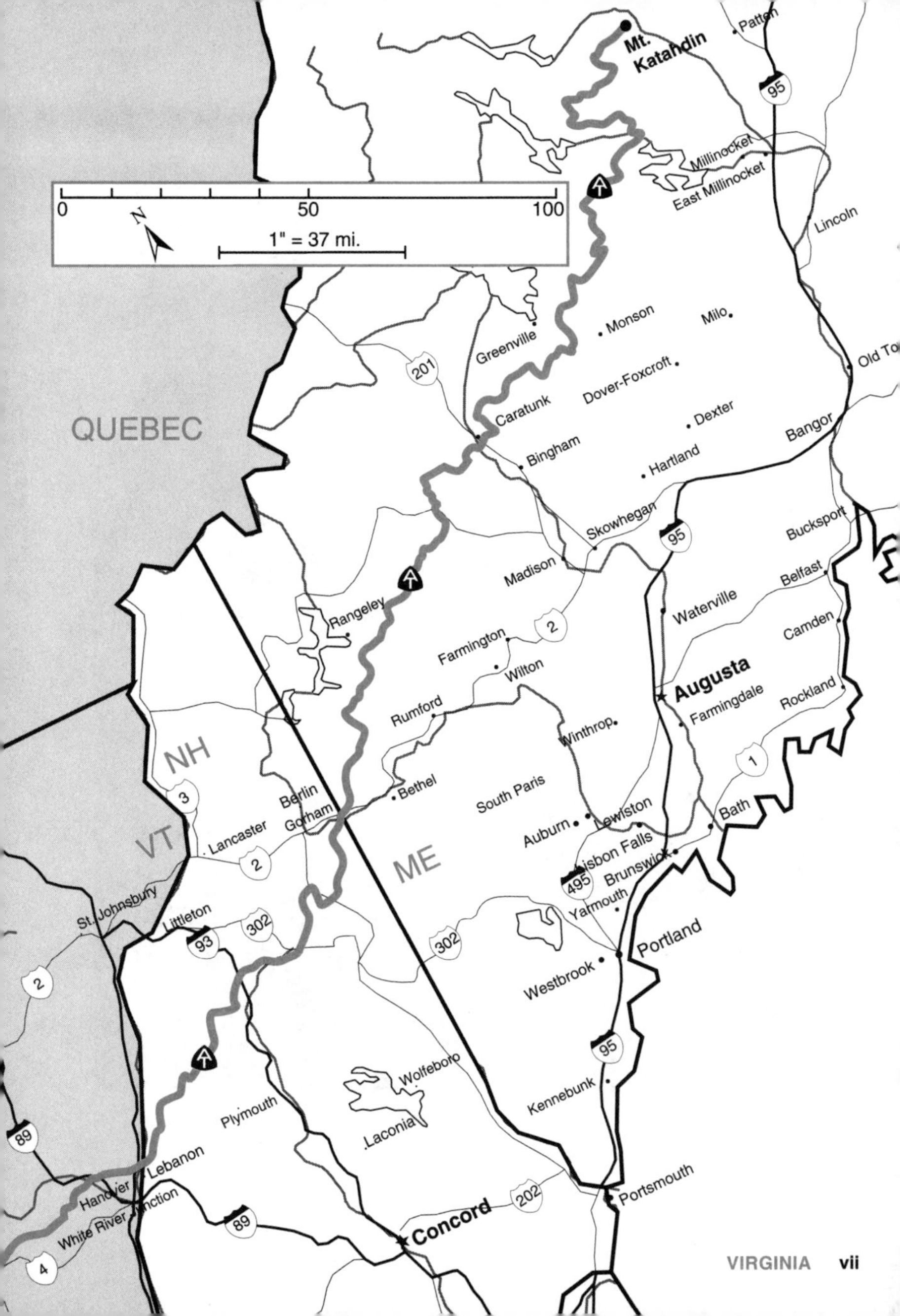
Mt. Katahdin
Patten
95
Millinocket
East Millinocket
Lincoln
0
50
100
N
1" = 37 mi.
Greenville
Monson
Milo
Old To
201
Dover-Foxcroft
QUEBEC
Caratunk
Dexter
Bangor
Bingham
Hartland
Skowhegan
Bucksport
Madison
Belfast
Rangeley
Waterville
2
Camden
Farmington
Wilton
Augusta
Rockland
Rumford
Farmingdale
Winthrop
NH
1
3
Bethel
South Paris
Berlin
Gorham
Lewiston
Bath
Auburn
Lancaster
VT
ME
Lisbon Falls
Brunswick
495
St. Johnsbury
Yarmouth
Littleton
302
93
Portland
Westbrook
Wolfeboro
Kennebunk
Plymouth
Laconia
89
Lebanon
Portsmouth
Hanover
White River Junction
202
Concord
4

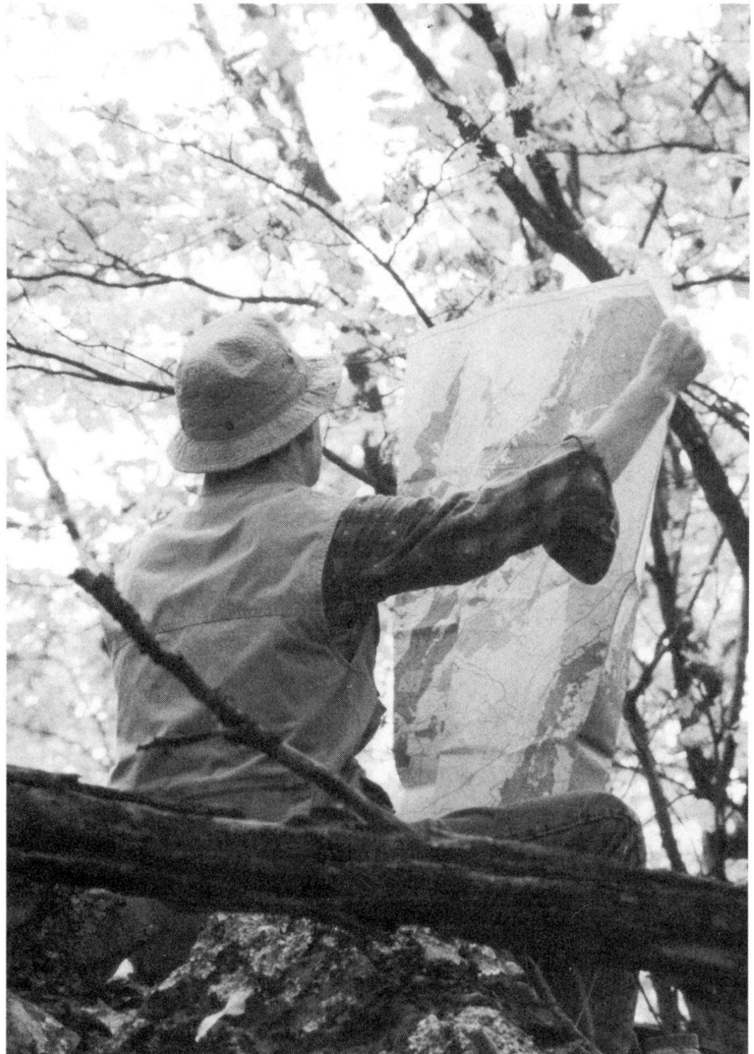

Contents

New Hampshire

Maine

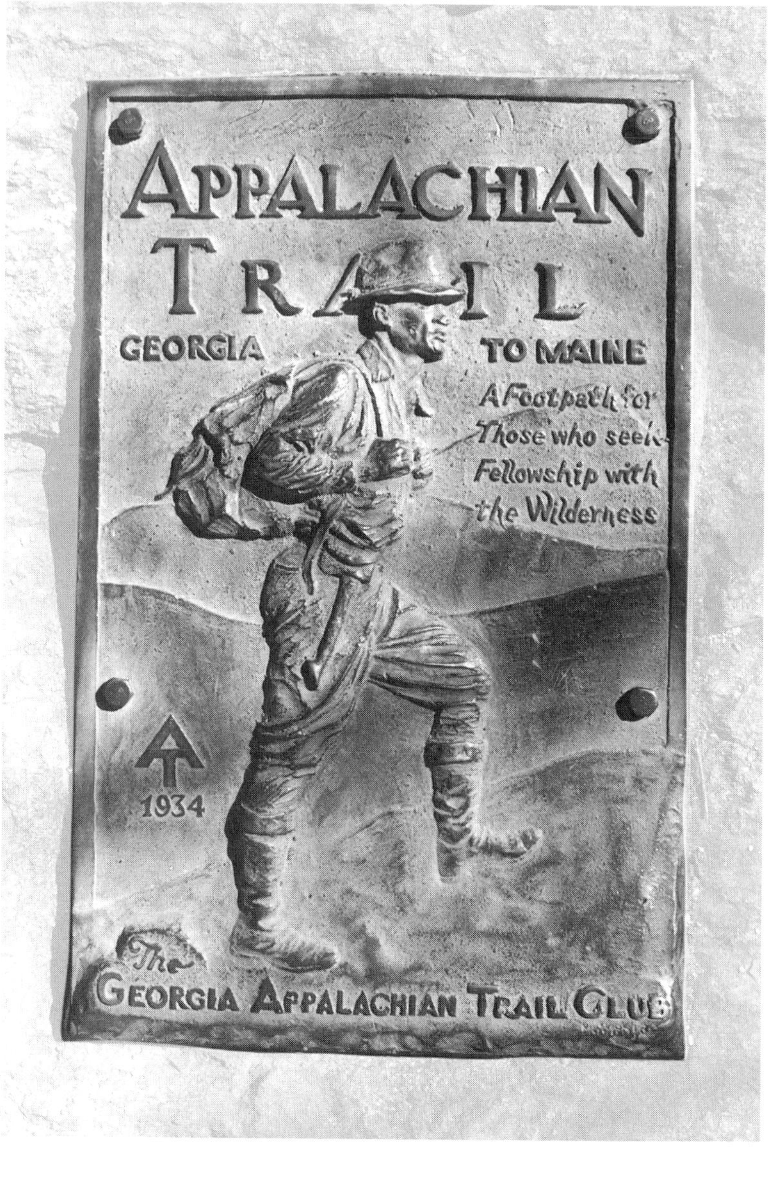

APPALACHIAN
TRAIL

GEORGIA TO MAINE

A Footpath for
Those who seek
Fellowship with
the Wilderness

1934

The
GEORGIA APPALACHIAN TRAIL CLUB

Introduction

Welcome to *Exploring the Appalachian Trail.* We're glad to have you join us for what promises to be a fine outdoor adventure.

Michael Kodas was the lead author for this volume, and covered New Hampshire and the Mahoosucs (Hikes #1 through 19). Glenn Scherer (who also wrote part of Volume 3: Mid-Atlantic States) covered Maine's 100-Mile Wilderness (Hikes #31 through 36). Andrew Weegar and David Emblidge (Hikes #20, 22, 24, 26, 28, 29, 38), and Mark Condon (Hikes #21, 23, 25, 27, 30, 37) wrote the remaining Maine hikes.

You may not have realized it when you bought or borrowed this book, but if the truth be told, it's all about a long-standing love affair. The authors of the hiking guides in this series have been in love with the Appalachian Trail since before we can remember. And we've come to believe that if you truly love something, you will probably act positively to protect it. So when we invite you to join us in walking on the trail, we're also inviting you to let yourself be seduced, indeed to go ahead and take the leap into a sweet and enduring love affair of your own. But then be sure to act on the responsibility created as a by-product of that love. It's called service and support. In the section below called "Joining Up," you can read more about how each of us can contribute to the health and continuing life of the trail. The Appalachian Trail will give you many gifts. Be sure you give some back.

Unlike other good books about walking the Appalachian Trail, this one will encourage you to slow down, to yield to the many temptations offered up freely by nature and by the social-historical world along the trail. Benton MacKaye, considered by most to be the chief visionary of the early Appalachian Trail, once defined the purpose of hiking on the AT as "to see, and to see what you see." MacKaye was something of a romantic, and we know he read Emerson, who instructs us all to "Adopt the peace of Nature, her secret is patience." We can't improve on that.

Our intention is to help you plan and carry out a wide variety of hikes on the nation's longest continuously marked footpath, surely one of the most famous walking trails in the world. We'll guide you from point A to point B, to be sure, but as far as this book is concerned, it's what happens for you between points A and B that counts the most.

If the goal of hiking on the Appalachian Trail is to come home refreshed in body, rejuvenated in mind, and renewed in spirit, then along with the fun of being outside in the mountains, a little work will be required. The most obvious work is of the muscular variety. Less obvious but just as rewarding is the mental kind, and it's here that the books in this series will help you the most. The famous world traveler Sven-Olof Lindblad said, "Travel is not about where you've been but what you've gained. True travel is about how you've enriched your life through encounters with beauty, wildness and the seldom-seen."

In these AT hiking books, we'll pause to inspect the rocks underfoot and the giant folding and crunching of the entire Appalachian landscape. We'll take time to listen to birds and to look closely at wildflowers. We will deliberately digress into the social history of the area the AT passes through, thinking sometimes about industry, other times about politics, and now and then about a well-known or an obscure but colorful character who happened to live nearby. We'll explore trail towns and comment on trail shelters and campsites (they're not all alike!). And to help make you a savvy hiker (if you aren't already), we will offer up some choice bits of hiker wisdom that just might get you out of a jam or make your load a bit lighter to carry.

This is a participatory book. You will enjoy it and profit from it most if you carry a small notebook and a pen or pencil, if you bring along a camera and perhaps a birding book or a wildflower guide or a guide to some other aspect of the natural world (see the Bibliography for suggestions). Bring a compass and use our maps, or better yet, supplement the maps in this book with the more detailed ones available from the Appalachian Trail Conference and other local sources (see page 9 and the Bibliography).

Chatting with your walking companions is a delightful thing to do some of the time while out on the trail, but the more noise you make, the less wildlife you'll see, and besides, it's hard for anyone to be both in conversation and simultaneously in close observance of the real details of the natural realm. Try hard to make some part of every hike a silent walk, during which you open all your senses and your imagination to drink in the marvelous environment of the Appalachian Trail.

The Appalachian Trail in Northern New England

The states covered by this book—New Hampshire and Maine—make up what the Exploring the Appalachian Trail series calls "northern New England." The previous volume, Southern New England, covers Vermont, Massachusetts, and Connecticut.

In northern New England the AT ranges from a low of about 500 feet at Antlers Campsite near the northern terminus on Mt. Katahdin to 6288 feet atop the spectacular alpine peak of Mt. Washington. There are about 440 miles of AT in northern New England, divided here into 38 hikes. In the White Mts. of New Hampshire, hundreds of miles of side trails link with the AT to form a vast network of hiking possibilities. The options are more limited in Maine, where fewer side trails access the AT.

The region shows dramatic contrasts in plant and animal life, weather, and degrees of challenge to the hiker. A few of the woodland walks here are benign enough for a toddler, while the abundant mountain climbs are ambitious enough to satisfy the most robust hiker. There are remote wilderness sections where backpackers can spend several days in deep forests and on remote alpine peaks, but there are also areas where regular road crossings make it easy to plan day hikes. The low elevations of New Hampshire's river valleys have rich hardwood forests where sugar maples are tapped for their sweet sap in winter, whereas even high-elevation species like red spruce and balsam fir cannot survive in the fierce weather encountered atop the alpine summits of the White Mts. and Mt. Katahdin. The alpine flowers, like diapensia and Lapland rosebay, found atop these summits are normally seen in the Arctic, hundreds of miles to the north. The AT hiker in northern New England enjoys the opportunity to explore these spectacular alpine summits and vast woodlands as well as several historic "trail towns" where services, supplies, and distractions are readily available. If you have never visited the region, a colorful armchair traveler's introduction awaits you in Northern New England in The Smithsonian Guide to Historic America series.

Joining Up

We urge you, our fellow hikers, to honor the thousands of volunteers and paid workers who built and who nowadays maintain the Appalachian Trail by becoming a volunteer and a financial supporter yourself. Join your local hiking club and join any or all of the following organizations, each of which contributes to the survival of the Appalachian Trail:

Appalachian Trail Conference, P.O. Box 807, Harpers Ferry, WV 25425

Appalachian Mountain Club, 5 Joy St., Boston, MA 02108

American Hiking Society, 1422 Fenwick Lane, Silver Spring, MD 20910

Walking Lightly on the Land

On behalf of the hiking community, we urge all hikers to manage their behavior in the woods and mountains so as to have a minimal impact on the land. The old adages are apt: Take only pictures, leave only footprints. Pack out whatever you pack in. Leave no trace. Indeed, be a sport and pack out some other careless hiker's garbage if you find it along the trail. The National Park Service, which maintains a protective corridor along the Appalachian Trail, estimates that between 3 and 4 million people use the trail every year, and the numbers are growing. In many places the ecology of the AT landscape is fragile. But fragile or not, every one of its 2150 miles is subject to abuse, even if unintended. Leave the trail a better place than you found it, and you'll take home better memories.

NOLS Soft Paths is a good general introduction to the principles of leave-no-trace hiking and camping. See the Bibliography.

We wish you good weather, warm companionship, and a great adventure, be it for 6 hours, 6 days, 6 weeks, or 6 months on the trail. The Appalachian Trail belongs to all of us. Treat it as you would something precious of your very own.

Reader Participation

Readers are invited to respond. Please correct our mistakes, offer your perspectives, tell us what else you'd like to see in the next edition. Please also tell us where you bought or borrowed this book. Write to: Editors, Exploring the Appalachian Trail, Stackpole Books, 5067 Ritter Rd., Mechanicsburg, PA 17055.

Acknowledgments

The authors and editors of each of the volumes in the series have helped strengthen and enrich this book.

Many others have my sincere thanks: Assistant Editor Marcy Ross, for dogged research and map management with good humor; Kathie Ness, Chief Copy Editor, for admirable competence and grace under pressure; Peter Jensen and Kathy Orlando, of OpenSpace Management, for carefully drawing the corrected AT on our maps and profiles; Austin Sass and the employees of Maptech for their assistance in creating the trail profiles; Maptech's TopoScout® CD-ROMs allowed us to create profiles of the AT with detailed accuracy. Thanks also to Letitia Mutter, Indexer, for her efficiency; Barbara Zheutlin, for keyboarding without tears; and Chris Blair for ever-patient computer support. Thanks as well to each photographer. Special thanks to Doris Gove for sharing her sidebars.

Trail clubs provided important assistance. Particular thanks go to Kevin Patterson of the Appalachian Trail Conference, David O. Hooke of the Dartmouth Outing Club, and Carl Demrow of the Appalachian Mountain Club for their advice on trail issues.

Special thanks also to Paul Johnson, Jr. of the Maine Appalachian Trail Club for his careful review of the 100 Mile Wilderness chapters and to Dean Cilley and Rick St. Croix of the MATC for supplying trail information.

Thanks also go to Jim Ecker of the Maine Bureau of Parks and Lands for clarifying road names and crossings; and to Dave Field, AATC Board of Managers Chair, for his generousity in supplying detailed cultural and historical research data.

USE THIS BOOK as you would the counsel of a wise friend. Absorb the information that seems noteworthy to you; take heed of opinionated statements; consider the logic behind suggested strategies for getting into, and through, the kind of hike you want. But remember that your own personal preferences for length of hike, amount of effort, and things to see along the way will be just as important as—or even more than—any information you may find in these pages. Walking and hiking in the forest and mountains are intensely personal activities. There are few rules to follow, and it's not a competitive game with winners and losers. What works well for Hiker A will be a disappointment for Hiker B. This book should indicate that there are many ways to complete and enjoy a hike on the AT.

How Hike Information Is Displayed Here

INFORMATION BLOCK: The hike's first page, a snapshot of the hike in the form of data and directions. Here you'll find road access information, elevation gain, distance to be walked, names of shelters, and so on. This first section gives an objective overview of the hike.

NARRATIVE: The full story—the hike you're likely to have on this section of the AT. Conditions vary widely depending on season and weather, depending on whether you're a robust 18-year-old, a tottering little kid, or a slow-but-steady octogenarian. Our description of the hike aims for a middle-range hiker, in good shape, with modestly ambitious goals but not with an eye on the stopwatch or the pedometer.

Throughout the hike's narrative we cite mileages at the major waypoints and landmarks. Occasionally we indicate the amount of time needed to go from one point to another. Generally, however, we stick to mileage as a reference point because each hiker's pace is different.

The narrative also pauses to describe rocks, plants, animals, vistas, and social history seen along the way... and then picks up the hike again with further directions toward its destination.

TRAIL PROFILE: A rendering of the trail's up-and-down travels over the landscape, suggesting graphically how easy or challenging sections may be. The profiles are based on USGS digital elevation maps. The linear scale on the profiles does not match the scale on the hike's topographic map (see below). Instead, the profile gives a cross-section view of the mountains and valleys with the trail running up and down as if on a straight line across the landscape. Trail profiles entail a certain degree of vertical exaggeration to make the rendering meaningful, and they do not show every hill or knob in the path.

Topographic map: Based on USGS 1:100,000 scale maps, the hike topo map also draws on information provided on AT maps published by the Appalachian Trail Conference and its member trail clubs. Our scale is usually 1 inch to 1 mile—or as close to that as the page trim size and length of the hike will allow. These maps show actual elevations (read about contour lines on page 8), usually in feet. They also show the compass direction (north) and important waypoints along the trail. See the map legend on page 7. For most day hikes, the maps in this book will serve well. For extended backpacking in the wild backcountry or high mountains, we recommend using Appalachian Trail Conference or Appalachian Mountain Club maps.

Note: Some USGS maps have not been updated for several years and may not show recent trail relocations. Follow the dark green line of the AT on the maps in this book. You may see the old AT outlined in gray on the map. In some cases the old path is open and usable, but in many it's not. Check the narrative and consult local trail clubs before hiking on discontinued sections of the AT.

Itinerary: A summary of the hike in table format, listing important waypoints noted in the narrative and shown on the topo map and/or the trail profile. Both the narrative and the itinerary describe the hike as either a south-to-north (most common) or north-to-south walk. Thus, in a S-N itinerary, directions to turn left (L) or right (R) mean "left when walking northward on the trail" and "right when walking northward on the trail," respectively. On a N-S itinerary, the reverse is true.

Bear in mind that "north" and "south" as used along the AT are not always literally true. The trail is said to run north from Georgia to Maine, but at any given point, even if you're walking "northward toward Maine," the footpath may veer to the west or east, or even southward to skirt a difficult mountain before resuming its generally northward direction. That's why in the narrative and itinerary we generally use "left" and "right" rather than compass directions. Inexperienced AT hikers simply have to orient themselves correctly at the start of the hike: Make sure you know whether you're following the trail to the north or south, and keep that in mind as you proceed. Then, "left" and "right" in the narrative and itinerary will be easy to follow. In any case, always carry a compass.

Note: In keeping with the tradition of showing north at the top of maps, we structure the itineraries with north always at the top of the table, south at the bottom. Thus, for a S-N hike, you will find the "Start" at the bottom (south) end of the itinerary, and you should read upward. "End" will be at the top (north) end of the table. We give mileage in both directions: the left-hand column goes S-N; the right-hand column goes N-S. Remember that access trail mileage must be added to miles walked on the AT itself. We total both mileages for you on the itinerary. Elevations are given in both feet and meters (feet elsewhere in this book). To construct our itineraries, we relied on walking the trail, taking careful notes, and then verifying by reference to other trail guides, especially the Appalachian Trail Conference and member club trail guides. Published trail guides, USGS maps, and ATC maps sometimes disagree by as much as a few tenths of a mile (distance) or a few feet (elevation).

Sidebar: In some hikes, special topics are discussed in a box set off from the narrative. The sidebars are listed in the table of contents.

Abbreviations

Abbreviations commonly used:

AHS, American Hiking Society
AMC, Appalachian Mountain Club
ATC, Appalachian Trail Conference
CCC, Civilian Conservation Corps
DOC, Dartmouth Outing Club
MATC, Maine Appalachian Trail Club
RMC, Randolph Mountain Club
SPNHF, Society for the Protection of New Hampshire Forests
USFS, U.S. Forest Service
USGS, U.S. Geological Survey
WMNF, White Mt. National Forest

Geographic Organization

The hikes included in this volume follow the Appalachian Trail from south to north. Most of the hikes are described as south-to-north walks, but many are suitable to walking the opposite way, too. A few hikes are best done from north to south. We have avoided some wicked climbs by bringing you down, rather than up, certain nasty hills.

Maps: Legends, Skills, Sources

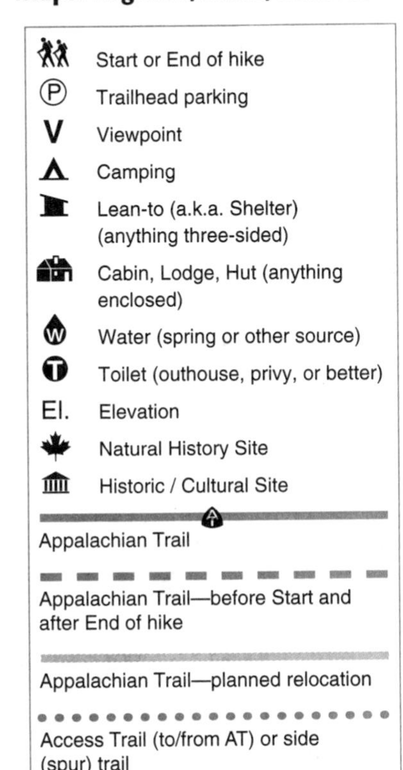

SCALE—Unless otherwise noted, approximately 1 inch = 1 mile.

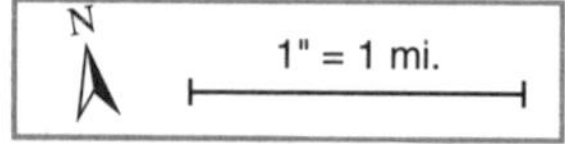

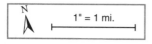

COMPASS DIRECTION AND DEVIATION—The scale bar shows the compass direction North. The north shown on the map is "true" or "grid" north, essentially a straight line to the north pole, whereas the north you see on your compass is "magnetic" north, usually a few degrees different due to the earth's magnetic field. Along the AT, magnetic north deviates from true or grid north by several degrees west. The farther north one goes, the greater the deviation. At the Vermont/New Hampshire state line the deviation is 15.5° west; throughout Maine it is about 18°.

CONTOUR INTERVAL—See "Contour Lines" below. Contour intervals on the USGS topographic maps used as the base for the hiking maps in this book are either 10 meters (33 ft.) or 20 meters (66 ft.) depending on the map (see "List of Maps" under "Useful Information").

Reading and planning your hikes with topographic maps can be fun and is certainly useful. Every hiking party should have at least one competent map reader. Often, if there are children aboard, they will be eager to follow the hike's progress on the topographic map. Here are a few pointers for beginning map readers.

CONTOUR LINES—All the hiking maps in this series of guides are based on official topographic maps which represent the three-dimensional shape of the land with contour lines (CLs). Typically, CLs are drawn at fixed intervals, for example, 20 meters, meaning that between each pair of lines in our example there is a rise or fall of 20 meters in the landscape.

In this example, the CLs are close together, suggesting a steep climb or descent:

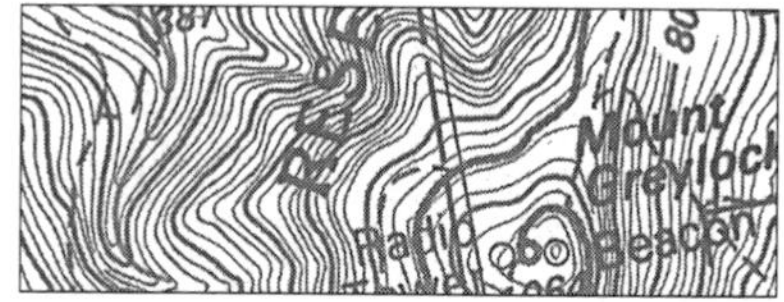

In this example, the CLs are farther apart, suggesting a gently sloping or nearly flat landscape:

LINEAR SCALE—To understand CLs fully, they must be related to the linear scale of the map. This relationship gives a sense of vertical rise or fall as it spreads out horizontally across the landscape. Thus, if 1 inch = 1 mile and if there are many CLs clustered in, say, a $^{1}/_{2}$-inch section of trail, then it's safe to assume that this $^{1}/_{2}$-mile section of the trail will be steep, going up or down depending on your direction.

Map Sources—All maps in this series are derived from United States Geological Survey topographic maps. Each of our maps is a small slice of a USGS topo map. We have updated relevant AT information (some USGS maps are 10 or more years old; the AT has moved at several points). The original map scale of 1:100,000 is enlarged here generally to about 1:62,000 (around 1 inch = 1 mile) for readability. A 1:100,000-scale map is not practical to carry on the trail. USGS maps scaled at a more convenient 1:62,000 are easy to read as trail maps, but a day's hike may cut across several maps or use only a tiny portion of one large map, an unwieldy affair when hiking.

For short day hikes, use the maps in this book. For longer hikes, overnight trips, or serious backpacking, use official AT maps from the Appalachian Trail Conference or supplementary maps from Trails Illustrated, the Appalachian Mountain Club, the Dartmouth Outing Club, or the Maine Appalachian Trail Club (see below).

Bookstores and outdoor outfitters near the Appalachian Trail usually stock the USGS quadrangles (1:62,500) for the local area. USGS maps can also be ordered by telephone (see "Useful Information" and the Bibliography). If you do not know the USGS map number (see the "Useful Information" list for maps used in this book), be sure to indicate (a) the portion of the AT you want to hike by providing nearby cities, towns, rivers, or other landmarks and (b) the scale you prefer. Anything over 1 inch = 1 mile will be impractical for hiking.

The Appalachian Trail Conference publishes a set of color-shaded topographic hiking maps for almost the entire length of the trail (excluding the national parks through which the AT passes). The scale is generally 1:38,750. This translates to about 1 5/8 inches = 1 mile. In other words, much more detail than on the USGS quadrangles and more than we can show in a book of this size. See your local bookseller or outdoor outfitter, or call the ATC (see "Useful Information"). A catalogue is available. For serious hikers and for any overnight or backcountry hiking on the Appalachian Trail, we strongly recommend these fine maps.

Trails Illustrated (distributed by National Geographic) publishes more than fifty maps of national parks; these include important sections of the Appalachian Trail in Great Smoky Mts. National Park and Shenandoah National Park. These full-color, large-format maps (printed on waterproof, tear-resistant recycled paper) provide detailed topographic information and descriptions of local flora and fauna. A 3-D overview map is an enjoyable bonus. These are metric maps. The scale is 1:100,000, roughly 5/8 inch = 1 mile. A metric conversion chart is provided. See your local bookseller or outdoor outfitter, or contact Trails Illustrated (see "Useful Information" and the Bibliography).

For most of the AT in New Hampshire, you'll want some of the excellent maps published by the Appalachian Mountain Club. A variety of AMC maps are available, covering all of the White Mts. in New Hampshire and Maine. The two- or three-color maps are made in both waterproof/tear-resistant (we recommend these) and paper versions. They are included in many of the club's hiking guides but are also available individually. The scale is usually 1:125,000, or 1/2 inch to 1 mile; however, more specific maps to popular areas like Mt. Washington are also available. These maps are particularly useful: they show not only the AT but many miles of other trails, too. The maps are also sold separately. The maps are available at many booksellers and outdoor outfitters, or from the Appalachian Mountain Club, Box 298, Gorham, NH 03581 (800-262-4455).

The section of the AT between the Connecticut River and Mt. Moosilauke (the first four hikes of this volume) is covered by Dartmouth Outing Club maps, available from the Director of Trails and Shelters, Box 9, Robinson Hall, Dartmouth College, Hanover, NH 03755. Mt. Moosilauke is covered by both AMC and DOC maps.

Maps of the AT in Maine can be ordered from the Maine Appalachian Trail Club, P.O. Box 283, Augusta, ME 04330.

Driving Time to the Trailhead

A factor frequently overlooked when planning a hike is the driving time required to reach the trailhead or to get back to civilization at day's end. When a substantial number of miles must be traveled from a major highway or town to get up into the mountains to the trailhead, we tell you in the information block. You must be sure to leave sufficient time to get to the starting point. Positioning two cars (finish and start) takes even longer.

Remember that many Appalachian Trail access roads are "secondary" at best. Some are decidedly unkind to low-chassis, two-wheel-drive cars. Some are impassable in wet weather (the entire spring mud season). Travel to the trailhead can be slow and dicey. Read our instructions carefully. Plan ahead.

Choosing Your Hike / Effort Required

In this book we rate hikes by three levels of "effort required": easy, moderate, and strenuous. Some hikes are a mix of easy, moderate, and strenuous sections.

New Hampshire and Maine are generally more challenging than the rest of the Appalachian Trail. All but two of this book's hikes in New Hampshire are rated "strenuous" as are many in Maine.

If little kids or folks with disabilities might find a hike too rugged, we tell you. If there are difficult water crossings, perhaps varying seasonally, we say so.

But remember, our judgments are somewhat subjective.

Easy: gentle ups and downs, fairly smooth path, few obstacles

Moderate: elevation gain or loss of up to 1000 feet.; narrower, rocky path; some obstacles (for example, brook crossings with no bridge)

Strenuous: elevation gain or loss of more than 1000 feet.; steep ups and downs; difficult, challenging path; numerous obstacles; possibly unsuitable for young children or the infirm.

Blazing

A "blaze" (from the Old English bloese, meaning "torch") is a bright painted mark (about 6 inches x 2 inches) on a tree, post, or rock indicating the path of a hiking trail. The Appalachian Trail is blazed in white (rather easy to see even in fog, though tough to follow in brightly dappled sunlight), all the way from Georgia to Maine. It's the same in each direction, south–north or north–south.

Side trails are often but not always blazed in a different color—generally blue, orange, or yellow. AT blazes are usually spaced 30 to 50 yards apart. In some sections overzealous trail maintainers have blazed at shorter intervals, while in other areas blazing has faded and may be hard to follow. If you haven't seen a white blaze for several minutes, backtrack and make sure you're still on the white-blazed AT, not an unmarked side trail or logging road.

Two blazes, one above the other, indicate a turn coming in the trail. In some states, if the upper blaze is positioned to the left, look for a left turn, and vice versa.

Estimating Hiking Times

An average adult hiker's pace is about 2.0 miles per hour on the flat. For every 1000-foot gain in elevation, add 30 minutes of time to your estimate. Thus an 8-mile hike up a 2500-foot mountain might take you 5 1/4 hours. This formula does not account for rests, mealtimes, or lollygagging to smell the flowers or talk to the bears. With a full backpack, little kids in tow, or slippery conditions, obviously you would add more time.

We recommend that you keep a record of your time and distance and the hiking conditions for a half dozen hikes, and then compare your averages to ours. You'll soon see whether our numbers match yours and if not, how much time you need to add or subtract from our estimates.

Day Hikes / Overnight Backpacking Hikes

The majority of the hikes in this book can be done as day hikes. Some day hikes can be conveniently strung together to make overnight backpacking trips of 2 or more days' duration. And some hikes are manageable only as overnight backpacking trips. The general rule: the more wilderness there is to traverse, the less likely it is that you can pop in and out for a day hike only. Read the information block carefully, and look at the hike south or north of the one you're considering to see whether a linkage is feasible.

Avoiding the Crowds

A great debate is raging: Is the AT now overused, too busy to be enjoyable, too tough on the land to be justifiable? Are we approaching, or are we already at, the point where reservations will have to be made for floor space in an AT shelter? (In fact, in some southern sections—Great Smoky Mts. National Park, for example—shelters are reserved for thru-hikers or other long-distance hikers only, not the casual weekender.) We don't mean to equivocate, but the answer seems to be yes and no. Collectively, the authors of this series have hiked thousands of AT miles over several decades. Far more often than not, we have had the trail essentially to ourselves, passing only a few people per day. Inevitably, however, certain sites on the trail (beautifully located shelters, or summits with great views or symbolic significance, for example) attract crowds, especially on weekends, and most especially in midsummer or at fall foliage time. The southern section of the AT is busy with hundreds of would-be thru-hikers in early spring. Don't expect to be alone on Springer Mt. in April.

It does not require a graduate degree in engineering to figure out a plan to avoid these crowds or to avoid swelling them yourself. The best times to be alone on the trail are midweek. No offense to kids or parents (we love 'em all), but June, before the kids leave school, and September, after they're back in, are great times to find warm-weather solitude on the AT. If you can swing it, why not work on Saturday (or even Sunday) and hike on Sunday and Monday (or better yet Monday and Tuesday). We've tried it with success.

If you cannot hike midweek and are headed for peaks or shelters likely to be overcrowded, start out early enough to permit you to move on to another site in daylight if your first target has already hung out the "No Vacancy" sign. When the shelter or official tent sites are full, accept the bad news and walk on. Carving out an impromptu tent site is generally forbidden except in extremely bad weather. Carry a detailed map. Study it carefully before leaving home to find the alternative site you may need in a pinch.

Circuit or Loop Hikes / Shuttle Services

Ideally you have a limousine with built-in hot tub and cold drinks awaiting you at the end of the trail. Short of that, you may have to improvise a way to get back to your starting point. Whenever it's convenient and sensible from a hiking viewpoint, we have suggested how to make the hike into a circuit or loop, bringing you back, on foot, to your car or pretty close to it. There are many hikes, however, especially those in wilderness areas, where this is simply not feasible.

It's usually best if you can work out a two-car team for your hike, with one car dropped at the finish line and another driven to the starting trailhead.

Out and back: Most of our hikes are described as linear—from A to B to C. Hikers with only one car available can make many fine hikes, however, by simply going out to a well-chosen point (the mountaintop, the pond) and then reversing direction to the starting point. The mileage indicators in the Itineraries will help you decide on a turnaround point. You may be pleasantly surprised to find that when walked in the opposite direction, the same section of trail yields a very different experience—especially if one direction is steeply up and the other sharply down.

Shuttles: In some areas, and through the auspices of some local hiking clubs, shuttle services are available. For example, the Green Mountain Club in Vermont provides to its members a list of shuttle drivers, although they are few in number and require early notice and modest fees. In this book, when we know there is a reliable shuttle service that is useful on a particular hike, we tell you. If we don't make a shuttle suggestion, it's often worth asking your motel or bed-and-breakfast keeper, or calling the local Chamber of Commerce or even the local taxi company. A hunting-lodge manager helped us one time at a good price. Ask around, make new friends.

Some hikers like to position a bicycle (locked) at the end of a hike so they can ride back to their car at the starting point.

If your hiking group consists of, say, four or more people and two cars, you might swap extra car keys at the beginning of the day and send people, a car, and a key for the other car to each end of the trail. You all meet somewhere in the middle of the hike, trade stories, and perhaps share lunch. And each group finds a car waiting at day's end. Depending on roads and distances to trailheads, this system can shave a good deal of time off the car travel at the start and end of your hiking day. This is especially helpful for very long day hikes and even more so in early spring or late fall when days are short. Besides, meeting friends deep in the forest or on a mountaintop is great fun.

Early Exit Options

Our hikes range from 5 to 15 miles per day. When road crossings and parking facilities permit, we indicate points where you could leave the AT before finishing the entire hike.

Sometimes such exits are convenient and safe; sometimes they should be used only for emergencies. Heed our advice. If we do not say good parking is available, don't assume there's a parking lot.

The Early Exit Options can often be used to make a loop hike out of an otherwise longish linear hike. To see your options clearly, study a good local road map.

Camping

Camp only in designated camping areas unless you know for sure that free-for-all camping is permitted. In most sections of the AT the land is too heavily used to permit improvisatory camping. We indicate official campsites. The rules may vary as you pass through state forest, national forest, or national park. In some areas, especially national parks, camping permits may be required and campsite reservations may be possible. See "Shelters and Campsites" in "Useful Information."

Shelters

The names may vary but the accommodations are much the same: Along the AT, about every 10 to 15 miles, you'll find three-sided lean-tos with minimalist interior decorating. Bunk beds or no beds at all, just floor space. Possibly a picnic table, a fire ring, an outhouse, a water source nearby. Many of these shelters have well-maintained facilities, charming names, and equally charming views. Some you wouldn't let your dog sleep in. We tell you which ones we like. Shelters usually have a few tent sites surrounding them.

Except in the two national parks through which the AT passes (Great Smoky Mts., Shenandoah) and in New Hampshire's White Mt. National Forest, where shelters are reserved for thru-hikers (for a fee), the "reservations policy" is first come, first served. Certain rules apply, however: Maximum stay, 3 nights. If it's raining, squeeze in and make room for late arrivals. Clean up after yourself, and respect others' needs for quiet and privacy.

Trail Registers

At shelters and occasionally at trail junctions, you'll find notebooks where you can, and should, write a few words for posterity and for practicality's sake. Logging in your arrival and departure time will help searchers find you if, unluckily, you get lost or hurt on the trail. But the real fun of the trail registers is adding your own thoughts to the collective wisdom and tomfoolery other hikers have already scribbled in the notebooks. The registers make great reading. A whole new literary genre! Go ahead, wax poetic or philosophical. Surely there's at least one haiku in you to express your joy at the view from the mountaintop or the first time you shook hands with a moose....

Trail registers also sometimes provide helpful warnings about trail conditions (recent mud slides or bridge washouts, for example). If the weather has been wild of late, read back a few days in the register to see what previous hikers may have said about what lies ahead of you.

HIKING: THE BASICS

WHILE IT'S TRUE that we go to the woods and the mountains to get away from the trappings of civilization, few of us really want to put our lives in jeopardy. Here are some recommendations every adult hiker (and Boy or Girl Scout-age youngster) should follow.

When the subject is equipment, we suggest you visit your outdoor outfitter to ask for advice or that you read back issues of *Backpacker* magazine, in print or on-line (see "Useful Information"). *Backpacker*'s annual "gear guide" sorts through hundreds of choices and makes useful recommendations. For the truly hiking/camping gizmo-obsessed, there are on-line chat rooms (again, see *Backpacker*) where you and other similarly gadget-crazed friends can compare notes.

Boots / Shoes

Nothing is more important to a hiker than the condition of his or her feet. From this axiom derives an important rule: Wear the right boots or shoes for hiking, or stay home. Some of the easier sections of the AT can be hiked in firm running shoes or high-top basketball sneakers, but most sections require a tougher, waterproof or water-resistant boot providing nonslip soles, toe protection, and firm ankle support. Shop carefully. Go to an outdoor outfitter rather than a regular shoe store. Try on several pairs of boots, with the actual socks you intend to wear (two pair: one thin, one thick). If you buy boots by mail, trace your foot size with those socks on your feet. Save your pennies and buy the best you can afford. Gore-Tex or one of its waterproofing clones is worth the money. Check the hiking magazines' annual gear reviews (in print or on-line) for ratings of comfort, weight, durability, and price. Think of the purchase as a multiyear investment. Shop long before the hiking season starts, and wear your boots for a good 10 to 20 miles of everyday walking before hitting the trail. Your feet will thank you.

Caveat for kids: The better discount stores carry boot brands that are quite sufficient for a season of hiking by young people whose feet are still growing. Parents, buy your own boots first and then use your shopper's savvy to find inexpensive boots for the kids.

Clothing

Bring sufficient clothes, appropriate for rain and cold. Layers work best. Gore-Tex and other waterproof fabrics are miraculous, but a $3 emergency poncho will do in a pinch. Think about what you would need to get through a rainy night, even if you're just out for a short, sunny day hike.

A visored hat. The top of your head is the point of major heat loss, whether you're bald or not. Inexpensive Gore-Tex hats can be found. Cruise the catalogues.

Sunglasses, in a protective case.

Cotton socks, sweatshirts, and T-shirts: avoid them. Blue jeans (essentially cotton): avoid them. Cotton is comfortable until it gets wet (from rain or perspiration). Then it's your enemy. It dries slowly and does not wick away perspiration. There are extraordinary synthetic fabrics nowadays for shirts, underwear, and long johns that will keep you warm or cool and will let the moisture leave your body. Visit your outdoor outfitter for a wardrobe consultation. Money well spent.

Wool is a miracle fabric from nature. Especially good for socks and gloves. Polartec is a miracle fabric from the high-tech world (recycled plastic bottles!). Jackets and pullovers in these miracle fabrics are what you want.

Food

Hiking eats up calories. Cold weather demands body heat, which demands calories. Diet at home. Eat high-energy foods on the trail. Carbohydrates are best. Sweets are less helpful than you might think, though a chocolate or energy bar to help you up the hill is sometimes right. It's better to eat several smaller meals en route than to gorge on a big one, unless you plan for a siesta. Digestion itself takes considerable energy. You'll find it hard to climb and digest at the same time. The hiker's fallback snack plan: (1) "Gorp," a mix of nuts, granola, chocolate chips, dried fruit, and whatever else you like. Mix it yourself at home—much cheaper than the ready-made variety at the store. (2) Peanut butter on anything. (3) Fruit. Heavy to carry but oh so refreshing. The sugar in fruit is fructose, high in energy but it won't put you to sleep.

And remember the miracle food for hikers, the humble banana. Or dried banana chips (crunch them or add water). High in potassium, bananas are your muscles' best friends because the potassium minimizes aches and cramps.

Planning menus and packing food for extended backpacking trips is a subject beyond the scope of this book. Several camping cookbooks are available, and *Backpacker* frequently runs how-to articles worth reading. Search their Web site for articles you can download. Advice: Whatever you plan to cook on the trail, try it out first, on the backpacking stove, at home. Make a list of cooking gear and condiments needed, and if the list looks long, simplify the menu unless you have willing friends along who will carry a gourmet's kitchen for you. Over time you'll find camp food tricks and tastes to add to your repertoire, such as bagging breakfast granola with powdered milk in self-seal bags (just add water and stir), or choosing tough-skinned veggies like carrots, celery, or snow peas that can be eaten cooked or raw and won't turn to mush in your pack. The ever popular macaroni and cheese (available nowadays in many fancy permutations from Lipton, Kraft, et al.) can be dressed up in countless lightweight, quick-cook ways. The camper's most important kitchen tool is imagination.

Whatever you plan to eat or cook on the trail, be prepared to clean up spotlessly. Leave no mess—indeed, no trace.

Food Storage

You're not the only hungry critter in the woods. Everyone from the bears to the squirrels and mice would like to breakfast on your granola and snack on your Oreos. Never keep food in your tent overnight. It's an invitation for unwanted company in the dark. Use a drawstring food sack, wrapped in a plastic garbage bag, which you hang from a sturdy branch on a nearby tree, keeping the sack several feet out on the branch, about 10 feet off the ground and several feet below the branch. Obviously this means you must carry about 50 feet of lightweight cord (useful in emergencies too).

Don't store your food in your backpack, either, indoors or out. Those cute little chipmunks and their bigger friends will eat a hole right through that expensive high-tech fabric.

Water

Keep drinking a little at a time all day while you hike. Dehydration is the major cause of hiker fatigue. Double or triple your normal daily intake of water.

Sadly, most of the water flowing in streams the AT crosses is polluted to one degree or another, sometimes by industry or agriculture, often by wild animals such as beavers upstream. The most common problem is a nasty protozoan known as giardia from which we get stomach cramps, fever, and the runs. Trust us: you don't want it. The rule is, unless an official sign says the water has been tested and is pure, assume the water must be treated with either iodine tablets or a water filter. Iodine is cheap and lightweight but slow, and it leaves a somewhat unpleasant taste in the treated water (Potable Aqua is an iodine treatment that minimizes the bad taste). Hiker water filters are faster-acting but more cumbersome.

They are useful elsewhere too—on boats, at freshwater beaches, and so forth. A good investment. Look for one that screens out most bacteria, is lightweight, and pumps quickly. The most convenient water bottles are (a) wide-mouth, facilitating refill and filter attachment, and (b) eqipped with a drinking tube or nipple, eliminating the need to open the bottle itself.

When Nature Calls

Every hiker—day only or overnight backpacker—must come prepared to deal appropriately with disposal of human waste in the woods. At most shelters and many campsites along the AT there are outhouses. Please help to keep them clean. Gentlemen especially are encouraged to urinate in the woods, a few hundred feet off the trail. Urine in the outhouse pit adds to the bad aroma.

Believe it or not, there's an entire book on the subject of defecating in the woods (see the Bibliography). Good reading on a slow day in camp, perhaps. This much you must know to do: Bring biodegradable white single-ply toilet paper in a plastic bag. Bring a little shovel (a plastic garden trowel will do). Bring a strong self-seal plastic bag to carry out used toilet paper, tampons, etc. If the woods is your toilet, get at least 100 feet off the trail and at least 200 feet away from any water. Dig a hole at least 8 inches deep, and cover your waste firmly. A squat is the time-tested position.

Weather

Basic precautions include a careful review of weather forecasts and typical conditions in the area you're hiking—before you pack your pack or leave home. See "Useful Information" for a weather Web site. If you go adventuring outdoors frequently, you'll enjoy and benefit from a lightweight battery-operated weather radio that provides access to several NOAA (National Oceanic and Atmospheric Administration) channels, offering detailed forecasts 24 hours a day, with special recreational forecasts emphasizing conditions at elevations of 3000 feet and above.

Learn to forecast weather yourself by reading the clouds (particularly cumulous clouds with towering thunderheads) and by noticing changes in animal and plant behavior that may telegraph the advent of a storm. Make it a habit to do a 360-degree sky check every hour or so to see what's coming and from which direction. If trouble is heading your way, plan ahead for emergency shelter. Get off the mountaintop or exposed ridge, where high winds and lightning are most likely to hit. Don't sit under a big rotting tree with branches waiting to clunk you on the head. When lightning is likely, avoid all metal objects (fire towers, tent poles, pack frames, etc.). Do find a dry, wind-protected spot (the downwind side of overhanging boulders is good), and lay a plan to make it your home for a few hours.

Wet weather often brings cool or cold temperatures. Wet clothing or a wet sleeping bag can exacerbate your sense of chill. Hypothermia can set in quickly, especially if you're fatigued or anxious. Even day hikers should carry extra clothing and something, if only a big plastic garbage bag, to cover themselves and their pack. Overnight backpackers, anywhere on the AT, must be ready for the worst. Keep rainwear light and simple so you won't resent carrying it on a sunny day.

See "Surviving Mt Washington," in Hike #12.

First Aid

Outfitters such as Campmor and L.L. Bean (excellent catalogs) offer first-aid kits for everyone from the day hiker to the Mt. Everest climber. Buy from them or patch together your own kit, based on the contents listed in the catalogues. A waterproof container is a must. Be prepared for cuts, scrapes, burns, blisters, sprains, headache. Sunscreen if exposure is likely. A very lightweight first-aid manual is not a bad idea either.

One essential is moleskin, a skin-covering adhesive, thicker than a Band-aid but soft enough to wrap around an unhappy toe. Many a hike has been ruined by blisters. At the first sign (heat, burning, tingling feelings on toes or heels), slap on the moleskin and leave it there until you're back home. Insurance against blisters is cheap: two pairs of (dry!) socks. And break in your new hiking boots thoroughly before you hit the trail.

Further insurance: bring a few feet of dental floss. If your teeth don't use it, a sewing job might.

Include a little but loud whistle in your first-aid kit. You might need to call for help.

If first aid is foreign to you, by all means take a course, with CPR (artificial respiration) training, from the local Red Cross. For parents hiking with kids, this is a must. For kids, join the Scouts and earn that First Aid merit badge.

Hiking Alone

There are real pleasures to be had from hiking alone. Generally, however, it's not recommended. Whether you hike alone or in a group, take pains to let someone know your plans (route, estimated times of departure and arrival, what to do if you don't check back in). Often a hiker who wants to walk alone can have that pleasure, letting fellow hikers know that by day's end he or she will rejoin the group.

Hiking in Groups

Keep your group size down to fewer than ten people. Even that many is stretching what the trailside facilities can bear. Large groups tend to overwhelm smaller ones, yet everyone has the same rights to enjoy the space and the quiet on the trail. Don't take a busload of kids on the trail. Find volunteers who will lead sections of a group with at least a mile or 30 minutes between them.

Women Hikers

Statistically, the Appalachian Trail is one of the safest places a woman (or a man) can be in the United States. But there have been some problems with harrassment, and there have been some cases of violence, even a few tragic murders. Play it safe. Don't hike alone. Be sensible—inappropriate clothing may attract the wrong kind of attention. Avoid the rowdy set sometimes found at shelters near road crossings or towns. Move on.

Taking Children on the Trail

By all means, do take the kids. The environment of the Appalachian Trail and the activities of climbing, exploring, and camping will engage the imagination and channel the energies of almost every kid, including those whose regular turf is the city street. Adult hikers just need to remember that a few things are different about kid hikers. Kids' attention spans are (usually) shorter than grown-ups'. Plan to break your hike into smaller units with something special to do in each part—birds here, lunch there, rock collecting next, photography from the mountaintop, writing messages in the trail registers. Give a kid a short-term achievable project linked to today's hike (such as collecting as many different-shaped leaves as you can from the ground beneath the trees), and you'll probably have a happy, satisfied kid hiker by evening.

Most kids love hiking and camping gear. Get them involved in planning, shopping, packing for, and executing the hike, especially the camping portion. Let them make breakfast. Teach them to set up the tent; then get out of the way. Take pictures and make a family hiking photo album: it's a memory bank for years to come. Put a map on your children's wall at home and mark the trails they have hiked, the peaks they have climbed. A sense of accomplishment is priceless.

Be realistic, too, about what kids can endure on the hiking trail. Their pain (and boredom) thresholds are lower than most adults'. Don't let blisters happen to kids; check their feet at lunchtime. Bring a book to read in case of rain, or a miniature chess set if they're old enough to play. Anticipate your own behavior in an emergency situation. If you panic, the kids will. If you're calm, know where to go for help, and know how to keep dry and warm, most kids will rise to the occasion and come home strengthened by the adventure.

Parking

Do not leave a sign on your car saying where you're going or when you'll return. Try not to leave anything (visible) in your car that might interest burglars. Avoid camping at shelters located very close to easily accessible parking lots. Respect the AT's immediate neighbors by not parking on their private property.

Backpacks and Day Packs

It's not quite a science but it's certainly an art. An incorrectly loaded backpack (badly packed on the inside or poorly fitted or adjusted to your torso and shoulders) can wreck even a sunny day on the world's loveliest trail. Some tips: Fanny packs, worn at hip level, are great for short day hikes as long as you can carry sufficient water, food, clothing, first aid, and map and compass. Less than that and the pack is too small.

Day packs carry proportionately more but without the frame that supports a backpacking pack. For both day packs and true backpacks, similar packing rules apply. Start at the outdoor outfitter. Have a knowledgeable salesperson fit the pack (with realistic dummy weights inside) to your specific torso. Walk around, bend over, squat, and be sure you're comfortable and stable.

At home, make a packing list with items categorized carefully (food, kitchen, first aid, clothes, stove and fuel, etc.). Jettison anything unnecessary. Roll your clothes. Pack one thing inside another (the Chinese box method). Then use the following scheme for stuffing the pack.

Keep weight distributed equally on the horizontal plane, but on the vertical, pack the lightweight items (such as sleeping bag) down low and the heavyweight items (food, water, tent) up high. Keep the heavier items close to your body. But be sure to pad any sharp-edged items so as not to poke you or to rip the pack fabric. Use the pack's outside pockets for a water bottle, fuel bottles, and smelly garbage.

Last, buy a rainproof pack cover or make one from a heavy-duty plastic garbage bag. Your clothing and sleeping bag will be glad you did.

Flashlight

Even a day hiker ought to carry a lightweight flashlight, just in case. In winter, early spring, and fall, daylight can disappear quickly, especially if the weather turns bad or you lose time by being temporarily lost. A slim flashlight that's portable in an elastic headband is a good investment.

Check the batteries before leaving home. Bring an extra bulb.

Matches

Even if you do not intend to cook or camp out and have a campfire, bring a supply of waterproof matches or a cigarette lighter. If you're forced to overnight in the woods, a fire may be good company indeed.

Jackknife

A multipurpose pocketknife will do. It needn't have a built-in chain saw or an eyebrow pencil, but a can opener, a Phillips screwdriver, and a tweezers are handy.

Weapons
We strongly discourage hikers from carrying any kind of weapon.

Cellular Phones
People have been hiking safely and contentedly in the woods for several thousand years without the aid or comfort of cellular phones. This is still possible. Many people come to the trail to get away from the electronic web in which we all are increasingly caught up. Here's a way to win friends on the trail: Keep your cell phone, if you bring one, out of sight, beyond earshot, and out of mind for everyone else. Don't use it except for emergencies, and do use it only when you're far away from other hikers. Domino's Pizza does not deliver to most AT shelters anyway. So why even call them?

FINDING YOUR WAY

Map and Compass
Don't go hiking without a map and compass and the skills to use them. In the fog, in the dark, in a storm, even familiar territory can seem like a directionless wilderness. Many hiking clubs offer map and compass (a.k.a. "orienteering") workshops. Map skills are fun to develop and highly useful. Many of the best natural history observations described in this book depend on your ability to locate a spot on the map and to orient yourself once you're there.

At the very least, be sure everyone in your party knows the compass direction of your intended hike, the cars' locations on the map, and the most likely way toward help in an emergency. *Backpacker* has run articles on map and compass skills (check the index on their Web site). The venerable *Boy Scout Handbook* has a good chapter on these skills. Or see Karen Berger's *Hiking & Backpacking: A Complete Guide.*

Being Lost and Getting Found
If you have studied your map before starting the hike, and if you faithfully follow the AT's white blazes or the access trails' blue (or red or yellow) blazes, the chances of getting lost are just about zero. With a map and compass in hand, there's no good excuse for being lost while you're on the AT itself. Your group should have a leader and a backup leader, and both should know the route. Because hikers sometimes get separated on the trail, everyone should know the direction of the hike, the major landmarks to be passed, the estimated timetable, and how to use the sun and the clock to keep themselves oriented.

But mistakes do happen. Inattention and inadequate planning are the enemies. Sometimes nature conspires against us. Fog (or snow) may obscure the blazes or the cairns above treeline. Autumn leaves or a snowfall may obliterate the well-worn trail that otherwise would guide your eyes as clearly as the blazes themselves.

If you are lost, the first thing to do is to decide that you will not panic. You probably have not been off the trail for long. Stay where you are and think. Keep your group together. Study the map and note the last landmark you're sure you passed. Get reoriented with the map and compass, and try to go in a straight line back toward the trail. Do not wander. Be especially observant of details until you regain the trail.

If all else fails, let gravity and falling water help you out. Except in the deepest wilderness of Maine or the Smoky Mts., at most places along the AT streams flow eventually to brooks, then to rivers, and where there's a river there will soon enough be a house or even a village. If you have to bushwhack to get out of the woods, and if you're really not sure where you are on the map, follow the water downstream. Patience and a plan will get you out.

Common Sense / Sense of Humor

Taking care of yourself successfully in the woods and on the mountains is not rocket science. It starts with preparedness (physical and mental), appropriate equipment, sufficient food and water. It continues with a realistic plan, guided by a map and compass, a guidebook, a weather report, and a watch. It gets better if you and your companions resolve ahead of time to work together as a team, respecting each other's varying needs, strengths, and talents. And it goes best of all if you pack that one priceless essential hiker's tool: a ready sense of humor.

APPALACHIAN TRAIL HISTORY

AT LEGEND HAS it that the 2150-mile footpath from Georgia to Maine is an ancient Native American walkway. Not so. In fact, the AT, as a concept, leapt from the imagination of one federal government civil servant who in 1921 had already recognized that Americans were too citified for their own good and needed more nearby, convenient opportunities for outdoor recreation.

In 1921, Harvard-educated forester and self-styled philosopher Benton MacKaye, of Shirley, Massachusetts, published an article ("An Appalachian Trail, A Project in Regional

Planning") in the *Journal of the American Institute of Architects*. His was a revolutionary idea: a linear park, extending from Georgia to Maine. The concept germinated in a hotbed of idealistic left-wing social thinking that called into question many of the assumed values of the capitalist workaday world. Look a little more deeply into MacKaye's thinking and the roots lead directly to the 19th-century romantics and Transcendentalists, Thoreau and Emerson. MacKaye had read his John Muir, too.

A whirlwind of self-promoting public relations energy, MacKaye set the ball rolling to develop the AT. Thousands of volunteers and many legislators helped make it a reality. Two other key players were Judge Arthur Perkins of Hartford, Connecticut, who helped found the Appalachian Trail Conference in 1925, and his successor as president of the Conference (1931-1952), Myron Avery, of Maine and Washington, D.C. By 1937, with major assistance from Civilian Conservation Corps workers under President Roosevelt's New Deal Works Progress Administration, the complete trail was essentially in place, though by today's standards much of it was rugged and unblazed.

Thru-hikers are an admirable but increasingly common breed these days. Yet it wasn't until 1948 that anyone walked the entire trail in one season. The first thru-hiker was Earl Shaffer, who hiked the trail end-to-end again in 1998 at age 79. The first woman to thru-hike in one season was Emma "Grandma" Gatewood, in 1955. By the mid-1990s the National Park Service was estimating that between 3 and 4 million people per year used the trail. In its first 75 years, from MacKaye's brainstorm to today, the AT has gone from a concept about escaping urban crowding to the point where crowding on the trail itself is a big issue.

In 1968, Congress put the AT under the authority of the National Park Service by passing the National Trails System Act. Overall, the story of the AT is a sweet tale of success. Occasionally there has been a sour note when the government's right of eminent domain has been used to take land required to create a 1000-foot-wide corridor of protection for the trail. By 1995 fewer than 44 miles of the trail remained unprotected by the Park Service corridor. In the 1990s, environmental impact concerns (wear and tear, sustainability) and hiker management issues (overuse, low-impact camping and hiking, safety) fill the pages of AT magazines and spark many a late-night campfire conversation. While the educational and environmental protection efforts of the Appalachian Trail Conference, the Appalachian Mountain Club, and all the regional hiking clubs improve yearly, adding strength to an admirable history, the erosion of financial support from Congress in a budget balancing era threatens to undermine many good efforts at a moment when user demands are growing exponentially. It is a time of fulfillment and challenge for all who use and manage the Appalachian Trail.

Note: A more detailed history of the AT can be found in any of the Appalachian Trail Conference's hiking guides. Colorful lore about the earliest days of trailblazing in New England appears in *Forest and Crag: A History of Hiking, Trail Blazing and Adventure in the Northeast Mountains*, by Guy and Laura Waterman. And *The Appalachian Trail Reader*, edited by David Emblidge, contains a diverse collection of writings about the AT.

The Appalachian Trail in New Hampshire and Maine

New Hampshire and Maine played opposite roles in the history of the AT. By the time Benton MacKaye proposed the creation of the AT in 1921, most of the route the trail would follow across New Hampshire was already blazed as part of a network of trails cut by the Appalachian Mountain Club in the White Mts., and another group of trails was maintained by the Dartmouth Outing Club on the western side of the state. Plans to connect the New Hampshire trails of the AMC and the DOC were already being considered by the New England Trail Conference when MacKaye wrote his famous proposal. In Maine, however, there were few trails cut and no hiking clubs to cut them. By 1932, the more than 250 miles of AT planned between the Mahoosuc Range and Mt. Katahdin remained to be blazed, while only about 26 miles needed to be blazed to connect the trail through the 13 other which the AT passes through. In fact, MacKaye's proposal neglected Maine altogether, and he originally suggested Mt. Washington as the northern terminus of the AT.

Much of the credit for bringing the AT across Maine and onto the summit of Mt. Katahdin lies, like so many of the developments of the AT in the 1930s, with Myron Avery. A Maine native, Avery was simultaneously the chairman of the Appalachian Trail Council, the president of the Potomac Appalachian Trail Club, and the first supervisor of trails for the Maine Appalachian Trail Club, which was formed in 1935. He worked tirelessly to bring about the completion of the AT, and was especially dedicated in his efforts to bring the AT across Maine. Also in 1935, the Civilian Conservation Corps agreed to complete cutting and blazing the trail, and on August 14, 1937, the AT's route from Georgia to Maine was completed when the CCC blazed the last 2 miles of the trail on Spaulding Mt., Maine.

The AT's route across the rugged and remote wilds of Maine continued to be complicated by the amount of private land it crossed. Although in the last 25 years more than two-thirds of the AT's original route across Maine has been rerouted onto protected land, the state still has the most unprotected miles of the trail.

Today the Maine Appalachian Trail Club maintains the AT between Grafton Notch and Mt. Katahdin. The Appalachian Mountain Club, the largest and oldest outdoor organization of its kind in the U.S., takes care of the section between Kinsman Notch and Grafton Notch, and the Dartmouth Outing Club maintains the section between the Connecticut River and Kinsman Notch, as well as a substantial portion of the AT in Vermont.

HIKE #1

Velvet Rocks

Maps: ATC N.H. and Vt. #4

Route: From Hanover over Velvet Rocks to Three-Mile Rd.

Recommended direction: S to N

Distance: 8.2 mi.

Elevation +/-: 500 to 1250 to 860 ft.

Effort: Easy

Day hike: Yes

Overnight backpacking hike: Optional

Duration: 4 to 5 hr.

Early exit option: Trescott Rd. Spur Trail, at 1.8 mi.; Etna Hanover Center Rd, at 5.7 mi.

Natural history features: Connecticut River valley; Velvet Rocks

Social history features: Dartmouth College and the Dartmouth Outing Club

Other features: University town shopping, dining, and entertainment

Trailhead access: *Start:* Hiker parking is provided in a Dartmouth College parking lot (specific lot varies). Stop at the DOC office in Robinson Hall on the green for parking instructions. (There is no parking on Lebanon St. and metered parking elsewhere.) From Dartmouth College green, at intersection of West Wheelock St. and Main St., the AT follows Main St. S to NH 120 (Lebanon St.) and turns L. It follows NH 120 for 0.6 mi. to service station on L where trail turns L off Lebanon St., skirts playing field, and then turns into woods. *End:* Follow East Wheelock St. E from Hanover for 2.8 mi., turn R on Trescott Rd., and drive 1.3 mi. to Etna-Hanover Rd. Turn R and follow Etna-Hanover Rd. (called Two-Mile Rd. on some maps) 1.8 mi. to Wolfeboro Rd. in Hanover Center. Turn R on Wolfeboro Rd. and go 1.0 mi. to Three-Mile Rd. Turn R and go 0.8 mi. to a parking lot on R where AT crosses Wolfeboro Rd.

Camping: Velvet Rocks Shelter

The Velvet Rocks may not be as plush as the name implies, but the stories they tell are rich with detail. Here, only a few miles from New Hampshire's western border, northbound AT hikers receive a polite introduction to the stone for which "the Granite State" is named. In future encounters, the rock will be far less courteous.

Hanover, at the southwestern end of this hike, is a popular trail town anchored by Dartmouth College and its famous Dartmouth Outing Club, which maintains 75 mi. of the AT in Vermont and New Hampshire. A stop at the DOC office will provide not only maps and advice, but also a glimpse of the character of this revered outdoor organization (see "What's Up DOC?"). Long-distance hikers can usually arrange to stay at Foley House on campus, or at the coed fraternity houses Alpha Theta,

Tabard, and Panarche, which offer hikers accommodations for a small fee or a few chores.

While some day hikers will head straight into the woods, most spend a little time lunching, shopping, or absorbing the Ivy League culture in what many hikers believe is the most sophisticated town on the AT. From the luxurious Hanover Inn, across the street from the Dartmouth Green, the AT cruises down Main St. past boutiques, restaurants, outfitters, pubs, bookstores, and a movie theater. Few long-distance hikers can pass up the Ben and Jerry's ice cream shop on Lebanon St.

Some hikers, intent on walking past every white blaze, begin their hike at the Connecticut River, which adds 1.2 mi. to the total distance of this hike. We'll start at the corner of E. Wheelock and Main streets, where a plaque in the sidewalk notes that the spot is 432 mi. from Mt. Katahdin and 1713 mi. from Springer Mt. (Reroutes have added some mileage in both directions since the plaque was donated by the Dartmouth class of 1954.) Follow Main St. south to the next traffic light (Lebanon St.), turn left, and walk 0.6 mi. to a service station on the left, where the AT turns left and this hike heads for the woods.

The AT skirts the right side of a playing field and steps through a gate, where it joins the Velvet Rocks Trail, turns right into the woods, and then climbs gradually to the left across the northwest slope of a ridge. An unreliable spring sometimes pools to the right of the trail here.

Lowland flowers like red trillium, painted trillium, and lady's-slipper are common amid the rich hardwood forest surrounding Velvet Rocks. Watch the base of trailside sugar maples for the pale purple flowers of great-spurred violets, which bloom in May and have a 1/4-in. spur on the back of the blossoms.

At 0.8 mi. a side trail on the left leads 0.2 mi. to Velvet Rocks Shelter, a popular overnight stop for locals as well as long-distance hikers because of the site's proximity to Hanover. Some visitors feel the campsite is too close to town, but compared to the shelter's birthplace, this location is remote: the structure was originally built on Boston Common as part of a DOC exhibit. The small shelter has room for four campers, and there is room for two or three tents in front.

For the few hikers who find the location of the shelter and tent space too rugged, the DOC trail sign that marks the northeast end of the shelter loop trail, 1.3 mi. into this hike, lists the posh Hanover Inn, 2.0 mi. away, as an alternative via the Old Velvet Rocks Trail. Another sign at the same junction marks Ledyard Spring Trail, which descends steeply to the sometimes unreliable spring in 0.2 mi. A glance at the trickling covered spring will make you glad you filled your bottles in Hanover.

At 1.8 mi. the Trescott Rd. Spur Trail, a former AT route and an early exit

What's Up DOC?

In 1771 four students stepped from a log hut in the wilds of New Hampshire as the first graduating class of Dartmouth College. In December 1909, Fred Harris, a student at the by-then-esteemed Ivy League institution, led the student body back into the wilderness with a letter in the student newspaper proposing the creation of a ski and snowshoe club that would hold weekly ski tours, ski jump competitions, and a winter carnival. "Dartmouth might well become the originator of a branch of college organized sport hitherto undeveloped by American colleges," Harris wrote.

A month later sixty students attended a meeting at which the Dartmouth Outing Club was organized and Harris was elected its first president. In 1911 the first Dartmouth Winter Carnival was held, with Harris winning the first ski jump competition. Two years later he and two DOC contemporaries claimed the first ski ascent of Mt. Washington, which tops a list of dozens of significant firsts credited to the club.

Today the DOC is the oldest college outing club in the United States and the largest student organization on the campus, composed of eleven specialized clubs. The Mountaineering Club has produced climbers of the stature of Barry Bishop and his son, Brent, both of whom have summited Mt. Everest. The Biathlon Club, the only collegiate club of its kind, has included a number of Olympic athletes. Cabin and Trail, the most active DOC club and the one that holds the most interest to AT hikers, is responsible for maintaining the DOC's 75-mi. section of the AT and for building cabins and shelters.

The DOC, in fact, is one of the godparents of the AT. Early trails blazed by the club provided one of the first links in the AT when they were connected with the trails of the Green Mt. Club in Vermont and the Appalachian Mt. Club in the White Mts.

Mt. Moosilauke, the first alpine summit crossed by the northbound AT in the White Mts., is largely owned by the college, and more than 90 percent of Dartmouth's incoming freshmen visit the mountain. The college's Moosilauke Ravine Lodge sits at the foot of the Jobildunk Ravine.

During a visit to the DOC, located in Robinson Hall on the Dartmouth campus, visitors can sign up for club membership, purchase copies of the club's maps and guidebooks, rent space in the club's cabins or at Ravine Lodge, or just feel the pulse of this unique organization while hanging out with students from the various clubs.

Contact the DOC at 603-646-2428, or write to the Dartmouth Outing Club, Robinson Hall, Box 9, Hanover, NH 03755.

option, descends 0.6 mi. to Trescott Rd., a continuation of E. Wheelock St., at a point 2.3 mi. east of Hanover (good roadside parking here). The AT/Velvet Rocks Trail climbs to the top of Velvet Rocks and curves to the right near the summit (approximately 1250 ft.).

Between Hanover and Glencliff, about 40 mi. away, the AT follows what was once the coastline of North America: the edge of the continent followed the Connecticut River valley north to the Hanover area, then cut diagonally across northern New Hampshire and Maine. The Velvet Rocks are the tip of a dome of coarse pink and gray granite that was formed when volcanic islands in the proto-Atlantic ocean overrode the ancient coastline and pushed it deep into the earth during the Acadian Orogeny, about 380 million years ago. The rocks of the coastline melted, then rose and cooled as domes of granite. Similar collections of domes can be found to the east of the entire Appalachian chain. Although the formation is small by New Hampshire standards, Velvet Rocks provides the only real opportunity for northbound AT hikers to get acquainted with the Granite State's namesake rock before they cross Kinsman Mt.

Large cracks in the exposed surface allow the overlying rock to be eroded in a process called exfoli ation—something like the rock shedding its skin. Large ledges and slabs hint at the true size of the dome, while horizontal bands of darker

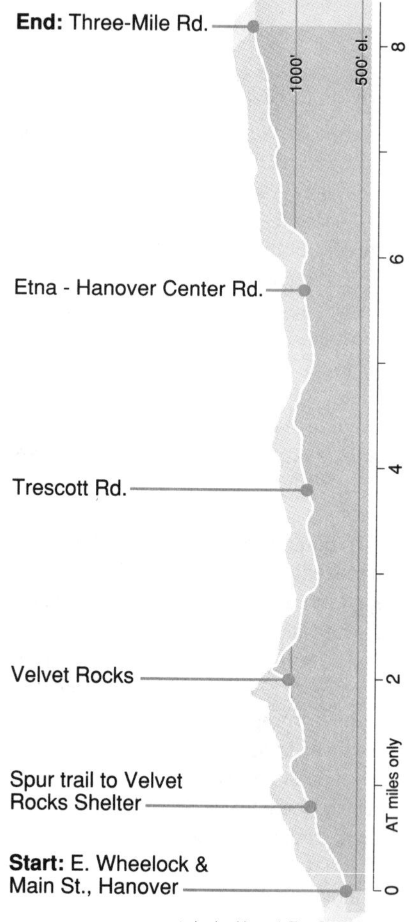

minerals show the flow patterns of the molten rock as it forced its way through the overlying rock.

The trail cuts sharply left off the ridge from the summit, then descends a number of slabs to a logging road that leads to a set of switchbacks over more granite.

The trail crosses a beaver pond, then passes through a pine farm. At 3.8 mi. it reaches Trescott Rd., which marks the end of the Velvet Rocks Trail. The AT crosses the road and climbs through a field to the woods, where more granite can be found—this time as part of a number of old

HIKE #1 Itinerary

Miles N	NORTH	Elev. (ft/m)	Miles S
8.2	**End: Three-Mile Rd.,** parking.	860/262	0.0
5.7	**Etna-Hanover Center Rd.,** early exit option, no convenient parking.		2.5
3.8	Cross **Trescott Rd.**		4.4
2.0	**Velvet Rocks.**	1250/381	6.2
1.8	**Trescott Rd. Spur Trail,** early exit option.		6.4
1.3	**Ledyard Spring Trail,** water.		4.5
0.8	Side trail to **Velvet Rocks Shelter.**		0.5
0.0	**Start: E. Wheelock and Main streets;** parking at Dartmouth College lot.	500/152	15.4

SOUTH

stone walls. Don't let the stacks of New Hampshire's state rock keep you from watching out for the state mammal, the white-tailed deer, which tend to hang out at the forest's edge at dawn and dusk. After a short walk on a logging road, the trail climbs to the left, then follows a stone wall on the right to Paine Rd. Follow this road to Dogford Rd., turn right, and then turn right onto Etna-Hanover Center Rd. One hundred yards past a cemetery, at 5.7 mi., turn left and climb a hill to a large grassy meadow. Beneath the old farm fields crossed by the AT here lies the wreckage of the volcanic islands that crushed the prehistoric coastline, as well as a lip of bedrock, once joined with the rock beneath Hanover, through which a tongue of molten granite pushed through to form Velvet Rocks.

After crossing the old farmland, the AT swings to the right and meets an old trail. At 8.2 mi. the AT reaches a small parking lot on Three-Mile Rd., where your waiting car will return you to the comforts of Hanover in just a few minutes.

HIKE #2

Moose Mt. and Holts Ledge

Maps: ATC N.H. and Vt. #4

Route: From Three-Mile Rd. over Moose Mt. and Holts Ledge to Lyme-Dorchester Rd.

Recommended direction: S to N

Distance: 9.0 mi.

Elevation +/-: 1400 to 2300 to 950 to 2100 to 880 ft.

Effort: Moderate

Day hike: Yes

Overnight backpacking hike: Optional

Duration: 5 to 5 1/2 hr.

Early exit option: Goose Pond Rd., at 5.5 mi.

Natural history features: Moose Mt.; Holts Ledge, peregrine falcon nesting area

Social history features: Dartmouth Skiway; the old Province Rd.

Trailhead access: *Start:* Follow East Wheelock St. E from Hanover for 2.8 mi., turn R on Trescott Rd., and drive 1.3 mi. to Etna-Hanover Rd. Turn R and follow Etna-Hanover Rd. (called Two-Mile Rd. on some maps) 1.8 mi. to Wolfeboro Rd. in Hanover Center. Turn R on Wolfeboro Rd. and go 1.0 mi. to Three-Mile Rd. Turn R and go 0.8 mi. to parking lot on R where AT crosses Wolfeboro Rd. *End:* From Lyme, go 3.2 mi. E on NH 10 to fork in road. The Dartmouth Skiway has abundant parking 0.1 mi. ahead on R.

Camping: Moose Mt. Shelter; Trapper John Shelter

You would expect to encounter moose during the AT's crossing of Moose Mt.—and you might. However, a few lucky hikers on this route have glimpsed far rarer wildlife: the peregrine falcons of Holts Ledge.

The vast majority of visitors to the ledge must content themselves with the knowledge that the peregrines are there, and that by keeping their distance from the cliffs, hikers are helping to ensure that they stay. Those who aren't treated to a sighting of the falcons will still be entertained by a variety of neotropical migrant birds—including bobolinks, indigo buntings, red-eyed vireos, and scarlet tanagers—that visit during the summer. The short, enjoyable climbs over Moose Mt. and Holts Ledge provide ample reward to most AT trampers and are an excellent warm-up for the higher mountains farther north.

From the Three-Mile Rd. parking area, the northbound AT is contiguous with Moose Mt. Trail for 5.5 mi. From Three-Mile Rd., the trail climbs briefly, then descends to a crossing of Mink Brook at 0.2 mi. At 0.4 mi. the trail reaches a woods road where it

Dale Gelfand

Downy woodpecker

meets the Fred Harris Trail, named for the founder of the Dartmouth Outing Club, which maintains this section of the AT. (The Harris Trail, which can be difficult to follow, takes the woods road to the left and rejoins the AT in 4.6 mi. at Goose Pond Rd., avoiding the climb over Moose Mt. and cutting 0.5 mi. off the length of our route on the AT.)

Soon after passing the junction with the Fred Harris Trail, the AT begins its sometimes steep climb to the south peak of Moose Mt., the first New Hampshire mountain crossed by northbound AT hikers.

About 420 million years ago you would have been strolling on a sandy beach that marked the coast of the continent rather than climbing over the quartzite mountain that rises here now. Moose Mt. is the first in a chain of three peaks that includes Mt. Cube and Smarts Mt., both crossed by the AT. These mountains are the exposed portion of a band of massive quartzites that crystallized, under immense heat and pressure, when the sandy shoreline was crushed by the colliding tectonic plates that created most of New Hampshire.

After passing through a clearing with views to the southeast, the AT reaches the south peak (2290 ft.) of Moose Mt. at 1.8 mi. From the summit, the trail descends into the col between the mountain's peaks. At 2.3 mi., it crosses a woods road.

This, the old Province Rd., was cut in 1772 by the order of Sir John Wentworth, the last of New Hampshire's royal governors. Sir John took over the governorship after the death of his uncle, Gov. Benning Wentworth, who had governed the province for 25 years. After taking office, the younger Wentworth purchased a 36-mi. tract of land on the shore of Lake Winnipesaukee, where he established an estate with the appropriately royal name of Kingswood. Winds of the coming revolution inspired tensions between the Connecticut Valley towns and the royal government, and Wentworth had the Province Rd. cut to allow better access to the rebellious towns from Kingswood. When the American Revolution began in earnest, Gov. Wentworth fled to Nova Scotia, where he got a second

The Return of the Peregrine Falcon

It only takes one sighting of a peregrine falcon in flight to understand why their disappearance was felt so deeply and why their reintroduction to the Northeast is monitored so diligently.

Adult peregrines are crow-size—about 15 to 20 in. long—with a slate-blue back and a white breast marked with bars and spots. Black stripes below their eyes, called mustaches in the birding world, actually resemble misplaced sideburns. Possibly the fastest bird on the planet, a peregrine can fly at speeds exceeding 150 mph in pursuit of prey. They eat many other birds, including the occasional duck, hawk, and, when nesting on city skyscrapers, pigeon, which they pluck from the sky during their high-speed dives. They also prey on small mammals and insects. Peregrines nesting in cities such as Springfield, Massachusetts; Hartford, Connecticut; Pittsburgh, Pennsylvania; and New York City are treated as celebrities, and the birth of chicks is often front-page news. A record-high 16 fledgling falcons took flight over New Hampshire in 1997.

Peregrine falcons are found worldwide, but their populations suffered a severe crash earlier this century, believed to be the result of pesticide poisoning, primarily from DDT. Since the banning of DDT and the founding of a reintroduction program in 1972 by the Peregrine Fund, a private group that breeds and releases the birds, this endangered species has made a dramatic comeback. In the lower 48 states the population of peregrines has risen from 39 pairs in 1970, the year the raptor was given federal protection, to 1,600 breeding pairs. The reintroduction has been so successful that Interior Secretary Babbitt announced plans to remove the bird from the endangered species list. The falcon should be "delisted" by the end of 1999.

chance to rule: he served as lieutenant governor there until his death in 1820. The town of Wolfeboro and Wentworth State Park occupy the land that once made up Kingswood.

Today the old Province Rd. is the path of the Clark Pond Loop, which leads 0.6 mi. left to Fred Harris Trail, or 0.5 mi. right (east) to Moose Mt. Shelter, a slopeside lean-to with space for six campers and reliable water from a nearby spring. Some level ground for tents can be found with a search of the nearby woods. Those who wish to get to know this historic road better can follow it 15 mi. to the east, where it rejoins the AT on Smarts Mt.

From its junction with the Old Province Rd., the AT/Moose Mt. Trail climbs the ridgeline of Moose Mt. to the north, then follows it as it swings to the east and climbs gradually to the north peak (2300 ft.). The trail continues along the ridgeline, heading northeast, makes a brief steep descent, then drops gradually until a sharp switchback to the right leads to a steep southerly descent off the ridge.

Moose Mt. Trail ends at Goose Pond Rd., 5.5 mi., which the AT follows to the left for about 50 ft. (there's limited roadside parking here). The AT now joins Holts Ledge Trail, which steps to the right off Goose Pond Rd. and follows a narrow road until it ends. After crossing a beaver dam, head left and begin the long, occasionally steep, climb up Holts Ledge. After passing the ledge's high point, about 2100 ft., you'll reach a junction, at 7.5 mi., where the AT descends to the left. A spur trail continues 0.1 mi. straight ahead to an overlook atop the ledge and the top of the Dartmouth Skiway.

One of the eleven pairs of peregrine falcons known to be nesting in New Hampshire in 1997 was located here, and young falcons have been spotted taking their first flights annually since 1988. These elegant raptors are sensitive about their privacy and won't return if intruded upon by humans, especially during their nesting season, which runs from spring through mid-July. Please take heed of the "No Trespassing" sign and chain-link fence that mark the birds' territory on the ledge. A nearby cabin is also off-limits to hikers. While sightings of falcons are rare, a careful eye

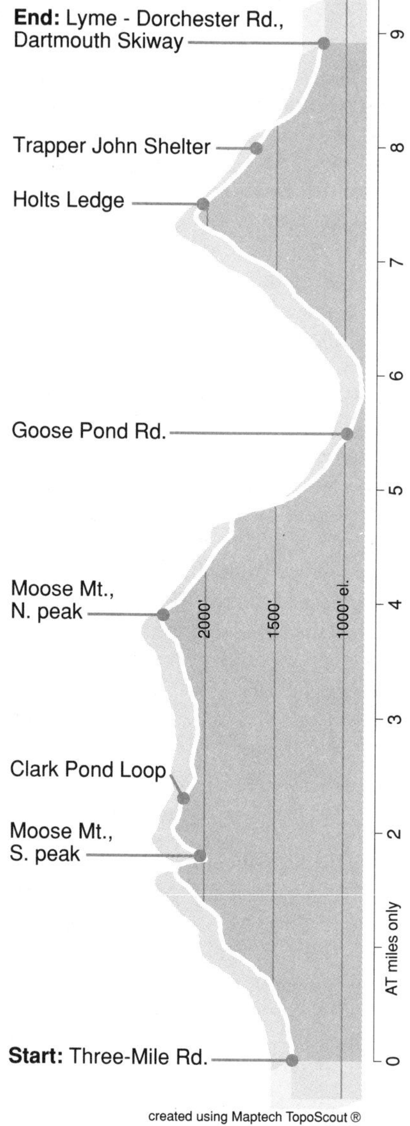

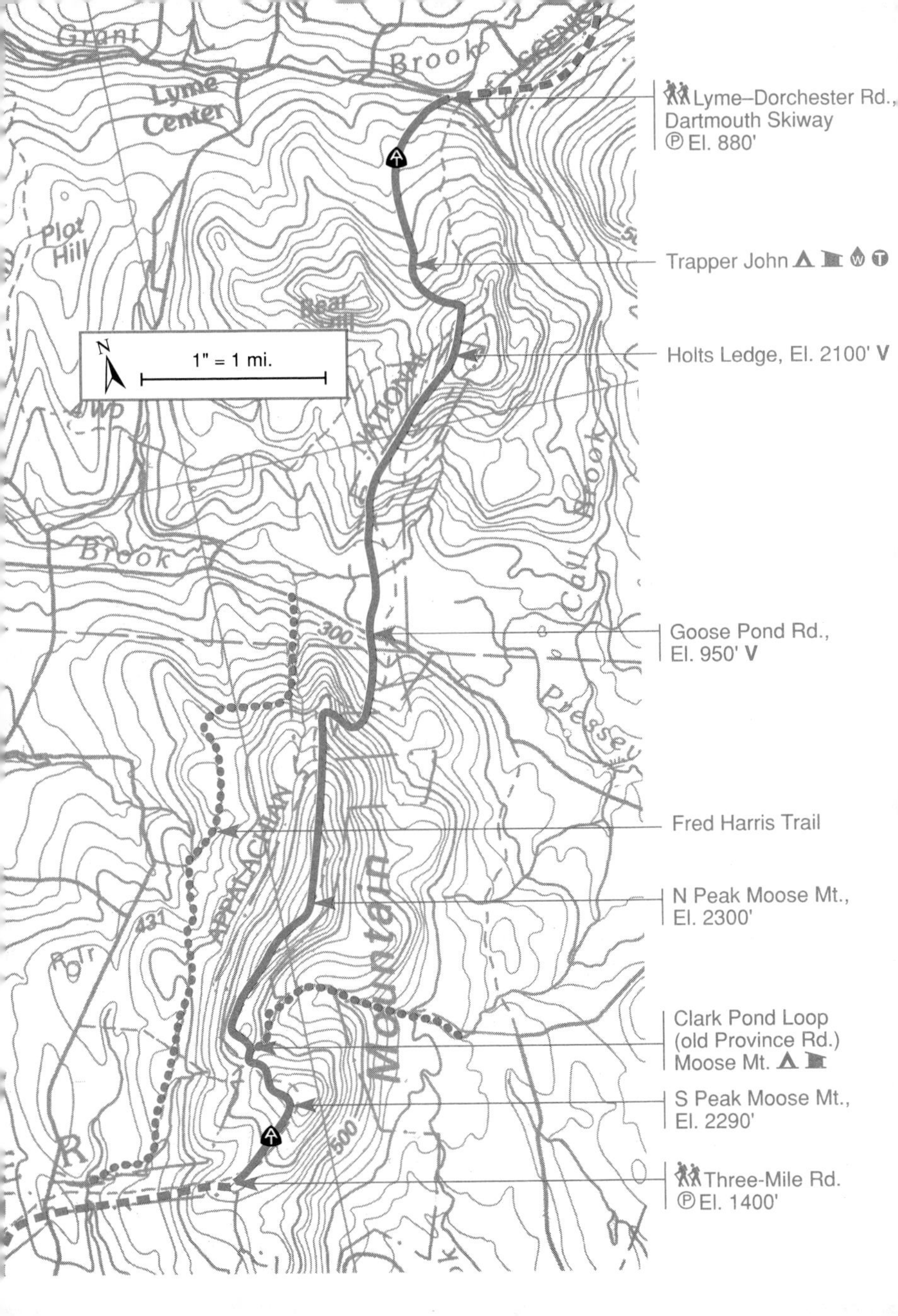

Grant
Brook
Lyme Center
Plot Hill
Bear Hill
Brook
Moose Mountain
APPALACHIAN
Pressey
Clark Brook
Lyme–Dorchester Rd., Dartmouth Skiway
Ⓟ El. 880'
Trapper John
Holts Ledge, El. 2100' V
1" = 1 mi.
N
Goose Pond Rd., El. 950' V
Fred Harris Trail
N Peak Moose Mt., El. 2300'
Clark Pond Loop (old Province Rd.) Moose Mt.
S Peak Moose Mt., El. 2290'
Three-Mile Rd.
Ⓟ El. 1400'

can usually find the orange whorl of the wood lily or the nodding scarlet flower of wild columbine near the ledges.

The AT makes a series of steep descents to the west from Holts Ledge, crosses an occasionally flowing brook, then drops gradually to the right. At 8.0 mi. a side trail leads 0.2 mi. to the left to Trapper John Shelter, which is named for the character from the popular movie and television program M*A*S*H, who, as the plot would have it, had studied medicine at Dartmouth. Dr. John McIntyre would be proud of the irreverent Dartmouth trail worker who used a Hitchcock chair for seating in the privy here, although the throne is not as comfortable as it is classy. The stone fireplace and chimney of the cabin that was once here stand in front of the shelter. A nearby creek provides water, but it has occasionally quit running in very dry years. The comfortable shelter accommodates eight people.

From the junction with the Trapper John spur trail, the AT descends gradually through the woods in a long eastward curve. It reaches Lyme-Dorchester Rd. at 8.9 mi.

The parking area at the Dartmouth Skiway is 0.1 mi. to the right (south) on Lyme-Dorchester Rd. In 1933 pioneering skiers in the Dartmouth Outing Club hiked up the flanks of Mt. Moosilauke to hold the first U.S. National Downhill Championships (see Hike #5). Since the boom in lift-service skiing, the Dartmouth Skiway has become the college's schussing center. Ski runs rise from both sides of Lyme-Dorchester Rd., where the skiway's rustic lodge is located. The runs to the south pass within 0.2 mi. of the AT on Holts Ledge. In February the skiway hosts a variety of events in the famed Dartmouth Winter Carnival.

HIKE #2 Itinerary

Miles N	NORTH	Elev. (ft/m)	Miles S
8.9	**End: Lyme-Dorchester Rd.,** Dartmouth Skiway, parking, 0.1 mi. R (S).	880/268	0.0
8.0	Side trail to **Trapper John Shelter,** privy, water.		0.9
7.5	**Holts Ledge,** spur trail to overlook, view.	2100/640	1.4
5.5	**Goose Pond Rd.** AT follows road, L, for 50 ft., then turns R off road.	950/290	3.4
3.9	**North peak of Moose Mt.**	2300/701	5.0
2.3	**Clark Pond Loop** to **Moose Mt. Shelter,** 0.3 mi. E.		6.6
1.8	**South peak of Moose Mt.**	2290/698	7.1
0.4	Junction with **Fred Harris Trail.**		8.5
0.2	Cross **Mink Brook.**		8.7
0.0	**Start: Three-Mile Rd.,** parking.	1400/427	8.9

HIKE #3

Smarts Mt. and Mt. Cube

Maps: ATC N.H. and Vt. #4

Route: From Dartmouth Skiway over Lambert Ridge and Smarts Mt., across Eastman Ledges and Mount Cube, to NH 25A

Recommended direction: S to N

Distance: 16.0 mi.

Elevation +/-: 880 to 3240 to 1400 to 2900 to 900 ft.

Effort: Moderate

Day hike: Optional

Overnight backpacking hike: Yes

Duration: 12 to 14 hr.

Early exit option: South Jacobs Brook logging road (unmarked), at 9.7 mi.

Natural history features: Smarts Mt.; Mount Cube

Social history features: Mount Cube Sugarhouse

Other features: Smarts Mt. fire tower

Trailhead access: *Start:* From NH 10 in Lyme, drive 3.2 mi. E on Lyme-Dorchester Rd. to fork in road. The Dartmouth Skiway has abundant parking 0.1 mi. farther on the fork to the R off Lyme-Dorchester Rd. Or continue W 0.1 mi. and turn R on Lyme-Dorchester Rd.; go 2.0 mi. to small parking lot at Smarts Mt. Ranger Trail. *End:* Drive N on NH 10 about 7 mi. to NH 25A. Turn R and drive 7.5 mi. to the AT crossing; limited roadside parking.

Camping: Smarts Mt. Tentsite and fire warden's cabin; Hexacuba Shelter

---

The AT's route over Smarts Mt. would be a favorite among hikers for its convenience—even if it didn't also offer some spectacular views.

The route offers two areas for overnight backpackers, which spreads out the crowd and allows various options for splitting up the days of hiking. Those who choose to stay on Smarts Mt. save the lion's share of the walking for the second day, while those who stay at Hexacuba Shelter finish most of it during the first day.

The accommodations are more than just convenient. The Smarts Mt. fire warden's cabin and tent sites are just steps away from the panoramic views atop the mountain's fire tower. Hexacuba, on the other hand, has some of the most interesting architecture on the AT.

A popular round-trip loop climbs northward up the AT to the summit of Smarts Mt., then follows the Smarts Mt. Ranger Trail south from the summit back down to the AT and Lyme-Dorchester Rd. From the Dartmouth Skiway parking lot, the circuit is about 12.0 mi. If you are able to park in the small parking lot (day and overnight) at the junction of the AT and the ranger trail, the loop will be about 8.0 mi.

Hikers who take the one-way option—which Hike #3 will follow—will reach NH 25A in 16.0 mi. from the Skiway parking lot and 14.0 mi. from the Ranger Trail parking lot.

From the parking area of the Dartmouth Skiway, home to events in the famed Dartmouth Winter Carnival, walk 0.1 mi. west, then turn right on Lyme-Dorchester Rd. Follow the road for about 200 yd. to a blazed post in a field on the right. The trail turns to the east here and climbs over the northwest shoulder of Winslow Ledge, crosses a stream in a col, then descends back to Lyme-Dorchester Rd. at 2.0 mi. (The Smarts Mt. parking area is to the left.) Here the AT/Lambert Ridge Trail heads north up Lambert Ridge, while the Smarts Mt. Ranger Trail cuts right and follows the gully between the ridge and Cole Hill to the east.

The AT route winds up along switchbacks past ledges and large red maple and American beech trees, reaching an outlook to the east at 2.8 mi. At 3.8 mi., ledges provide views to the northeast, onto the long ridgeline of Smarts Mt., 2.0 mi. away. Few parties can pass the spot on a clear day without taking off their packs and stopping a while to admire the peak—the first in New Hampshire to exceed 3000 ft. on the northbound AT.

From the ledges, the AT/Lambert Ridge Trail descends to the north, then swings east onto the flank of Smarts Mt. The ascent begins gradually amid hemlock and red maple, then steepens as the trail rises into the red spruce and balsam fir that thrive at higher altitudes.

At 5.3 mi., the Smarts Mt. Ranger Trail rejoins the AT for the steepest part of the climb to the summit. Hikers planning to do the loop back to Lyme-Dorchester Rd. will pick it up here after their visit to the summit. At 5.7 mi. a side trail on the right leads about 0.1 mi. to the scenic Smarts Mt. tent site, which occupies the floor of the dismantled Smarts Mt. Shelter. The nearby privy offers spectacular views to the south as a bonus. There's a fairly reliable spring near the trail junction.

The AT passes just east of the summit of Smarts Mt at 5.8 mi., where a steel fire tower rises from a clearing in the spruce trees. The fire tower is no longer used to search for fires but still provides the best views in the region. The Dartmouth Skiway, Moose Mt., the Connecticut River valley, and the Vermont peaks of Ascutney, Killington, and Camel's Hump lie to the southwest. Mt. Cube is 4.2 mi. away in the north, and the White Mt. peaks of Moosilauke and the Franconia Ridge rise to the northeast. Beyond them looms Mt. Washington, 48 mi. away.

At 5.9 mi. the Clark Pond Loop Trail descends to the east from the summit, reaching Moose Mt. col in approximately 15 mi. via the path of the old Province Rd., which connected the estate of Sir John Wentworth, the last royal governor of New Hampshire, with rebellious towns in the Connecticut River valley (see Hike #2).

Just below and east of the Smarts Mt. summit, the Dartmouth Outing Club maintains the fire warden's cabin as a shelter. The nearby fire tower's views, along with the convenient loop trails, make these accommodations quite popular, despite the dilapidated condition of the rotting and vandalized shack.

The Daniel Doan Trail, marked with blue blazes, leads northwest from the cabin to the Mike Murphy Spring, in 0.1 mi., and in 3.5 mi. to Doan's old stomping grounds in Quinttown and Orford. The trail was known as the Mousley Brook Trail in Doan's day, but it was renamed to honor the revered woods writer after he died in 1993.

From the north side of the summit the AT follows the J Trail, which must be named for the shape it draws on its way to Eastman Ledges. The path descends the summit ridge to the east, then swings sharply left and drops into the wooded valley to the north.

In his book *50 More Hikes in New Hampshire*, Daniel Doan describes finding the tracks of bears, drawn to this side of the mountain by the ripe

Continued on p. 44

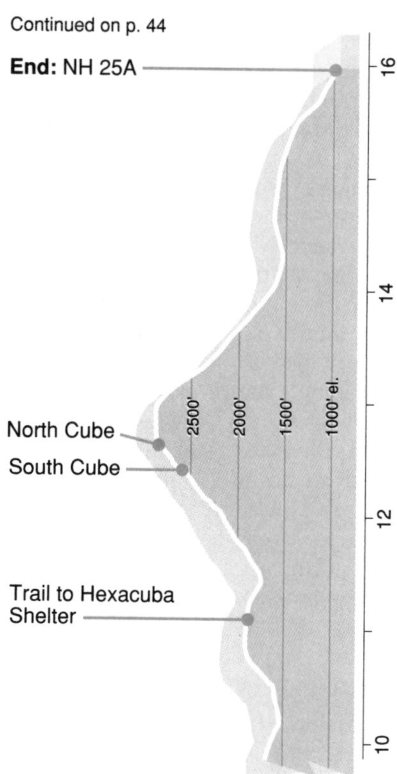

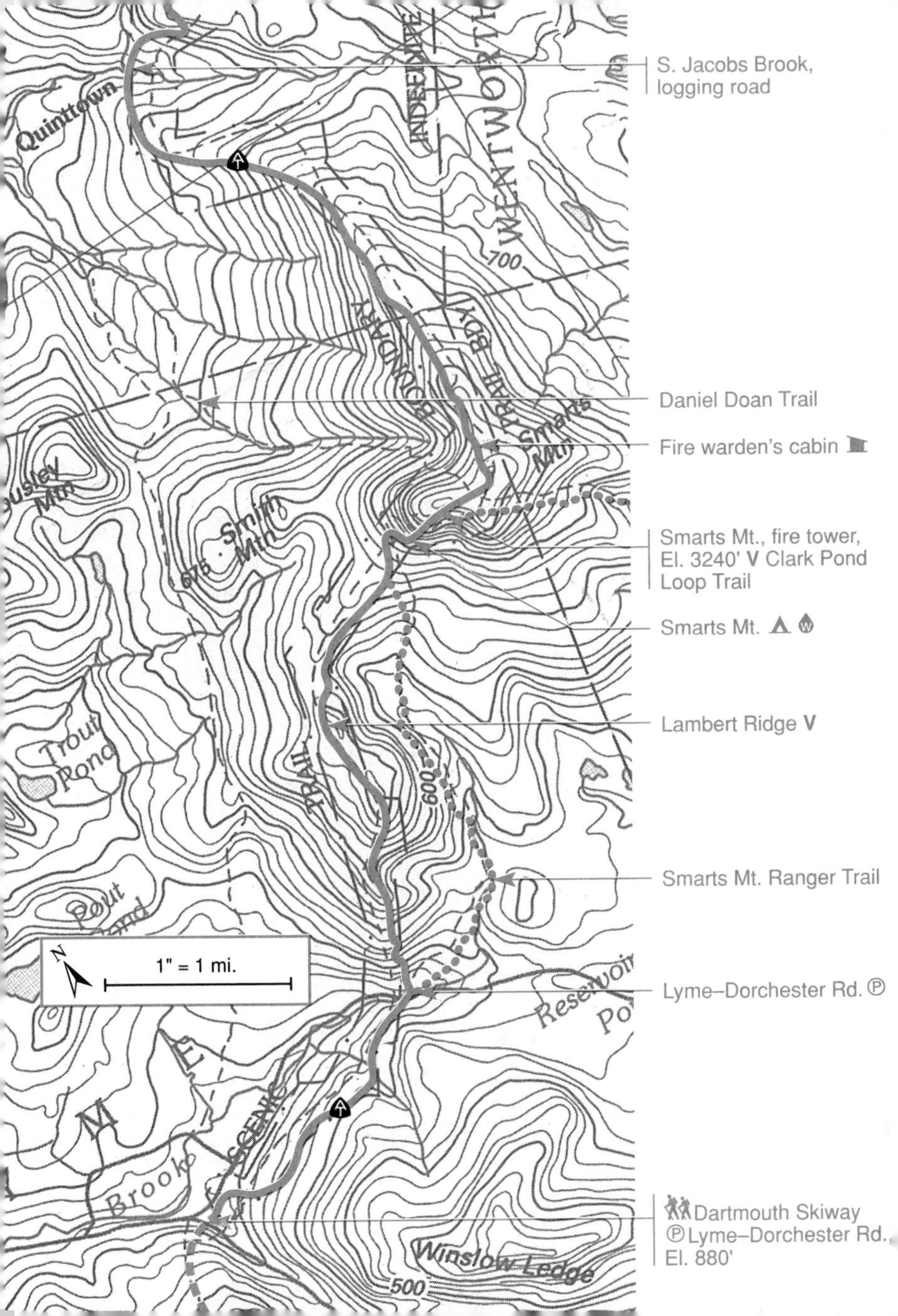
S. Jacobs Brook, logging road
Daniel Doan Trail
Fire warden's cabin
Smarts Mt., fire tower, El. 3240' V Clark Pond Loop Trail
Smarts Mt.
Lambert Ridge V
Smarts Mt. Ranger Trail
Lyme–Dorchester Rd. Ⓟ
Dartmouth Skiway
Ⓟ Lyme–Dorchester Rd.
El. 880'
1" = 1 mi.
N
Quinttown
Trout Pond
Smarts Mtn
Smith Mtn
Winslow Ledge
Reservoir
700
600
500
675

shadberry bushes in the first week of August.

During our late-August visit to Smarts Mt., a juvenile barred owl perched in a tree just above the trail to watch our descent. These, the most common owls in the woods of the Northeast, have a distinctive "barred" pattern on their chest and back and resemble a great horned owl without the horns. You are more likely to hear the broken rhythm of their "hoo, hoo, h', hoooo" than to see them.

Short-tailed weasels, which grow up to 9 in. long with a 4-in. tail, are also fond of the woods here too. Also known as ermines, they are brown with white feet in the warmer months, but turn completely white in winter. These bold and inquisitive relatives of the mink and the marten will dash in and out of cover to keep an eye on the humans they encounter.

The AT curves gradually to the left toward the floor of the valley, then swings back to the northeast. It crosses the fascinating A-frame of McGee's Bridge over South Jacobs Brook, then at 9.7 mi. crosses the South Jacobs Brook logging road, which leads 1.2 mi. west to Quinttown Rd. to provide an early exit. Quinttown was named for Benjamin Quint, who cleared his farmland there after sailing under John Paul Jones in the American Revolution. The forest has reclaimed both the farm and the town.

After crossing the logging road, the AT follows the Kodak Trail, which

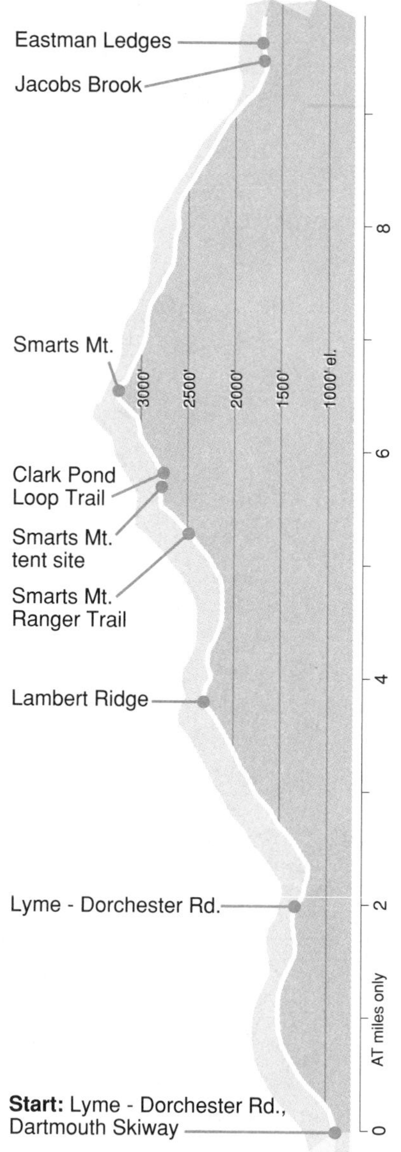

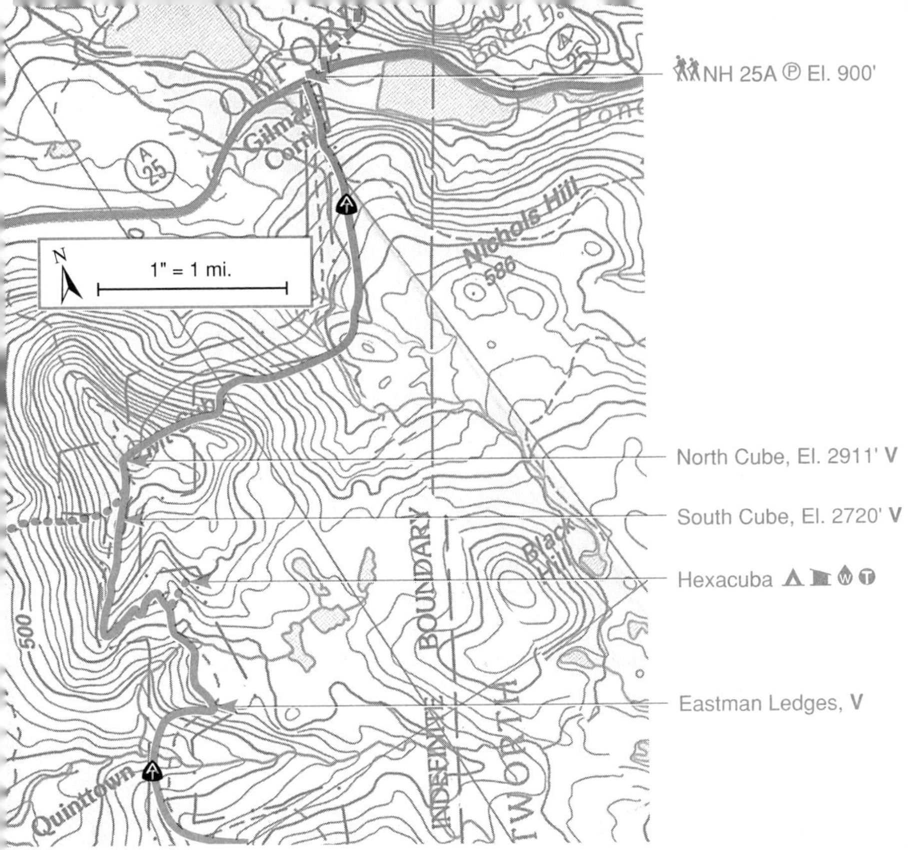

NH 25A Ⓟ El. 900'
1" = 1 mi.
N
Nichols Hill
586
North Cube, El. 2911' V
South Cube, El. 2720' V
Hexacuba
Eastman Ledges, V
Black Hill
BOUNDARY
500
Quinttown

continues to swing rightward as it makes a rocky climb to the southeast up Eastman Ledges, which provide a snapshot view of Smarts Mt. between South Jacobs Brook and Mt. Cube. At the crest of the ledges, a switchback to the left leads to a ridgeline, which the trail descends to the north. After crossing North Jacobs Brook the AT traverses a hillside. Then, at 11.1 mi., a side trail on the right climbs 0.3 mi. to Hexacuba Shelter. Water is available from North Jacobs Brook, 50 ft. beyond the junction on the AT.

Jim De Carlo, a Dartmouth physics major, oversaw the construction of the six-sided shelter and matching pentaprivy in 1990. The shelter's shape is both the topic and the venue for some lively conversations, but it can be tricky to divvy up the oddly shaped floor space when it's crowded.

From North Jacobs Brook, the AT climbs switchbacks to the west onto ledges, then hairpins back to the northeast and climbs a ridgeline that leads to Mt. Cube. At 12.5 mi. an unnamed side trail leads 1.5 mi. left to Baker Farm Rd., which in turn leads 1.5 mi. north to NH 25A. The AT bears right across the open summit of South Cube (2911 ft.), which looks out on Smarts Mt., the Connecticut River valley and, in Vermont, Mt. Ascutney. Here the quartzite that forms Mt. Cube, Smarts Mt., and Moose Mt. is dramatically exposed. Subtle swirls in the coarse-grained white rock show the flow patterns formed when the quartzite, once the sand of a prehistoric shoreline, was melted under tremendous pressure. The stripes of quartz are a younger rock that filled cracks in the older quartzite.

At 12.7 mi. the AT begins a steep descent on switchbacks to the right but hikers willing to take 0.6 mi. of extra steps should consider following another spur trail, part of a former AT route, that leads straight ahead to the summit of North Cube, which provides magnificent views of the White Mts. in the north.

Back on the present AT route, a stone chair on the left at 13.5 mi. provides a rest from those extra steps. At 14.2 mi., a log bridge leads over Brackett Brook, and at 15.5 mi. the AT bears to the left and crosses a gravel logging road. Smart Smarts Mt. hikers will slow down during the northernmost 0.5 mi. of this hike, where an old cellar hole, the remains of an early farm, can be found among ancient stone walls next to the logging road that will gradually bring them down to NH 25A.

HIKE #3 Itinerary

Miles N	NORTH	Elev. (ft/m)	Miles S
16.0	**End: NH 25A,** limited parking.	900/274	0.0
15.5	Gravel logging road.		0.5
14.2	Log bridge over **Brackett Brook.**		1.8
12.7	Saddle between North Cube and South Cube summits, side trail to North Cube summit, views.		3.3
12.5	Switchbacks to **South Cube** summit, views.	2911/887	3.5
11.1	Side trail to **Hexacuba Shelter,** water, privy.		4.9
9.7	Logging road, early exit option. Climb up Eastman Ledges.		6.3
9.6	Bridge over **South Jacobs Brook.**	1400/427	6.4
5.9	**Clark Pond Loop Trail,** then fire warden's cabin.		10.1
5.8	**Smarts Mt.,** fire tower, views.	3240/987	10.2
5.7	Side trail to **Smarts Mt. Tentsite.**		10.3
5.3	**Smarts Mt. Ranger Trail** rejoins AT.		10.7
3.8	**Lambert Ridge,** view.		12.2
2.0	**Lyme-Dorchester Rd., Ranger Trail,** parking. Junction of **Smarts Mt. Ranger Trail.** AT heads N.		14.0
0.1	**Lyme-Dorchester Rd.,** trail turns E.	880/268	15.9
0.0	**Start: Dartmouth Skiway** parking area.		16.0

SOUTH

HIKE #4

Wachipauka Pond and Webster Slide Mt.

Maps: ATC N.H. and Vt. #4
Route: From NH 25 over Wyatt Hill to Wachipauka Pond, up Webster Slide Trail to Webster Slide Mt., and back by same route
Recommended direction: N to S
Distance: 6 mi. round-trip
Elevation +/-: 1074 to 2260 to 1074 ft.
Effort: Moderate
Day hike: Yes
Overnight backpacking hike: No
Duration: 4 hr.
Early exit option: None
Natural history features: Webster Slide Mt.; Wachipauka Pond, glacial tarn
Social history features: Roger's House of Weather
Trailhead access: From Glencliff, follow NH 25 0.5 mi. NW to roadside parking.

Hikers headed from the quartzite mountains of western New Hampshire to Mt. Moosilauke are often so eager to reach the gateway to the White Mts. that they hardly remember passing Wachipauka Pond. Those who take the time find that the tarn is unforgettable when seen from the top of Webster Slide Mt., where they will also receive an early introduction to Moosilauke. Fortunately for those who have hurried past, the pond and the mountain can be reached easily in this circuit hike from Glencliff.

Most day hikers here choose to forgo the 8.0 mi. of AT between Wachipauka Pond and NH 25A to the southwest. Some are not interested in a long, largely flat woods walk when so many mountains beckon nearby; other are put off by Ore Hill, 5.0 mi. south of the pond, where an old mine has leached acid. Neither the roads crossed by the southbound AT in those 8.0 mi. nor the three DOC trails that between them carry the AT —Wachipauka Pond Trail, Ore Hill Trail, and Atwell Hill Trail—offer the rewards we will find when we turn right at Wachipauka Pond and follow the former AT route that leads up Webster Slide Trail.

From the roadside parking in Glencliff, follow NH 25 0.1 mi. northwest to a woods road in Oliverian Notch. The AT follows this road to the left (south) into the White Mt. National Forest. After approximately 0.2 mi. the trail begins a steady climb up Wyatt Hill on the Wachipauka Pond Trail. The woods surrounding the path are soon thick with red maple, suger maple, yellow birch, and American beech. At 1.2 mi. the AT reaches the top of Wyatt Hill. From here it descends gradually

The Weather Man

Thru-hikers arriving in the town of Glencliff on NH 25 are often sheltered in "Roger's House of Weather," the home of Roger Brickner, himself a 2,000-miler. Brickner, a historian and founder of the Museum of American Weather, provides mattresses in his barn, along with hot showers, hearty meals, and an analysis of upcoming weather on the trail. The trampers' pub in the basement displays a 36-ft. mural of the AT, which trail alumni might recognize from the yard of Brickner's previous home, the Appalachia Cottage in New York. The hostel is available irregularly from late July until September, and is never open on Wednesdays. Hikers can call Brickner at 603-989-3167 to see if he is taking guests. Day hikers and long-distance hikers alike will find a visit to the House of Weather fascinating.

west, then levels out and curves slightly to the southwest through boggy woods, where marsh marigolds and red-spotted newts can occasionally be found amid the skunk cabbage along the trail.

At 2.0 mi. the AT reaches Wachipauka Pond on the left. The pond almost seems to hide amid the thick hardwood forest. This is the southernmost of New Hampshire's glacier-made lakes on the AT. A 1000-ft.-thick sheet of ice that extended from Canada gouged a depression in the granite bedrock, then filled it with meltwater when it retreated.

The AT walks southwest along a finger of the lake pointing northeast toward Mt. Moosilauke. The route closely follows the northwest shore, passing Hairy Root Spring, which is as unreliable as its name is unappetizing. It is, however, the only source of water on this hike, other than the pond. Water from either source should be treated.

In the summer, watch the trail for signs of mink, which leave roundish tracks that are about 1 1/4 in. in diameter, with small claw marks. Minks grow up to 17 in. long with an 8-in. tail and dark brown fur. They are excellent swimmers and spend most of their time in the water. You might hear the spooky call of the common loon here, which actually uses four calls to communicate. During the summer day loons sing in falsetto wails, strange yodels, and maniacal, tremulous laughs. At night their call is a quavering "ho-oo." The beautiful black and white birds are long-bodied swimmers with stout, knife-like bills. They have a black head, white belly, a collar of white stripes, and white checks on their backs.

Should you be lucky enough to see one, keep your distance, as the birds are quite shy and easily disturbed. You are more likely to see a merganser, a diving duck with a spikelike bill and slender body.

At 2.3 mi. the AT/Wachipauka Pond Trail reaches Webster Slide Trail. Turn right off the AT onto this spur trail, which follows a logging road to the west, up a gully onto the southern flank of Webster Slide Mt. After 0.2 mi., Webster Slide Trail turns right and begins a somewhat steep climb onto Webster Slide Mt., then swings back to the east for the final push onto the summit. At 2.9 mi. you will climb onto the broad, rounded summit of the mountain.

The summit viewpoint is 0.1 mi. farther east, past the ruins of a summit shelter. The eastern ledges hang directly over Wachipauka Pond, and although the tarn seemed to hide in the woods when you were beside it, you can now see the glacier's magnificent work. From the beckoning finger of water in the north, the pond is cut in an easterly crescent through the lush, forested valley.

Mt. Moosilauke, 4802 ft., is even more impressive now as it looms over the lowlands to the south. The overlook provides an introduction to this historic White Mt. (see Hike #5).

From the summit of Webster Slide Mt., return to Glencliff by reversing your path. Give an appreciative glance at Wachipauka Pond as you pass it, remembering how it looked from the ledges above.

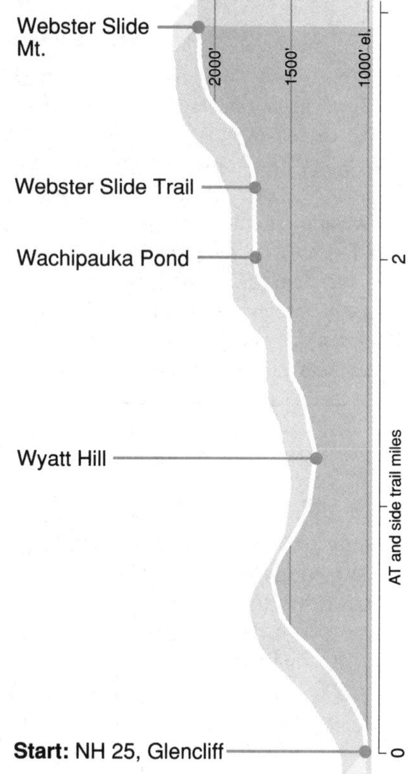

created using Maptech TopoScout ®

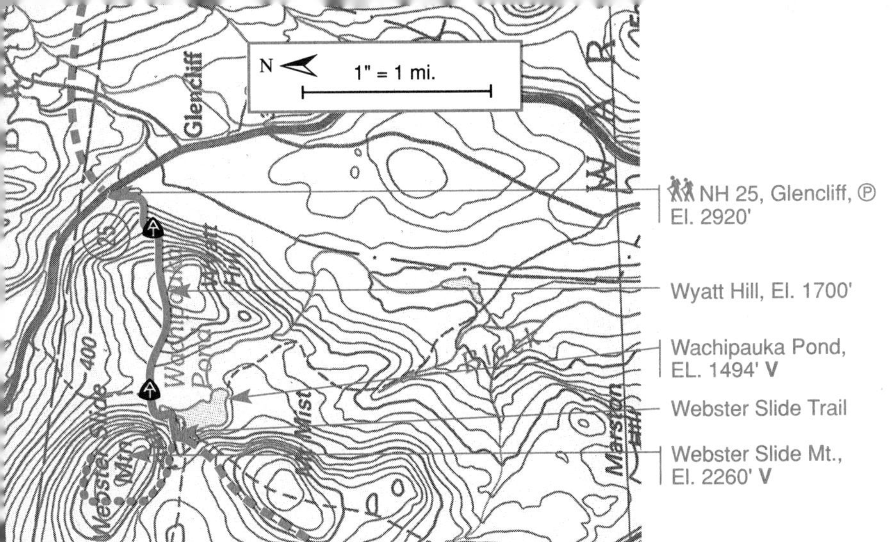

N
1" = 1 mi.
Glencliff
NH 25, Glencliff, Ⓟ
El. 2920'
Wyatt Hill, El. 1700'
Wachipauka Pond,
EL. 1494' **V**
Webster Slide Trail
Webster Slide Mt.,
El. 2260' **V**

HIKE #4 Itinerary

Circuit Hike

Miles N		Elev. (ft/m)	Miles S
	Start: NH 25, 0.5 mi. NW of Glencliff, roadside parking.	1074/327	0.0
	Woods road; follow road L (S) into White Mt. National Forest.		0.1
	Begin climb up **Wyatt Hill** on AT/Wachipauka Pond Trail.		0.2
	Crest of **Wyatt Hill.**	1700/518	1.2
	Wachipauka Pond; trail follows shoreline, passes spring.	1494/455	2.0
	Turn R onto **Webster Slide Trail;** begin climb to summit.		2.3
	Summit of **Webster Slide Mt.,** views 0.1 mi. farther E.	2260/689	2.9
	REVERSE DIRECTION. Go north. Read from bottom up.		
5.8	**End: NH 25,** roadside parking.	1074/327	
5.7	**Woods road;** turn R onto NH 25.		
4.6	Crest of **Wyatt Hill.**	1700/518	
3.8	**Wachipauka Pond;** trail follows shoreline; gradual ascent begins.	1494/455	
3.5	Turn L onto **AT/Wachipauka Pond Trail.**		
2.9	Begin descent from **Webster Slide Mt.**	2260/689	

Circuit Hike

HIKE #5

Mt. Moosilauke

Maps: ATC N.H. and Vt. #3
Route: From Glencliff over Mt. Moosilauke to Kinsman Notch
Recommended direction: S to N
Distance: 9.5 mi.
Elevation +/-: 900 to 4802 to 1870 ft.
Effort: Strenuous
Day hike: Yes
Overnight backpacking hike: Optional
Duration: 7 to 8 hr.
Early exit option: Snapper Trail, at 4.9 mi.
Natural history features: Alpine environment
Social history features: Remains of summit hotel
Trailhead access: *Start:* From Glencliff follow NH 25 0.5 mi. NW. Park in Glencliff or on the W side of NH 25 near intersection of southbound AT. *End:* Day and overnight parking on L (W) side of NH 112, 0.5 mi. N of Lost River Reservation in Kinsman Notch.
Camping: Jeffers Brook Shelter; Beaver Brook Shelter

Standing guard on the southwestern edge of the White Mts., Moosilauke is both a friendly concierge and a stern sentinel for the high peaks beyond. Its summit lays the rest of the mountain range and the Connecticut River valley at hikers' not-too-weary feet. The first peak to break treeline on the northbound AT, Moosilauke has some of the most spectacular views in the Whites. Although the east side of the mountain is relentlessly steep, from the west, Moosilauke's summit is easier to reach than most of the high peaks deeper in the range. A sunny walk to the Moosilauke summit from Glencliff is like getting a room at the Ritz for the price of a Motel 6.

But the mountain is also subject to the full force of New Hampshire's violent storms. Hundreds of hikers have been lured to Moosilauke by its panoramic views only to be turned away from the summit by its fickle and ferocious weather. Make sure to get a weather report for the White Mt. summits before heading up Moosilauke (or any alpine summit), and be prepared for the worst.

Were it not for the weather, Moosilauke's spectacular views and moderate difficulty would make it one of the best introductions to alpine hiking offered in the Whites. Perhaps the weather is just part of the introduction.

For many hikers another part of the introduction is a disagreement about how to pronounce "Moosilauke." Some say that the name finishes with

The AMC

Before the trail traversing the Appalachian Mts. was even a dream, New England hikers knew the chain well through the efforts of its namesake club. The Appalachian Mt. Club was born in a classroom at the Massachusetts Institute of Technology in January 1876, the brainchild of a few dozen Boston-area White Mt. hikers.

Today the AMC, the oldest continuously operated outdoor organization in the U.S., boasts a membership of more than 64,000 and is one of the most active organizations of its kind in the world. Along the more than 350 miles of AT maintained by the club, the AMC offers the widest range of services available anywhere on the trail.

Foremost among these are the AMC's eight alpine "huts"—Lonesome Lake, Greenleaf, Galehead, Zealand Falls, Mizpah, Lakes of the Clouds, Madison, and Carter Notch—all on or near the AT. The huts (lodges really) offer bunks and meals to overnight guests and comfortable pit stops to daytime visitors. Rates in the full-service huts run between $56 and $62 a night per person, with discounts for children, club members, and visits during less popular times of the year. Carter Notch Hut, which offers bunkrooms and a self-serve kitchen, charges between $16 and $18. Most of the huts are open from mid-spring through mid-autumn, and Zealand Falls and Carter Notch are open year-round. The comfortable accommodations and spectacular locations of the huts have made them overwhelmingly popular, so book your stay well in advance by contacting AMC reservations at 603-466-2727.

Accommodations are also available at the AMC's Joe Dodge Lodge at Pinkham Notch on NH 16, and at the Crawford Notch Hostel on US 302.

a "key," while others believe there is only a "lock."

However you say it, Moosilauke remains one of the most popular peaks in the White Mts. and receives thousands of visitors every year. Weekdays and early mornings are the best times to find solitude. No matter when you visit, be kind to the mountain by staying on the trail, leaving all alpine vegetation untouched, and picking up any garbage you find.

To the Pemigewasset Indians, who centuries ago christened the mountain with their word for "high bald place," Moosilauke was a favorite hunting ground. To the European settlers of the 1700s, it provided farmland and wood. To tourists in the 1850s, the mountain was a popular resort, with a bridle path, a carriage road, and a summit hotel called Prospect House. To 19th- and 20th-century paper companies, Moosilauke was a supply of timber. They stripped virtually the entire western side of the mountain between 1890 and 1940.

The AMC hiker shuttle—one van based at Pinkham Notch Visitor Center and another at Crawford Notch Hostel—runs between a dozen of the most popular trailheads from late spring through early autumn. Because of the vans' limited hours of operation (between 9 a.m. and 4 p.m.), they are usually best used to reach the start of your hike in the morning so that your car will be waiting for you at the end point—you won't have to worry about catching the shuttle by mid-afternoon. Reservations, which cost about $7, should be made at least a day in advance, as the vans are often full. Call AMC reservations to check the current shuttle schedule, price, and availability.

Although the AMC is still based in Boston, the Pinkham Notch Visitor Center is its hikers' headquarters. The visitor center's Trading Post sells a wide variety of hiking supplies and books, puts out an early morning breakfast buffet in a large dining room, and provides extensive information on the White Mts., including daily weather reports and trail condition updates. The pack room downstairs is open 24 hours a day to allow hikers a place to meet, shower, repack their gear, warm up or cool down. The Joe Dodge Lodge, next door to the Trading Post, can accommodate more than one hundred guests ($27 to $30 a night per person), and has an extensive library and a conference room.

The Crawford Notch Hostel accommodates forty guests in the renovated Shapleigh studio and eight people each in the two nearby cabins, which are heated with wood stoves. A self-serve kitchen is available for hostel guests. Dollar showers, weather reports, and trail condition updates are also provided here. Last-minute hiking supplies can be purchased at the AMC's store at nearby Crawford Depot.

To the students and staff of Dartmouth College, Moosilauke is an outdoor classroom and sports complex. Nearly all of the incoming freshmen meet the mountain through an outing to the Moosilauke Ravine Lodge, which the college owns and operates, at the base of the mountain on the southeast (the lodge, which features eighty bunks, hearty family-style meals, and evening programs, is open to the public from late May through mid-October). The college also owns the summit, where its outing club operated the summit hotel, renamed the Tip Top House, as a hikers' hut until it burned in 1942. Between the summit and the lodge, the college owns 4500 acres of the Baker River watershed. The rest of the massif is owned by the U.S. Forest Service.

From Glencliff, which provides ample and secure parking, walk 0.5 mi. northeast on NH 25 to its junction with the southbound AT (there is some additional parking here on the left). Follow the northbound AT, known for the next mile as the Town

Line Trail, turning right into the woods 100 yd. farther north.

Shortly after entering the woods, the AT crosses Oliverian Brook, a formidable obstacle in high water, and briefly follows the brook downstream before climbing a ridge. (If the brook is too high to cross safely, follow Sanitarium Rd. from Glencliff to the Glencliff Trail.) After a mile in the woods, the trail crosses a bridge over a Jeffers Brook tributary, then intersects a side trail that leads 0.1 mi. to Jeffers Brook Shelter. In warmer weather small cascades and kettles in Jeffers Brook provide a welcome spot to cool off.

Moosilauke merits some contemplation, and Jeffers Brook Shelter provides a convenient and comfortable setting to ponder the upcoming adventure. For most hikers a breakfast stop at the shelter will provide more than enough time to meet the mountain with their minds. Those searching for deeper meditation should consider camping at Jeffers Brook. There is plenty of space for tents, so day hikers can leave the shelter to long-distance backpackers.

From the shelter, the AT leads 0.2 mi. to USFS 19, which it follows for 0.1 mi. to Sanitarium Rd. This road serves the New Hampshire Home for the Elderly and provides a shortcut for hikers who want to skip the first 1.7 mi. of the hike. Parking for four or five cars is available at a small U.S. Forest Service parking area off Sanitarium Rd., just beyond the Glencliff Trail trailhead.

The AT follows Glencliff Trail for the next 3 mi. After leaving Sanitarium Rd., it passes through a gate into a pasture, crosses a brook on a bridge, and follows first a farm road and then a cart track through farm fields.

At the site of an old camp 0.4 mi. from Sanitarium Rd., the AT turns left and climbs into the woods. Hurricane Trail soon forks off to the right and climbs over Hurricane Mt. to Ravine Lodge. Although its name is ominous, on many days Hurricane Trail may be a better choice than the AT. You are more likely to encounter hurricane-force winds atop Moosilauke, where the gusts above treeline often top 60 mph, than you are on Hurricane Mt. (Hurricane Mt. and the Hurricane Trail commemorate the hurricane of 1938, which blew down most of what remained of Moosilauke's old-growth forest.)

Following the AT uphill, imagine the farmland below as part of the homestead of one of those early settlers. Imagine Pemigewasset braves prowling the woods in search of deer and moose. Imagine the woods road being used to clear the forest, and what the slope looked like when it was bald.

Today these woods are dominated by American beech, sugar maple, yellow birch, and paper birch trees, although hemlocks, aspens, poplars, and red oaks can be found here as well. The woods road soon fades, and about 3 mi. into the hike, the AT turns right and begins to ascend steeply, moving from the hardwood forest to the spruce and fir forest typically found above 2500 ft. Higher-elevation hardwoods, like striped maple, with red-and white striped bark; mountain ash, with white flowers in the spring and orange berries in the fall; and paper birch can still be found among the red spruce and balsam fir as the AT approaches the 3000-ft. elevation. But by the time it reaches 3500 ft., most of the hardwoods have vanished.

As you climb through the conifers, watch the understory for goldthread, with three leaves and white flowers; Indian pipes, which are white, hanging, bell-shaped flowers that grow in clusters around tree roots; and wood sorrel, an edible plant with heart-shaped leaves and white flowers striped with pink.

At about 4.0 mi., the AT begins its steepest climb on this side of Moosilauke. It quickly ascends above 4000 ft., where the weather is too harsh and the soil too poor to support even the red spruce trees. Here only the balsam fir survive, and their distinctive aroma sweetens the air as it is huffed and puffed by hikers on this section of the trail. Don't be surprised if gusting wind drives mist through the small conifers, which shrink as the rocky path continues to climb.

During our hike here, we encountered a camp stove burning in the middle of the steepest pitch of the trail. Beside it a college professor and his elderly father huddled in a stand of small fir trees. Their down coats, wool caps, and fleece gloves seemed out of place in August. We figured they had already been to the summit.

The pitch relents after 0.5 mi., and at 4.7 mi. the AT intersects an 0.2-mi. spur to the South Peak's overlook, as well as the carriage road that the Moosilauke Mountain Road Company built to carry tourists to the Tip Top House nearly 150 years ago. The point where the AT/Glencliff Trail meets the carriage road was the starting point for America's first downhill ski race, which took place in April 1927, one of many notable dates in ski history marked on the the flanks of Mt. Moosilauke by the DOC. About fifteen skiers competed in the Moosilauke Down Mountain Race, with the winner reaching the bottom of the carriage road in about 21 min. In March 1933, the first U.S. National Downhill Championships were held on the carriage road, with DOC skier Henry "Bem" Woods reaching the finish in about 8 min. to take first place. Another Dartmouth student, Harry Hillman (for whom Hillman's Highway, a ski run in Mt. Washington's Tuckerman Ravine, is named), finished second.

By the time the racers in that first national championship were struggling down the narrow, winding switchbacks of the carriage road, some DOC skiers had seen a faster future. The first race on Cannon Mt.'s Richard Taft Trail, which was steeper, wider, and more open than Moosilauke's carriage road, had been held earlier in the winter of 1933. Determined to keep Mt. Moosilauke on the cutting edge of downhill racing, DOC skiers cut Hell's Highway during the following summer. The trail started just below South Peak, plunging more than 900 ft. in 0.5 mi. down the west side of Gorge Brook Ravine across the 38-degree incline of the "Rock Garden," then following what is now the Gorge Brook Trail to the Ravine Lodge. DOC skiers became known as "Hell Divers," and Hell's Highway was considered the steepest, most challenging ski run in New England, but only for 5 years. The hurricane of 1938 caused a landslide in the Rock Garden that exposed bedrock too steep to hold snow. The Slide Trail, a now abandoned hiking trail, followed the approximate route of Hell's Highway from a point just south of the junction of the Glencliff Trail and the carriage road. The Snapper Trail, which drops off the carriage road 2.0 mi. below the summit and connects to the Gorge Brook Trail, was also originally cut as a ski trail by the DOC.

Lights, a 25-meter ski jump, and a small ski tow occupied Moosilauke briefly in the late 1940s, but most skiers headed to more developed ski fields elsewhere in the Whites. Skiers (and snowmobilers) still travel the carriage road on occasion, but most of its traffic nowadays is on foot. The AT follows the carriage road 0.2 mi. to the ruins of the summit hotel.

Stepping past treeline, frigid air may blast you from your footing as the trail climbs gradually out of the krummholz—balsam firs and black spruces so gnarled and stunted by the fierce weather that they resemble bonsai. Legend holds that famed German skier Otto Schniebs, hired in 1930 to coach DOC skiers, was disappointed in the stature of Mt. Moosilauke until, during his first hike up the mountain, he was forced to crawl along the summit ridge by its fierce weather.

Take care to keep your feet between the stones that mark the edges of the path. A single step could kill the trailside cushions of mountain sandwort, which shows white flowers with five petals in July, August, and September; and mountain cranberry, an evergreen mat with pink, urn-shaped flowers in June and bright red berries in August and September.

The rock here is schist, which was exposed when an overlying layer of granite was eroded away. Moosilauke rises from an arm of the Littleton Formation, which also provides the bedrock of the Presidential Range, and the rocks here are quite similar to those found atop Mt. Washington.

The 5-ft. cairns that mark the path across the summit might seem excessive on a clear day, but they can fade like ghosts in rain or fog, making it difficult to see from one to the next.

The 4802-ft. summit, at 5.7 mi., provides a true panorama on a clear day. Vermont's tallest peaks lie in the distance—Mansfield and Camels Hump in the northwest, Stratton and Killington in the southwest, and the Lake Willoughby gap to the north. The

White Mts, to the northeast, are mesmerizing. The peaks crossed by the AT are lined up like soldiers: South Kinsman, Lafayette, Lincoln, South Twin, Liberty, Washington, Hight, Carter Dome.

On July 4, 1860, more than 1000 people came to the summit of Mt. Moosilauke for the opening of the Prospect House, where they were entertained by a brass band, Native American dancers, and speakers. The old hotel continues to be one of the best lunch stops in the state, although today's visitors must make themselves comfortable on the relics of the stone foundation, bring their own food, and let the view entertain them.

On other days, Moosilauke's legendary weather will provide the entertainment. Gusts of wind often slap hikers like pinballs blowing through the foundations of the old hotel and of a dismantled emergency shelter nearby.

Geologist J. H. Huntington and photographer Amos Clough spent the winter of 1869-70 in the Summit House (originally Prospect House) after their proposal to study the winter atop Mt. Washington was turned down by the owners of the Tip Top House. After their successful studies of the winter environment on Mt. Moosilauke, they easily raised the funds and support needed to conduct a study on Mt. Washington's summit the following winter.

Don't worry if the weather turns while you are on the summit. As opposed to the other alpine peaks in the White Mts., a few minutes of quick walking will bring you down into the shelter of the trees.

The route you have just completed, following the Glencliff Trail and the carriage road, provides the most direct return back down the west side for a round-trip hike of 11.4 mi. For those looking to return to Glencliff via a different route, Gorge Brook Trail is a beautiful, though often steep, alternative. Gorge Brook Trail gradually descends 3.7 mi. from the carriage road just east of the summit, down the southern flank of the mountain to Ravine Lodge Rd., where a second car can be left to make a 9.4-mi. hike. From Ravine Lodge Rd., Hurricane Trail leads west 4.3 mi. back to Glencliff Trail and Sanitarium Rd., making a complete loop hike. Be forewarned, however: this circuit is more than 13 mi. long and may take up to 10 hr. to hike.

On the left side of the AT, at 6.1 mi., Benton Trail descends 3.1 mi. to Tunnel Brook Trail, which leads north to Tunnel Brook Rd.

The AT turns a sharp right at the junction with Benton Trail and takes a wild ride 3.7 mi. down Beaver Brook Trail, the most difficult path on the mountain. Like any good carnival thrill, the excitement builds slowly, as the trail drops gradually for more than a mile before veering along the brink of Jobildunk Ravine, which provides some beautiful views and tough terrain. The ravine is one of the best examples of a glacial cirque this side of the Presidential Range. Snow in the valley below accumulated over years and was eventually compressed into a small glacier that carved the steep-walled ravine more than 50,000 years ago. Legend holds that the ravine is named for three brothers who were early loggers in the region—Joe, Bill, and Duncan.

At 7.9 mi., a spur trail on the left (west) leads 200 ft. to Beaver Brook Shelter, which was relocated in 1993 from the bottom of Beaver Brook Cascades to this high terrace with its gorgeous outlook through yellow birch trees onto the ranges to the east. The shelter sleeps ten, and there is space for two tents on nearby platforms. The site has a composting toilet, and water is available from a nearby brook accessed by a spur trail.

Below the shelter the trail steepens as it follows a tributary to Beaver Brook. Here the path drops like a roller-coaster back into the hardwood forest. The trip up this path from Kinsman Notch is a thigh-pumping grunt; the trip down to the notch is like trying to walk on a waterslide. Be particularly careful when it is wet.

Steep granite slabs run most of the last mile down the mountain to Kinsman Notch. On the left they are filled by the spectacular Beaver Brook Cascades. The right-hand side is filled with stone footholds, wooden steps, and iron rungs placed by DOC trail crews. The descent is steep, slow, and scary. Boulders in the brook and ledges beside it provide seats for watching the water show and a

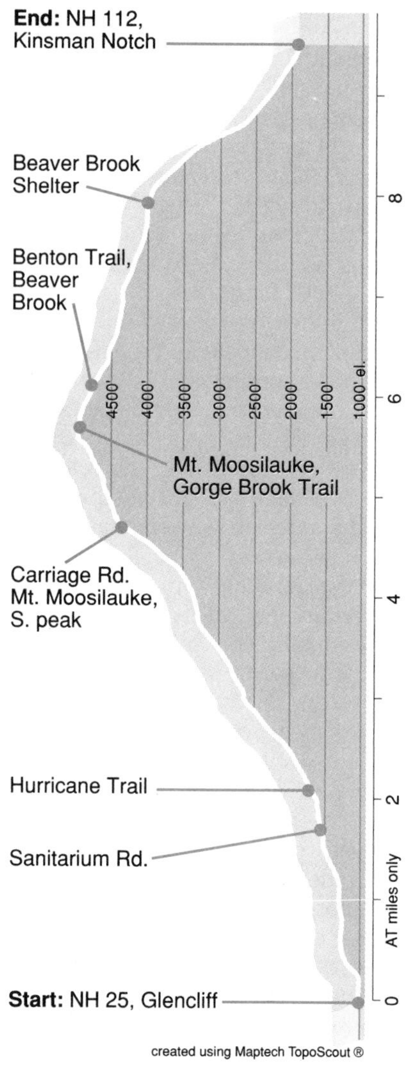

created using Maptech TopoScout ®

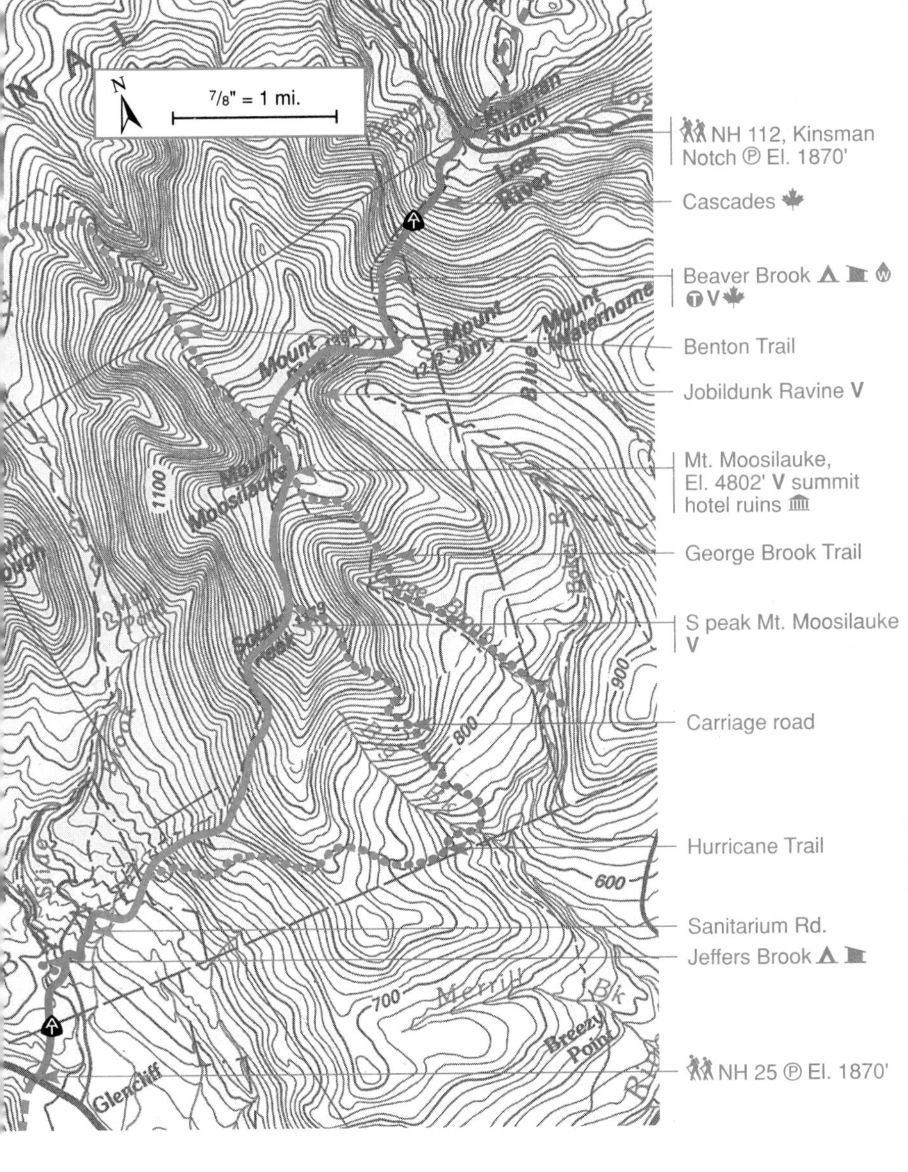
7/8" = 1 mi.
N
NH 112, Kinsman Notch Ⓟ El. 1870'
Cascades
Beaver Brook
V
Benton Trail
Jobildunk Ravine V
Mt. Moosilauke, El. 4802' V summit hotel ruins
George Brook Trail
S peak Mt. Moosilauke V
Carriage road
Hurricane Trail
Sanitarium Rd.
Jeffers Brook
NH 25 Ⓟ El. 1870'
Kinsman Notch
Lost River
Mount Moosilauke
Mount Jim
Mount Watername
Breezy Point
Glencliff
Merrill Bk
1100
900
800
600
700

HIKE #5 Itinerary

Miles N	NORTH	Elev. (ft/m)	Miles S
9.5	**End: NH 112,** Kinsman Notch parking lot.	1870/570	0.0
7.9	Spur to **Beaver Brook Shelter,** tentsites, view, water.		1.6
6.1	Junction with **Benton Trail;** AT turns sharp R; difficult descent on **Beaver Brook Trail** to Jobildunk Ravine.		3.4
5.7	Summit of **Mt. Moosilauke,** views; **Gorge Brook Trail,** 3.7 mi. to Ravine Lodge Rd., alternative descent.	4802/1464	3.8
4.7	Carriage road and spur to **South Peak** overlook, views.		4.8
4.0	Steep climb begins.		5.5
2.1	AT heads into woods. **Hurricane Trail** forks R to Ravine Lodge; follow AT uphill.		7.4
1.7	**Sanitarium Rd./Glencliff Trail junction,** limited parking; follow AT/Glencliff Trail.		7.8
1.1	Spur trail to **Jeffers Brook Shelter,** tentsites.		8.4
0.6	Cross **Oliverian Brook.**		8.9
0.5	**Junction with AT,** limited roadside parking; walk N on road.		9.0
0.0	**Start: NH 25, Glencliff,** roadside parking.	1074/327	9.5

SOUTH

welcome rest for aching knees. A variety of ferns grow along the cascades among the beech, birch, and maple trees. Look for the triangular fronds of long beech fern and the broad, toothed fronds of mountain wood fern.

The trail levels out quickly at the bottom of the cascades, crossing two bridges over Beaver Brook before meeting NH 112 and the Kinsman Notch parking lot, where hikers can catch their breath, put their feet up, and once again contemplate Moosilauke's welcome to the Whites.

HIKE #6

Kinsman Mt.

Maps: ATC N.H. and Vt. #3

Route: From Kinsman Notch, over the south and north peaks of Kinsman Mt., down past Lonesome Lake to Franconia Notch

Recommended direction: S to N

Distance: 17 mi.; 16.3 mi. on AT

Access trail name & length: Whitehouse Trail (0.7 mi.)

Elevation +/-: 1870 to 3478 to 2400 to 4358 to 1450 ft.

Effort: Very strenuous

Day hike: Optional

Overnight backpacking hike: Yes

Duration: 10 to 13 hr.

Early exit option: Dilly Trail, at 0.7 mi.; Gordon Pond Trail, at 3.3 mi.; Reel Brook Trail, at 6.5 mi.

Natural history features: Lost River glacial gorge; Eliza Brook cascades; Lonesome Lake; The Flume

Trailhead access: *Start:* From North Woodstock go W on NH 112 for 6.2 mi. to Kinsman Notch. Hikers' parking lot is located on L (W) side of road 0.5 mi. N of Lost River Reservation. *End:* From North Woodstock, drive 5.8 mi. N on US 3; hiker parking on R (E) side of road, adjacent to NH State Park Flume complex in Franconia Notch State Park.

Camping: Eliza Brook Shelter; Kinsman Pond Campsite; Lonesome Lake Hut

Among the many fierce peaks and famous names that create the lure of the White Mts., Kinsman is often forgotten. Rugged reputations put mountains like Washington and Moosilauke high on hikers' hit lists. Names like Crawford and Guyot turn up in many a campfire tale. But Asa Kinsman—who is said to have homesteaded near the notch only because he was lost—seems equally lost in the local lore. Likewise, his namesake notch seems a poor brother to the triumvirate of Franconia, Crawford, and Pinkham. Kinsman Mt. isn't even a mark on the Rand McNally road atlas. Hikers, however, will find the mountain staunch and spectacular, full of cascading brooks, high mountain tarns, hand-over-hand climbs, and top-of-the-world views. Those who meet this mountain with their feet will not soon forget it, even if they can't remember its name.

Kinsman Notch also marks the southern boundary of the Appalachian Mt. Club's maintenance of the AT within the White Mt. National Forest, an area that is more intensively managed than other areas of the trail. Trailside camping is carefully restricted throughout the White Mts. and is prohibited in some places, so thorough planning of overnights is required here. (See "The AMC" in

Hike #5 and "White Mt. National Forest" in Hike #7.)

From Kinsman Notch the hike north over the mountain is long and committed, and all but the fittest hikers should plan for one or two overnights. It is 7.5 mi. to Eliza Brook Shelter, 10.0 mi. to the south summit, and 11.5 mi. to the Kinsman Pond Campsite. Only four side trails intersect the AT in that distance, and the only one that returns to the Notch is less than a mile from the start of the hike.

From the hikers' parking lot in Franconia Notch, however, the southbound AT meets the summit of South Kinsman in 6.3 mi., putting it within the reach of ambitious day hikers. A variety of trails on the Franconia side of the mountain—Kinsman Pond Trail, Kinsman Ridge Trail, Lonesome Lake Trail, and Hi-Cannon Trail—allow hikers to return to Franconia Notch on a different path than they took up the mountain.

From the Kinsman Notch hikers' parking lot, the AT follows Kinsman Ridge Trail, which climbs sidehill north from NH 112, then turns right and ascends quite steeply into the woods. Although the grade relents shortly after entering the woods, hikers should take this first ascent as a wake-up call. The terrain on this trail is consistently challenging, with constant ups and downs over steep and rocky ground.

Watch and listen for rose-breasted grosbeaks, red-eyed vireos, and wood thrushes in the hardwood forest here, and blackpoll warblers in the evergreen forest higher up. Magnolia warblers and hermit thrushes can be found in both.

The Kinsman Ridge Trail/AT intersects Dilly Trail 0.7 mi. from NH 112. A hike up Kinsman Ridge Trail and back down Dilly Trail will leave hikers 0.5 mi. from their car, making a convenient loop involving an hour or so of hiking for those who want to spend most the day exploring Lost River. Dilly Trail descends for 0.8 mi., past an overlook of Kinsman Notch, to the Lost River Reservation. Here the aptly named Lost River disappears into a huge gash in the granite of Kinsman Mt. The narrow valley is filled with enormous boulders that fell from the sides of the cirque above when the glacier receded, 12,000 to 20,000 years ago. The boulders have created caverns and cliffs, and in many places have completely buried the river. Where the rushing waterway is exposed, it gives a wondrous performance, carving giant circular holes, called potholes, into the granite and falling occasionally in beautiful waterfalls. Trails, ladders, and boardwalks allow visitors to explore the geologic wonderland for a fee. The Society for the Protection of New Hampshire Forests maintains the area, as well as an extensive garden of native plants, an ecology trail, and a museum. Tickets for admission to the gorge can be purchased in the reservation's main building, which also houses the entrance to the gorge, a cafeteria, and a gift shop.

The Franconia Notch Geology Show

Most backpackers headed down from an overnight on Mt. Kinsman or the Franconia Ridge step into Franconia Notch by the early afternoon. That leaves plenty of time to explore the state park's three-ring circus of geology.

For AT hikers, the first stop is usually **The Flume,** a dramatic gorge formed by granite, glaciers, and gushing water. The 800-ft.-long Flume, 1.0 mi. south of the AT on the east side of I-93, carves through the base of Mt. Liberty like an alleyway between skyscrapers. Rock walls 12 to 20 ft. apart rise 70 to 90 ft. above Flume Brook. The gorge lies where a dike of basalt eroded more quickly than the Conway granite that surrounded it. The Pool, a deep, glacier-carved basin, lies 0.5 mi. from the Flume. "Aunt Jess" Guernsey discovered The Flume and The Pool in 1808 when, at age 93, she was searching for some new fishing holes in Franconia Notch. Admission has been charged to visit the Flume since the 19th century, when entrepreneurs built a boardwalk to allow tourists a walk through the gorge. Now managed by the state, The Flume has bus service, guided tours, a snack bar, souvenir stand, and visitors' center. In 1997 admission was $7 for adults, $4 for children aged between 6 to 12, and free for children under 6.

The Basin, a giant pothole carved by glacial runoff, lies 1.0 mi. north of the AT on the west side of I-93. A paved path leads past a variety of cascades, waterfalls, and smaller potholes before arriving at The Basin itself. Sand swirling in the Pemigewasset River has carved what began as a small crack in the granite bedrock into a pool that is 15 ft. deep and more than 30 ft. wide. Resist the temptation to join the bold youths who, on hot summer days, ignore the park rules and jump from the small overhanging cliff into the water below.

You will undoubtedly see the **Old Man of the Mountain,** the ringmaster of the Franconia Notch geology show, on postcards and state highway signs before you arrive in the Notch. A viewing area for New Hampshire's most famous face, the profile atop the cliffs on the side of Cannon Mt., is located about 5.0 mi. north of the AT on I-93. Today turnbuckles, tie rods, cables, and cement hold together the ledges that form the face. Writers and painters have been stopping here for nearly two centuries to take in the "Old Man." Bring a copy of Nathaniel Hawthorne's "Great Stone Face" to the overlook to compare your impressions with those of the famous author.

Another popular literary site lies in the town of Franconia, just north of the state park, where the New Hampshire home of poet Robert Frost is maintained as a memorial. Readings, lectures, and concerts are held here in the summer.

From the junction with Dilly Trail, the AT heads northeast over the bumps, humps, and hills of Kinsman Ridge, past brooks and overlooks. At 3.3 mi. it reaches Gordon Pond Trail—which leads to Gordon Pond (0.3 mi.), Gordon Falls, and finally to NH 112, where a second car can be left to allow an 8.2-mi. walk.

From the junction with Gordon Pond Trail, the AT/Kinsman Ridge Trail climbs in spurts for the next 0.7 mi. to the west knob of Mt. Wolf (3360 ft.). At 4.6 mi. a 200-ft. spur trail heads up to the summit of the east knob (3478 ft.), where there are fine outlooks onto the ranges to the east.

Black bear, moose, and red fox can be found in the diverse woods of beech, maple, birch, aspen, hemlock, and spruce. The trees are home to porcupines, along with one of their few predators, the fisher. The largest member of the weasel family, fishers grow to 25 in. long with a 14-in. tail and dark brown fur. They feed on mammals, not fish, and kill porcupines by flipping them upside down and slashing their unprotected bellies. At 6.5 mi. Reel Brook Trail, an early exit option, descends left 4.0 mi. to NH 115 near Easton, where Asa Kinsman built his homestead. Shortly after the junction, the AT/Kinsman Ridge Trail drops into the col between Mt. Wolf and Mt. Kinsman.

At Eliza Brook, 7.5 mi. into the hike, a short side trail on the left leads to Eliza Brook Shelter, nestled in the woods at about 2400 ft. The musical sound and beauty of the brook make the shelter an ideal spot to refill water bottles or have some lunch. Hikers who prefer a more leisurely pace may choose to spend a night at this shelter and a second night at Kinsman Pond. This would provide an entire day to enjoy the 4 mi. of spectacular scenery and arduous hiking between Eliza Brook and Kinsman Pond. The lean-to has space for eight.

From Eliza Brook Shelter the trail crosses back over the brook, follows a logging road left, then turns from it after about 0.3 mi. to rejoin the brook amid a stunning series of cascades and pools. At 8.9 mi., after again crossing Eliza Brook, the trail climbs to log bridges across the east end of Harrington Pond, at about 3400 ft.

The pond seems to hide in the woods and will probably disappear altogether in centuries to come, as sediments collecting in the glacier-carved tarn gradually transform it into a bog. Lack of adequate drainage and an abundance of spaghnum moss make the soil very acidic, so the bacteria needed for decomposition have a hard time surviving here. Consequently the soil has little of the nitrogen needed to nourish most plant life. Insectivorous plants, however, gather their nitrogen from the insects they consume and thrive in this environment. Look for sundew, which has a spike of small flowers rising above small leaves on long stems covered with sticky, knob-topped hairs; and pitcher plant, with vase-shaped leaves that often hold water below a dark reddish flower on a 1-ft.

stem. Both can be found among the black spruce and tamarack trees that grow around the edges of alpine bogs and ponds.

From the pond it is just over a mile to the summit of South Kinsman. But between you and the top lie nearly 1000 ft. of some of the most difficult climbing on the AT.

The path is soon filled with a jumble of blocks and boulders shaped like the granite kitchen appliances in a *Flintstones* cartoon—a microwave stacked atop a dishwasher perched on a refrigerator. Pull-ups and boot edges will bring you to the top of the pile, where you will be confronted with more of the same.

Glaciers littered Kinsman with these granite blocks, but their arrangement on the trail is largely the result of the Herculean efforts of AMC trail crews. The blocks themselves are checkered with rectangular crystals up to 3 in. long. These large feldspar crystals, distinctive of Kinsman granite, cooled faster than the surrounding rock when the molten granite was still deep in the earth.

Climbing over this blocky trail is a strenuous but enjoyable romp on a sunny day, but be wary on a wet one. These climbs are treacherous when they are damp, and Kinsman offers no detour to avoid them in inclement weather. Each pitch seems steeper and more spectacular than the last. As the boulders in the middle of the trail get larger, the spruce and fir trees beside them shrink with the approaching treeline. Behind you, the Franconias and the ranges beyond appear like a violet mural.

At the summit of South Kinsman Mt. (4358 ft.), 10.0 mi., the Franconia Ridge, across Franconia Notch, dominates the eastern horizon while Mt. Wolf and Mt. Moosilauke stand to the southeast and the valley of the Pemigewasset River speads out to the southeast.

The summit cairn sits on more than an acre of open tundra covered with a variety of alpine plants, mosses, and lichens. In August look for urn-shaped fruits on the low sweet blueberry, which has narrow leaves with fine teeth, and the mountain cranberry, which has red berries and thick, waxy leaves. Both are edible, but the blueberries are much tastier. Labrador tea, another perennial shrub found here, has thick leaves with woolly undersides; native Americans steeped the leaves to make a medicinal tea.

From the summit of South Kinsman, the trail descends back into gnarled black spruce and balsam fir trees, crosses a col, then climbs to the wooded summit of North Kinsman (4293 ft.), about 1.0 mi. away. The ridge between the peaks is part of the divide between waters that flow west, to the Connecticut River, and east, to the Merrimack River. A side trail on the right near the North Kinsman summit leads to two lovely overlooks, the first of the Franconias and the second of Kinsman Pond, 500 ft. below, where the Kinsman Pond Campsite is located.

On the descent from North Kinsman the AT passes a junction with Mt. Kinsman Trail on the left, then reaches Kinsman Junction at 11.5 mi., where Kinsman Pond Trail leads right 0.1 mi. to the campsite.

There is an AMC caretaker stationed at Kinsman Pond through the summer, and a fee is charged to stay overnight. On a busy weekend it's easy to see why. The shelter and tent sites are spread out in an acre of woods and bogs next to the scenic pond. The campsite can comfortably accommodate two dozen people, but is often crowded with more than thirty overnight visitors during the peak months. Large groups are encouraged to contact the AMC with their overnight itineraries in order to prevent sites from becoming overwhelmed.

Plan your stay at Kinsman Pond for a weekday or an off-peak weekend, and avoid visiting on holidays. Arrive early if you hope to get a spot in the comfortable shelter, which has space for fourteen but fills quickly. The campsite also has five tent platforms.

Bicknell's thrushes, boreal chickadees, white-throated sparrows, and gray jays are all common in the surrounding woods.

Although the pond is lovely, it hides an ugly secret: the contents of the campsite's privy were accidentally dropped into the pond from a helicopter several years ago. Make sure to purify any water taken from the pond, or better yet, get your water from one of the brooks crossed by

Continued on p. 70

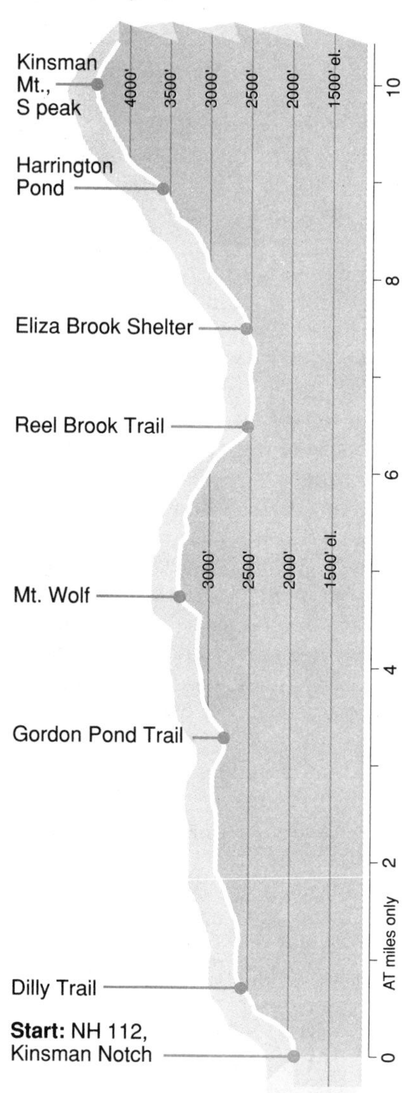

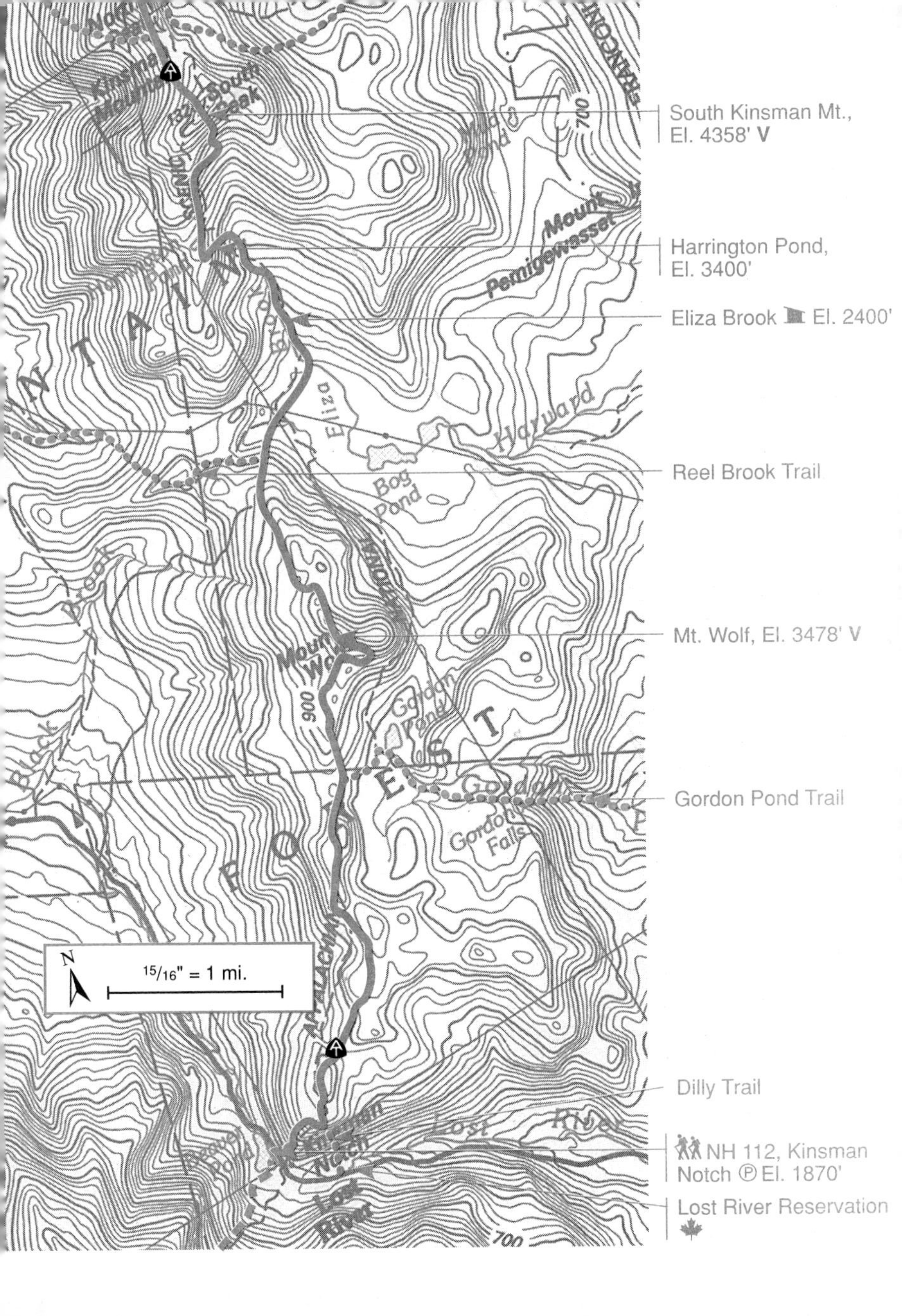

South Kinsman Mt., El. 4358' V
Harrington Pond, El. 3400'
Eliza Brook El. 2400'
Reel Brook Trail
Mt. Wolf, El. 3478' V
Gordon Pond Trail
Dilly Trail
NH 112, Kinsman Notch Ⓟ El. 1870'
Lost River Reservation
15/16" = 1 mi.
N
South Peak
Pemigewasset
Eliza
Harward
Bog Pond
Gordon Pond
Gordon Falls
Black Brook
Lost River
700
900

the AT/Fishin' Jimmy Trail 1.0 mi. to the north (but still purify it).

From Kinsman Pond several trails bearing the Kinsman name head away from the AT:

1) Kinsman Ridge Trail, which the AT has followed from Kinsman Notch to Kinsman Junction, veers northeast over hills called the Cannonballs, then over Cannon Mt. in 3.2 mi., and in another 2.2 mi. heads into the tramway parking lot beneath New Hampshire's most famous profile, the Old Man of the Mountain.

2) Mt. Kinsman Trail heads northwest, to NH 116 near Easton, where Asa Kinsman built his homestead.

3) Kinsman Pond Trail descends to the southeast and rejoins the AT on the Cascade Brook Trail.

The AT, on the other hand, spends the next 2 mi. on a trail with a name that is hard to forget: Fishin' Jimmy, after a story Annie Trumbull Slosson set in Franconia Notch. Although the Connecticut author's fiction has long been out of print, she is well remembered for her work as an entomologist in the White Mts., where, among other accomplishments, she recorded more than 500 species of flies atop Mt. Washington. The hero of her story knew these woods better than any real-life woodsman could, but wanted to be more than just a fisherman—he yearned to serve Christ as a "fisher of men."

Few have read his tale, but many have walked his trail, and despite his noble aspirations, some hikers find Jimmy to be a slippery character.

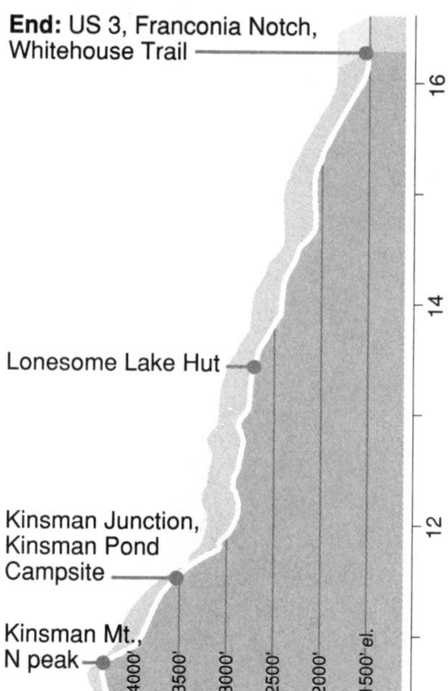

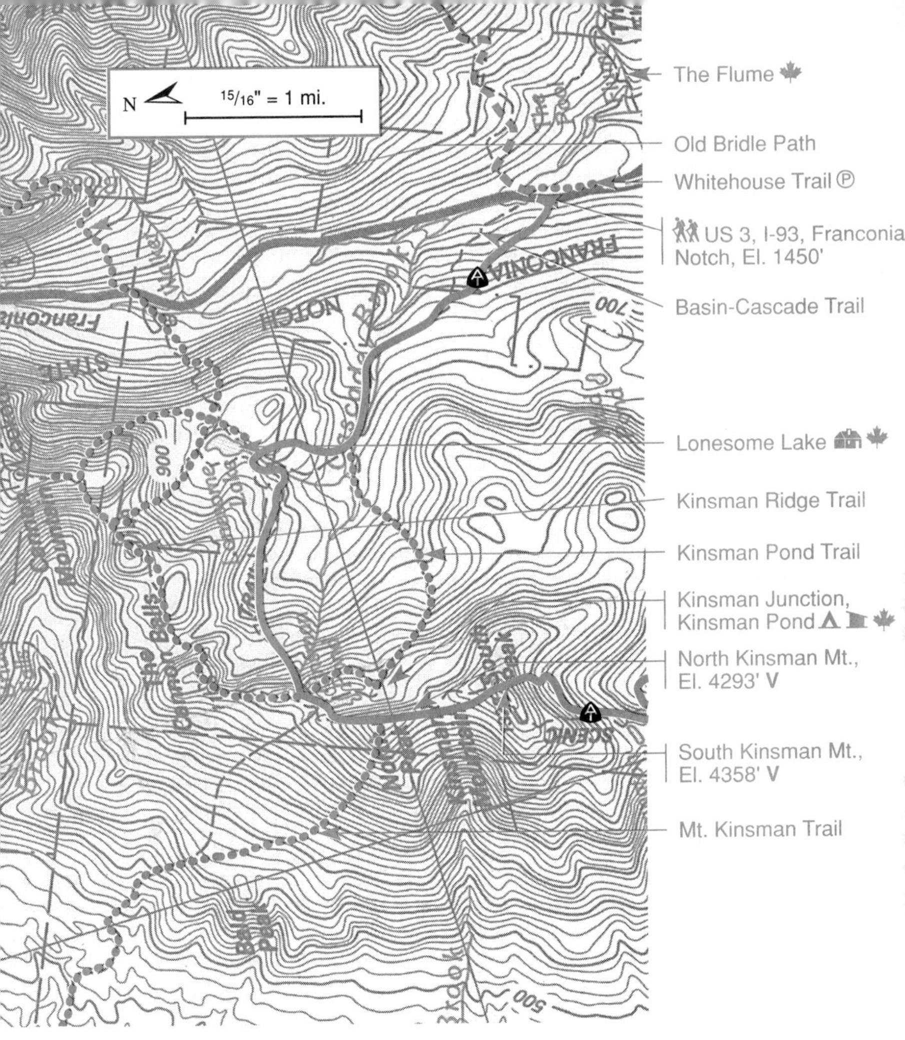
N
15/16" = 1 mi.
The Flume
Old Bridle Path
Whitehouse Trail Ⓟ
US 3, I-93, Franconia Notch, El. 1450'
Basin-Cascade Trail
Lonesome Lake
Kinsman Ridge Trail
Kinsman Pond Trail
Kinsman Junction, Kinsman Pond
North Kinsman Mt., El. 4293' V
South Kinsman Mt., El. 4358' V
Mt. Kinsman Trail
FRANCONIA
NOTCH
STATE
900
700
500

Rains can make the path slick and muddy, and the wooden steps occasionally attached to the steepest parts may do little to slow your slide. After several steep pitches and brook crossings, the AT/Fishin' Jimmy Trail descends into Franconia Notch State Park and arrives at Lonesome Lake, a pastoral mountain tarn surrounded by trails with wonderful views of the Franconia Ridge (see Hike #7).

The Lonesome Lake Hut, at 13.4 mi., is the first AMC "hut" met by the northbound AT. It is the easiest of the AMC's huts to reach and offers a number of programs for families and children. The hut, with its eight-sided skylighted roof, was built on the western shore of Lonesome Lake in 1964, making it one of the newest of the AMC huts. It is open from May until mid-October, with space for forty-six overnight guests in small family-size bunkrooms. Meals are provided for overnight guests in June, July, and August, but plan on bringing your own food and doing your own cooking in May, September, and October, when the "croo" is replaced by a caretaker. Reservations can be made by calling AMC's Pinkham Notch Visitor Center (603-466-2727). Hot drinks, baked goods, and basic hiking supplies are available to visitors throughout the day, and the hut is a fine spot to take a load off. Camping, however, is not permitted around the lake, hut, or anywhere else in Franconia Notch State Park outside of Lafayette Campground.

Continuing from Lonesome Lake, the AT takes the Cascade Brook Trail southeast, first following a rough logging road, then hopping rock-to-rock across Cascade Brook at 14.8 mi., near a junction with the Basin-Cascade Trail. Sixty yards downstream from the brook crossing there is an overlook of Rocky Glen Falls.

From Cascade Brook the trail continues at a moderate grade over a wide and often muddy path. The path may be crowded here, so be prepared to step aside. Shortly after crossing Whitehouse Brook—again on rocks—the trail announces its return to civilization by turning into a paved bike path and passing under the US 3 overpass. After the overpass, Whitehouse Trail turns right from the AT and leads 0.7 mi. to the Flume complex and the hikers' parking area.

To the east, the AT heads up Liberty Spring Trail to the Franconia Ridge, some of the most famous miles of the entire trail. But hikers who have had the rocky climb to the summits of Kinsman and their spectacular vistas to themselves will be thankful that this mountain keeps its secrets well.

HIKE #6 Itinerary

Miles N	NORTH	Elev. (ft/m)	Miles S
Total: 17.0 mi. with access trail.			
0.7	Access: **Whitehouse Trail** S to Flume hiker parking, US 3, 5.8 mi. N of North Woodstock		0.7
16.3	**End AT miles: US 3** overpass.	1450/442	0.0
14.8	**Cascade Brook,** crossing, overlook.		1.5
14.3	**Kinsman Pond Trail** rejoins AT.		2.0
13.5	AT follows **Cascade Brook Trail.**		2.8
13.4	**Lonesome Lake Hut,** food, supplies, program.	2760/841	2.9
11.5	**Kinsman Junction; Kinsman Pond Campsite,** shelter, tent sites, caretaker.		4.8
11.3	Junction with **Mt. Kinsman Trail.**		5.0
10.9	Summit of **North Kinsman Mt.,** overlooks.	4293/1309	5.4
10.0	Summit of **South Kinsman Mt.,** views.	4358/1328	6.3
8.9	**Harrington Pond,** then difficult boulder-strewn climb.	3400/1036	7.4
7.5	**Eliza Brook Shelter.**	2400/732	8.8
6.5	**Reel Brook Trail,** early exit option.		9.8
4.6	East peak of **Mt. Wolf,** views.	3478/1060	11.7
3.3	**Gordon Pond Trail,** early exit option		13.0
0.7	**Dilly Trail,** route to Lost River, early exit option.		15.6
0.0	**Start: Kinsman Notch** parking area, NH 112, 6.2 mi. E of North Woodstock.	1870/570	16.3

SOUTH

HIKE #7

Lonesome Lake and The Basin

Maps: ATC N.H. and Vt. #3
Route: Circuit from Lafayette Place Campground (Franconia Notch) around Lonesome Lake to Kinsman Falls and The Basin, and back to Lafayette Campground
Recommended direction: S to N
Distance: 6.0 mi.; 4.1 mi. on AT
Access trail name & length: Basin-Cascade Trail, 1.0 mi.; Pemi Trail, 1.9 mi.
Elevation +/-: 1450 to 2760 to 1450 ft.
Effort: Moderate
Day hike: Yes
Overnight backpacking hike: Optional
Duration: 4 to 5 hr.
Early exit option: None
Natural history features: Lonesome Lake; Upper, Middle, and Lower Kinsman Falls; Cascade Brook; The Basin
Social history features: New England Ski Museum; Cannon Mt. aerial tramway and rock climbing
Trailhead access: Hikers' parking area at Lafayette Place Campground in Franconia Notch State Park, 7.7 mi. N of North Woodstock on US 3
Camping/Lodging: Lafayette Place Campground; Lonesome Lake Hut

In the White Mts. the AT has a lust for summits that often makes it charge like a drill sergeant at the most difficult terrain. Certainly the alpine peaks offer the most fantastic reward to hikers here, but they come at a high price, requiring a substantial commitment of time and effort. The punishing New Hampshire mountains climbed by the AT offer few opportunities to take it easy on a relaxing stroll.

But for those who are not obsessed with bagging a peak, Franconia Notch supplies many ambles through the woods, including this one, which connects an AT route with Lonesome Lake Trail, Pemi Trail, and Basin-Cascade Trail to make a loop from the Lafayette Place Campground. The footing is occasionally rough, but with no mountains to climb, this hike allows plenty of time to explore Lonesome Lake, The Basin, and anything else that strikes the wayfarer's fancy.

There's no significant advantage to heading N – S or S – N, but most hikers will choose to follow the route counterclockwise (S – N), which will lead more quickly into the deep woods of Franconia Notch State Park. ATC maps present the trail section from Lafayette Place west to Lonesome Lake as part of a foul-weather AT bypass (it also continues east from the campground directly to the summit of Mt. Lafayette to bypass the Franconia Ridge in severe weather).

In 1925 Philip Ayres, head forester of the Society for the Protection of

New Hampshire Forests, led a national campaign to save Franconia Notch from clearcutting. The land within the Notch was purchased with funds raised by the Society's "Buy a Tree" campaign, state taxes, and private contributions (largely raised by Ayres). In 1928 Franconia Notch was dedicated as a state park and forest reservation in a ceremony at Profile Lake, below Cannon Mt.

Today the the park comprises 6441 acres between North Woodstock to the south and the town of Franconia to the north. The controversial Franconia Notch Parkway—the 8-mi. section of US 3 that passes through the Notch—was completed in 1988 after a nearly 30-year battle between environmental groups, the New Hampshire legislature, and U.S. transportation officials. Completion of the parkway brought a number of amenities to the park, including a new visitors' center for the Flume gorge (see Hike #6), a parking lot from which to view the Old Man of the Mountain, a 10-mi. bike path through the Notch, and a campground at Lafayette Place that offers spacious campsites, showers, bathrooms, a camp store, and hikers' parking lots. You can pick up a map of the trails in Franconia Notch at the Lafayette Place trading post or the Flume visitors' center.

From the south parking lot at Lafayette Place, follow Lonesome Lake Trail as it heads west across a bridge over the Pemigewasset River, crosses the Pemi Trail, and follows yellow blazes through the campground. From the campground, the trail climbs steadily on an old bridle path, crossing a brook on a bridge, then turning sharply left to a junction with the Hi-Cannon Trail, which leads right. From here the trail climbs three switchbacks, each around 0.1 mi. long.

At 1.2 mi. the bridle path reaches Lonesome Lake, where it ends at a junction that presents a number of options. Cascade Brook Trail heads left here and provides the shortest route south to Lonesome Lake Hut; the Dodge Cutoff leads right 0.3 mi. to Hi-Cannon Trail; and Lonesome Lake Trail follows the shore of Lonesome Lake to the north.

Having spent only an hour or so in the woods, most walkers will choose to put off their arrival at the hut and continue on Lonesome Lake Trail, now a footpath. Another 0.2 mi. to the north, follow Around Lonesome Lake Trail as it forks to the left off Lonesome Lake Trail (which continues 0.9 mi. to Kinsman Ridge Trail). From this junction follow Around Lonesome Lake Trail, an 0.8-mi. loop—surprise! —around the lake, reaching Lonesome Lake Hut in 0.2 mi.

This pastoral loop provides many beautiful glimpses of the Franconia Ridge to the east. Note the red spruce and balsam fir trees, and the bogs on the edge of Lonesome Lake. Look for the Indian Head, a stone face carved by a glacier into the side of Mt. Pemigewasset (2554 ft.), about 2.5 mi. due south of the lake. Legend tells of an Abenaki chief who waited

White Mt. National Forest

Between Mt. Moosilauke and the Androscoggin Valley most of the land crossed by the AT is protected as part of the White Mountain National Forest, which was established by the Weeks Act in 1911 in response to the devastation brought to the White Mountains by unrestricted logging. Today WMNF encompasses about 730,000 acres of woodlands in New Hampshire, and about 47,000 acres in Maine.

Unlike national park lands, which the National Park Service manages with the goals of preservation and recreation, national forests are managed by the Forest Service, part of the Department of Agriculture, for multiple uses, which include timber harvesting, hunting, and fishing as well as watershed protection and wildlife propagation.

Severe cuts in federal spending on public lands since the mid-1990s have hindered the Forest Service's ability to repair and maintain trails and facilities while, at the same time, outdoor recreation is booming. Nearly 7 million people visit WMNF every year. Heavy use of the backcountry trails and facilities in the White Mountains has eroded trails, killed vegetation, and gutted campsites prompting the Forest Service to adopt a variety of regulations to protect the land, improve the wilderness experience and raise funds.

User Fees: Since May, 1997 WMNF has charged a user fee in the form of recreation passports, which are required for parking on National Forest land and at Forest Service trailheads. Weekly vehicle passes cost $5; annual vehicle passes cost $20; annual 2-car passes cost $25. Visitors who cannot afford a passport can earn one from the Forest Service with 16 hours of volunteer work. Passports will not be required at areas that already charge a fee, such as campgrounds, and visitors passing through the area but not stopping will not need to buy a passport.

Areas where the passports are required are marked by signs, and trail-

through the winter at Lonesome Lake for his Algonquin bride to return from a visit to her ailing father. The following spring Abenaki braves found Chief Pemigewasset's bones next to the lake, then saw his profile carved in the stone of the mountain, where he still waits for the return of his bride.

Lonesome Lake is actually a tarn, a dark lake gouged into a mountain cirque by a more-than-1000-ft.-thick glacier and filled by the melting ice. Sundew, a small carnivorous bog plant, grows abundantly here and can be identified by the sticky red knob-topped hairs that grow on its round, long-stemmed leaves. A curving one-sided spike of flowers grows about 3 in. above the insect-eating leaves. Hikers more interested in their own meals can often find

head bulletin boards carry information about the program. Passports can be purchased at Forest Service offices, the Pinkham Notch and Crawford Notch visitor information centers in the White Mountain National Forest, and at many local businesses and hiking clubs. Passes can be purchased through the mail by sending a check to: White Mountain NF Fee Program, Androscoggin Ranger Station, 300 Glen Rd., Gorham, NH 03581.

The WMNF user fee is part of a 3-yr. program to test fees on federal land, including 100 national forest sites. WMNF officials hope to raise a minimum of $500,000 a year and plan to spend 95 percent of the revenues on the Forest (80 percent on maintenance and improvements, and up to 15 percent on administration and fee collecting).

Restricted Use Areas: Fragile ecosystems and those in recovery are protected as Restricted Use Areas (RUA) by the national forest. Camping and fires are prohibited above treeline (where the trees are less than 8 ft. tall), and campsites and fires elsewhere in RUAs must be at least 200 ft. off the trail and 0.25 mi. from huts, shelters, campsites, roads, lakes, and streams.

Wilderness Areas: The AT's route in WMNF passes through the Great Gulf Wilderness, on Mt. Washington, and follows the northern boundaries of the Presidential-Dry River Wilderness and the Pemigewasset Wilderness. No logging, road building, machinery or mechanical vehicles are permitted in wilderness areas; visitors to these areas enjoy quiet, undisturbed forests. Shelters and other structures are also prohibited in wilderness areas to ensure a rugged experience.

Visitors will usually be notified by a small, trailside sign when they enter an RUA or a Wilderness area. Be sure to get a copy of the brochure, Backcountry Camping Rules, available at WMNF ranger stations or from the WMNF office, 719 N. Main St., Laconia, NH 03246; 603-528-8721.

mountain wood sorrel in the grass here. The cloverlike plant shows three heart-shaped leaves. Don't eat any wild plants unless you have a made a positive identification of what they are. A variety of songbirds can be found here in summer, including white-throated sparrows, yellow-rumped warblers, and dark-eyed juncos. On the water, watch for American black ducks, mergansers, ring-necked ducks, and, on rare occasions, green-winged teal.

You'll find it difficult to be lonely at Lonesome Lake, particularly on a summer weekend. Its ease of access and proximity to US 3 make it an unlikely place to find solitude, especially as you approach the hut, at 1.6 mi., where snacks, hot drinks, and shelter draw a steady stream of visitors.

The AMC's second-newest hut, built in 1964, has space for forty-six overnight guests in small bunkrooms and is the only accommodation for visitors to Franconia Notch State Park outside of Lafayette Place (no camping is permitted around the lake or elsewhere in the park). The distinctive hut has an eight-sided, eight-peaked, skylighted roof and offers many hands-on programs for families and children. Swimming in the lake is allowed from a nearby dock. Reservations can be made by calling the AMC's Pinkham Notch Visitor Center (603-466-2727).

From the hut, step onto the AT, which follows Fishin' Jimmy Trail 0.1 mi. south to its junction with Cascade Brook Trail. The AT follows Cascade Brook Trail to the right, parallel to the outlet of Lonesome Lake. Here the trail follows an old logging road that occasionally presents difficult rocky footing, particularly when wet. At 2.6 mi. Kinsman Pond Trail enters from the right, and the logging road narrows to a footpath that descends along the northeast bank of Cascade Brook.

At 3.1 mi. the AT/Cascade Brook Trail skips on rocks across Cascade Brook, which may be hazardous if the water is at all high. A 60-yd. detour downstream, along the opposite bank of the stream, leads to an overlook of Rocky Glen Falls. The route to the falls can be treacherous, so walk carefully.

From the edge of the brook, the AT follows Cascade Brook Trail 1.5 mi. to the junction with Whitehouse Trail/

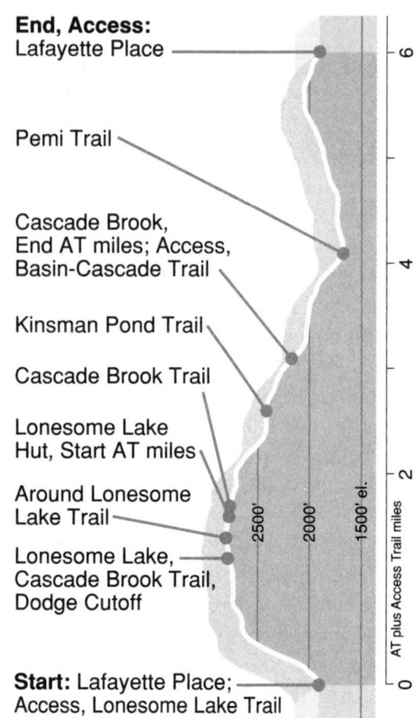

Liberty Spring Trail on the east side of I-93. Our route follows Basin-Cascade Trail, which forks left off the AT here and provides a scenic ride 1.0 mi. to The Basin, one of Franconia Notch's geologic wonders.

Basin-Cascade Trail reaches Rocky Glen Falls 0.1 mi. below its junction with the AT, after passing through a narrow gorge. From the falls it continues to follow Cascade Brook, which provides an almost nonstop water show. The trail descends steeply to an

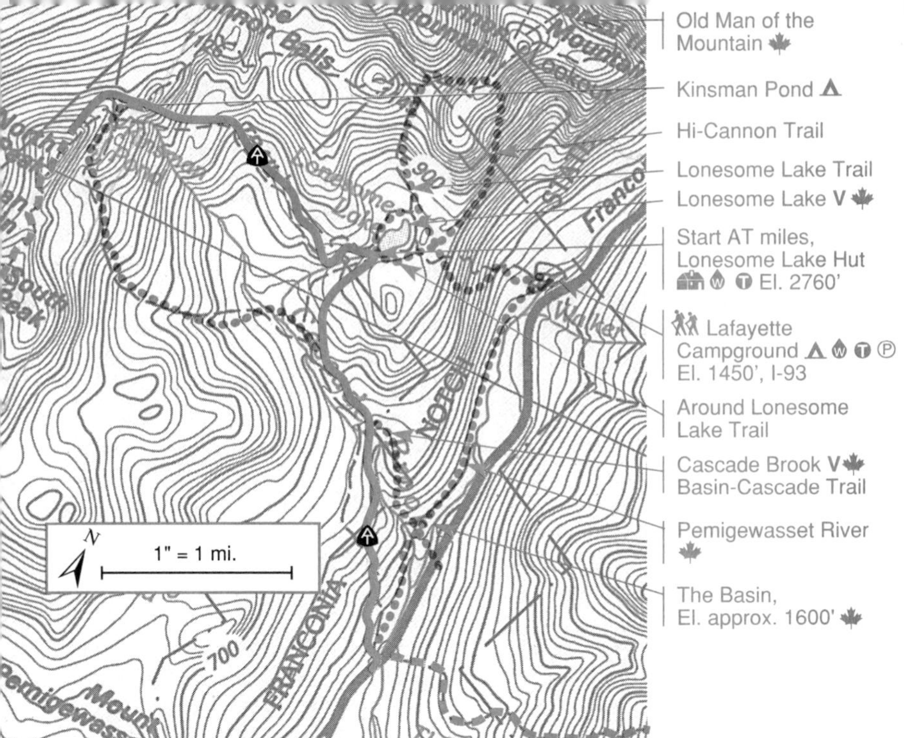

excitingly high bridge over the brook, and 100 yd. lower, a ledge on the right provides the first view of Kinsman Falls tumbling amid large hemlock trees. In another 50 yd., at 3.7 mi., a rough spur trail leads to another outlook over the falls. During the 0.4-mi. descent to The Basin, several other unmarked side trails lead to views of the Franconia Range, with the peaks of, from left to right, Lafayette, Lincoln, Little Haystack, and Liberty, lining up in a dramatic alpine ridgeline. Below the views of the Franconias, Cascade Brook continues its plunge into the Notch.

Basin-Cascade Trail reaches a junction with Pemi Trail at 4.1 mi. Pemi Trail will return you to Lafayette Place. Before hopping on the trail, however, continue on Basin-Cascade Trail 20 yd. to the trailhead. From here a labyrinth of paved tourist paths explore The Basin and the flumes and waterfalls that surround it.

The Basin, a pothole 40 ft. in diameter and 15 ft. deep, was carved over the course of some 25,000 years by sand and gravel swirling in the Pemigewasset River as it gushed through Franconia Notch. Where the river rushes across the granite bedrock nearby, many smaller potholes show what The Basin must have looked like thousands of years ago.

From The Basin, Pemi Trail makes an easy cruise 1.9 mi. north to its junction with Lonesome Lake Trail in the campground at Lafayette Place. Most of the way it parallels the Pemigewasset River. Although here the river doesn't quite live up to its name—an Abenaki word for "rapidly moving"—it provides some pleasant company and masks the sound of traffic on the nearby highway as you head back to the campground. Look for signs of raccoons, otters, and minks along the riverbank.

Many other attractions in the state park are within walking distance of Lafayette Place. A paved bike path less than 1.0 mi. north of the campground leads to the 1000-ft. cliffs of Cannon Mt. This rock face is home of some of America's oldest rock climbs, and is still popular with climbers today. A series of ledges at the top of the right end of the cliff (now held together with tie rods, turnbuckles, cables, and concrete) form New Hampshire's most famous profile, the Old Man of the Mountain. He is visible, however, only from viewing areas about 1.5 mi. to the north on the east side of US 3. About 1.8 mi. from the campground the bike path arrives at pretty Profile Lake and then at the Cannon Mt. aerial tramway, which occupies the spot where the Profile House, one of New Hampshire's grandest hotels, burned in 1923. The tramway, open year-round, leads to spectacular views from the summit walking paths atop Cannon Mt. (about 4200 ft.). The New England Ski Museum, located at the base of the state-run ski area, is a worthwhile stop for dedicated schussers.

HIKE #7 Itinerary

Miles N	Circuit Hike	Elev. (ft/m)	Miles S
Total: 6.0 mi. with access trail			
1.9	Access: Follow **Pemi Trail** N to **End:** at junction with **Lonesome Lake Trail** at **Lafayette Place Campground,** parking.		
4.1	Junction with **Pemi Trial;** paths explore **The Basin.**		
3.1	**End AT miles:** Cross **Cascade Brook** and follow **Basin-Cascade Trail** 1.0 mi. to The Basin; steep descent, views.		
2.6	**Kinsman Pond Trail** enters from R.		
1.7	**AT/Cascade Brook Trail;** occasionally difficult footing.		
1.6	**Lonesome Lake Hut,** shelter, snacks, programs, swimming. Start AT miles, AT/Fishin' Jimmy Trail 0.1 mi. S.	2760/841	
1.4	Turn L at fork onto **Around Lonesome Lake Trail** for loop around lake.		
1.2	**Lonesome Lake;** junction with Cascade Brook Trail and dodge Cutoff; follow Lonesome Lake Trail.	2760/841	
0.0	**Start: Lafayette Place,** S parking lot, US 3. Follow **Lonesome Lake Trail** W.	1450/442	

Circuit Hike

HIKE #8

Franconia Ridge

Maps: ATC N.H. and Vt. #3

Route: Circuit Hike from Lafayette Place Campground up Falling Waters Trail to AT/Franconia Ridge Trail, along ridge to Mt. Lafayette, down to Greenleaf Hut, the Old Bridle Path, and back to Lafayette Place Campground

Recommended direction: S to N

Distance: 8.9 mi; 1.6 mi. on AT

Access trail name & length: Falling Waters Trail, 3.2 mi.; Greenleaf Trail/Old Bridal Path, 4.1 mi.

Elevation +/-: 1450 to 5249 to 1450 ft.

Effort: Strenuous

Day hike: Yes

Overnight backpacking hike: Optional

Duration: 7 to 9 hr.

Early exit option: None

Natural history features: Alpine ridgeline; alpine flora

Social history features: AMC hut; Col. Greenleaf and Profile House

Trailhead access: Hikers' parking area at Lafayette Campground in Franconia Notch State Park, 7.7 mi. N of North Woodstock on US 3

Camping/Lodging: Lafayette Campground; Greenleaf Hut

The most spectacular miles of the AT?

While even the most stubbornly opinionated hiker is loath to speak in such absolutes, the Franconia Ridge makes it onto everyone's top-ten list. Many thru-hikers have chosen this alpine ridgeline as their favorite 5 mi. of the more than 2150 that make up the AT. Some hole up for days in the Notch, waiting for a sunny day to put its summits in the right light, while others make regular pilgrimages to the path along the skyline. Its popularity is easy to understand.

The rocky spine stretches over the most alliterative combination of peaks in the Whites—Liberty, Little Haystack, Lincoln, and Lafayette—the western slopes of which fall precipitously into Franconia Notch State Park, with the 1000-ft. granite face of Cannon Mt. rising on the other side. The eastern slopes spill into the vast woods of the White Mt. National Forest's Pemigewasset Wilderness. Mt. Washington and the Presidential Range loom in the distant northeast.

This trail passes through an alpine zone similar to that of the Presidential Range, but much easier to reach. Six miles' worth of walking will bring hikers from the Notch to the ridgeline and back down again, leaving them the better part of the day to explore the 3.5 mi. of glorious knife-edge AT. For a few weeks in June the bright blossoms of alpine flowers—including diapensia, Lapland rosebay, and mountain avens—paint constellations of color on its summits, just as they do on the Presidentials.

The popularity and accessibility of the Franconia Ridge has made it one of the most traveled routes in the White Mts. In the alpine world, that much traffic isn't good. The wear of boots is more evident here than in any other place in the Whites. In many places the ridgeline is badly eroded. Much of the delicate vegetation has been trampled, and some of the rarest species have disappeared. Rock borders and steps now help mark the path, and crews have worked since 1977 to stabilize the erosion. To prevent further deterioration to the ridgeline and damage to the flora, stay on the path and leave all plant life undisturbed. If you must take steps off the trail, do so carefully on bare rock to avoid additional erosion of the thin soil.

The ridgeline is fully exposed to violent weather, including regular lightning strikes. Be especially wary of electrical storms here, and descend quickly below treeline should the weather turn bad. Carry warm clothing and rain gear, even on a hot summer day, and get a weather report for the mountain summits before ascending.

Most day hikers will choose to ascend the ridge by the most direct route: Falling Waters Trail. This trail is rougher than Liberty Spring Trail, but as the name implies, it rewards visitors with a collection of waterfalls and cascades that seldom fail to impress, especially in late spring and early summer when they are gorged with meltwater. It's easier to climb this steep route than to descend it, so take it up and descend via the somewhat easier Old Bridle Path at the other end of the loop. A paved connector, 0.1 mi. long, passes under US 3 from the west-side parking area and the campground to the east side, where Falling Waters Trail and the Old Bridle Path travel together onto the lower flank of the Franconias. At 0.2 mi. Falling Waters Trail forks right from the Old Bridle Path and crosses a bridge over Walker Brook, which cuts through a diverse forest of mature hardwoods. American beech, sugar maple, and yellow birch are abundant in the lower elevation woods of Franconia Notch, but watch for red maple, black cherry, red oak, poplar, paper birch, and white pine as well. Black bears prowl the woods here; one dashed across the highway in front of our car during our drive to the trailhead for an early October hike on the ridge.

Dry Brook, which is crossed by the Falling Waters Trail 0.5 mi. beyond Walker Brook, probably won't live up to its name. This will be a blessing when you arrive at the cascading Stairs Falls and, slightly farther up the trail, cross back beneath Swiftwater Falls. Switchbacks and a logging road climb into the boreal forest of spruce and fir trees, characteristic of the higher elevation. Listen for the flute-like song of Bicknell's thrush as you climb higher in the woods; watch for gray jays, bold 12-in. birds with a gray back and lighter belly, and boreal chickadees, a 5-in. gray bird with a brown cap. The trail then climbs steeply to the 80-ft.-tall Cloudland Falls and an overlook toward 4802-ft. Mt. Moosilauke in the distance. Two more waterfalls, the right one originating on Little Haystack Mt. and the left on Mt. Lincoln, cascade parallel to each other atop Cloudland Falls. More brook crossings, logging roads, and switchbacks lead to the final climb onto Little Haystack Mt., but at 2.8 mi. consider detouring on the 100-yd. spur to the right that leads to the Shining Rock overlook of the Notch. Be careful on this slippery perch—that mirrorlike shine seen from the bottom of the Notch is caused by water seeping from springs onto the steep, 200-ft.-tall ledge.

If the final charge up Falling Waters Trail onto the summit of Little Haystack Mt. at 3.2 mi. doesn't leave you breathless, your arrival on the Franconia Ridge will. The ridgeline winds from the summit of Little Haystack, about 4760 ft., to the summit of Mt. Lafayette, 5249 ft., like the top of China's Great Wall. Tiny hikers can be seen in the distance, marching along the knife-edge with the mountainsides falling away precipitously below them.

On rare days the summits have 100-mi. visibility that can make you dizzy. On others 100-mph winds will try to blow you from the ridge. In either case, you shouldn't dally here too long. Retreat if the weather is foul, and be especially wary of electrical storms that may be brewing. In clear weather don't be fooled by the optical illusion that makes the ridgeline's other summits appear close. You will need to keep your break short here if you want plenty of time atop Mt. Lincoln and Mt. Lafayette.

From Little Haystack the trail runs almost flat to the foot of Mt. Lincoln, then climbs steeply up the sharp ridgeline between the two mountains and, at 3.9 mi. (0.5 on the AT), reaches the summit of Mt. Lincoln at 5089 ft.

You are walking on some of the youngest bedrock on the AT here, part of a vast ring dike formed by intruding molten rock that surrounds the western lobe of the Pemigewasset Wilderness. As you walk, look off into the bowl-shaped wilderness on the eastern side of the ridge. It's actually a caldera that was raised into a dome by the pressure of molten rock rising below it. When the dome collapsed, between 150 and 200 million years ago, molten rock escaped through cracks along its edges, forming the granite mountains of the Franconia Ridge on the western side of the caldera as well as Twin Mt., Mt. Guyot, Mt. Bond, and Bondcliff, which are visible from north to south overlooking the eastern side of the caldera. The broad, flat mountain in the middle of the caldera is Owl's Head.

The trail descends from the summit cairn of Mt. Lincoln into a sag, then crosses a hump that is more of

Granite and Glaciers: Geology of New Hampshire

New Hampshire has long been known as "the Granite State," but granite is just one chapter in the story of the state's geology. Dramatic glimpses into the anatomy of the earth provided by such wonders as the Franconia Ridge, Crawford Notch, and the Presidential Range are made even more amazing by what can no longer be seen—the colliding continents, volcanic islands, and rivers of ice that created them.

Like many good epics, the story of New Hampshire's creation actually begins on another continent. Most of what is now New Hampshire was part of the Eurafrican plate or was lying beneath the ocean that separated it from the North American plate 600 million years ago.

The two continents drifted a few inches toward each other every year, squeezing uplifts from the floor of the ocean between them, and eventually raising an arc of volcanoes off the North American coast.

As Europe collided with North America in the Acadian Orogeny 350 million years ago, it pushed the volcanic islands, and the sea floor they rose from, onto the eastern edge of North America, which probably followed today's Connecticut River valley. The islands bulldozed onto Vermont and pushed the lighter rock that was already there deep into the earth, where it melted and formed domes of granite that were later exposed by erosion.

The first granite that northbound AT hikers encounter are these domes, at Velvet Rocks near Hanover. Wreckage of the volcanoes is largely buried under pastoral farmland northeast of Velvet Rocks. The AT then crosses Moose Mt., Holts Ledge, and Mt. Cube, which are made of a Silurian quartzite, more than 400 million years old, that was formed when the sands of the ancient shoreline melted beneath the pressure of the overriding islands.

Mt. Moosilauke, the southernmost peak to rise above treeline on the AT, is the northbound AT's introduction to the White Mts., a range with a geology as complex as it is dramatic. Noble Moosilauke is actually made up largely of mud that was washed into the sea floor and hardened into a variety of rocks during the Acadian Orogeny.

Moosilauke tells little of New Hampshire's namesake rock, but it provides a dramatic introduction to the more recent chapters in the creation of New Hampshire—the glaciers.

Two types of glaciers carved the face of the White Mts. Valley, or alpine, glaciers formed from snow that accumulated over hundreds of years in small valleys, eventually compressing into glaciers that carved the gentle slopes of the mountains into cirques—bowl-shaped valleys with steep walls and flat

(continued)

(continued)

bottoms. Jobildunk Ravine and Gorge Ravine on Mt. Moosilauke are the first examples of glacial cirques encountered by the northbound AT hiker.

The continental ice sheets, up to a mile thick, spread southward from the Arctic across New England all the way to Long Island and the Delaware Water Gap, polishing the mountains and carving the valleys between them into steep-walled notches. The steep, bare-rock trails encountered below treeline on Mt. Moosilauke and elsewhere in the White Mts. are a testament to the polishing of these glaciers. The soil the ice left behind is so thin that it will erode away after only a few footsteps, leaving trailblazers no choice but to charge straight up the steep slopes on the smooth rock.

Glaciers are responsible for most of the landscaping in the White Mts. Standing atop Webster Cliff or the Franconia Ridge, it is easy to imagine the river of ice carving its way through Crawford Notch and Franconia Notch. Glacial tarns, such as Lonesome Lake in Franconia Notch and Lost Pond in Pinkham Notch, are depressions carved into the bedrock by the ice sheet, then filled by the melting ice of the retreating glacier. The dramatic boulder fields of Carter Notch and Mahoosuc Notch (in Maine) are made up of rocks that fell from the cliff walls when the glacier retreated. Whalebacks, or *roches moutonées,* are large rocks that are polished on one side and jagged on another; they were formed in the Presidential Range by the ice sheet, which polished the upstream side of the rock but cut chunks from its downstream side.

Mt. Washington and the Presidentials are supported by the erosion-resistant rocks of the Littleton Formation, more mudstones metamorphosed into mica schists which are characterized by distinct folding and layering. The ankle-challenging felsenmeer—literally "sea of rocks"—that covers the top of Mt. Washington was formed by the alpine environment's constant freezing and thawing of water that seeps between the layers of the schists, causing the rock to fracture into thousands of irregular blocks and plates.

Between Lonesome Lake, on the western side of Franconia Notch, and the Webster Cliffs, on the east side of Crawford Notch, the White Mts. sit on a pedestal of volcanos. The Franconia Ridge is a massive ring dike, where rising molten rock raised the landscape above into a dome, the top of which collapsed, allowing the molten rock to escape through cracks at the edge of the dome.

Hikers who want to see more of the state rock should head to Kinsman Mt., which provides the best example of the Granite State's granite (see Hike #6).

an obstacle than it appears, and drops into scrub which may provide some shelter in foul weather. From here the trail rises more than 400 ft. in a steep and steady climb to the summit of Mt. Lafayette at 4.8 mi. (The AMC sign at the summit indicates an elevation of 5225 ft.; the ATC maps add another 24 ft.) The foundation stones, all that remain of the summit house, which operated in the mid-1800s, make a fantastic lunch spot on a clear, warm day but provide little protection in severe weather.

Early White Mt. botanists like Edward Tuckerman and William Oakes found many rare alpine plants, such as dwarf cinquefoil, mountain heath, and mountain sedge, on what was then called Great Haystack. (The name was changed to honor the French hero of the American Revolution after his visit to New Hampshire in 1825.)

The alpine zone atop the Franconias, only 5 mi. long, is a fraction of the size of the zone surrounding Mt. Washington, but there are still many lovely alpine plants to be found on Mt. Lafayette, and some rare ones have been rediscovered here in recent years. Watch for the white flowers and evergreen cushions of diapensia and the small pink flowers and needlelike leaves of mountain heath. Mountain avens, which has long-stemmed yellow flowers that resemble buttercups, is found only on White Mt. summits and on Briar Island, Nova Scotia. Be extremely careful when investigating these fragile and slow-growing alpine plants. A few misplaced boot soles could spell the extinction of some rare and endangered plants.

From the summit of Mt. Lafayette, Greenleaf Trail and the Old Bridle Path link up (extending from Lonesome Lake to Mt. Lafayette, this trail forms the AT's foul-weather bypass of the Franconia Ridge). Greenleaf Trail descends gradually 1.1 mi. west from the summit to the AMC's Greenleaf Hut, at about 4200 ft., which is visible in clear weather from the ridgeline. Shelter and snacks can be had here, but you will need a reservation if you plan to be one of the thirty-four overnight guests. The hut is open in May on a caretaker basis and offers full service, including breakfast and dinner, from June through mid-October. In the late 1920s, Col. C. H. Greenleaf gave the AMC the money to build the hut, and appropriately, the hut overlooks the site at the base of Cannon Mt. where Greenleaf's grand hotel, the Profile House, was located until it burned in 1923. The hut's perch above Eagle Lake, to the east, also provides outlooks onto Eagle Cliff to the northwest, where an 18-ft.-tall wooden panther was built in the 1800s for the amusement of guests at the hotel, and along the length of Franconia Notch. The cliffs of Cannon Mt. rise directly across the Notch from the hut. In early summer a pair of binoculars might help you catch a glimpse of Franconia Notch's peregrine falcons on Cannon Mt. or Eagle Cliff.

From the hut, Greenleaf Trail continues to the northwest, descending to US 3 at Profile Clearing in 2.2 mi. However, our hike follows the Old Bridle Path instead, as it descends to the southwest. Much of this trail follows the horse trail that led to the summit of Mt. Lafayette in the early 1800s, and which burros used to deliver supplies to the hut in the 1930s. The horse trail and several subsequent paths that followed its route were repeatedly obliterated by logging in the late 1800s and early 1900s.

While this route is less steep than the Falling Waters Trail, don't let the fact that it once carried horses deceive you. The trail crosses features with names like Agony Ridge and the Three Miseries that will give your knees a pounding. Your suffering will be rewarded with fine views of the mountains to the west, particularly Moosilauke, Kinsman, and Cannon.

A side path loops from Old Bridle Path 0.5 mi. below Greenleaf Hut, passes two viewpoints, then rejoins the bridle path. At 7.4 mi. the trail steps to the edge of Walker Ravine, which it overlooks for the next 0.2 mi. Walker Brook, the first brook crossed by this hike, runs through the ravine.

At 8.7 mi. the terrain will begin to look familiar as the trail rejoins Falling Waters Trail and continues the final 0.2 mi. to Lafayette Place, where you can relax on the porch of the trading post and watch the setting sun paint the ridgeline of the Franconia Range.

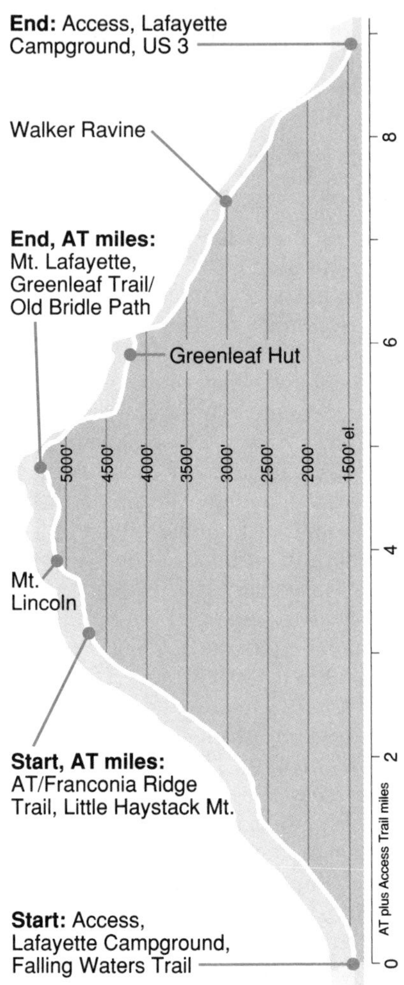

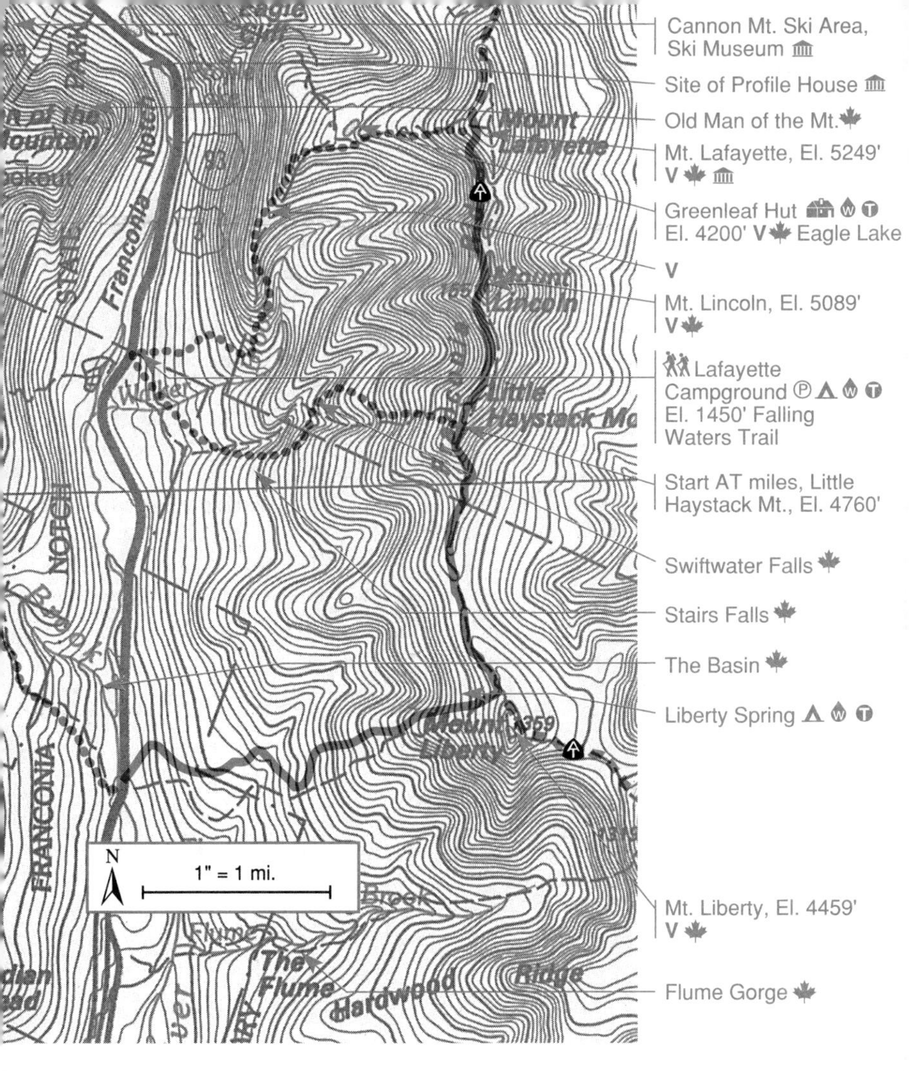

Cannon Mt. Ski Area, Ski Museum
Site of Profile House
Old Man of the Mt.
Mt. Lafayette, El. 5249' V
Greenleaf Hut El. 4200' V Eagle Lake
V
Mt. Lincoln, El. 5089' V
Lafayette Campground El. 1450' Falling Waters Trail
Start AT miles, Little Haystack Mt., El. 4760'
Swiftwater Falls
Stairs Falls
The Basin
Liberty Spring
Mt. Liberty, El. 4459' V
Flume Gorge
Mount Lafayette
Mount Lincoln
Little Haystack Mt
Franconia Notch
Mount Liberty
The Flume
Hardwood Ridge
N
1" = 1 mi.

Optional Extended Hike: The Lafayette Place Campground parking area in Franconia Notch provides an excellent staging area for a variety of day and overnight hikes in the Franconias. An expanded version of our loop hike could follow Liberty Spring Trail up to the ridgeline: From the Lafayette Place Campground, follow the paved bike path 2.3 mi. south on the east side of US 3. (Hikers on this route can also park in the hikers' parking lot at the Flume complex, near the start of the Liberty Spring Trail.) The Liberty Spring Trail makes a steep but secure ascent of Mt. Liberty, at the southern end of the Franconia Ridge, to the Liberty Spring Tent Site at 2.6 mi. from the bike path and 4.9 mi. from Lafayette Place. There is space for forty-two people on eleven tent platforms, convenient water, and a caretaker at this popular campground, where a fee is charged during the busy spring, summer, and fall months. Visit on weekdays to avoid the crowds. At 5.3 mi. Liberty Spring Trail joins Franconia Ridge Trail, at about 4200 ft. Here the AT turns left and follows Franconia Ridge Trail north, reaching a short side trail to the summit of Mt. Liberty (4459 ft.) at 5.6 mi. The AT follows the ridge for another 3.1 mi. to the summit of Mt. Lafayette, where Greenleaf Trail heads left (west), reaching Greenleaf Hut in 1.1 mi. From the hut the Old Bridle Path/Falling Waters Trail reaches Lafayette Place in 2.5 mi. The round-trip is 12.3 mi., including 6.4 mi. on the AT.

HIKE #8 Itinerary

Miles N	Circuit Hike	Elev. (ft/m)	Miles S
	Access: Follow **Greenleaf Trail/Old Bridle Path** left.		4.8
	Greenleaf Hut; food, shelter (reservations required), views. Continue on Old Bridle Path.	4200/1280	5.9
	Side loop trail to viewpoints.		6.4
	Walker Ravine.		7.4
	Join **Falling Waters Trail.**		8.7
	End: Lafayette Place, parking; US 3, 7.7 mi N of North Woodstock.	1450/442	8.9
	Route now turns south. Read from top down.		
4.8	**End AT miles:** Summit of **Mt. Lafayette.**	5249/1600	
3.9	Summit of **Mt. Lincoln;** followed by descent, then steep climb.	5089/1551	
3.2	**Start AT miles:** Junction with **AT/Franconia Ridge Trail.** Summit of **Little Haystack Mt.** Level to foot of Mt. Lincoln; then steep climb.	4760/1451	
2.8	Spur to **Shining Rock** overlook.		
0.2	**Falling Waters Trail** forks R (S) from Old Bridle Path; steep climb, switchbacks, waterfalls, views.		
0.0	**Start (Access): Lafayette Place,** parking; US 3, 7.7 mi. N of North Woodstock; 0.1-mi. connector to **Old Bridle Path/Falling Waters Trail.**	1450/442	

Circuit Hike

HIKE #9

Pemigewasset Wilderness and Zealand Notch

Maps: ATC N.H. and Vt. #3

Route: From Gale River Loop Rd. up Garfield Trail to the AT, along Garfield Ridge Trail to Galehead Hut, over South Twin Mt. and Mt. Guyot to Zealand Hut, Ethan Pond Trail, through Zealand Notch, to Crawford Notch

Recommended direction: S to N

Distance: 23.2 mi.; 17.6 mi. on AT

Access trail name & length: Garfield Trail, 4.8 mi.

Elevation +/-: 1500 to 4902 to 1277 ft.

Effort: Strenuous

Day hike: No

Overnight backpacking hike: Yes

Duration: 16 to 20 hr.

Natural history features: Alpine peaks and ridgelines; forest recovery; waterfalls; Zealand Notch

Social history features: Logging of Pemigewasset Wilderness and Zealand Mt. areas; Arnold Guyot

Trailhead access: *Start:* Drive 4.0 mi. N on US 3 from I-93 in Franconia Notch to small picnic area 0.3 mi. S of Trudeau Rd. at Five Corners. Follow Gale River Loop Rd. (FR 92) S from the picnic area for 1.2 mi. past a right fork; then turn L and cross bridge to parking lot on R. Parking area for Gale River Trail, an early exit option, is 1.6 mi. ahead. *End:* Parking in lot at end of Willey House Rd., 0.3 mi. W of US 302, about 1 mi. S of Willey Recreation Area in Crawford Notch and 1.5 mi. N of Dry River Campground.

Camping/Lodging: Garfield Ridge Campsite; Galehead Hut; Guyot Campsite; Zealand Hut; Ethan Pond Campsite

Between Franconia Notch and Crawford Notch lies the longest unbroken section of wilderness crossed by the AT in New Hampshire and Vermont. The 18,560-acre Pemigewasset Wilderness, which borders the southern side of the AT between Mt. Liberty and Ethan Pond, is filled with spectacular scenes—alpine summits, rock-walled notches, roaring waterfalls, and looming cliffs.

Among these sights, it is the woods that are most impressive. From the Pemigewasset's highest peaks hardly a building or road can be seen. The vast forest seems infinite. The true wonder of these views, however, is best seen by those who can look into the past, for early this century, there was no sea of trees here. On most of the land there were no trees at all. Logging and fires had turned the Pemigewasset into a barren wasteland.

Many of today's trails follow the paths of the seventeen railways that carved their way through the mountains to retrieve the cut timber. Whitewall Brook in Zealand Notch ran with so much tannic acid from felled trees that nothing could live in it or beside it. Forest fires left entire mountains clothed only in cinder and ash. Until recently, guidebooks to the area placed the word *wilderness* in quotation marks to note the irony of the title.

Today the Pemigewasset is a tribute not only to the beauty of the forest but also to its ability to rise from its own ashes. The plight of these forests brought the timber industry under heavy scrutiny and inspired the Weeks Act, which created the White Mt. National Forest in 1911. The U.S. Forest Service turned portions of the Pemigewasset into the Lincoln Woods Scenic Area, and in 1986 Congress approved it as a wilderness area.

The AT circles the northern lobe of the wilderness on a ring dike of mountains—the edge of a giant volcanic caldera that includes the Franconia Ridge in the west and extends to Mt. Guyot in the east. From Mt. Guyot the trail descends Zealand Ridge to Zealand Notch and then Crawford Notch. Hikers who cross this wilderness must plan for one or two overnights, and the AMC provides several options, from the rustic luxury at either Galehead Hut or Zealand Falls Hut to the chilly tent sites at Guyot Campsite. The huts are well located for hikers preferring to spread out this hike's 23 mi. over 3 days. An overnight each at Galehead Hut, on the western side of the wilderness, and at Zealand Falls Hut, at the head of Zealand Notch, allows for 3 days of evenly spaced walking. Garfield Ridge Campsite, at the northwest corner of the wilderness, and Ethan Pond Campsite, near Crawford Notch, are also well located for hikers who want to spend more than one night out, although the 14 mi. between the two campsites make for a full day of walking.

The Franconia Ridge portion of the AT is the favorite route for entering the Pemigewasset, but Hike #9 shaves off a few miles by approaching the wilderness on Garfield Trail, which provides a quick, only occasionally difficult route 4.8 mi. straight up to the AT and the magnificent summit of Mt. Garfield. The Forest Service provides campsites along Gale River Loop Rd. near the trailhead, which will help hikers get an early start. Garfield Trail generally follows a logging road leading to the fire tower that once occupied the peak of Mt. Garfield and gives a good introduction to the forest. The trail follows the Gale River during the first mile, then turns away from it and crosses Thompson and Spruce brooks, then recrosses Spruce Brook at 1.2 mi. Moose are occasionally seen near these waters in early morning and evening during the spring and summer.

Large hemlocks dominate the lower forest. Higher on the mountainside, pretty stands of yellow and paper birch highlight areas along the trail where the forest is still recovering from a 1902 fire. Areas logged near the trail as recently as the 1970s show earlier stages of forest succession (the order in which tree species arrive and replace one another as a forest matures). The trail rises into the spruce/fir forest zone, but yellow birch continue to punctuate the woods beside the path long after other hardwoods have dropped out. These deciduous trees hang on stubbornly in the higher elevations where coniferous forests thrive. By the time the trail charges up the steep finale of Garfield, the forest is occupied only by red spruce and balsam fir. It reaches the AT at 4.8 mi., but before following the white blazes back down (left) into the woods, at 4.6 mi. head up (climb about 490 ft., 0.2 mi.) on the rocky finish of Garfield Trail onto the summit (4488 ft.), where you will become acquainted with the adventure that lies ahead. You will have to retrace your steps back to the AT, but the detour is worth it.

The concrete foundation is all that remains of the fire tower that once occupied the summit of Garfield, and while it doesn't improve the view, it does break the wind on gusty days. The gray jays that frequent the summit will try to steal your lunch from your hand. To the south the Pemigewasset Wilderness spreads out in a giant bowl of spruce and fir where it was once barren. Stripes in the forest show the location of overgrown logging roads. In 1907 a lightning strike to Owl's Head, due south of Mt. Garfield, ignited a fire in the slash left by timber baron J. E. Henry's loggers. The ensuing inferno devoured more than 25,000 acres of the wilderness.

The massive peaks of the Franconia Ridge, on the western edge of the wilderness, seem close enough to touch while Galehead Hut, the next stop on most hikers' itineraries, can be seen to the east, nestled beneath South Twin Mt. It may appear close, but the hut is still at least 2 hours away, as the next section of the trail is the most difficult of the trip. The hiking on the AT here is far more strenuous than that surrounding Zealand Notch, so be prepared to pay your dues between Mt. Garfield and Mt. Guyot.

Our AT mileage count starts at the junction of Garfield Trail and the AT.

The 3.1-mi. trip from the summit of Mt. Garfield to the hut begins with a harrowing 1000-ft. descent, often on steep slabs slick with flowing water. During our early October visit to the Pemigewasset, the hardwood forest lower on the mountain showed peak fall color but the steep rocks here were covered with thick ice. Fall and spring hikers should be well aware of recent weather to judge trail conditions.

At 0.2 mi., where a spring-fed brook flows beside the AT, a spur trail leads left 0.1 mi. to Garfield Ridge Campsite. The campsite has space for twelve in its shelter and another twenty-four on six tent platforms. A fee is charged, and there is a caretaker in residence during the summer. Water is available from the spring beside the AT. As many as seventy campers, nearly twice the site's capacity, have overrun this campground on popular nights during recent years. Although the site is lovely, it is obviously best avoided on weekends and holidays. At 0.7 mi., the AT finally levels out in a large col, then reaches a junction where Franconia Brook Trail leads 2.2 mi. south down to the Thirteen Falls Shelter.

Black-capped chickadees, boreal chickadees, purple finches, nuthatches, gray jays, and dark-eyed juncos live in these woods year-round. They are joined by a wide variety of migrant songbirds in the summer.

The AT here trudges over dozens of short, steep, rocky hillocks that cover the ridgeline. Gale River Trail comes in from the left at 2.3 mi., and the AT climbs Galehead Mt. at a moderate grade until a steep push brings it to the Twinway and Frost trails at 2.9 mi. and, 40 yd. to their right, Galehead Hut.

While we sipped hot tea a crew member pointed out the "hutmaster" to us—a small peak overlooking the hut from the southeast. South of it rises the "assistant hutmaster" and the "croo." Turning back to the east he showed us several small fir waves on the side of Galehead Mt. Fir waves, crescent-shaped stands of dead fir trees with dying trees on one side and new trees on the other, move slowly through the balsam fir forest zone as part of the life cycle of the woods.

Galehead Hut was built in 1932 and sits at about 3800 ft. It sleeps thirty-eight in two bunkrooms that are situated on either side of the dining room and kitchen. Known for its friendly crews, it is open from mid-May until mid-October. Hikers who plan to stay at the hut will need a reservation. Those who don't should plan on staying at Guyot Campsite and will need an extra couple hours of daylight to reach it.

The AT hops on the Twinway 40 yd. east of the hut, passes an outlook to the south, and makes a rocky drop to the pool that provides the hut with water. Then the trail charges straight up the side of South Twin Mt., ascending more than 1000 ft. in 0.8 mi. and passing through one of the fir waves visible from the hut. It reaches the south knob of the summit (4902 ft.) at 3.7 mi., where dozens of peaks and ridges spread out like a charcoal-pencil drawing. The Presidentials rise 10 mi. to the northeast, the Franconias are 5 mi. to the southwest, and Mt. Monadnock is 96 mi. away to the south.

Near the south knob of the summit, North Twin Spur leads to the north knob and North Twin Mt. and, beyond, to North Twin Trail. The AT drops south from the south knob onto the flat alpine ridge that leads to Mt. Guyot. At 5.7 mi. the AT/Twinway heads left to the summit of Mt. Guyot while the Bondcliff Trail descends 0.5 mi. south to a spur trail leading 0.2 mi. to Guyot Shelter and campsite.

Swiss scientist Arnold Henri Guyot's name (pronounced "Gee-yo") is also attached to a mountain crossed by the AT in the Great Smoky Mts., as well as others in New York, Colorado, Utah, California, and Alaska, not to mention a crater on the moon and a street on the campus of Princeton University! The beloved professor was already well known for his study of glaciers when he emigrated to the United States in 1848, but it was his intensive exploration, measurement, and mapping of the entire Appalachian mountain chain that made his name so popular a title for American peaks. Guyot's explorations in the Northeast, where he climbed scores of previously untouched mountains, were particularly thorough, and his strict scientific methods produced the first accurate map of the Whites and corrected many errors, including the belief that Mt. Washington was the highest mountain east of the Mississippi (North Carolina's Mt. Mitchell, 6684 ft., holds that honor). The campsite that bears his name here is notoriously frigid, but wakes its visitors with one of the best sunrises in the Whites.

From the junction with Bondcliff Trail, the AT/Twinway heads east over stepped ledges to the bare, flat summit of Mt. Guyot, 4560 ft., at 5.8 mi., then drops back into the krummholz. Aside from a steep pitch here and there, the trail takes a long, moderate cruise down the Zealand Ridge to Zealand Falls Hut, 4.0 mi. away. At 7.0 mi. the trail passes a knob where a spur trail cuts left to the summit of Zealand Mt., and soon after the trail passes an overlook of Zeacliff Pond. After climbing down a ladder and stone steps over steep ledges, the AT/Twinway flattens out again.

Most of the forest on the Zealand Ridge is still in succession from the lumberjacks and forest fires that destroyed it at the turn of the century, but the forest here has almost recovered fully and is now again filled with red spruce, balsam fir, and yellow birch along with the occasional striped maple and mountain ash.

At 8.2 mi. a side trail leads 0.1 mi. right to Zeacliff Pond, and at 8.5 mi., Zeacliff Trail drops 1.5 mi. right (east) to rejoin the AT on the Ethan Pond Trail. This shortcut nips 1.5 mi. off the hike but is terrifyingly steep in good weather and downright deadly in the rain.

The AT follows sidewalk-like slabs from the Zeacliff junction, then crosses bog bridges to another junction at 8.7 mi., where a loop leads 100 yd. right to a magnificent overlook of Zealand Notch from a granite patio atop the Zeacliff. In clear weather from this vantage you will see Ethan Pond Trail, an upcoming portion of this hike, running atop the talus below Whitewall Mt. across the notch. On warm days there is no finer place to lunch than the Zeacliff patio, but many parties will choose to wait until they reach the next hut, a mile farther down the trail.

The loop heads north from the viewpoint and rejoins the AT/Twinway, which now descends at a steeper grade. It crosses Whitewall Brook, among cascades and flumes, at 9.8 mi. The strange birdcalls you hear as you cross the brook are actually a hydroelectric pump that supplies the nearby hut with water. Lend-a-Hand Trail merges from the left 200 ft. farther along, and at 9.9 mi. the trail arrives at Zealand Falls Hut.

Built in 1932, the hut sits at about 2700 ft. beside Zealand Falls on Whitewall Brook. It sleeps thirty-six in two bunkrooms and provides full service, including meals, from May to October. It is one of two huts that are open through the winter with a caretaker on duty, making it very popular with cross-country skiers. Several moderate trails connect this hut with the highway, making it a bustling resort compared with the remote solitude of Galehead.

The AT continues to follow the Twinway 0.2 mi. east to its end at Ethan Pond Trail, which the AT follows sharply to the right down Zealand Notch. (Zealand Trail heads left here, leading 0.3 mi. to A-Z Trail, which reaches Zealand Rd. in 2.5 mi., allowing for a quick exit from Hike #9 with little elevation change. A-Z Trail also provides an alternate route to the AMC's Crawford Notch Hostel by way of Avalon Trail, 5.1 mi. in all. This route bypasses the Ethan Pond and Webster Cliffs trails.)

For the next 1.7 mi. the AT cruises through Zealand Notch on the bed of the Zealand Valley Railroad, which hauled timber out of the notch until 1900. To the east the cliffs that give Whitewall Mt. its name hang above the trail, while to the west rises the Zeacliff. Aside from an occasional speed bump of boulders, the walking is fast and easy here, allowing plenty of time to search for relics of the old railroad, which can still be found occasionally in the woods beside the trail. Parallel piles of talus above and below the trail make the notch resemble a quarry, while stands of birch show that the forest here is still recovering from the fires that raged through the notch after the logging finished. Huge fires in 1886 and 1903 destroyed more than 20,000 acres of the forest on Zealand Mt. and in Zealand Notch. A variety of birds can be found in the notch, including black-throated green warblers, black-throated blue warblers, and common yellowthroats.

At 11.4 mi. Zeacliff Trail merges from the right, and 0.3 mi. later the AT/Ethan Pond Trail begins to curve eastward around the southern end of Whitewall Mt. At 12.2 mi. Thoreau Falls Trail leads right to falls that the writer never claimed to have visited, and 0.2 mi. later, the trail crosses a wooden bridge over the North Fork and continues on the wooded west bank of the brook. The trail continues its curve east toward Crawford Notch and at 12.7 mi. crosses Shoal Pond Trail, which forks off to the south, heading for Wilderness and Carrigain Notch trails. The AT now rises slightly but steadily on bog bridges over creekbeds and woods roads.

At 14.2 mi. a side trail leads 200 yd. left to Ethan Pond Campsite, which has a shelter with space for ten, five tent platforms, and convenient water from a nearby brook. M. F. Sweetser's 1891 guide to the White Mts. reported that Ethan Allen Crawford spent a single night at the pond, during which he caught several trout, shot two moose, and slept among howling wolves. Moose and trout are still common here, but the wolves were driven from the Whites long ago.

A mile past Ethan Pond, Willey Range Trail leads off to the north to Mt. Willey, Mt. Field, and A-Z Trail. The AT/Ethan Pond Trail turns sharp right here and begins the final descent into Crawford Notch, a leisurely stroll during which the abundance of trail junctions and an occasional train whistle will prepare campers for their return to civilization.

At 16.0 mi. Kendron Flume Trail drops steeply left to the Willey Recreation Area, at the site of the Willey house (food, drinks, AMC shuttle service, fishing pond for kids), 1.3 mi. away on US 302. The AT continues to descend from the junction down a steepening woods road through hardwood forest. At 17.1 mi. Arethusa-Ripley Falls trail cuts right 0.3 mi. to Ripley Falls, named by Rev. David Starr King for his friend Henry Wheelock Ripley, and 2.5 mi. to Arethusa Falls, the highest in New Hampshire, probably named for the nymph who

Continued on p. 100

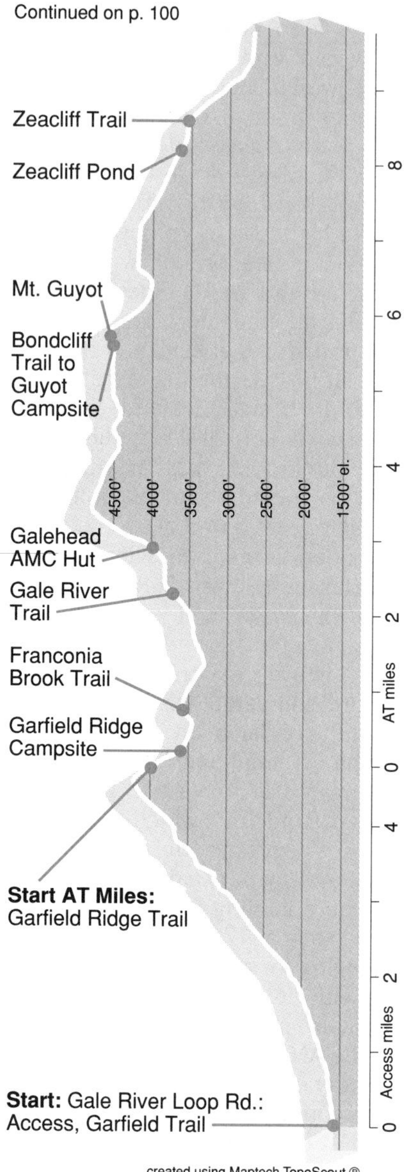

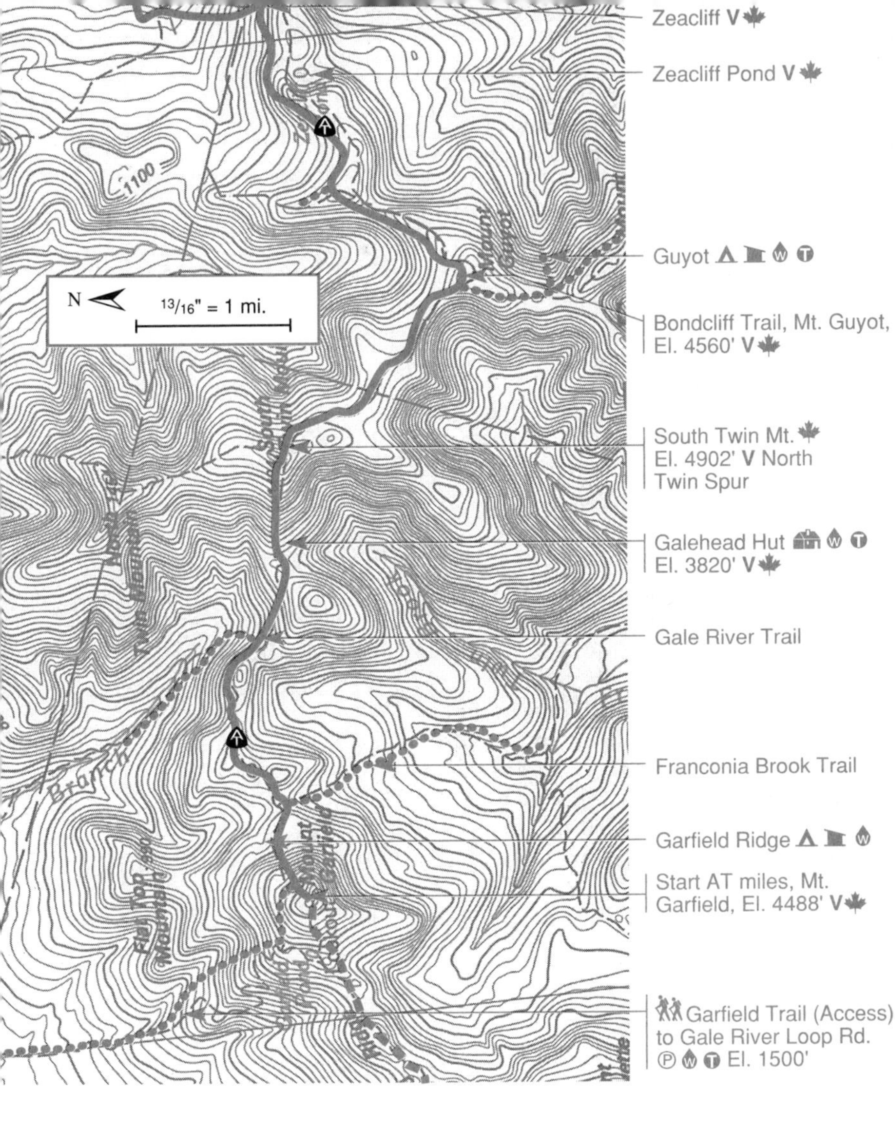
Zeacliff V
Zeacliff Pond V
1100
N
13/16" = 1 mi.
Guyot
Bondcliff Trail, Mt. Guyot, El. 4560' V
South Twin Mt.
El. 4902' V North Twin Spur
Galehead Hut
El. 3820' V
Gale River Trail
Branch
Franconia Brook Trail
Garfield Ridge
Start AT miles, Mt. Garfield, El. 4488' V
Garfield Trail (Access) to Gale River Loop Rd.
Ⓟ El. 1500'

is transformed into a fountain in a poem by Percy Bysshe Shelley.

A few hundred yards past the junction, a sign marks the edge of Crawford Notch State Park, and a short distance later, the trail crosses the tracks of the Maine Central Railroad and reaches the parking lot at the end of Willey House Rd., which leads 0.3 mi. north to US 302 and Crawford Notch, about 1.0 mi. south of the Willey house site.

Optional Shorter Hike: Hikers looking to spend only a day or two on the AT in the Pemigewasset Wilderness should consider hiking in on Gale River Trail 4.0 mi. from Gale River Loop Rd. to the AT/Garfield Ridge Trail, then heading east on the AT 0.6 mi. to Galehead Hut. From the hut, follow the AT/Twinway 0.8 mi. to the top of South Twin, where the North Twin Spur leads 1.3 mi. to the summit of North Twin and then North Twin Trail, which descends 4.3 mi. to Haystack Rd. This 11.0-mi route climbs more than 3500 ft., so only ambitious hikers will want to walk it in a day. Others can easily spread this hike over 2 days with a stay at Galehead Hut.

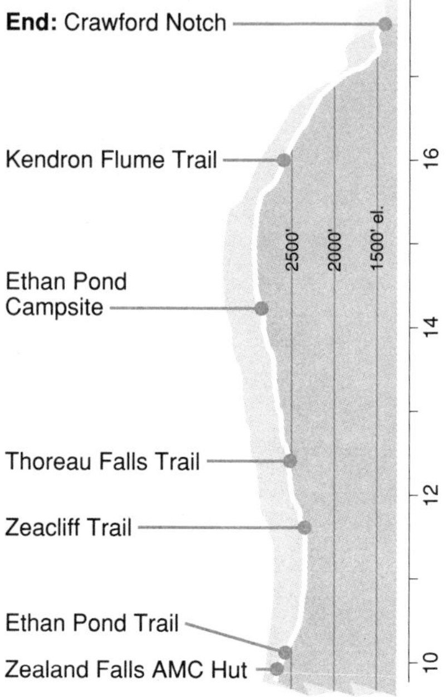

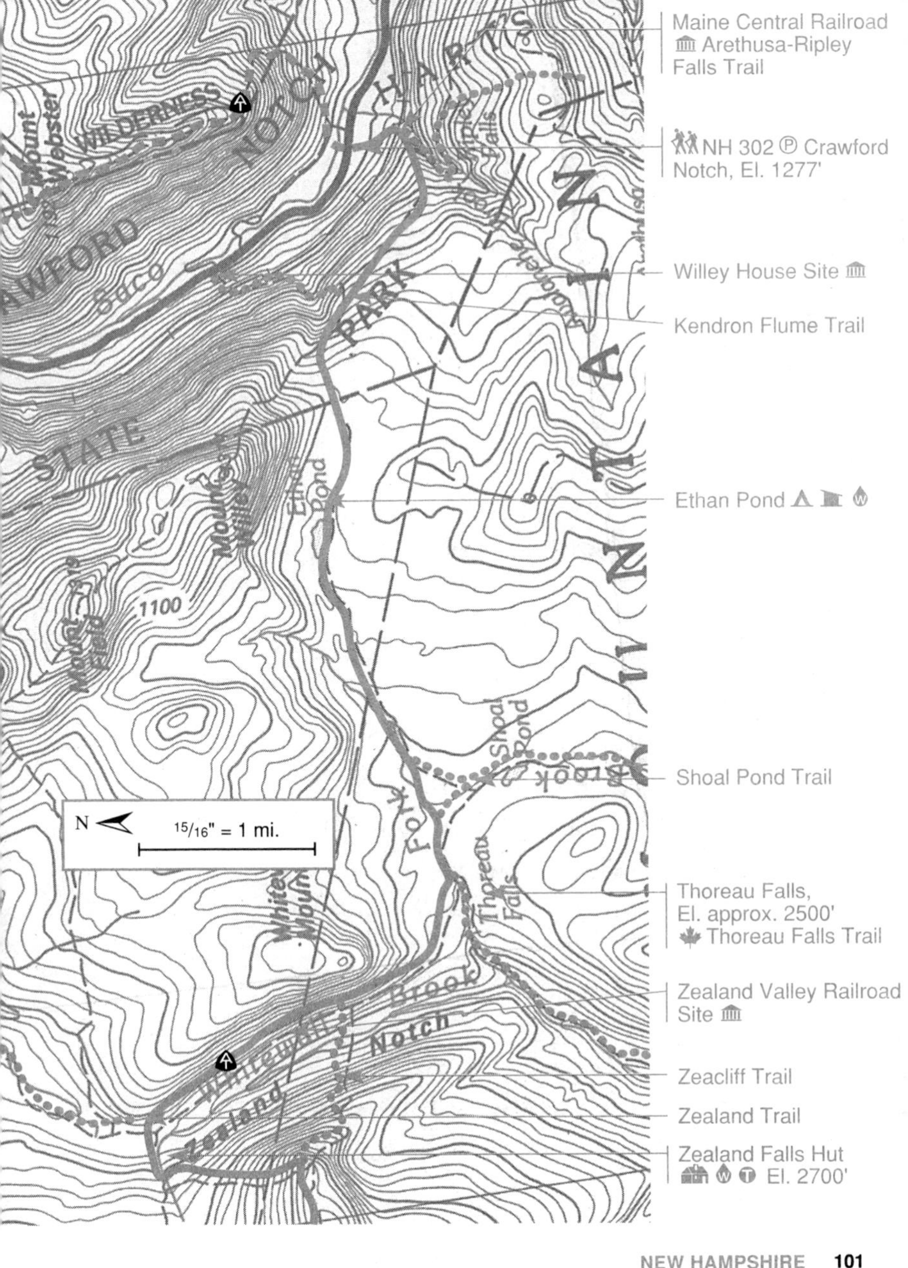

Maine Central Railroad
Arethusa-Ripley Falls Trail
NH 302 Ⓟ Crawford Notch, El. 1277'
Willey House Site
Kendron Flume Trail
Ethan Pond
Shoal Pond Trail
Thoreau Falls, El. approx. 2500'
Thoreau Falls Trail
Zealand Valley Railroad Site
Zeacliff Trail
Zealand Trail
Zealand Falls Hut El. 2700'
N
15/16" = 1 mi.
WILDERNESS
NOTCH
STATE
PARK
Saco
Mount Webster
Mount Willey
Mount Field
1100
Ethan Pond
Shoal Pond
Thoreau Falls
Zealand Notch
Brook

HIKE #9 Itinerary

Miles N	NORTH	Elev. (ft/m)	Miles S
Total: 22.4 mi. with access trail			
17.6	**End: Crawford Notch,** parking on Willey House Rd., 0.3 mi. W of US 302.	1277/389	0.0
17.1	**Arethusa-Ripley Falls Trail** leads to waterfalls (2.5 mi.).		0.5
16.0	Pass **Kendron Flume Trail** (1.3 mi.) to historic site at Willey House.		1.6
14.2	**Ethan Pond Campsite,** shelter, platforms, water.		3.4
12.7	Pass **Shoal Pond Trail.**		4.9
12.2	Pass **Thoreau Falls Trail.**		5.4
11.4	**Zeacliff Trail** merges; trail curves E.		6.2
10.1	AT follows **Ethan Pond Trail** down to Zealand Notch.		7.5
9.9	**Zealand Falls AMC Hut,** bunkrooms, full service, reservations needed.	2700/823	7.7
8.7	Spur trail to **Zealand Notch** overlook.		8.9
8.5	**Zeacliff Trail,** 1.5 mi. to Ethan Pond Trail (extremely steep descent).		9.1
8.2	Side trail to **Zeacliff Pond,** 0.1 mi.		9.4
7.0	Spur trail to **Zealand Mt.** summit.		10.6
5.8	**Mt. Guyot,** followed by long easy ridge walk.	4560/1389	11.8
5.7	**Bondcliff Trail** to **Guyot Campsite,** shelter, spring, fee.		11.9
3.7	South Knob of **South Twin Mt.**	4902/1494	13.9
2.9	**Galehead Hut,** bunkrooms, full service, reservations needed.	3800/1158	14.7
2.3	**Gale River Trail.**		15.3
0.7	**Franconia Brook Trail.**		16.9
0.2	Spur trail to **Garfield Ridge Campsite.**		17.4
0.0	**Start AT miles: Garfield Ridge Trail;** steep descent.	4000/1219	17.6
4.8	**Access: Garfield Trail;** parking on Gale River Loop Rd. Moderate climb to summit of Mt. Garfield.	1500/457	0.0

SOUTH

HIKE #10

Webster Cliff Trail

Maps: ATC N.H. and Vt. #2

Route: From Willey Station in Crawford Notch up Webster Cliff Trail to Mizpah Hut, then Crawford Path West to Crawford House site on US 302

Recommended direction: S to N

Distance: 10.2 mi.; 7.3 mi. on AT

Access trail name & length: Crawford Path, 2.9 mi.

Elevation +/-: 1277 to 4310 to 1879 ft.

Effort: Very strenuous

Day hike: Yes

Overnight backpacking hike: Optional

Duration: 7 to 8 hr.

Early exit option: Webster-Jackson Trail, at 3.4 mi. or 4.7 mi.

Natural history features: Webster Cliffs; Crawford Notch; mountaintop views; Gibbs Brook falls and cascades

Social history features: Willey slide site; Crawford family

Trailhead access: *Start:* Park at junction of road to Willey House Station and US 302, about 1.0 mi. S of Willey Recreation Area in Crawford Notch and 1.5 mi. N of Dry River Campground. Additional parking is available 0.1 mi. N on road to Willey House Station. *End:* Park in lot on Mt. Clinton Rd. near junction with US 302. The Crawford Connector leads 0.2 mi. S to the Crawford Path. The Crawford Path joins US 302 across from the Crawford House site, 0.1 mi. N of the AMC Crawford Notch Hostel and the Crawford Depot AMC Information Center.

Camping/Lodging: Mizpah Spring Hut; Nauman Tentsite

The cliffs of Mt. Webster loom over Crawford Notch like fortress walls. Hidden behind them stand the Presidentials, the crown jewels of the White Mts.

From here, AT hikers who aspire to an audience with Jackson, Pierce, Monroe, or the great Washington must first negotiate the AT/Webster Cliff Trail, which, after 2 mi. of strenuous walking, will have them standing atop the forbidding cliffs overlooking the Notch. Later it will take them over Mt. Webster, Mt. Jackson, and Mt. Pierce, give them a few glimpses of Mt. Washington, then merge with the oldest continuously used hiking trail in the country, the Crawford Path, which provides a gradual descent back into the Notch.

Be careful not to let your impending brush with the great Presidentials keep you from enjoying the nature and history lessons along the way. The trail passes through some of the most diverse ecosystems of the Presidential Range, and the AT's perch atop Webster Cliffs provides not only spectacular views of Crawford Notch but also some insight into the birthplace of tourism in the White Mts. Avoid this trail in foul weather, however, as the ridgeline is prone to lightning strikes and serious falls have occurred from rain-slicked cliffs.

At US 302 the AT is at its low point in the Presidential Range (1277 ft.), and the trail here is surrounded by northern hardwood forest, giving the woods a substantially different character than the forest found at the higher elevations encountered on the Crawford Path and in Pinkham Notch. In late September and early October the sugar maple, American beech, and yellow birch trees in this area are fiery with color. A sharp eye can find red oak, red maple, black cherry, hemlock, and aspen here as well.

Watch the trunks of the beech trees for the scratches of bear claws. Black bears have a taste for beechnuts, which they collect in platforms that they build in the branches of trees. Elsewhere in the branches you can find yellow-rumped warblers, white-throated sparrows, golden-crowned kinglets, red-breasted nuthatches, and dark-eyed juncos.

Enjoy this forest while you can, for the trail ascends quickly after it heads east from Rte. 302 and crosses a bridge over the Saco River at 0.1 mi. Steepening switchbacks lead toward the southern end of the line of cliffs.

Paper birch trees often drop pieces of their parchment-like bark on the trail here, like notes telling of their presence. Balsam fir, on the other hand, announce themselves with their delicious alpine scent as the trail approaches 2,500 ft. in elevation. This marks the beginning of the transition to the spruce/fir forest zone.

Aside from an occasional muddy dip, the trail climbs steeply and steadily through dense woods. At 0.6 mi. it curves to the north and reaches the western edge of the Presidential – Dry River Wilderness, which the AT follows from the border of Crawford Notch State Park to Lakes of the Clouds. At 0.8 mi. the trail turns sharply northwest below a cluster of boulders and runs parallel to Rte. 302. Here the trail works in short zigzags of suffering and relief toward the ridgeline. It flattens out long enough to allow you to catch your breath when it progresses parallel to the Notch but climbs arduously when it turns to the east.

The trail becomes increasingly rocky, but don't become discouraged by the difficult ascent. At a large slab halfway through the climb, there's some foreshadowing of the rewards ahead: a glimpse through the trees of the Notch below and the peaks to northwest. Rest up here, because now the trail becomes still steeper and rockier on its final grunt onto the ridge of Mt. Webster. Steps of rock and wood improve the footing through the toughest sections, but the grade is unrelenting.

At 1.8 mi. the final obstacle, a ledge more than 4 ft. tall with the white blaze of the AT in its center, blocks the trail. Scramble over it to where the trail swings a few feet west to the first

The Crawfords

Ethan and Abel Crawford, two of America's first tourism boosters, cut what is now this country's oldest continuously maintained hiking trail in the state where, every four years, the country begins its process of selecting a president. Soon the peaks crossed by the Crawford Path were named for our first presidents, and not long afterward, real presidents began visiting Crawford Notch, the Crawford House, and the Crawford Path.

"I now mustered all my courage, as I was then lame, took a load on my back and a cane in my hand to help my lame foot.... We ascended at six o'clock in the morning, and reached the summit just as the sun had got to the meridian. What a wonderful sight! We could look over the whole creation with wonder and surprise, as far as the eye could extend, in every direction, and view the wonderful works of God."—as told by Ethan Allen Crawford in *Lucy Crawford's History of the White Mountains.*

Amid the White Mts., whose summits are named for the fathers of the nation, no name is more fabled or revered than that of the pioneering family who helped bring the names Washington, Adams, Jefferson, Monroe, and Madison to the peaks.

Abel and Hannah Crawford, along with their young sons Ethan Allen and Erastus—who would later be followed by six more brothers—occupied a settlers' cabin at the south end of their namesake notch about 1791. Hannah's parents arrived in the remote and rugged notch a year later, setting up house at the upper end in Nash and Sawyer's Location. The families carved out farms, persevering through severe hardships.

In 1803 state funding helped the Crawfords to improve the road through the notch and to focus on earning a living as innkeepers for the drivers of freight-filled sleds and wagons, which passed through the notch on the way to northern New Hampshire and Vermont. As the year-round business provided by teamsters and farmers grew, a new type of traveler began to appear in the notch —the tourist. In taking advantage of this new market, the Crawfords established themselves as the godparents of White Mountain tourism and America's first alpine guides.

Strapping Ethan Allen Crawford, known as the Giant of the Mountains, recognized that his colorful family was as big a draw to many of their visitors as the mountains themselves. He missed few opportunities to build their reputation as innkeepers and guides.

In 1819 Ethan and his father cut the Crawford Path to the summit of Mt. Washington, which—although not the first trail to the summit of the awesome peak—outlived its predecessor, the Gibbs Path, and is now considered the oldest continuously maintained footpath in the United States. Ethan soon cut a second Crawford Path up Mt.

(continued)

(continued)
Washington, and this one, now the route of the cog railway, was what he used to guide most of his clients to the summit. In 1820 he took a festive group from Lancaster, New Hampshire, that included Philip Carrigain, who had recently published the first accurate map of New Hampshire. After a healthy dose of Crawford's "Oh-Be-Joyful," the party named Mts. Washington, Adams, Jefferson, Madison, Monroe, Franklin, and Pleasant (now Mt. Eisenhower).

After Ethan and his cousin, Lucy Howe, married and took over their grandfather's house at the top of the notch, the floor was was regularly filled with sleeping pallets for visitors who would be spellbound by Ethan's tales. Most of his stories were true, aside from a hefty spicing of hyperbole; however, some tales proved tall enough to make P. T. Barnum proud. His claim that he found the Devil's Den, a cave in the side of Mt. Willard, filled with human bones would not be contradicted until a geologic survey in the 1870s.

In 1828 the family built a third house, this one at the gateway of the notch, halfway between their earlier homes, which Thomas Crawford, another of Abel's eight sons, ran as a profitable inn. This, the Crawford House, grew into a major resort and flourished until it was destroyed by a fire in the 1970s. The present AMC Crawford Hostel is located just south of the site of Crawford House.

of many terraces, at about 3000 ft., overlooking Crawford Notch. The second viewpoint, a few dozen yards farther along the trail, is a giant patio of schist that back in civilization would hold half a dozen umbrella-topped tables. From this vantage point it is easy to imagine the glacier that turned a V-shaped river valley into the U-shaped notch that stretches below like a bowling-alley gutter.

At the bottom of the Notch, 2000 ft. below, the engine of the Conway Scenic Railway's "Notch Train" whistles as it pulls its vintage coaches over the Frankenstein Trestle and Willey Brook bridges—engineering wonders of the early 20th century. These are the same tracks that brought early White Mt. tourists to the famous Crawford House inn more than a hundred years ago. Rising above the tracks at the bottom of the Notch, to the south, are the Frankenstein Cliffs, which, although they are as intimidating as Mary Shelley's monster, are actually named for the founder of the Cincinnati Academy of Art, Godfrey Frankenstein, who visited the area regularly to paint. At the top of the Notch, to the north, the train passes beneath the sheer bluffs of Mt. Willard. Mt. Field stands behind Mt. Willard's left shoulder and Mt. Tom looks over its right. The clearing on its summit, an overlook which guests of

Crawford House rode to in carriages, is the top of Mt. Willard Trail.

For the next 1.5 mi. the ridgeline provides countless perspectives over the Notch as the trail dips into woods and bogs, then veers back to the cliffs for yet another view on the way to the summit of Mt. Webster.

At 2.4 mi. a ledge looks down onto the Crawford Notch State Park buildings at the site of the Willey House. In August 1826, heavy rains brought a massive landslide down onto the site. Apparently fearing the slide would bury the house, the family fled, leaving an open Bible on the kitchen table. Samuel Willey, his wife, their five children, and two hired hands were killed by the rockfall. The house, however, was protected by a rock outcrop, and the family dog, left inside the house, was the only survivor. Nowadays novice ice climbers flock to Willey's Slide to get their own "case of the Willeys."

The scars of more recent slides can be seen on mountainsides in Crawford Notch and throughout the White Mts. They occur when the thin soil on steep slopes becomes waterlogged by heavy rains and tears loose from the bedrock, releasing a flood of mud, trees, and rock down the mountain. They are marked by vertical stripes of rock and debris on the sides of steep mountain slopes.

For the next 0.9 mi. the trail climbs and descends steeply over rocky ledges filled with fins and wings of schist, which resembles the granite found elsewhere in New Hampshire but contains much more mica. The rock fractures along the layers of shiny mica into the distinctive plates found here.

At 3.3 mi. the trail reaches the summit of Mt. Webster at 3910 ft., which not only affords another look at the south side of Crawford Notch but also provides a peek at Mt. Washington and the southern Presidentials to the northwest, as well as the Mt. Washington Hotel, about 6 mi. to the north, and the north side of the Notch.

The barren rocks at this final lookout over Crawford Notch might make you think you are entering the alpine zone, but the summit of Mt. Webster is actually almost 1000 ft. below treeline. Still, plenty of lovely alpine vegetation can be found here, particularly in the form of lichens. Look for map lichen, a bright yellow crust; target lichen, in pale green concentric circles; and rusty rock lichen.

From the Mt. Webster summit the trail descends 0.1 mi. into the woods to its junction with the Webster branch of Webster-Jackson Trail, which offers an early exit from the hike, descending 2.3 mi. past the Elephant Head spur and Silver Cascade Brook to US 302, 0.4 mi. south of the Crawford House site.

Spruce trees dominate spruce/fir forests, but that dominance is often challenged, usually by manmade forces. At lower elevations it was logging that devastated the spruce populations; along this section of the AT it is believed that acid rain, along with other blights, has attacked the trees.

Many of the red spruce here bear needles only on their uppermost and lower branches, like grotesque skeletons of once-mighty trees.

Watch the trunks of dead spruce trees for signs of the rare black-backed three-toed woodpecker, which is fond of bark insects that live in dead conifers. They peck the trees gently to flake off the bark, leaving reddish spots that can easily be recognized on the sides of the spruce trees. The bird is also easily recognized, if you have the luck to see one, by its black back and the male's yellow cap. Boreal chickadees, winter wrens, and Swainson's thrushes are also common in the woods here.

From the junction with Webster-Jackson Trail at 3.4 mi., the AT/Webster Cliff Trail turns away from Crawford Notch and heads east across numerous marshy sags, bog bridges, and several short slick declines that can be hiked on either mud or rock. Both methods often end in a tailbone slide.

At 4.7 mi. the trail climbs steeply onto the summit cone of Mt. Jackson (4052 ft.), where the Jackson fork of the Webster-Jackson Trail, another early exit option, descends to the west, joining the Webster fork and reaching US 302 in 2.3 mi. Like the mountains named Carter and Clinton, Mt. Jackson bears the name of a president but was not named for one. This peak honors New Hampshire state geologist Charles Jackson. A stroll around the summit of Mt. Jackson provides vistas onto every region of the Whites, making it an enticing spot for lunch. At 4000 ft., however, the weather can be windy, wet, and quite cold, even in the summer, and the AMC's Mizpah Spring Hut, visible to the northeast from the top of Jackson, may be a more appealing place to take a seat. Follow the cairns that swing northward down the ledges toward Mizpah and Mt. Pierce.

The trail quickly drops back into the trees, and at 5.2 mi., a side trail leads right about 40 yd. to another outlook over the Presidentials. The AT/Webster Cliff Trail descends into the woods to the left.

Once in the trees, the trail passes through several large bogs and marshy alpine meadows filled with colorful grasses, sedges, and reeds. The peat-filled bogs are fed entirely by rainwater. Several species of sphagnum moss usually lie beneath the bogs, and many bog plants can grow only in sphagnum. Cotton sedge and the aptly named hairlike sedge grow in the marshy meadows. Like all ecosystems at this elevation in the White Mts., the bogs and marshes are more delicate than they appear. The climate is cold and wet, the growing season is short, and the soils and peats are low in nutrients and highly acidic. Hikers must stay on the footpath, even when it is knee-deep with water. On the path undulating down to Mizpah you may see where footsteps taken on the side of the trail to avoid the muddy channels have killed the delicate trailside vegetation and consequently made the

Cairn and trail signs on AT/Webster Cliff Trail

path wider and muddier. In other areas new bog bridges will keep your boots from filling with mucky water and prevent further damage to the lush carpet along the trail.

The AT/Webster Cliff Trail intersects the Mizpah cutoff, a shortcut to the Crawford Path, at 6.3 mi., and 0.1 mi. later it arrives at Mizpah Spring Hut, where Mt. Clinton Trail leads off to the southeast, through Oakes Gulf to the Presidential Range – Dry River Wilderness.

Built in 1965 at 3800 ft., Mizpah Spring Hut is the newest of the AMC's huts and is probably named after the Hebrew word for watchtower. It sleeps sixty in eight bunkrooms, which are a little cozier than the larger bunkrooms at most other huts in the Whites. Skylighted and spacious, the hut has solar panels on its roof and high ceilings in its dining area. This modern hut is one of the most popular, and reservations are strongly recommended. It is open from mid-May until mid-October. There are several tent sites adjacent to the hut, for which reservations are also advised. Baked goods and hot drinks are usually available for day hikers to enjoy while they read leaflets detailing the condition of the red spruce. Trail conditions, weather reports, a trail register, and natural history reading can also be found at the hut, as well as lively conversations with the "croo" and other guests.

From Mizpah the trail climbs steeply over slabs and boulders through the thick spruce/fir forest toward Mt. Pierce and another series of spectacular outlooks onto the southern Presidentials and Mt. Washington to the northeast. At 6.6 mi. the trail clambers onto ledges, then heads right and ascends gradually onto the southwest knob of Mt. Pierce. Mt. Pierce is also known as Mt. Clinton—not for President Bill Clinton but for DeWitt Clinton, U.S. senator, mayor of New York City, and governor of New York State. The name was changed to Mt. Pierce by the New Hampshire legislature in 1913 to honor the president from New Hampshire.

At 7.2 mi. Hike #10 reaches its high point on the scrub-covered summit of Mt. Pierce, which, at 4310 ft., is just below treeline. From the summit the AT/Webster Cliff Trail descends 0.1 mi. northeast to its junction with the Crawford Path, where there are still more views of the Presidential range to the east, the Abenaki Ravine to the north, and the Mt. Washington Hotel in the northeast. The northbound AT spends most of the next 12.7 mi. above treeline as it follows the Crawford Path (see Hike #11) east to Mt. Washington. Hike #10, however, turns left on the Crawford Path and follows it 2.9 mi. west into Crawford Notch.

Here the Crawford Path is an alternate route allowing AT hikers to avoid the AT/Webster Cliff Trail in foul weather. This wide path was blazed in 1819 by the legendary father-and-son guides and innkeepers Abel and Ethan Allen Crawford, pioneering mountaineers and unmatched promoters of tourism. In

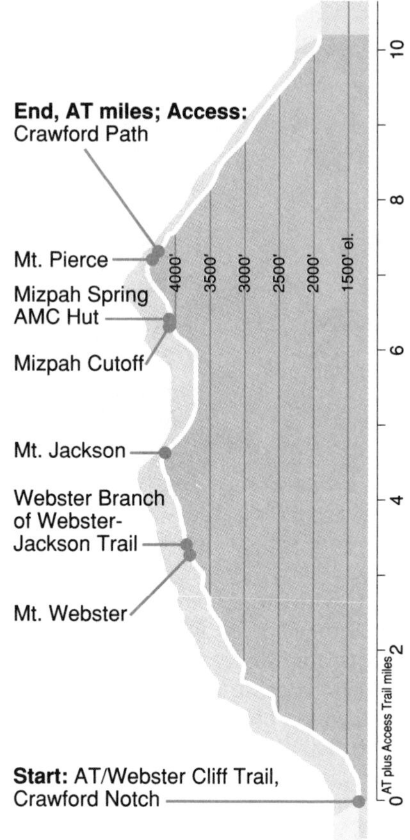

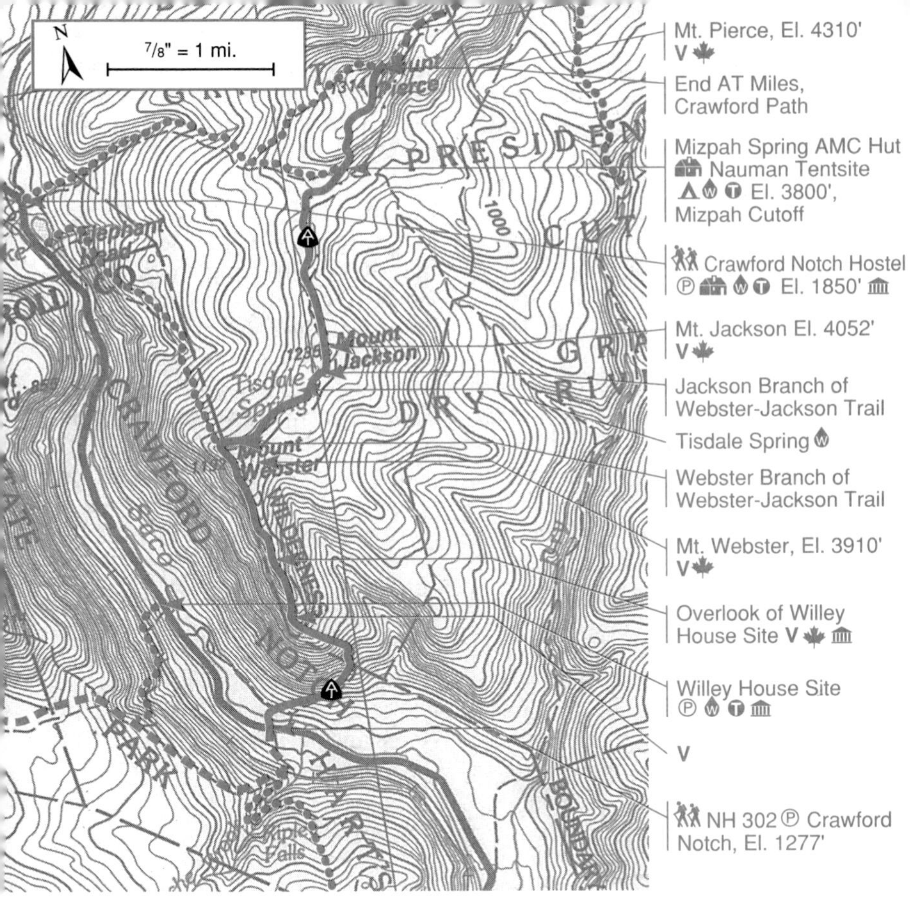

N
7/8" = 1 mi.
Mount Pierce
Mount Jackson
Tisdale Spring
Mount Webster
Elephant Head
DRY RIVER
CRAWFORD NOTCH
Saco
WILDERNESS
PARK
BOUNDARY
Ripley Falls
1000
Mt. Pierce, El. 4310'
V
End AT Miles, Crawford Path
Mizpah Spring AMC Hut
Nauman Tentsite
El. 3800',
Mizpah Cutoff
Crawford Notch Hostel
El. 1850'
Mt. Jackson El. 4052'
V
Jackson Branch of Webster-Jackson Trail
Tisdale Spring
Webster Branch of Webster-Jackson Trail
Mt. Webster, El. 3910'
V
Overlook of Willey House Site V
Willey House Site
V
NH 302 Ⓟ Crawford Notch, El. 1277'

1839 Thomas, a younger son of Abel, converted the trail into a bridle path. The wide, rocky path descends gradually from the evergreens into the higher reaches of the hardwood forest. At 8.5 mi. the Mizpah Cutoff joins the Crawford Path on the left, and at 9.8 mi., the trail passes an information sign for the Gibbs Brook Scenic Area, where rare old-growth forest can be found.

Slightly farther on, a short spur to the right leads to Gibbs Falls, and farther still, a plaque mounted on the rock wall next to the trail designates the oldest continuously maintained footpath in America a National Recreation Area. Just beyond, the path reaches a junction with the Crawford Cliff spur that leads north across Gibbs Brook (where the Mt. Clinton Rd. connector forks to the left and leads to the Mt. Clinton Rd. parking area in 0.2 mi.; a spur to the right off the connector makes a rugged climb past a flume and a pool, eventually reaching an overlook of Crawford Notch 0.4 mi. from the Crawford Path).

After another 0.2 mi. the Crawford Path meets US 302 in Crawford Notch, across from the AMC hostel and near the site of the original Crawford House. The hostel is a bargain compared with the AMC's mountain huts, and its convenient location near the AT, Crawford Path, and other trails makes it an ideal low-budget lodging option for the beginning or end of your hikes in Crawford Notch. It provides a clean, well-equipped self-serve kitchen, trail and weather information, a shuttle stop, dollar showers, a telephone, and bunks in several outbuildings. Its commodious library affords hikers the opportunity to continue their investigations of the ecology and history of Crawford Notch and the southern Presidentials without further strain on their legs.

HIKE #10 Itinerary

Miles N	NORTH	Elev. (ft/m)	Miles S
Total: 10.2 mi. with access trail			
2.9	Access: **Crawford Path,** wide bridle trail, gradual descent to US 302, parking, 0.1 mi. N of Crawford Depot AMC information center at Crawford Notch Hostel.	1879/573	0.0
7.3	**End AT miles:** Junction with **Crawford Path.**		0.1
7.2	Summit of **Mt. Pierce,** views.	4310/1314	0.9
6.4	**Mizpah Spring AMC Hut,** bunkrooms, full service, reservations advised; tent sites.	3800/1158	1.0
6.3	**Mizpah Cutoff,** shortcut to Crawford Path.		2.6
4.7	Summit of **Mt. Jackson,** Jackson fork of Webster-Jackson Trail, views.	4052/1235	3.9
3.4	**Webster Branch** of **Webster-Jackson Trail,** leads 2.3 mi. to US 302		4.0
3.3	Summit of **Mt. Webster,** views.	3910/1192	4.9
2.4	Ledge overlooking Willey House site.		5.5
1.8	**First overlook of Crawford Notch.**		6.5
0.8	NW turn below boulders, AT then zigzags to ridge.		7.2
0.1	Bridge over **Saco River;** steep climb begins.		7.3
0.0	**Start: AT/Webster Cliff Trail,** Crawford Notch, parking on US 302, 1.5 mi. N of Dry River.	1277/389	10.2

SOUTH

HIKE #11

Mt. Washington and the Southern Presidential Range

Maps: ATC N.H. and Vt. #2

Route: From the Crawford House site on US 302 up the Crawford Path, over Mounts Pierce, Eisenhower, Monroe, and Washington, to Tuckerman Ravine Trail and down to Pinkham Notch

Recommended direction: S to N

Distance: 12.4 mi.; 5.4 mi. on the AT

Access trail name & length: Crawford Path, 2.9 mi.; Tuckerman Ravine Trail, 4.1 mi.

Elevation +/-: 1879 to 6288 to 2032 ft.

Effort: Strenuous

Day hike: Optional; shorter loop options

Overnight backpacking hike: Yes

Duration: 8 to 10 hr.

Early exit option: Edmands Path, at 4.6 mi.; Ammonoosuc Ravine Trail, at 6.8 mi.

Natural history features: Highest peak in the Northeast; alpine peaks and ridgeline; rare alpine vegetation; glacial geology; old-growth forest

Social history features: Cog railway; Crawford Path; first alpine summit climbed in the Americas; Tuckerman Ravine skiing; visits by Thoreau

Trailhead access: *Start:* US 302, Crawford Notch, across the street from the Crawford House site, 0.1 mi. N of the AMC hostel and the Fabyan Station AMC office. Parking area on Mt. Clinton Rd., 0.1 mi. N of US 302. Mt. Clinton Rd. connector, 0.2 mi., joins Crawford Path 0.2 mi. from its junction with US 302. *End:* Pinkham Notch AMC camp, on NH 16 about 20 mi. N of North Conway and 11 mi. S of Gorham.

Camping: Mizpah Spring Hut and Nauman Tentsite; Lakes of the Clouds Hut; Hermit Lake shelters and tent sites (tent sites available in winter only)

Nearly two centuries after it was first blazed, the Crawford Path to the summit of Mt. Washington remains one of the grandest walks in America. The nation's oldest continuously maintained footpath passes through a diversity of natural and social history that is as rich as any in the country as it climbs to the summit of the most famous mountain of the eastern U.S. The 5.3 mi. of the Crawford Path between Mt. Pierce and Mt. Washington are shared by the AT.

Warning: Hiking up Mt. Washington requires more preparation than on any other section of the trail. Nearly two dozen of the more than 120 deaths that have occurred on the mountain were caused by exposure and hypothermia. Freezing temperatures and hurricane-force winds are common even in the summer, and weather conditions can deteriorate swiftly above treeline. Summit temperatures can drop a degree a minute for more than half an hour. No hiker should head above treeline in any season here without a weatherproof jacket, long pants, heavy sweater, winter hat, gloves or mittens, first-aid kit, water, and food. Carry a compass and a map, always be aware of the nearest trail that will take you below treeline, and take seriously the signs that advise you to "Turn Back Now If The Weather Is Bad."

From the col between Mt. Eisenhower and Mt. Franklin, the AT/Crawford Path is entirely above treeline and fully exposed to severe weather. The Lakes of the Clouds Hut provides the only refuge between Mt. Monroe and the summit of Mt. Washington. Ammonoosuc Ravine Trail, which meets the AT/Crawford Path at the hut, is the quickest foul-weather escape route for this part of the path.

The Lakes of the Clouds Hut is also the most convenient overnight stop for a two-day hike, covering 6.8 mi. on day #1 and 5.5 mi. on the next day. Mizpah Spring Hut and its Nauman Tent Sites, 2.4 mi. east of US 302 near the junction of the Crawford Path and Webster Cliff Trail, can provide a headstart at the southern end of this hike; and the Hermit Lake Shelters in Tuckerman Ravine, 2.4 mi. from NH 16 in Pinkham Notch, split up the miles on the north side. No camping is permitted above treeline (where the trees are less than 8 ft. tall) except in winter. Camping is also prohibited within 200 ft. of existing trails and within 0.25 mi. of huts or campsites. There are no longer any overnight accommodations on Mt. Washington's summit. See also "Surviving Mt. Wasington" in Hike #12.

Once you are prepared for the possibility of severe weather, prepare to enjoy the rich nature and heritage of Mt. Washington by packing a field guide or history book; then climb the wooden steps across US 302 from the AMC's Crawford Notch Hostel, or follow the 0.2-mi. connector from the Mt. Clinton Rd. parking area, to the Crawford Path to begin your own historic journey.

A spur just to the north off the Crawford Connector, the Crawford Cliff Trail, leads 0.4 mi. from the connector, to a cascade, a pool, and a view of Crawford Notch and the Willey Range. This lovely detour will add up to 0.8 mi. to your route. The brook is named for Joseph Gibbs, who purchased the Crawford House from Thomas Crawford and at one time also owned the Lafayette House in the Franconia area. Visitors to the Crawford House in the 1800s frequented this area for afternoon walks, during which they usually wore semiformal attire. (See Hike #10 for a portrait of the Crawfords.)

The Crawford Path continues along the south side of Gibbs Brook, past a rock-mounted plaque on the right commemorating the path as a National Recreation Area, and at

The Ice Storm of '98

It's not uncommon to encounter the wreckage of a winter storm during a mid-summer's hike in northern New England. Some storms mark the forest for decades to come.

The ferocious ice storm that fell upon northern New England and Quebec from January 5 through 9 of 1998 proved to be one of the most destructive weather events ever recorded in the region. In many areas of the White Mts. the damage surpassed even that of the infamous hurricane of 1938. But, like most northern New England weather, the storm was both fierce and fickle, devastating many areas while leaving others nearby nearly untouched. The spotty damage is attributed to the "microclimates" that are common in New Hampshire and Maine, causing storms to vary their intensity dramatically within small areas. The ice that coated roads and trees during the storm was caused by a layer of warm air sandwiched between two layers of cold air. Snow and sleet melted into rain in the layer of warm air, then froze again when it landed on surfaces in the layer of cold air below. The weather observatory on the summit of Mt. Washington recorded three record high daily temperatures in the 40s while the forest below 3500 ft. was being coated with ice. While the tough coniferous trees of the higher elevations have adapted to withstand the extreme weather of White Mts. summits, hardwoods characteristic of the lower elevations shattered under the weight of the ice.

The storm, which caused massive power outages in Quebec and New England, also devastated portions of the

0.4 mi. it reaches another spur trail on the left, this one leading about 100 ft. to Gibbs Falls. The view from the bridge overlooking the falls is well worth the short detour. Just beyond the spur trail, a sign identifies the Gibbs Brook Scenic Area. Parts of the forest along the brook have never been logged, which is rare at this low elevation in the White Mts.

Mt. Washington was first climbed in 1642 by Darby Field, who took 18 days to reach the summit from his home in Durham, New Hampshire. Field recruited a number of Indians for assistance in the southern foothills of the daunting mountain, but only two of them were willing to accompany him to the summit. Until recently his route was believed to have been up Boott Spur, Tuckerman Ravine, or the Montalban Ridge. In a recently discovered letter, Thomas Gorges, a magistrate in Maine in Field's day, describes the explorer crossing several smaller peaks on his way up Mt. Washington. Historians now believe that the smaller peaks were the

AT in areas scattered throughout New Hampshire, Vermont, and Maine. Trails in Pinkham Notch, on the east side of Mt. Washington, were particularly hard hit. Both the Old Jackson Rd., and the Lost Pond Trail, which together make up the AT's route through the notch, were badly damaged, along with such popular routes as the Tuckerman Ravine Trail. The Wildcat Ridge Trail, another link in the AT, was severely damaged, particularly between peaks C and D of Wildcat Mt. Heavy damage was also reported on the Garfield Ridge Trail, a section of the AT near Franconia Notch. South of the White Mts., significant damage was reported by the Dartmouth Outing Club on Moose Mt., Holts Ledge, Lambert Ridge, Smarts Mt., and Mt. Cube, all of which are crossed by the AT. Trail crews from the AMC, DOC, U.S. Forest Service, and other groups planned to have cleared most of the damage affecting the AT by the summer of 1998; however more than 100 trails in New Hampshire, Maine, and Vermont were damaged, and it will take years for all of the wreckage of the ice storm to be fully cleared away.

Trails damaged by the ice storm present several safety issues. Timber in damaged forests will fall—unpredictably—for years to come. Hard hit areas of the forest will have no canopy to shade the understory, which will allow sunlight to dry the forest floor and increase the threat of forest fires. Rescue help will be delayed by trail damage to some areas, and hikers should take this into account before passing beyond a significantly impacted section of an ice-damaged trail.

—Michael Kodas

Southern Presidentials, and that Field followed a route near that of the Crawford Path you are walking today.

Low on the mountain, the path blazed by Abel and Ethan Allen Crawford in 1819 is wide, its footing solid, and its grade moderate. It continues to follow the right (south) side of Gibbs Brook, then climbs away from it to the east. At 1.7 mi. it reaches the Mizpah Cutoff on the right, a shortcut leading 0.7 mi. to Mizpah Spring Hut (see Hike #10). From the cutoff, the Crawford Path continues its gradual climb onto the flank of Mt. Pierce, atop which it will join the AT.

Mt. Pierce is also known as Mt. Clinton (this, its original name, honors DeWitt Clinton, governor of New York, U.S. senator, and presidential wanna-be in the early 1800s—not the U.S. President of the 1990s). The New Hampshire legislature changed the name to Mt. Pierce in 1913 to honor native son, President Franklin Pierce.

The Crawford Path meets the AT/Webster Cliff Trail at 2.9 mi., on the shoulder of Mt. Pierce, just past a flat outlook where you will get your first views of the Southern Presidentials parading toward the northeast. From the junction—where our AT mileage count begins—the Webster Cliff Trail leads right 0.1 mi. to the summit of Mt. Pierce (4310 ft.), while the AT/Crawford Path goes left and swings gradually to the north, passing above the Abenaki Ravine, named for a tribe of Native Americans that inhabited the region. To the south lies the Presidential Range-Dry River Wilderness, whose boundaries the trail parallels between Mt. Pierce and Lakes of the Clouds.

On a clear day the views in all directions are dizzying as the AT/Crawford Path climbs gradually through scrub, following cairns between Mt. Pierce and Mt. Eisenhower. (Even better views are provided by the short loop trails that lead to the summits of Mts. Eisenhower, Franklin, and Monroe. These exposed summits, however, should be avoided in sketchy weather.) At 0.7 mi. the AT crosses a spring-fed brook, and at 1.2 mi. it reaches the base of the Mt. Eisenhower Loop, which leads to the summit of Mt. Eisenhower (4761 ft.) and rejoins the AT after 0.8 mi., adding only 0.2 mi. and 300 ft. of climbing to the trip.

The AT/Crawford Path runs flat to the southeast of Mt. Eisenhower and is met by the northeastern end of the Mt. Eisenhower Loop, along with the Edmands Path, at 1.7 mi. on a rocky shelf that overlooks the stagnant waters of Red Pond. From the junction, the Edmands Path—named for J. Rayner Edmands, a scientist, trailblazer, and one of the founders of the AMC—descends 2.9 mi. west to Mt. Clinton Rd., an early exit option. The AT/Crawford Path drops into the small sag between Mt. Eisenhower and Mt. Franklin, and then at 1.9 mi. reaches Mt. Eisenhower Trail on the right, which descends into Oakes Gulf and the Presidential Range-Dry River Wilderness.

Here the AT/Crawford Path makes a steepening ascent on a blunt ridgeline onto Mt. Franklin, passes a spring, then levels out and at 2.9 mi. passes just west of the flat summit of Mt. Franklin (5004 ft.). A short loop trail on the right leads to the summit, which offers magnificent overlooks of Oakes Gulf. This cirque, dropping to the east of Mts. Franklin and Monroe, is named for William Oakes, a botanist who first visited the White Mts. in 1825 and named Mt. Jackson and Mt. Clay. The reverent prose and large lithographic plates in Oakes's book *Scenery of the White Mountains*, published in 1848, inspired thousands of tourists to visit the region.

At 3.2 mi. the Monroe Loop forks off to the left and leads to more spectacular views atop the mountain's summit (5384 ft.) on a detour that adds 350 ft. of climbing but no substantial mileage to the hike. Mt. Monroe is actually a huge "roche moutonnée," also called a whaleback or sheepback, created by glaciers that polished the northeast side of the mountain into a smooth slope but cut the southeast side into a jagged face. The AT/Crawford Path passes and crosses many smaller roches moutonnées in this area.

The AT traverses the top of the northwest wall of Oakes Gulf, then crosses Monroe Flats, an excellent area to enjoy alpine flowers during their June bloom. Watch for diapensia, a mat of dark green leaves speckled with waxy white flowers; Lapland rosebay, with larger magenta flowers; and alpine azalea, with small pink star-shaped blossoms. The flats' botanical significance is matched only by the fragility of the plants, and hikers must be exceedingly careful to keep their boots on bare rock as they cross the area. A sign marks the spot where the trail has been moved away from the section where the federally protected dwarf cinquefoil, named by William Oakes, is being preserved. Be happy in the knowledge that by avoiding this area you are doing your part to preserve this five-petaled yellow flower, which is only found atop the Presidential and Franconia mountain ranges.

At 3.9 mi. the Monroe Loop rejoins the AT/Crawford Path, which then makes an easy descent to the AMC's Lakes of the Clouds Hut, overlooking the Ammonoosuc Ravine at 5050 ft., between the foot of Mt. Monroe and the hut's two namesake alpine lakes.

William Curtis and Allen Ormsbee, experienced hikers and respected members of the AMC, were caught in a severe storm here on the last day of June 1900 while hiking to an AMC meeting on the summit of Mt. Washington. Curtis died in the rocks surrounding the Lakes of the Clouds, where he had sought shelter. Ormsbee succumbed to the elements only a few hundred yards from the summit buildings. The AMC, hoping to prevent more tragic deaths, built a shelter near where Curtis's body was found. Although it was intended only for emergency use, by 1915 its popularity had spurred the club to build a hut supplied with bunks for thirty-six people and a caretaker to cook meals and manage the building. Today the "Lakes of the Crowds," as it is often called, is the closest public shelter to Mt. Washington's summit and the most popular of the AMC huts. The original stone building has been significantly expanded to hold ninety guests with an eight-person "croo." Space for backpackers is available at a reduced cost in the basement, but this option is generally reserved for long-distance hikers and is usually filled by early afternoon. The hut is open from June to mid-September; however, the "dungeon," a room in the cellar that will sleep six, is left open year-round for emergency shelter. The incredible popularity of this hut makes reservations a must for overnight visitors.

If the weather is good during your stay, a sunset trip to the summit of Mt. Monroe makes a magnificent finale to a day of hiking.

From the hut, Ammonoosuc Ravine Trail descends 2.5 mi. westward to the Cog Railroad Base Rd., providing the easiest direct access to the hut and the most convenient escape route for this part of the AT/Crawford Path. "Ammonoosuc" derives from an Abenaki word noting the river as a good place to find fish. Dry River Trail leads south from the hut to the Dry River Wilderness and US 302, 9.6 mi. distant.

The Crawford Path turns right at the hut, crosses the outlet of the larger of the Lakes of the Clouds, then climbs between it, at 5025 ft., and the smaller lake, which at 5050 ft. is the highest-elevation lake in New England. The research equipment that's set up between the dark waters of the lakes measures the effects of acid rain.

A few feet past the lakes, the AT/Crawford Path reaches a junction with Camel Trail to Boott Spur and the Tuckerman Crossover, both of which eventually lead to Pinkham Notch. The Tuckerman Crossover crosses Bigelow Lawn to Tuckerman Ravine Trail, cutting approximately 1.5 mi. from the length of this hike. Although this route is a good way to avoid the summit of Mt. Washington in a storm, it is also treacherously steep and exposed and must be traveled with extreme caution.

The AT/Crawford Path continues from this junction across the western end of Bigelow Lawn, another fine area to take in the alpine flower show in early summer. Dr. Jacob Bigelow, a Boston botanist and physician, teamed up with Dr. Francis Boott (Boott spur's namesake) to find plants native to Labrador, Siberia and Greenland on Mt. Washington. A careful eye will note striped soil that makes parts of Bigelow Lawn look like a recently plowed field. These features are actually made by the freezing and thawing of rocks and soil in a process called "solifluction," which creates soil stripes, circles of stone, and terraces.

At the base of the Mt. Washington summit cone, the Davis Path, which leads back south to the Tuckerman Crossover and Camel Trail, enters from the right, 5.1 mi. up the AT Crawford Path. A few feet beyond, Westside Trail, a shortcut to the Northern Presidentials, exits to the left. From here the summit of Mt. Washington, rising in front of you, seems but a short jog away—but don't be misled. It is farther away than it appears and is reached after some of the day's slowest walking. The final ascent crosses a sea of felsenmeer—large, jagged rocks that have been fractured at their joints by the cycle of freezing and thawing—which makes for difficult footing with a heavy pack or in high winds. The rime ice that often frosts the summit buildings can make travel on these rocks even more dicey.

You are likely to encounter the sulfuric odor and black smudge of coal smoke from the Cog Railway, chugging steeply up the northwest side of Ammonoosuc Ravine. The antennas and the summit buildings that become more obvious as you climb will be an incentive to those looking for a warm seat, a snack, or an easy ride down. Others will slow their stride, disappointed that the summit of this great mountain is so heavily developed.

At 5.2 mi. the AT/Crawford Path passes Gulfside Trail on the left, which the AT will soon join to traverse the Northern Presidentials. The AT swings to the right up the final climb onto the summit of Mt. Washington, passing through an old stone corral that held the horses ridden up the Crawford Path after Thomas Crawford, Ethan's younger brother, turned it into a bridle path in 1840. Abel Crawford, then seventy-five, was the first person to ride to the summit of Mt. Washington, and the bridle path was later immortalized in a painting by Winslow Homer.

Today the summit is a New Hampshire state park, covered with buildings, railroad tracks, antenna towers, an observation platform, and a parking lot. More than 250,000 people visit the summit of Mt. Washington during the summer, most of them arriving via the auto road or the cog railway. On a warm, clear day, the peak, reached at 5.4 mi. on the AT/ Crawford Path, has the atmosphere of a carnival.

The development here is anchored by the Sherman Adams Summit Building, which was dedicated in 1980 after the last of three summit houses was removed. Adams was a New Hampshire native and Dartmouth graduate who diligently advocated appreciation and protection of the White Mts. as a congressman, governor, and aide to President Eisenhower. The Adams building is a two-story crescent with large observation decks that overlook the Great Gulf Wilderness Area. The Mt. Washington Observatory fills the west side of the building, while a restaurant, museum, gift shop, and post office occupy the other half (open from mid-May to mid-October). The original stone Tip-Top House, built in 1853 and accommodating such diverse characters as President Franklin Pierce and confederate leader Jefferson Davis, remains on the summit—a counterpoint to the modern concrete summit building.

Several options present themselves now: (1) Finish the trip by boarding the Mt. Washington Cog Railway, just east of the summit building ($20 fare), for the quick ride down to Marshfield Station, 3.0 mi from Crawford Notch. The railroad, completed in 1869, was the first mountain-climbing rail line in the world. The 3.0-mi. run follows the route of another trail blazed up Mt. Washington by the Crawfords and was once descended in less than 3 min. by a workman on a slideboard, a small sled that rode the rails. (2) Continue on the AT, which horseshoes back to the northwest on the 0.1-mi. Trinity Heights Connector to Gulfside Trail and on into the Northern Presiden-

David Emblidge

Alpine azaleas and diapensia—alpine plants

tials (see Hike #12). Or (3) head south across the summit parking lots to Tuckerman Ravine Trail, another historic route, which leads down to Pinkham Notch.

Tuckerman Ravine Trail

Amherst College botanist Edward Tuckerman started studying plants on Mt. Washington in 1837, identified many of its unusual alpine species, and named four zones of mountain plant life: the alpine zone, the subalpine zone, the higher forest, and the lower forest. The trail through the ravine named in his honor is the shortest route to the summit of Mt. Washington and is steep, rugged, and spectacular. Pinkham Notch is only 4.1 mi. away from the top of Mt. Washington via this route, half the distance the Crawford Path takes to reach the summit.

Follow the cairns south over more jagged felsenmeer down the summit cone, where, on a clear day, you can see dozens of the large cones of rock stretching into the distance past Tuckerman Junction, across Bigelow Lawn, to the Lakes of the Clouds. At 0.4 mi., Lion Head Trail heads left off Tuckerman Ravine Trail. This trail rejoins Tuckerman Ravine Trail 1.5 mi. lower and provides an alternate route when Tuckerman Ravine Trail is closed due to snow. Lion Head Trail, named for the obvious ridge that hangs over the north side of Tuckerman Ravine, is particularly popular with climbers and skiers because it provides the easiest access to Mt. Washington's summit in winter, when

Plant Life in the Alpine Zone

To the careless eye the world above treeline in the White Mountains is a barren wasteland of dwarfed and deformed trees, broken rock, and tiny plants struggling to survive the harsh weather. Closer inspection, however, will reveal one of the most fascinating plant worlds on the entire AT.

Treeline–the point of elevation where severe weather prevents trees from growing more than eight-feet tall–occurs at about 4800 ft. on the north side of Mt. Washington and 5200 ft. on the south side of the mountain. Stunted spruce and fir trees will tell you when you have reached it. The altitude's high winds, short growing season, and increased precipitation (eight inches more for every 1,000 ft. of elevation gain) make it impossible for most tree species to survive and prevent those that do from growing taller or remaining straight. The rime ice that decorates the windward side of trees here in cold, wet weather is fascinating to the eye but damaging to the trees, hindering their production of food through photosynthesis and stunting new growth.

Higher still lie the krummholz–trees so dwarfed and twisted by the weather that they often grow horizontally along the ground rather than vertically. In places mats of the gnarled trees form impenetrable thickets called tuckamores, which proved the most difficult part of the first climbs to the summits. Black spruce dominates the krummholz on the eastern slopes of the Presidential Range, where there is some protection from the prevailing west wind, and often grows in large, ground-hugging mats. Balsam fir is more common on slopes exposed to the wind and tends to grow in clumps. The branches of both species grow new roots when they are pressed against moist soil in these conditions, allowing the tree to survive if its original trunk should die.

After seeing what the White Mountains' ferocious, alpine weather does to its trees, it's hard to believe that any more delicate plants can survive here at all. Yet an amazing collection of flowers, grasses, mosses and lichens not only endure these harsh conditions, but thrive only here.

No visitor to Mt. Washington's Alpine Garden, Bigelow Lawn or Monroe Flats during the two weeks in mid-June during which the alpine flowers bloom can fail to be impressed by their diverse abundance and flamboyant showmanship. Diapensia is one of the most common, with small, white flowers polka-dotting a mat of dark green evergreen leaves. Lapland rosebay, with one-inch-wide, magenta flowers, and alpine azalea, with smaller, pink flowers –both actually dwarf shrubs–bloom at the same time as diapensia and can often be found nearby. These plants not only survive the harsh mountain environment, but flourish in the most

(continued)

(continued)

exposed sites of the alpine zone. Like all of the plants in the alpine zone, they are perennial, storing food in the part of the plant that survives the winter. The mats of evergreen leaves of these hardy plants protect the root systems and, like the trees of the alpine summits, they grow close to the ground to stay out of the wind.

Mountain sandwort has a similar appearance to diapensia, but its flowers have longer petals and bloom from July until September. It is common along trails in the alpine zone and in areas that have been disturbed by frost and erosion. Three-toothed cinquefoil is more common than the federally protected dwarf cinquefoil and displays a white flower with five ("cinq") petals on a stalk above a mat of green leaves that turn red in the fall.

Bigelow's sedge, the most common of the grasses, sedges and rushes that cover the alpine summits, can be recognized by the dried, grass-like leaves at its base. Mosses, like woolly shag moss and the worm-like turgid bog moss, can be found on the rocks of the alpine zone and in every nook and cranny between them. Lichens cover rocks, trees and open ground. Map lichen, an obvious, yellow crust lichen, and rusty rock lichen, an orange crust on exposed rock, are two of the most common.

Alpine vegetation, while able to flourish in some of the fiercest weather on the planet, can be destroyed by single misplaced footstep, making it important for hikers venturing above treeline to stay on the path. When exploring areas off the path, take care to step only on bare rock, as even the mosses and lichens of the alpine zone are fragile. Avoid walking in any area where your footsteps will cause any erosion of the soil or rocks. Digging is devastating to the fragile soil and vegetation of the alpine summits, so all solid human waste should be carried out, along with any other garbage brought there. Under no circumstances should any vegetation be removed from the alpine zone.

Rare species (some unique in the world) are found in the Whites' alpine zone, including dwarf cinquefoil, a plant so vulnerable that its one habitat is now off limits to everyone. Other plants have become extinct due to careless human impact.

A highly recommended resource on the alpine environment is *Field Guide to the New England Alpine Summits* by Slack and Bell, published by AMC. The best time to see alpine plants in bloom is mid-June to early July, shortly after the snowcap melts away. For guided hikes through Mt. Washington's alpine flower zone, contact AMC at Pinkham Notch, NH (603-466-2727).

David Emblidge

Lapland rosebay—alpine plant

Tuckerman Ravine Trail is often closed.

Tuckerman Ravine Trail reaches Tuckerman Junction at 0.6 mi., turns left, and descends to the east, reaching Alpine Garden Trail at 0.8 mi. As the name implies, the Alpine Garden, a mile-long terrace above Huntington Ravine to the northeast of Tuckerman Ravine Trail, is a fine spot to see alpine flowers like diapensia and alpine azalea. It is also a great place to investigate Mt. Washington's rich insect life. On sunny summer days several types of butterflies can be seen in the area, including White Mt. butterflies, a variety that mates here in July and is found nowhere else in the world.

At 1.1 mi. Tuckerman Ravine Trail descends steeply into the ravine, then turns sharp left and passes a spot where an arch is often carved in the snow by an underlying waterfall. Stay well away from the arch and never pass below it, as chunks of snow and ice weighing thousands of pounds can fall at any moment! Be very careful not to dislodge any rocks that might fall on hikers below.

The trail turns back right, descending very steeply into the quintessential glacial cirque. To the left is the Lion Head, while just to your right is the headwall of the ravine and, on the southwest side of the ravine, the hanging cliffs of Boott Spur. Snow filling what was once a gentle bowl here was eventually compressed into a glacier that carved the steep walls you see today.

Snow continues to shape Tuckerman Ravine, and thousands of skiers hike into the ravine in spring and summer to test their mettle on the steep walls of corn snow that can last until late summer. The headwall is still considered one of the most demanding ski runs in the country. The "Inferno" ski race from the top of the headwall to Pinkham Notch was discontinued long ago, and the 6-min. 29-sec. record set by Toni Matt in 1939 was never broken. In 1858 Henry David Thoreau had his own inferno in the ravine when his party's campfire spread out of control, burning several acres of the nearby slopes before the blaze was fortuitously drowned by a sudden downpour.

The descent will pound your knees whether you descend on skis or on Vibram soles.

As the pitch eases, Tuckerman Ravine Trail passes to the right of a boulder field known as Lunch Rocks, which serves as bleachers for skiers and spectators, then follows the north side of the stream that flows out of the ravine. At 1.8 mi. you will arrive at the Hermit Lake Shelters' caretaker's residence, where you can purchase a few hiking supplies and relax on a popular deck. Tickets for space in the lean-to shelters, which can accommodate eighty-six people in all, are $5 per person per night and must be purchased at the Pinkham Notch Visitor Center in person. The shelters are scattered in the woods surrounding Hermit Lake, just east of the caretaker's residence, and are available year-round. Ten tentsites, accommodating forty people, are available in winter only.

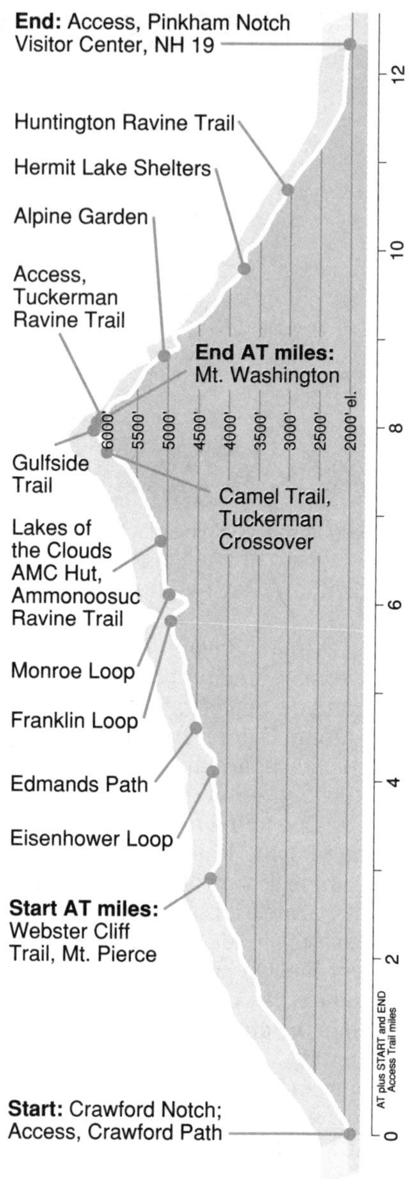

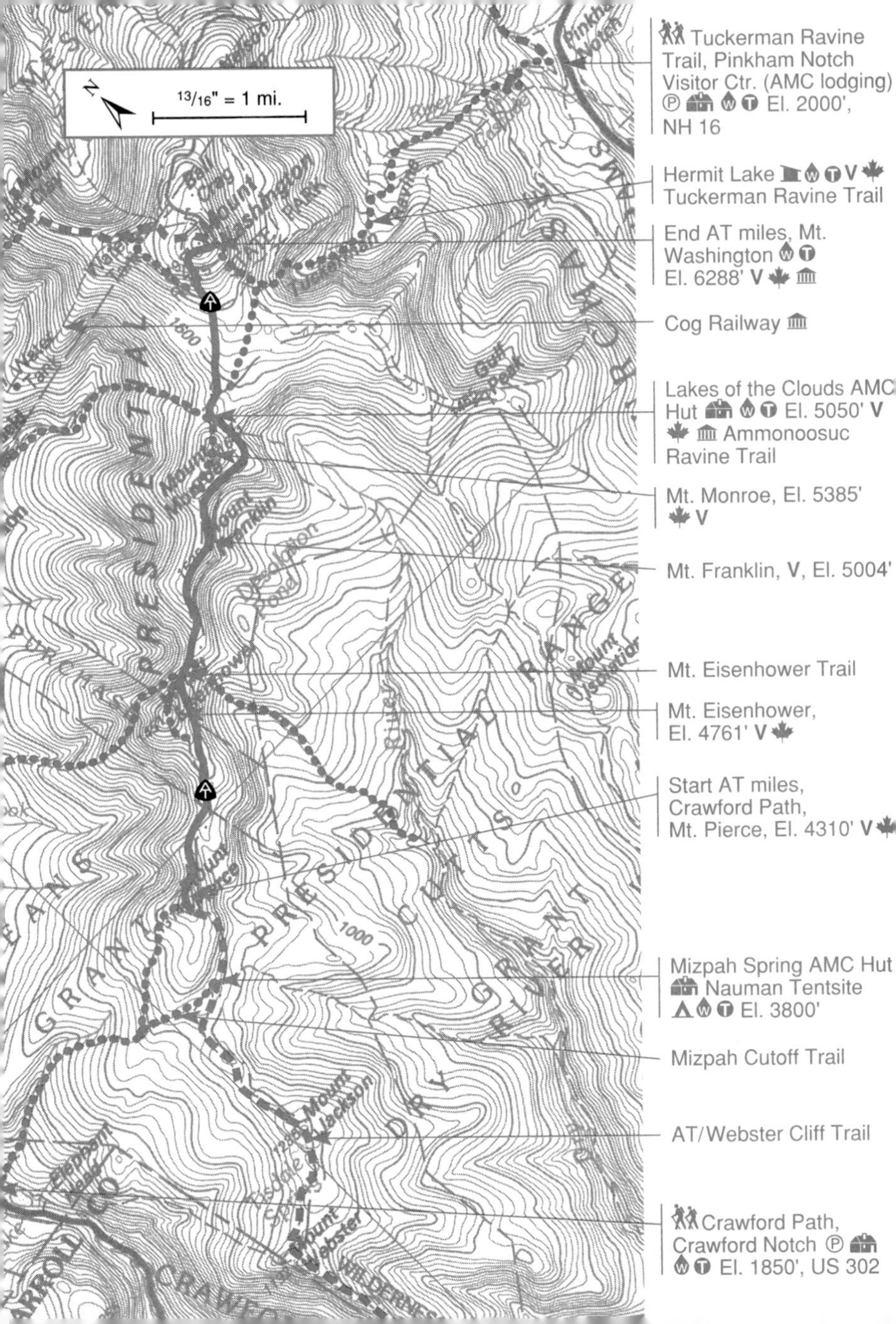

N
13/16" = 1 mi.
Tuckerman Ravine Trail, Pinkham Notch Visitor Ctr. (AMC lodging) Ⓟ El. 2000', NH 16
Hermit Lake V Tuckerman Ravine Trail
End AT miles, Mt. Washington El. 6288' V
Cog Railway
Lakes of the Clouds AMC Hut El. 5050' V Ammonoosuc Ravine Trail
Mt. Monroe, El. 5385' V
Mt. Franklin, V, El. 5004'
Mt. Eisenhower Trail
Mt. Eisenhower, El. 4761' V
Start AT miles, Crawford Path, Mt. Pierce, El. 4310' V
Mizpah Spring AMC Hut Nauman Tentsite El. 3800'
Mizpah Cutoff Trail
AT/Webster Cliff Trail
Crawford Path, Crawford Notch Ⓟ El. 1850', US 302
PRESIDENTIAL
PRESIDENTIAL RANGE
DRY RIVER
Mount Washington
Mount Monroe
Mount Franklin
Mount Pierce
Mount Jackson
Mount Webster
Gulf Peak
1600
1000

Lion Head trail rejoins Tuckerman Trail on the left just east of the last shelter, and the Boott Spur Link heads south here. From Hermit Lake, Tuckerman Ravine Trail descends a logging road parallel to the Cutler River, reaching the Raymond Path 0.3 mi. below Hermit Lake. The descent steepens somewhat, and although the grade remains moderate, it is unrelenting. During its final 2.0 mi., Tuckerman Ravine Trail intersects many logging roads and ski trails. At 2.5 mi. it crosses the river, and at 2.7 mi. it reaches Huntington Ravine Trail on the left. At 3.7 mi., at a sharp curve to the left, Boott Spur Trail diverges to the right. This trail honors Dr. Francis Boott, a botanist who explored the area in the early 1800s. Shortly before arriving in Pinkham Notch, at 3.8 mi., a side trail climbs 20 yd. to one last scenic stop, a stone-walled overlook of Crystal Cascade in the Cutler River. Rev. Manasseh Cutler, the botanist honored by the river's name, was a member of the first scientific expedition to Mt. Washington, led by Jeremy Belknap in 1784. Cutler was the first to study the mountain's alpine plants and was led by the severe conditions on the summit to gauge its elevation incorrectly at 10,000 ft.!

A few minutes later you will find yourself at the AMC Pinkham Notch Visitor Center, which offers a full range of services: lodging, food, hiking supplies, bookstore, natural history programs, pay showers, toilets, and overnight parking. With the south and north access trails, you have hiked 12.4 mi. and climbed over 5000 ft. If you're done in, the AMC shuttle will return you to Crawford Notch the easy way (reservations advised).

Day Hikes in the Southern Presidentials

There are many options, including:

- Up Crawford Path from US 302, south on Mizpah Cutoff to Mizpah Hut, then along AT/Webster Cliff Trail to Mt. Pierce. Return via Crawford Path for a 6.2-mi. round-trip.
- Edmands Path from Mt. Clinton Rd. to Mt. Eisenhower Loop Trail, 6.8 mi. round-trip.
- Ammonoosuc Ravine Trail from Marshfield Station (the base station of the Mt. Washington Cog Railway) to Lake of the Clouds Hut and back, 6.2 mi. round-trip.
- The ever-popular climb from Pinkham Notch Visitor Center to the summit of Mt. Washington via Tuckerman Ravine Trail (8.2 mi. round-trip), or via a combination of Tuckerman Ravine and Lion Head trails (8.4 mi. round-trip), or via Tuckerman Ravine Trail and Boott Spur (9.5 mi. round-trip).

HIKE #11 Itinerary

Miles N	NORTH	Elev. (ft/m)	Miles S
Total: 12.4 mi. with access trails at both ends			
4.1	**Pinkham Notch Visitor Center,** full service, parking, NH 16, AMC shuttle to Crawford Notch.	2032/619	0.0
3.8	Side trail to **Crystal Cascade.**		0.3
3.7	**Boott Spur Trail** goes S (R).		0.4
2.7	**Huntington Ravine Trail** enters from L (N).	3031/924	1.4
2.5	Cross **Cutler River.**		1.6
2.1	Junction with **Raymond Path.**		2.0
1.8	**Hermit Lake Shelters,** fee, caretaker, lean-tos, tent sites (winter only), supplies, water, privy. **Lion Head Trail** rejoins; **Boott Spur Link** heads south. Trail descends on logging road.	3877/1182	2.3
1.1	Sharp descent into ravine.		3.0
0.8	**Alpine Garden Trail.**		3.3
0.6	**Tuckerman Junction.**	5383/1641	3.5
0.4	**Lion Head Trail** heads L (E); alternate route.		3.7
0.0	Access: **Tuckerman Ravine Trail** (south across parking lots).		4.1
5.4	**End AT miles: Mt. Washington** summit, junction with cog railway and auto road, summit building, observatory, restaurant, museum, gift shop, post office.	6288/1917	0.0
5.2	Junction with **Gulfside Trail**; AT swings R, passes through stone corral.		0.3
5.1	**Davis Path** leads S to Tuckerman Crossover and Camel Trail; then **Westside Trail** exits L (W).		
4.8	Junction with **Camel Trail** and **Tuckerman Crossover;** bad-weather bypass to Pinkham Notch, use extreme caution. AT crosses W end of Bigelow Lawn.		0.6

Itinerary continued

HIKE #11 Itinerary *continues on previous page.*

Miles N		Elev. (ft/m)	Miles S
3.9	**Lakes of the Clouds Hut,** AMC lodging, water, toilet, reservations necessary; year-round emergency shelter. **Ammonoosuc Ravine Trail,** 2.5 mi. W to cog railway base, early exit option. AT turns R at hut and climbs between lakes.	5050/1539	1.6
3.2	**Monroe Loop** to summit of Mt. Monroe, views.	5034/1534	2.2
2.9	**Franklin Loop** to summit of Mt. Franklin, views.	5004/1525	2.5
1.9	Junction with **Mt. Eisenhower Trail.**		3.5
1.7	**Edmands Path** descends 2.9 mi. W to Clinton Rd., early exit option.		3.7
1.2	Junction with **Eisenhower Loop;** 0.8-mi. summit loop.	4461/1360	4.2
0.7	Brook.		4.7
0.0	**Start AT miles: Webster Cliff Trail, Mt. Pierce;** summit 0.1 mi. S	4310/1311	5.4
2.9	Access: **Crawford Path** from US 302 at Crawford Notch Hostel or on connector from Mt. Clinton Rd. parking area, along S side of Gibbs Brook to junction with AT/Webster Cliff Trail. Pass Mizpah Cut-off at 1.7 mi. (leading to Mizpah Hut, Nauman Tentsite at 2.4 mi., 3800 ft.).	1879/573	2.9

SOUTH

HIKE #12

The Northern Presidentials

Maps: ATC N.H. & Vt. #2

Route: Circuit hike up from Pinkham Notch via Tuckerman Ravine Trail to summit of Mt. Washington, north over Mts. Clay, Jefferson, Adams, and Madison, then south through the Great Gulf back to Pinkham Notch

Recommended direction: S to N

Distance: 17.5 mi.; 13.4 mi. on AT

Access trail name & length: Tuckerman Ravine Trail, 4.1 mi.

Elevation +/-: 2032 to 6288 to 2032 ft.

Effort: Very strenuous

Day hike: No

Overnight backpacking hike: Yes

Duration: 14 to 18 hr.

Early exit option: Jewell Trail, at 1.1 mi.; Sphinx Trail, at 2.0 mi.; Cornice Trail, at 2.5 mi.; Six Husbands Trail, at 2.9 mi.; Randolph Path, at 3.4 mi.; Israel Ridge Path, at 4.0 mi.; Lowe's Path, at 4.6 mi.; Air Line, at 5.2 mi.; Valley Way, at 5.6 mi.; Watson Path, at 6.1 mi.; Daniel Webster Trail, at 6.5 mi.; Great Gulf Trail, at 9.2 mi.

Natural history features: Alpine peaks and ridges; highest peak in Northeast; world's worst weather; alpine plants

Social history features: Mt. Washington weather observatory; Appalachian Mountain Club; Randolph Mountain Club

Trailhead access: *Start and End:* Pinkham Notch AMC camp, on NH 16 about 20 mi. N of North Conway and 11 mi. S of Gorham

Camping: Hermit Lake Shelters; The Perch; Crag Camp; Gray Knob; Valley Way Tentsite; Madison Springs Hut; Osgood Tentsite; Gray Knob cabin; Pinkham Notch Camp

---

The northern and southern ridgelines of the Presidential Range seem like twins at first glance, but they actually have distinct personalities. The Southern Presidentials, traversed by the venerable Crawford Path, seem older and friendlier. The Northern Presidentials, on the other hand, are taller, less cultured, more aloof. Indeed, the four highest mountains in the Northeast are crossed by the AT's route across the Northern Presidentials: Mt. Washington, Mt. Jefferson, Mt. Madison, and Mt. Adams. The northwest flank of the Presidential ridge has a density of footpaths achieved nowhere else in the White Mts., thanks to the efforts of the White Mt. National Forest (WMNF), the Appalachian Mt. Club (AMC), and the Randolph Mt. Club (RMC), centered in Randolph, on the north side of the range.

Day hikers visiting the Northern Presidentials should consider following one of the many popular trails

David Emblidge

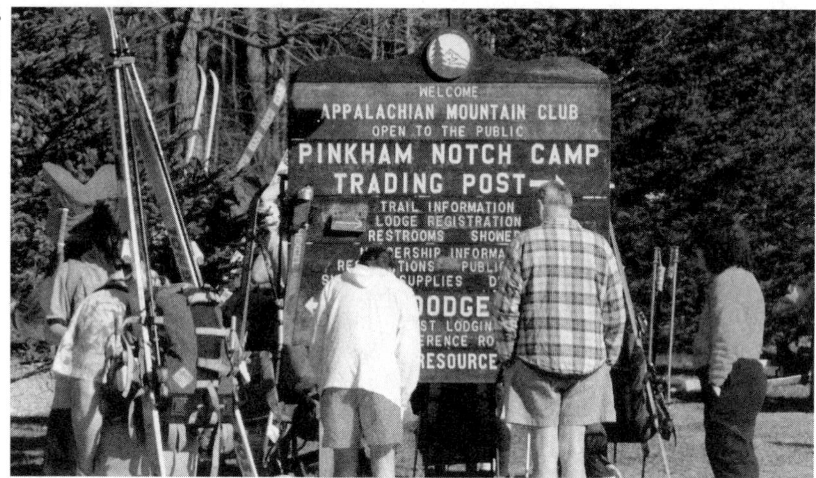

Spring hikers and skiers gear up at AMC's Pinkham Notch Camp

that lead up from US 2: Castle Trail to the summit of Mt. Jefferson; Lowe's Path and the Air Line to the summit of Mt. Adams; and the Valley Way to Madison Springs Hut.

Although it does not maintain the AT, the RMC takes care of nearly three dozen other trails in the area. The RMC brings a rugged flavor to their part of the Presidentials—no huts, shuttle buses, or visitor center complexes. The club's trailside accommodations in the Presidentials—The Perch shelter, Crag Camp, and Gray Knob cabin—are simple, rustic, and inexpensive. As opposed to the AMC huts, no meals are served at the RMC facilities and visitors must provide their own cookware and bedding.

The AMC's Madison Springs Hut and the U.S. Forest Service's Osgood Tentsite are located on the AT, while the Valley Way Tentsite, also run by the USFS, is located 0.6 mi. north of the AT and the RMC overnight options, noted above, are 0.9 mi. or more below the Presidential ridge. Madison Springs Hut, the Valley Way Tentsite, and the RMC facilities are between 7.8 and 10.2 mi. from the end of Hike #12. Osgood Tentsite is 4.8 mi. from the hike's finish. There are no overnight accommodations on the summit of Mt. Washington.

The Forest Service allows no shelters or tent sites in the Great Gulf Wilderness, which fills the giant bowl south of the Northern Presidential ridgeline, making it a distinct counterpoint to the north side of range. Between the Osgood Tentsite and the Mt. Washington auto road, the AT passes through the heart of the wilderness area.

On a clear day the Mt. Washington summit provides the most spectacular panorama on the AT. The Presidentials, however, can be frigid, violent, and deadly. Bring a weatherproof jacket, long pants, heavy sweater, winter hat, gloves, first-aid kit, water, and food whenever you climb above treeline in the Presidentials, regardless of the season. Carry a compass and a map, always be aware of the quickest route to get below treeline, and turn back at the first sign of foul weather. See sidebar in this hike.

The terrain above treeline in the Presidential Range is relentlessly rugged. Be prepared to keep a slower pace here than you would on a forest trail, and allow additional time to reach your destination.

Hike #12 makes a circuit, beginning and ending at Pinkham Notch Visitors Center. This loop can be hiked over two, three or four days, depending on the speed of the party and the amount of time the hikers would like to spend investigating the alpine summits. A stay at Madison Springs Hut, the Valley Way Tentsite, or the RMC overnight stops will split the hike nicely into two full days of walking. However, this option is suitable only for fit hikers with experience in the rugged environment above treeline. For the less ambitious, the trip can be spread over three days with a stay at the Hermit Lake Shelters or Lakes of the Clouds Hut on the first night, and another at Madison, Valley Way, the RMC facilities, or Osgood Tentsite. A four-day trip would include overnights at Hermit Lake or Lakes of the Clouds on the first night; Madison, Valley Way, or the RMC sites on the second night; and the Osgood Tentsite on the third night.

Our hike starts on Tuckerman Ravine Trail, the shortest and most popular route to the summit of Mt. Washington. (Those looking for a different route can take Lion Head Trail, which leaves Tuckerman Ravine Trail near Hermit Lake, or Boott Spur Trail, which starts near the bottom of Tuckerman Ravine Trail.) Step onto the woods road behind the Pinkham Notch Visitor Center, and after 50 yd., pass the junction with the AT/Old Jackson Rd., on which you will return to Pinkham Notch in a day or two (or three). Tuckerman Ravine Trail heads left here, away from the AT. For a description of this link to Mt. Washington, see the itinerary and Hike #11. These 4.1 mi. start out as a moderate climb and then become a steep haul to the summit, with the final stretch on the cone a slow and strenuous climb over felsenmeer rock fields.

Benton MacKaye originally proposed Mt. Washington as the northern terminus of the AT, but given the current amount of development on the summit, few hikers are saddened to see the trail continue on to Katahdin. Black smoke from the cog railway engine and a full parking lot are likely to provide your first impressions of the summit, which is a New Hampshire state park. The original stone Tip-Top house still clings to the rock, but the huge Sherman Adams Summit Building, dedicated in 1980, is where today's tourists head. A restaurant, museum, post office, and gift store are situated inside the building, which is open to the public from mid-May to mid-October. The Mt. Washington (Weather) Observatory occupies the western end of the building.

Aside from his work as a mayor, governor, and aide to President Eisenhower, Sherman Adams, a New Hampshire native, was renowned for his love of the outdoors and his skill as a woodsman. In 1920, while a student at Dartmouth College, Adams hiked the 83 rugged miles from Skyline Cabin, north of Franconia Notch, to Hanover in a single day!

Tourists brought to the summit by the cog railway and the auto road are often too chilly to appreciate the view from the summit as they race in to the building to warm themselves. Indeed, often there isn't much to see —the views are obscured by clouds during all or part of more than 300 days each year.

On a clear day, however, the vista is unsurpassed. The panorama stretches to the Atlantic Ocean, 76 mi. away, which can be seen when the sun reflects off the water: before 9 a.m. during late summer, above Peak D of Wildcat Mt., south-southeast on the horizon, or around 11 a.m. on the horizon left of Conway Lake in the southeast. Just right of due south, Joe English Hill stands as a bump on the horizon 93 mi. away. Your future route across the top of the Northern Presidentials, however, provides the best show, as Brent Scudder describes in *Scudder's White Mountain Viewing Guide:* "Most spectacular is the view to the north. Watch the Presidential peaks march away in the forms of Mounts Clay, Jefferson, Adams and Madison. Peer down into the deep abyss between here and Mount Adams, the so called Great Gulf. On the horizon is Quebec. See Hereford mountain on the left, Megantic in the center and Gosford on the right. Closer to us, the Mahoosuc Mountains start near Madison and draw away towards the northeast... Hayes, Baldcap, Success, Goose Eye and Old Spec.... The Appalachian Trail hiker will soon encounter these."

A fair-weather view of the Northern Presidentials entices many hikers to forgo a trip to the summit building and head right to the spectacular ridgeline to the north, which is above treeline for the next 7.0 mi. In deteriorating weather hikers should prepare to get below treeline fast. A dash back down Tuckerman Ravine Trail to Lion Head Trail is the quickest route below treeline from the summit. Hikers caught by the weather on the AT between the Mt. Washington summit and Mt. Clay can get below treeline quickly on Great Gulf Trail, 0.3 mi. north of the summit buildings, or on Jewell Trail, 1.1 mi. northeast of the summit.

From Mt. Washington, the northbound AT makes a horseshoe-shaped crossing of the range, leading back to Pinkham Notch; the total circuit is 13.4 mi. The mileage count for Hike #12 begins here.

The AT follows the Trinity Heights Connector 0.1 mi. northwest past the apex of the summit, then descends over rugged talus to Gulfside Trail. Rime ice, formed from droplets of water frozen onto rocks and structures, then shaped by the severe wind into fascinating one-sided sculptures, forms in all but the warmest months here. The decorative frosting of the buildings and the path can be as treacherous as it is beautiful, slowing an already difficult walk. The AT turns right on Gulfside Trail, which descends gradually, crosses the tracks of the cog railway, and reaches a junction with Great Gulf Trail at 0.2 mi., the first of more than thirty trail junctions the AT will encounter on its way to Pinkham Notch. The AT/Gulfside Trail turns left here while Great Gulf Trail descends to the right into the gulf, a giant glacial cirque. Spaulding Lake, at the bottom of the huge forested bowl, can be seen 2000 ft. below. During an October hike of the Northern Presidentials we paused here to watch a handful of migrating broad-winged hawks float over the ridge during their journey to the south.

At 0.6 mi. Westside Trail heads left to rejoin the AT on the Crawford Path 0.9 mi. to the south. From the northbound AT there is a view of Marshfield Station to the left, as the trail drops into the Clay-Washington col. The Mt. Clay Loop climbs rightward to the summit of Mt. Clay (5532 ft.) and rejoins the AT after 1.2 mi. Loop trails leading from the AT to six of the Presidential peaks allow hikers to climb quickly to the peaks on clear days—and to avoid the exposed summits in bad weather.

It's hard to take in Mt. Clay's spectacular overlook of the Great Gulf without feeling this peak has been shortchanged. Named for Virginia statesman and senator Henry Clay (a unionist and abolitionist in the 1830s and '40s) rather than a president, the summit is actually not recognized as a mountain because it doesn't rise the required 200 ft. above the ridge that connects it with Mt. Washington.

At 1.1 mi. Jewell Trail descends to the west, reaching Marshfield Station, the base of the cog railway, in 2.9 mi. While this is a scenic early exit option, you will be left with a long road walk to the highway if you haven't left a car in the hiker's parking lot and can't find a ride at the station. The AT descends gradually on rock slabs and boulders, passes a short loop trail to Greenough Spring (often dry), then meets the north end of the Mt. Clay Loop before reaching Sphinx Col at 1.9 mi. where Sphinx Trail, named for a rock profile overlooking the route, descends to the right (east) into the Great Gulf Wilderness. Sphinx Trail, although quite steep, is the best escape route for this part of the AT. (Getting back to Pinkham Notch from the Sphinx

Mt. Washington—Worst Weather in the World?

- Temperatures that can plummet 1 degree per minute for more than 30 minutes.
- An average annual temperature of 26° F.
- Winter temperatures as low as – 40° F.
- Hurricane-force winds (75 mph or faster) on more than 100 days in the average year.
- A world-record 231-mph wind speed recorded April 12, 1934.
- An average annual snowfall of 256 inches, with a record 566 inches in the 1968 – 69 season.
- A U.S. record of 49.3 inches of snow, ice, and hail falling in 24 hours (February 1969).
- Winterlike storms and snowfall twelve months of the year.
- Clouds covering the summit approximately 60% of the time.

Hikers caught on the summit of Mt. Washington will be even more impressed when, in an hour, a beautiful summer day deteriorates into a fierce storm with winds in excess of 100 mph, freezing temperatures, and near-whiteout visibility. Weather forecasts often fail to predict the mountain's deadly storms.

The mountain's climate, in many ways comparable to the conditions found in the Antarctic (although not quite as cold), can be attributed to its location at the intersection of major storm tracks from the south, the west, and the north. Air masses collide at the mountain, creating an air column that is forced over the summit. Temperatures drop 5.5 degrees for every 1000 feet the air mass climbs, and the altitude and lack of sun on the summit chill the air even more. Moisture in the cooling air is condensed as rain and snow, and

Trail requires a long circuitous route through the Great Gulf to Madison Gulf Trail.)

The AT/Gulfside Trail now traverses the east side of Sphinx Dome, and at 2.5 mi., Cornice Trail descends left to Caps Ridge Trail, (a much quicker early exit option than the Spinx Trail) which rides 2.4 mi. down the Ridge of the Caps to Jefferson Notch Rd. From here the AT climbs gradually onto Monticello Lawn, a large meadow on the flank of Mt. Jefferson whose name alludes to Jefferson's Virginia homestead. A rusted push mower once served as "lawn art" here. These fields of grass found high on the flanks of the Presidential Range are actually meadows of Bigelow's sedge, recognized by its haylike leaf bases and purple spikes; it flourishes in the constant exposure to fog and rain. The Jefferson Loop leaves the AT here, climbs to the left onto the summit of Mt. Jefferson (5715 ft.), and rejoins the AT 0.7 mi. farther on. Trails encircle Mt. Jefferson and climb it on all sides, making a map of the moun-

the air column is constricted as it forces its way over the mountain, creating violent, frigid winds.

In November 1870, a team led by J. H. Huntington, for whom Huntington Ravine is named, spent the winter atop Mt. Washington to study its arctic conditions. A weather observatory was then staffed on the summit by the U.S. Signal Corps until 1892. Forty years later, in 1932, the present weather observatory was established on the summit by Joe Dodge, the famed AMC hutmaster, and Bob Monahan, of Dartmouth College. In April 1934 the observatory recorded a wind speed of 231 mph, the greatest wind speed ever recorded on land in the world. A later relocation of the observatory building away from the edge of the summit plateau, where wind speeds are greatest, will probably ensure that the record is never broken, although wind speeds in excess of 120 miles per hour are still recorded regularly.

Today the observatory is staffed year-round to conduct research and to provide a report of the summit conditions each morning. The observatory itself, in the Sherman Adams Summit Building, is open to the public only for educational trips reserved in advance, but a museum in the basement of the building displays artifacts from its history. To learn more about the Mt. Washington Observatory, visit its office on Main Street in North Conway. The Mt. Washington Observatory is a private, nonprofit organization that offers a variety of memberships to the public to support its research. Information about membership, volunteer opportunities, and educational trips is available by writing to the observatory at P.O. Box 2310, North Conway, NH 03860; or by calling 603-356-8345.

tain's summit resemble the bull's-eye on a dart board. The summit makes a great spot from which to compare Mt. Washington and Mt. Adams, the Northeast's tallest peaks.

The AT traverses the east side of the mountain and at 2.9 mi. reaches Six Husbands Trail, which climbs to the left up Mt. Jefferson and descends steeply to the right into the Great Gulf. The trail takes its name from the life of Wetamoo, a polygamous Penacook Indian queen. At 3.3 mi. you will arrive at Edmands Col, where the Edmands Col Cutoff leads 30 yd. right to the Gulfside Spring. A plaque mounted near the trail in the col commemorates J. Rayner Edmands' dedication to blazing trails through the Presidential Range that were easy on both the delicate landscape and its visitors' knees. The Randolph Path heads left from the col, reaching Spaulding Spring in 0.2 mi., then descends 1.1 mi. to The Perch, the first overnight option for AT hikers north of Mt. Washington. The Perch, an open-faced log shelter at 4,300 ft., has space for eight, along with four tent platforms, all of which are located between the Israel Ridge and Randolph Paths on the Perch Path, which continues past Randolph Path to Gray Knob Trail. A fee is charged to stay at The Perch, which is the highest elevation tenting option in The Presidentials. From the col the AT/Gulfside Trail rises like a skywalk on the narrow ridgeline between Jefferson Ravine on the right and Castle Ravine on the left.

Don't worry if the rocky trail keeps you looking at your feet; there is plenty to see on the ground. Alpine flowers such as diapensia and lapland rosebay are often hidden between the rock steps, and chips of mica sparkle in the stones. Large bands of while quartzite near the trail here are often mistaken for snow banks. Mats of dwarfed black spruce and balsam fir spread out like lawns. The pale green tips of the evergreens show how much they have sprouted during the most recent growing season.

Even if you are enjoying the scenery at your feet, don't forget to stop walking regularly so you can take in the big picture. Mt. Adams rises like a great rock cairn before you and, to your left, it's easy to see how the Castle Ravine got its name. At 4.0 mi. the Israel Ridge Path, an early exit option, and foul-weather escape route, descends 0.9 mi. to The Perch and then 4.4 mi. to US 2. The AT passes several springs in the next 0.5 mi., then reaches its northern junction with the Israel Ridge Path, which climbs to the summit of Mt. Adams (5798 ft.), the second highest peak in the Northeast and perhaps the most dramatic in the Presidentials.

The summit of Mt. Adams looks back at Mt. Washington, Mt. Jefferson, and Mt. Clay across the vast wooded bowl of the Great Gulf. Many hikers prefer the perch atop this undeveloped peak to the busy summit of Mt. Washington. To make a loop of Mt. Adams's summit, take the Air Line, which rejoins the AT at the foot of Mt. John Quincy Adams, or Star Lake Trail, which rejoins the AT at Madison Springs Hut. Five summits bearing the name Adams (only Mt. Adams is recognized as a true mountain) and the half dozen trails that meet among them can cause some confusion here. The AT crosses a grassy col covered with Bigelow's sedge between Mt. Adams, on the right, and Mt. Sam Adams (5594 ft.), on the left, then reaches a towering rock cairn that marks Thunderstorm Junction at 4.6 mi. Two routes lead from the junction to RMC cabins: Lowe's Path descends to the left (west) here, passes over Adams 4, another member of the Adams family of peaks, and arrives at Gray Knob Cabin after 1.2 mi., at the Log Cabin at approximately 1.7 mi., and at Lowe's Service Station on US 2 in 4.5 mi. Spur Trail drops to the right off Lowe's Path 0.1 mi. below Thunderstorm Junction and leads 1.1 mi. to Crag Camp Cabin.

Gray Knob Cabin, a fully enclosed and winterized cabin with a gas stove and some cooking utensils, is the highest and most comfortable accommodation (other than the AMC Huts) in the presidential range. It's located at 4,400 ft. at the junction of the Gray Knob and Hincks Trails just east of Lowe's Path. The cabin has space for 14, has a caretaker year-round, and charges a fee. The Log Cabin, about 0.5 mi. north of Gray Knob on Lowe's Path, was first built around 1890. It was rebuilt in 1985, but is still quite rustic. It sits at about 3,300 ft. beside a spring, is partially enclosed with room for 10 guests. There is no stove and no fires are allowed in the area. A fee is charged, but there is no caretaker. Crag Camp is perched on the rim of King Ravine at 4,247 ft. Also recently rebuilt, the cabin here is fully enclosed and has a gas stove, some cooking utensils, and a caretaker in the summer. A fee is charged and visitors must limit the size of their groups to ten. The Gray Knob Trail connects Crag Camp with Gray Knob. To the east of the AT, Lowe's Path climbs directly to the top of Mt. Adams, while Great Gully Trail descends to the north into King Ravine. The AT continues to follow Gulfside Trail as it descends gradually to the northeast and crosses the left flank of yet another mountain named Adams, Mt. John Quincy Adams (5410 ft.).

At 5.2 mi. the Air Line, an early exit option descending from the top of Mt. Adams, joins the AT, which it follows briefly before diverging to the left and descending 3.3 mi. to the Appalachia parking lot on US 2. After crossing Snyder Brook, Gulfside Trail ends at 5.5 mi. at the AMC's Madison Springs Hut, nestled at treeline (4800 ft.) in the windswept saddle between Mt. Madison and Mt. John Quincy Adams. Built in 1888, Madison was the first in AMC's network of mountain huts. The current hut was built in 1940 out of the wreckage of the original, which had burned that year. The hut's two bunkrooms will accommodate fifty guests in quadruple-decker bunks. The hut, with a "croo" of five, is open only from June until mid-September due to the extreme weather of the Northern Presidentials. Snacks, drinks, and hiker supplies are available to day hikers. Reservations are strongly recommended for overnight stays (see "The AMC" in Hike #5).

Some of the most scenic areas of the Northern Presidentials are only a short walk away from this popular hut. Star Lake, a mountain tarn, lies 0.2 mi. due south, and the spectacular Knife Edge of the Durand Ridge crests 0.2 mi. to the northwest. The summit of Mt. Madison rises 0.5 mi. to the east and the cliffs of the Parapet, overlooking Madison Gulf, lie approximately 0.7 mi. from the hut past Star Lake. A variety of alpine flowers grow trailside everywhere near Madison Springs Hut, and as elsewhere above treeline, the rocks are bedecked with lichens in white, black, yellow, orange, and green. These are delicate and very slow growing, so treat them with care. Inquire at the hut for some suggestions on self-guided tours of alpine wildflowers between the hut and Star Lake.

Backpackers who would prefer to camp can descend 0.6 mi. north from the hut on the Valley Way to Valley Way Tentsite, accessed by a spur trail on the west side of the Valley Way, with four tent platforms and a spring (the Valley Way, an early exit option, continues 2.9 mi. to the Appalachia parking lot on US 2).

Northbound AT hikers who begin their day at Madison Hut shouldn't dally at breakfast—there is a feast for their eyes just 0.5 mi. away atop Mt. Madison (5363 ft.), the most northeasterly of the Presidential peaks, which the AT climbs on the steep and rocky Osgood Trail. The view of Mts. Adams and Washington, in the southwest, is spectacular from the summit of Mt. Madison, but it is the view to the northeast, where the mountainside plunges more than 4000 ft. into the Androscoggin River valley, that is unique. Nowhere else in the White Mts. does a valley fall away so dramatically beneath a high peak. Down below are the towns of Gorham and Berlin, and beyond them rises the Mahoosuc Range.

During foul weather the summit of Mt. Madison can be avoided by following Star Lake and Parapet trails around the south side of the mountain and rejoining the AT at Osgood Junction, 1.0 mi. away. The entire Osgood Ridge is avoided by descending the very rugged Madison Gulf Trail from Parapet Trail near Star Lake and rejoining the AT after approximately 2.0 mi. Be warned: the top portion of this trail is one of the most difficult in the White Mts. Descending the Madison Gulf headwall requires hand-over-hand climbing that may be difficult for short or inexperienced hikers. Buttress Trail, which diverges from Star Lake Trail near Madison Hut, connects with Six Husbands Trail and Great Gulf Trail to provide a shortcut to the AT's route through the Great Gulf Wilderness. This route, however, while less difficult than the headwall on Madison Gulf Trail, is more exposed to the weather and has two brook crossings that may prove difficult in wet weather.

From the summit of Mt. Madison, the Watson Path, an early exit option, leads 1.0 mi. north to the Valley Way. The AT continues on Osgood Trail as it descends steeply east on the spine of the Osgood Ridge, passing Howker Ridge Trail approximately 0.2 mi. below the summit, on the left. Below this junction on the east side of Mt. Madison, a small, flat col is filled with Bigelow's sedge, mountain cranberry shrubs, and mats of alpine flowers including New Hampshire's rarest alpine flower, the dwarf cinquefoil. During a snowy autumn hike here, groundpine and fir clubmoss pierced the snow. Club mosses like these look like evergreen branches growing from the ground, but are actually spore-bearing plants similar to ferns.

At 6.5 mi. the AT reaches Osgood Junction, where Parapet Trail enters from the right and Daniel Webster

Surviving Mt. Washington

In a country with nearly 80 peaks over 14,000 ft. high, few people would choose the 6288-foot Mt. Washington as the nation's deadliest. Yet Mt. Washington has claimed more than 120 lives—nearly 40 more than Alaska's Denali, which, at 20,320 ft., is North America's tallest peak.

The obvious difference is accessibility. While long climbs, thin air, glaciers, and remote locations keep the crowds away from most of the country's highest peaks, the short stature, easy road access, and convenience to the country's most populated region allow more than 250,000 people a year to reach the summit of Mt. Washington.

The alpine summits of the Presidential Range are easier to reach than any others in the country, but they are as just as unforgiving as the nation's tallest. In fact, a winter traverse of the Presidentials is considered excellent training for Mt. McKinley-Denali.

It is crucial that every visitor to Mt. Washington give the peak the respect it is due. Hikers should prepare for violent and frigid mountain weather, even on sunny summer days. Bring, as a bare minimum, a raincoat or windbreaker, wool sweater, hat, gloves, compass, map, first-aid kit, and flashlight, along with plenty of water and food. Check the weather report, but remember that few forecasts are intended to include mountain summits. It is often warm and sunny at the trailhead, but brutal above treeline. A weather report that includes the conditions on Mt. Washington is posted at the AMC Pinkham Notch Visitor Center and at Crawford Hostel every day at about 8 a.m. Turn back at the first sign of bad weather, and always be aware of the nearest route that will bring you below treeline. Let someone outside your party know your itinerary, get an early start, and allow plenty of time for any hikes in the Presidentials. Your party should stay together above treeline and keep an eye on one another for signs of hypothermia, a condition where cold wind and/or rain drains heat from the body to the point where it can no longer recover on its own. Uncontrollable shivering, lethargy, confusion, and slurred speach are signs of hypothermia, which can prove fatal if the victim is not sheltered from the elements and warmed immediately.

Above all, don't let Mt. Washington's short stature fool you into becoming an unhappy statistic. This mountain can be a killer.

Trail, and early exit option, descends 3.5 mi. left (east) to Dolly Copp Campground.

The pioneering Copp family carved out a life for themselves at the foot of Mt. Madison in the 1830s. Hayes Copp became known for his stern, quiet demeanor while his wife, Dolly, became famous for her impulsive high spirits. While Hayes worked to make their farm a success, Dolly transplanted wild apple trees to their yard, hived wild bees, and raised her own flax for linen. Their house eventually became a popular inn, and when the famous Glen House opened nearby, she sold her linens and cooking there.

On November 3, 1881, the Copps celebrated their fiftieth wedding anniversary, after which the couple announced their plans to separate. "Fifty years is long enough for a woman to live with any man" was Dolly's famous response to incredulous family and friends.

Hikers can be thankful that Ben Osgood didn't "cop out," as the saying now goes, when he cleared the Osgood Trail to the summit of Mt. Madison a few years after the Copps' separation. Osgood was a famous guide at the Glen House in the late 1800s, and his trail is the oldest route up the mountain.

Between treeline and the summit of Mt. Madison, the AT/Osgood Ridge Trail crosses a strenuous series of rocky humps and false summits that tax and tease hikers climbing this side of the mountain. For those descending from Osgood Junction, the AT/Osgood Trail makes a dramatic, rocky descent into the scrub above treeline. The grade relents as the trail drops below treeline, then plunges steeply through beautiful spruce woods filled with boreal chickadees and white-breasted nuthatches. It reaches Osgood Tent-

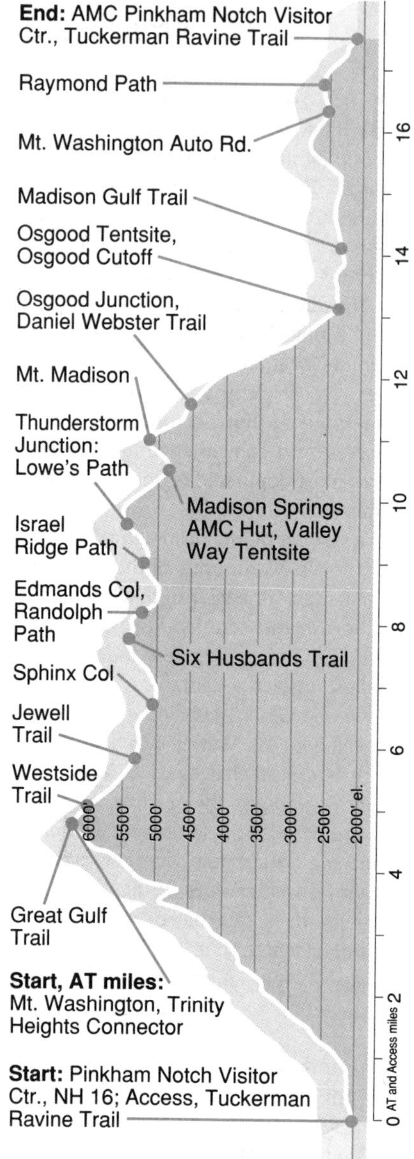

created using Maptech TopoScout ®

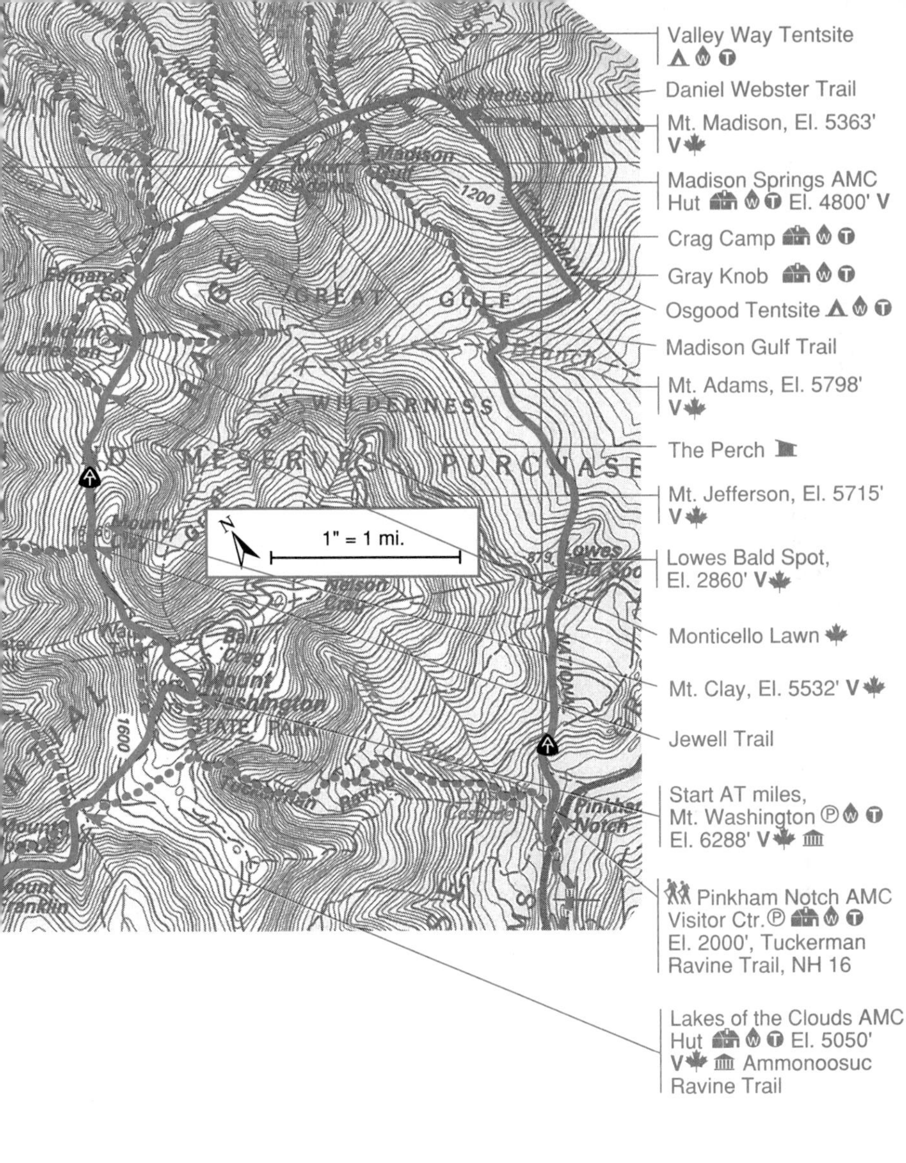
Valley Way Tentsite
Daniel Webster Trail
Mt. Madison, El. 5363' V
Madison Springs AMC Hut El. 4800' V
Crag Camp
Gray Knob
Osgood Tentsite
Madison Gulf Trail
Mt. Adams, El. 5798' V
The Perch
Mt. Jefferson, El. 5715' V
Lowes Bald Spot, El. 2860' V
Monticello Lawn
Mt. Clay, El. 5532' V
Jewell Trail
Start AT miles, Mt. Washington El. 6288' V
Pinkham Notch AMC Visitor Ctr. El. 2000', Tuckerman Ravine Trail, NH 16
Lakes of the Clouds AMC Hut El. 5050' V Ammonoosuc Ravine Trail
1" = 1 mi.
N
GREAT GULF
WILDERNESS
PURCHASE
Mount Washington
STATE PARK
Tuckerman Ravine
Pinkham Notch
Mount Adams
Madison
1200
1600

site, on the left, at 8.2 mi. A boulder marks the spring that provides water for the tent site, which has four tent platforms and a privy. The site's trail register, stashed in the corner of the privy, provides excellent bathroom reading. From here the AT follows the Osgood Cutoff to the right as it descends into the Great Gulf Wilderness (Osgood Trail continues 0.8 mi. to Great Gulf Trail).

Aside from the occasional steep bit, the AT's route through the Great Gulf Wilderness, the only WMNF Wilderness crossed by the AT, is moderately flat, allowing hikers to enjoy the beautiful forest of spruce trees punctuated by the occasional hardwood.

The Osgood Cutoff ends at Great Gulf Trail, which the AT descends to the right, crossing Parapet Brook before ascending a small ridge, where Madison Gulf Trail joins from the right at 9.2 mi. Just after the junction, the AT, Madison Gulf Trail, and Great Gulf Trail drop southward briefly to cross the Peabody River's West Branch on a suspension bridge, then climb back north to another junction. Here the AT follows Madison Gulf Trail on a gradual ascent to the south (Great Gulf Trail climbs west along the river). At 11.2 mi. a spur trail leads left to the fine views from Lowe's Bald Spot (2860 ft.), which stands like a podium beneath the balcony of the Northern Presidential Range. At 11.4 mi. the AT crosses the Mt. Washington auto road, the southern boundary of the Great Gulf Wilderness, and steps onto Old Jackson Road, a trail that continues the southerly course and generally moderate grade. At 11.6 mi. the AT passes junctions on the right, first with Nelson Crag Trail, which climbs to the auto road, then with the Raymond Path, which climbs to Tuckerman Ravine Trail. Between the east-side junctions with George's Gorge Trail, at 12.4 mi., and Crew Cut Trail, at 12.9 mi., the AT/Old Jackson Rd. descends at a moderately steep grade.

At 13.1 mi. the terrain begins to look familiar as the AT passes several ski trails, then the northernmost buildings of Pinkham Notch, and finally reaches Tuckerman Ravine Trail, where this journey's last few steps lead left to the welcoming Visitors Center and NH 16.

HIKE #12 Itinerary

Miles N	Circuit Hike	Elev. (ft/m)	Miles S
Total: 17.5 mi. with access trail			
13.4	**End: Tuckerman Ravine Trail** to **Pinkham Notch Visitor Center,** NH 16, full service, parking, AMC shuttle to Crawford Notch.	2032/619	0.0
13.1	AT passes ski trails, then Visitor Center buildings.		0.3
12.9	Junction with **Crew Cut Trail.**		0.5
12.4	Junction with **George's Gorge Trail.**		1.0
11.6	Pass junction with **Nelson Crag Trail,** then **Raymond Path.**		1.8
11.4	Cross **Mt. Washington Auto Road** and join **Old Jackson Rd.**		2.0
11.2	Spur Trail to **Lowe's Bald Spot,** views.	2860/872	2.2
9.2	**Madison Gulf Trail** joins AT; cross suspension bridge; follow **Madison Gulf Trail** to S.		4.2
9.0	AT joins **Great Gulf Trail.**		4.4
8.2	**Osgood Tentsite,** privy; AT follows **Osgood Cutoff** into Great Gulf Wilderness.		5.2
6.5	**Osgood Junction: Parapet Trail; Daniel Webster Trail** to Dolly Copp Campground.		6.9
6.0	**Mt. Madison,** views; AT follows **Osgood Trail.**	5363/1635	7.4
5.5	**Madison Springs AMC Hut,** supplies; **Valley Way Tentsite** 0.6 mi. N.	4800/1463	7.9
5.2	**Air Line** briefly joins AT.		8.2
4.6	**Thunderstorm Junction: Lowe's Path** leads L (W) to **Gray Knob Cabin** (1.2 mi.); **Spur Trail** descends R off Lowe's Path to **Crag Camp Cabin** (1.2 mi.).	5490/1673	8.8
4.0	**Israel Ridge Path** southern junction, leads to summit of Mt. Adams.		9.4

(continued on next page)

Miles N	Circuit Hike	Elev. (ft/m)	Miles S
3.3	**Edmands Col; Edmands Col Cutoff; Randolph Path** to **The Perch** (1.1 mi.).	4938/1505	10.1
2.9	Junction with **Six Husbands Trail.**	5350/1631	10.5
2.5	**Cornice Trail** descends L (W).		10.9
1.9	**Sphinx Col; Sphinx Trail** descends to E (escape route).	4959/1511	11.5
1.1	**Jewell Trail** descends to W (early exit option).		12.3
0.6	**Westside Trail** heads L (N).		12.8
0.2	Junction with **Great Gulf Trail;** AT/Gulfside Trail turns L.		13.2
0.0	**Start AT miles: Trinity Heights Connector** NW past apex; turn R on **Gulfside Trail.**	6288/1033	13.4
4.1	Summit of **Mt. Washington,** cog railway, auto road, summit building, observatory, restaurant, museum, gift shop, P.O.	6288/1917	0.0
3.8	**Lion Head Trail** joins Tuckerman Ravine Trail.		0.4
3.6	**Tuckerman Junction: Tuckerman Crossover, Lawn Cutoff.**		0.6
3.4	**Alpine Garden Trail.**		0.8
3.3	**Tuckerman Ravine,** headwall.		0.9
2.3	**Hermit Lake Shelters,** fee, lean-tos, tent sites (winter only), caretaker, supplies, water, privy. Junction with **Boott Spur Link** and **Lion Head Trail.**	3870/1180	1.9
2.1	Sharp L turn; **Raymond Path** enters on R.		2.1
1.7	**Huntington Ravine fire road** (unmarked).		2.5
1.3	**Huntington Ravine Trail** enters on R.		2.9
0.4	Junction with **Boott Spur Trail.**		3.8
0.3	Stone steps to overlook of **Crystal Cascade.**		3.9
0.0	Start: **Tuckerman Ravine Trail** from **Pinkham Notch Visitor Center,** NH 16, full service, parking, AMC shuttle.	2032/610	4.2

Circuit Hike

HIKE #13

Wildcat Mt.

Maps: ATC N.H. & Vt. #2
Route: Pinkham Notch to Wildcat Mt., along Wildcat Ridge and Nineteen-Mile Brook to NH 16
Recommended direction: S to N
Distance: 9.2 mi.; 5.7 mi. on AT
Access trail name & length: Nineteen Mile Brook Trail, 3.5 mi.
Elevation +/-: 2032 to 4380 to 2000
Effort: Very strenuous
Day hike: Optional
Overnight backpacking hike: Yes
Duration: 7 to 9 hr.
Early exit option: Wildcat Mt. ski trails and gondola, at 2.7 mi.
Natural history features: Views of the Presidential Range; dramatic geology; glacial tarns
Social history features: Wildcat ski area; visit by Guyot
Other features: Observation tower
Trailhead access: *Start:* AMC Pinkham Notch Visitors Center on NH 16 about 20 mi. N of North Conway, 11 mi. S of Gorham. *End:* NH 16 about 3 mi. N of Pinkham Notch Visitors Center. Parking at Nineteen-Mile Brook trailhead.
Camping: Carter Notch Hut; Pinkham Notch Camp

Hundreds of boots are laced tight every day at the AMC's Pinkham Notch Visitors Center (see "The AMC" in Hike #5). The majority of those toes will point toward Mt. Washington and the Presidential Range. A few, however, will turn away from the most famous summits of the White Mts. and head to the five peaks of Wildcat Mt., which, like any good neighbors to the famous, have plenty of light to shed on the prominent residents across the street.

The ski resort saddled to its flank might appear to have tamed Wildcat Mt. Maps showing a ridgeline that barely breaks treeline might make it appear less rugged than its Presidential neighbors. Don't be fooled. This cat is feisty and the precarious and strenuous climb up Wildcat requires clawing, pawing, and the occasional snarl. The ledges and slabs that climb Peak E are treacherous when wet or icy and can expose hikers to serious falls.

However, at the outset, between Pinkham Notch Visitors Center and Wildcat Ridge Trail, the AT follows the gentle Lost Pond Trail for 0.9 mi., which makes for a fine warm-up to the upcoming difficulties and a lovely 1.8-mi. round-trip day hike on its own.

From the visitors center, head southeast across NH 16 and follow the AT Lost Pond Trail into a marsh

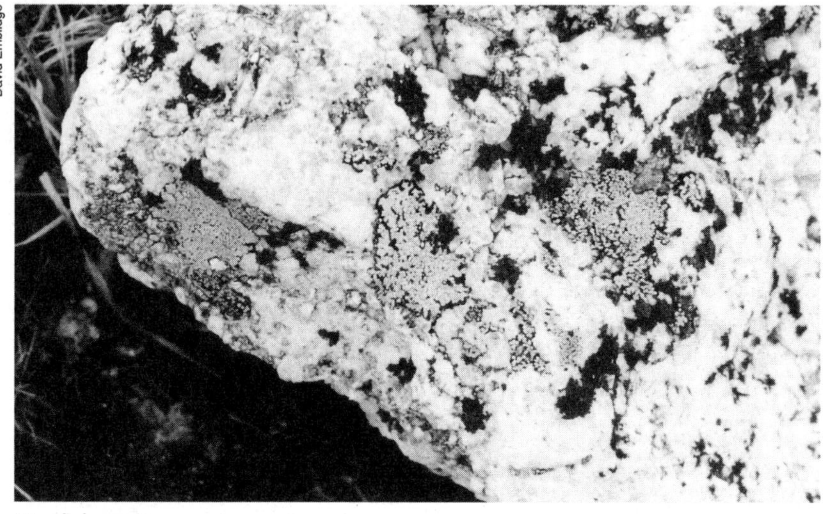

Map lichen

on bog bridges that lead in turn to a large footbridge over the Ellis River. Moose are frequently seen in the vicinity of an old beaver pond near the start of the trail, and the tracks of beaver and otter can often be found on the riverbank. Most of the warblers in the area have blackened names: black-throated blue, black-throated green, black and white, and Blackburnian warblers can all be heard singing in the woods here, along with the "Old Sam Peabody, Peabody, Peabody" call of the white-throated sparrow.

The trail crosses another, smaller footbridge, passes Square Ledge Trail on the left, and heads south along the eastern edge of the Ellis River, which makes its own lazy stroll over the stony riverbed. (The Ellis perks up a bit farther north when it meets the larger Cutler River.) At 0.5 mi. the AT makes a short, rocky climb to Lost Pond, where it follows the eastern shore, lined with northern hardwoods, fir trees, and boulders. At the south end of the pond a flat slab extending into the water provides a beautiful spot to snack and sunbathe.

The trail meanders away from the pond through a labyrinth of granite boulders that fell from the pockets of the retreating glacier. Bright green mosses and lichens cover the boulders and small bogs are scattered about the maze. Watch for bog laurel, a shrub up to 2 ft. tall with evergreen leaves with whitish undersides and showy pink flowers from mid-May through July. Leatherleaf, a shrub with tough, leathery leaves and white bell-shaped flowers from May through June, can also be found in the area.

At 0.9 mi. Lost Pond Trail arrives at the Wildcat Ridge Trail, which the AT follows to the left. To the right, Wildcat Ridge Trail leads away from the AT to a difficult crossing of the Ellis River, and after 0.1 mi. meets a paved path leading to Glen Ellis Falls, one of the most scenic and easily reached waterfalls in the Whites. Most hikers, however, will choose to approach the falls from the Glen Ellis Falls parking area on NH 16 rather than take on the hazardous river crossing.

From the Lost Pond Trail, the AT/ Wildcat Ridge Trail climbs 2000 ft. onto Peak E, then works its way backward through the alphabet. The trail introduces itself with steep steps onto a jumble of large wet rocks that climb the southern end of the ridge. Wildcat Mt. has a fierce reputation, but the bumps crossed during the climb to Peak E, the "Wild Kittens," have most of the bite. Follow the first dozen blazes carefully—in the next 0.2 mi. the path is easily lost as it makes a box-shaped pair of left turns that swing it nearly 180 degrees back to the northeast and onto Wildcat's stony spine.

Wooden stairs, then switchbacks, lead to the top of a huge block, nearly 40 ft. tall, overhanging the woods. Large gouges cut in the block match up with stone steps that appear in a steep V-groove that the trail climbs above it. Continuing up rocky switchbacks, the AT arrives at a rounded ledge, the first of many overlooks of Pinkham Notch. The trail becomes dramatically steep here as it climbs through triangular gullies past boulders, cliffs, and blowdowns. Short flat sections provide a chance to catch your breath between the steep bits. At 1.8 mi. a ledge looks south down the notch and onto cliffs carved into the side of the mountain.

The famed swiss geologist Arnold Guyot (see Hike #9) named Wildcat Mt., probably because he or a friend saw one of the predatory cats while hiking here. Bobcats still prowl the region, but it is rare to see one, as they are nocturnal and secretive. Bobcats grow to 30 in. long and have a short tail, 1-in. ear tufts, and brown fur with spots. Rabbits, which they hunt by creeping low through cover until they are close enough to pounce, provide the lion's share of their diet. Debris—fur, bones and scat—from one of their meals can occasionally be found near the trails in the area.

At 2.1 mi. pass a crevicelike cave that at one time was probably a wildcat's lair and will provide comfortable shelter to a hiker brave enough to venture inside. Slightly higher, the AT climbs to a long boulder that forms a wall along the left side of the trail, then turns right, directly away from the boulder. A side trail continues forward along the wall to a spring.

Amid the boulders and crags that surround the trail like a sculpture garden, another cave beneath a block on the left would provide protection from a storm. The trail continues to climb over steep slabs and occasional stair steps past magnificent views of Mt. Washington and Pinkham Notch Camp, the best from a ledge at 2.4 mi.

During the final ascent to the summit of Peak E, the trail receives the full force of the weather, making the insecure footing on the steep slabs even more treacherous. After rolling over a series of rocky bumps, the trail reaches a lower summit, then the top of Peak E (4,041 ft.), at 2.7 mi., finally descending to the summit station of Wildcat Mt. ski area in the small col between Peaks E and D. The gondola, which operates in the summer from 10 a.m. to 4 p.m., except in high winds, and a number of ski trails descend northwest from the ski area summit to NH16 in Pinkham Notch. The northern ski trails are the easiest to hike down as an early exit option and will bring hikers to the ski area's base lodge in 2.6 mi. A one-way ride on the gondola costs $3.50; a round-trip is $7.00.

The col here overlooks the ranges to the south, and a sign along the AT helps hikers identify S. Baldface Mt. in the east, Mt. Chocorua in the south, and a number of peaks in between. An observation tower with a 25¢ telescope provides a closer look at the southern ranges and at Mt. Washington to the west.

From the col the trail makes a short, rocky climb to the summit of Peak D (4000 ft.), which has the White Mts.' best view of the southeast face of Mt. Washington. Another observation

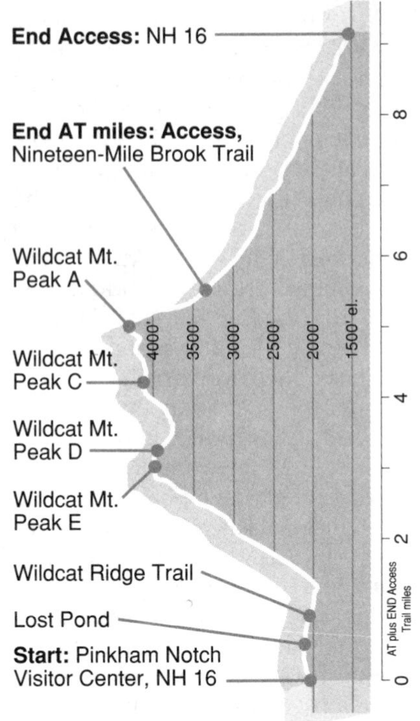

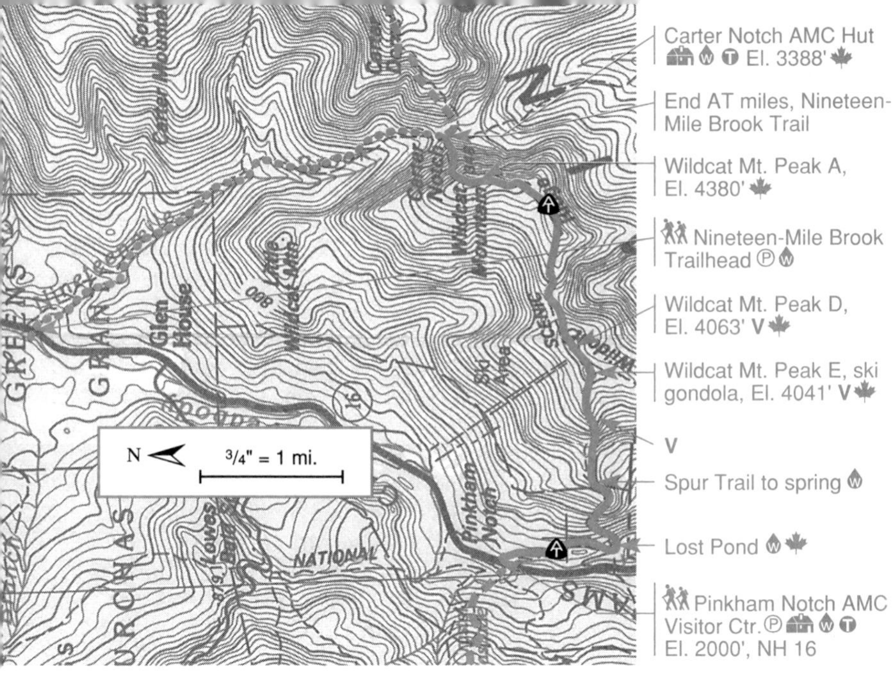

platform lifts spectators out of the trees to check out Tuckerman Ravine, below and left of the 6288-ft. summit of Washington; Huntington Ravine, below and right of the summit; the Gulf of Slides and Glen Boulder, on the far left; and the Mt. Washington Auto Road, on the right. A keen eye can even find the Boott Spur and Lion Head trails winding up New England's most massive mountain.

From Wildcat Peak D the AT drops steeply into Wildcat Col, the ridgeline's deepest decline. Winds gusting through the fir trees here can sound like breaking surf. You may relish the savage feel of the surrounding woods after your brief stop on the commercially developed summit. Pointed rocks and slippery bog bridges in the col, and in the sag that follows it, make the walking here difficult and slow. After passing through a small boulder field, the trail climbs in steep spurts over slick rock and polished tree roots to the summit of Wildcat Peak C (4270 ft.), with an outlook to the east, at 4.2 mi. It then drops into another col before climbing to Peak B (also 4270 ft.), where, apart from a slight dip into a smaller col, the trail makes a lovely cruise through the rich spruce-fir forest that is a welcome relief to battle-weary legs. Sphagnum moss carpets the ground beside the trail, lichens clothe the trees, and balsam firs sweeten the air. The songs of Bicknell's thrushes and boreal chickadees often provide accompaniment for the walk here, and a waddling spruce grouse or curious gray jay occasionally accompanies the walker.

At 5.0 mi. the trail completes a gradual climb to Peak A (4380 ft.). On this, the tallest summit on Wildcat Mt., you are just reaching treeline (the point where trees are no more than 8 ft. tall), but Wildcat Mt. never actually breaks treeline, and although the trees become smaller, they never vanish from the summit altogether. Don't let Wildcat Mt.'s lack of an alpine zone cause you to hurry down from Peak A. Instead, follow a spur trail near the summit 20 yd. east to a breathtaking overlook of the wilds of Carter Notch. The Carter Lakes, directly below the summit of Wildcat Peak A, are enclosed between the notch itself and the Rampart, a rocky wall to the south. A glacier gouged the notch between Wildcat Mt. and the Carter Range. When it retreated, blocks of rock fell into the notch below as they were quarried from the notch walls by freezing water, filling this rugged landscape with boulders and caves.

From Peak A the trail makes a long, steep descent of 0.7 mi. to its junction with Nineteen-Mile Brook Trail, which it reaches after passing through tangle of blowdowns.

From this junction, those with an extra hour or so might consider a quick side trip to explore the wilderness of Carter Notch: Follow Nineteen-Mile Brook Trail to the right (south), reaching Carter Moriah Trail in 0.2 mi. and following that trail for 0.3 mi. to Carter Notch Hut (see Hike #14).

Our hike turns left (north) onto Nineteen-Mile Brook Trail, makes a brief, steep descent, then turns into a romp through the woods along the eastern bank of the brook. Watch for mountain aster, with hairy stems and purplish flowers in leafy bracts; the buttercup-like yellow flowers of mountain avens; and the nodding, bell-shaped flowers of bluebell while you are looking for a spot to soak the wounds left by Wildcat. At 3.5 mi. you'll arrive at the Nineteen-Mile Brook trailhead parking area on NH 16.

HIKE #13 Itinerary

Miles N	NORTH	Elev. (ft/m)	Miles S
Total: 9.2 mi. with access trail			
3.5	Access: **Nineteen-Mile Brook Trail,** brief steep descent, then *wooded streamside walk* to NH 16, parking (3 mi. N of Pinkham Notch AMC Visitor Center).	2000/610	3.5
5.7	**End AT miles:** Junction of **Nineteen-Mile Brook Trail** and AT. Follow Nineteen-Mile Brook Trail L (NW).	1500/457	0.0
5.0	**Wildcat Mt. Peak A,** spur trail to overlook of Carter Notch; long steep descent.	4380/1335	0.7
4.2	**Wildcat Mt. Peak C,** then col, Peak B, and gradual climb.	4270/1301	1.5
3.0	**Wildcat Mt. Peak D,** observation platform, then steep descent.	4000/1219	2.7
2.7	**Wildcat Mt. Peak E,** observation tower, ski trails, gondola, early exit option.	4041/1232	3.0
2.4	Pinkham Notch overlook.		3.3
2.1	Spur trail to spring.		3.6
1.8	Ledge, overlook.		3.9
0.9	Turn L onto **Wildcat Ridge Trail,** begin steep climb.		4.8
0.5	**Lost Pond.**		5.2
0.0	**Start: AMC Pinkham Notch Visitor Center,** NH 16, parking.	2032/619	5.7

SOUTH

HIKE#14

Carter Moriah Range

Maps: ATC N.H. & Vt. #2

Route: From US 2 along Rattle River over Mt. Moriah, through Zeta Pass, to Carter Notch, then along Nineteen-Mile Brook to Pinkham Notch

Recommended direction: N to S

Distance: 18.7 mi.; 15.2 mi. on AT

Access trail name & length: Nineteen-Mile Brook Trail, 3.5 mi.

Elevation +/-: 800 to 4832 to 1500 ft.

Effort: Very strenuous

Day hike: Optional

Overnight backpacking hike: Yes

Duration: 15 to 19 hr.

Early exit options: Carter-Moriah Trail, at 5.7 mi.; Stony Brook Trail, at 7.1 mi.; North Carter Trail/Imp Trail, at 9.7 mi.; Carter Dome Trail/Nineteen-Mile Brook Trail, at 12.4 mi.

Natural history features: Androscoggin Valley; Moriah Range; Carter Range; Carter Notch, The Imp; views of Presidential Range

Social history features: Oldest AMC Hut

Trailhead access: *Start:* The AT intersects US 2 at 3.6 mi. E of Gorham, NH, and 19 mi. W of Bethel ME. Parking lot at trailhead. *End:* NH 16 approximately 3 mi. N of Pinkham Notch Visitors Center and 8 mi. S of Gorham. Parking lot at trailhead.

Camping: Rattle River Shelter; Imp Campsite; AMC Carter Notch Hut

For most White Mt. hikers, the Carter Moriah Range is just a small part of the panorama from the top of Mt. Washington. The half dozen alpine peaks crossed by the AT between Carter Notch and the Androscoggin Valley are overshadowed, literally and figuratively, by the Northern Presidential cirque, which rises nearly 1,500 feet higher on the west side of Pinkham Notch.

But AT connoisseurs know that this path offers something difficult to find on the trail in this area—the chance to be alone in the woods. While the AT through the Presidentials often seems to be a freeway of feet, backpackers in the Carter Moriah Range occasionally hike for entire days without having to step aside for an oncoming walker.

And what a landscape these lucky few woodspeople have to themselves! Between the rugged spectacle of Carter Notch and the bucolic Androscoggin valley, the trail crosses four mountains bearing the name Carter and two bearing that of Moriah. Each of these provides spectacular vistas, particularly of the Presidentials, but perhaps the most spectacular peak belongs to neither of these clans. The wildly steep and rocky climb up Mt. Hight is rewarded with an incredible panorama, where a glance across Pinkham Notch at the Mt. Washington Auto Road can't help but bring appreciation for this peak's seclusion.

The AMC's Carter Notch Hut, at the southern end of the hike, provides bunkhouses and a self-serve kitchen, but otherwise there are no comfortable accommodations to lure crowds into these woods. Instead, the Imp Campsite provides overnighters with a cozy lean-to and the best bench in the Whites for viewing the north country.

Day hikers can follow the AT/Rattle River Trail for 5.9 mi. to the northbound Carter Moriah Trail, which makes a short, rocky climb over the 4049-ft. summit of Mt. Moriah, then leads 4.5 mi. north to US 2 in Gorham. For this 10.5-mi. day hike, you will need to leave a second car in Gorham or plan on finishing the day with a 3.6-mi. road walk from Gorham back to the trailhead.

Near the beginning of Hike #14, the White Mt. National Forest's Rattle River Shelter provides a headstart for hikers who get to the trailhead the evening before they plan to start their adventure. With an hour or so of daylight, hikers can comfortably cruise the first 1.7 mi. from the AT/Rattle River Trailhead parking area on US 2 to the shelter on the AT/Rattle River Trail. From the parking area, the trail follows a logging road south along the left (east) bank of the Rattle River. As the trail climbs gradually out of the valley, the river accompanies hikers' footsteps with its own relaxing beat, making it easy to see how it got its name. Walkers, however, should not be rattled, even in approaching darkness, because the path here is wide, the footing easy, and the route easy to follow.

Hardwoods dominate the forest at this elevation. American beech, sugar maple, yellow birch, and hemlock are the most common here, but paper birch, aspen, red oak, and black cherry are also easy to find. The aptly named interrupted fern, with black pinnae resembling dying leaves in the middle of its long fronds; and the poisonous Indian poke, with large pleated leaves that resemble skunk cabbage and clusters of yellow-green flowers, can be found amid the rich understory. Wildflowers like red trillium, Canada lily, clintonia, and dogtooth violet are also found along the trail by the river, which has several good swimming holes as well.

A snowmobile trail joins from the right at 0.3 mi. and accompanies the AT across a tributary of the river at 0.6 mi, then splits off to the left. At 1.7 mi. the trail reaches Rattle River Shelter on the left, in an area of open woods. No fee is required to use the shelter and that, along with its proximity to the road, make it an unfortunately popular site for parties. On quiet nights, however, the rhythm of the river encourages a great night's sleep. The shelter holds eight, and there is abundant space for tents nearby.

If you arrive at the shelter without enough daylight to explore the area, don't fret about taking the time to get to know the river in the morning. While the miles between the Rattle River Shelter and Imp Campsite, the next recommended overnight stop, are more difficult than the first 1.7, there are only 6.1 of them, so you can take the time to enjoy them.

From the shelter the AT/Rattle River Trail continues along the west bank, then skips across rocks to the other side of the Rattle River (this may be hazardous in high water) and makes a short steep climb up the east bank. The trail makes sweeping S-curves through small gorges back down to the river, which pools to provide a beautiful spot for a swim on hot days. A few dozen steps farther along, the trail hops back across a fast branch of the river that, barely a foot wide, is cutting its own, as yet miniature, gorge in the schist bedrock. From the crossing the trail climbs the triangle of land formed by the merging waterways, crosses bog bridges, then rides the right side of a ridge. As the brook rises to the level of the trail, the path becomes rocky, then climbs again to an area of blowdowns. Make sure to fill your water bottles before the AT leaves the Rattle River altogether.

At 3.2 mi. the trail again crosses the river and begins a steady climb through birch, beech, and maple trees, with occasional overlooks of the river. At 3.7 mi. a small cascade falls from boulders and the trail soon turns away from the Rattle River, climbing steeply onto the sag between Shelburne Moriah Mountain, to the east, and Middle Moriah Mountain, to the west.

As the trail levels out in the sag, which is about 2500 ft. above the valley where the hike began, it crosses dozens of bog bridges, beside which the tracks of moose can often be seen puncturing the lush green carpet of sphagnum moss. The cloven hoofprints, 5 to 7 in. long, will fill with water like an hourglass, giving a good gauge of the proximity of their maker. If the prints are less than a quarter full, keep your eyes peeled as you continue. Watch the trunks of trees in the area, especially the maple and aspen that moose snack on year-round, for tooth marks or areas where the bark has been stripped away. Clearings left by timber harvests are good places to see moose—they eat the abundant small trees and shrubs. In summer the animals prefer to dine in swamps and bogs, where they can find succulent sodium-rich aquatic vegetation. Moose may look mellow, but they are wild and unpredictable, especially in the September – October rutting season. The largest member of the deer family, they are often more than 6 ft. tall at the shoulder and can weigh 1200 lb. A blow from the broad antlers of the male can be fatal. If you are lucky enough to see a moose, be extremely careful. Keep your distance, and avoid making sudden movements or loud noises.

At 4.3 mi. Rattle River Trail ends at its junction with Kenduskeag Trail, which the AT follows to the right up

Henry Lafleur

Carter Notch AMC Hut

Middle Moriah Mt. and, in 1.4 mi., to Carter-Moriah Trail. (Mt. Moriah and its lesser peaks are believed to be named after a hill in Jerusalem.)

The AT makes its first steps on Kenduskeag Trail, at 3300 ft., over large stone steps and soon passes just right of a huge boulder with a 50-ft. vertical face hanging over the trail. The trail then levels out and, in 0.4 mi., passes 0.1 mi. south of the summit of Middle Moriah Mt. Here the trail turns left and drops down into a series of bogs. Then, 0.3 mi. farther on, the trail climbs onto a rocky ridge between Middle Moriah Mt. and Mt. Moriah, where slabs provide the first of many breathtaking outlooks onto the ranges to the north and the west.

At 5.7 mi. the AT/Kenduskeag Trail arrives at the junction with Carter-Moriah Trail; follow either of the two paths that climb a steep jumble of boulders to the panoramic summit block of Mt. Moriah (4049 ft.), 0.1 mi. to the north. The peak provides excellent views of the Presidential Range to the west and the Mahoosuc Range to the northeast. (Day hikers should climb to the summit of Mt. Moriah, then continue on Carter-Moriah Trail another 4.4 mi. north to Gorham. Hikers continuing on the AT will want to check out the views atop Mt. Moriah, then return to this junction.) The AT now follows the Carter-Moriah Trail south, then west, to Imp Campsite in 1.9 mi.

From the junction, the AT/Carter-Moriah trail follows a ridgeline through the woods, then follows cairns across a rocky knob before descending to the south cliffs of Mt. Moriah, which offer an excellent outlook onto the ranges to the north and west. The gradual descent into the scrub allows hikers to turn their gaze from their feet to the Northern Presidentials, which hang above the trail like a city skyline. Dikes of white quartz stripe the slabs and cliffs in the woods below the trail like lines painted on a highway.

During a fall excursion on this hike, ice filled sags in the trail on the north side of Mt. Moriah, but on the south side, the sun warmed the path enough to lure a garter snake out for a sunbath.

At 7.1 mi. the AT/Carter-Moriah Trail reaches junctions, first with the Moriah Brook Trail, which leads left (SE) 5.5 mi. to Wild River; then with Stony Brook Trail, which leads right 3.5 mi. to Gorham. Stony Brook Trail allows for a 10.6-mi. day hike from the Rattle River trailhead parking area.

From this junction, the AT climbs over a knob, then descends to a clifftop overlooking a stand of paper birch. Here the trail turns right and continues to descend to a sag at 7.8 mi., where a spur trail leads 0.2 mi. right to Imp Campsite, at about 3200 ft. This AMC campsite has a comfortable shelter with space for ten, platforms for five tents, and water from a brook near the shelter. A fee is charged for overnights during the late spring and summer, when a caretaker manages the site. While you cannot see the Imp (the spooky 600-ft.-tall rock profile in the side of North Carter Mt. is best viewed from Dolly Copp Campground off NH 16), Imp Campsite's oversized log bench, at an overlook onto the Androscoggin valley and the ranges to the north, provides a spectacular seat for dining, stargazing, or lounging during an overnight. Imp Mt., 3708 ft., is 0.3 mi. west of the campsite.

Between Imp Campsite and Carter Notch lie this hike's most difficult miles—7.2 of them. The incredible vistas of Mt. Hight and the wild labyrinth of Carter Notch make these miles the hike's most rewarding as well, so it's good to get an early start, particularly if you plan to hike the Nineteen-Mile Brook Trail out to NH 16, which will give the day a hefty 10.7 mi. of rigorous walking. Those who prefer a shorter day should make arrangements to stay at the AMC's Carter Notch Hut for a second (or third) overnight.

From the Imp Campsite spur trail, the AT/Carter-Moriah Trail climbs moderately, crossing a long series of bridges over bogs and a brook, which provides a last chance for hikers who forgot to top off their water bottles at the campsite. The next reliable water source is 4.6 mi. away, so make sure to fill up before heading on.

The trail crosses a plateau, drops into a sag, and then, at 9.1 mi., presents an arduous hand-over-hand climb up the rocky side of North Carter Mt. Turn around as you gasp for breath between the steep pitches to behold your companions from the day before, the Moriah Mts. At 9.5 mi. reach the top of North Carter, which at 4530 ft., is still wooded. Poke around a little in the clearing at the summit and you will find fine views of the Northern Presidentials and the ranges to the east. The trail continues on past several outlooks to the south.

At 9.7 mi. North Carter Trail descends right 1.2 mi. to its intersection with Imp Trail. Both north and south legs of Imp Trail lead to NH 16 in about 2.5 mi., but the northern route leads to a spectacular overlook from atop the cliffs that form the Imp.

Following bog bridges through gnarled red spruce trees, then passing over several bumps and knobs, the AT/Carter-Moriah Trail crosses the slabs of Mt. Lethe, where more fine vistas are available a few steps to the left of the trail, just before ascending to the summit of Middle Carter Mt. (approx. 4600 ft.) at 10.3 mi.

From the summit of Middle Carter Mt., where other outlooks can be found, the trail follows a rocky spine through the spruce-fir forest, descends to a col, and then, at 11.6 mi., climbs to the top of South Carter Mt. (4458 ft.). The trail descends from the summit, with occasional steep drops, into Zeta Pass (3990 ft.) which it reaches at 12.4 mi. Here the westbound Carter Dome Trail, on the right, provides an excellent 1.9-mi.-long shortcut to Nineteen-Mile Brook Trail, which in turn leads in another 1.9 mi. to NH 16. This route will cut 2.7 mi. off the length of the hike, ending at the same point as the complete route. Water can often be found on a side path that intersects Carter Dome Trail just below the junction.

The southbound Carter Dome Trail shares the path with the AT/Carter-Moriah Trail as they begin the ascent of Mt. Hight during the next 0.2 mi. The AT/Carter-Moriah Trail then turns left to claw its way up Mt. Hight while Carter Dome Trail heads southwest, bypassing Mt. Hight and rejoining the AT/Carter-Moriah Trail on Carter Dome. This alternative shaves off a difficult 0.5 mi.. Both shortcuts provide a foul-weather bypass of the hike's most difficult climb, but skip what most visitors consider the Carter Range's most spectacular summit.

The 600-ft. climb to the exposed summit of Mt. Hight (4675 ft.) is rocky, steep, and relentless. Be especially careful at the top of the climb, where precariously placed boulders provide a final challenge. The clear summit offers a fine reward. Mt. Washington, the Northern Presidentials, and Madison Gulf spread out majestically in the west. Carter Dome rises in the southwest, and the washboard landscape of Maine rolls away to the northeast.

At the summit of Mt. Hight, 13 mi., the trail makes an extremely sharp right turn, which is easy to miss, particularly in poor visibility. The *AMC White Mountain Guide* provides the compass bearings of southbound 2401 magnetic and northbound 2901 magnetic for the AT from the summit cairn.

At 13.4 mi. Carter Dome Trail rejoins the AT/Carter-Moriah Trail from the right, and 100 ft. farther, Black Angel Trail descends, left, 4.6 mi. to Wild

River Trail. From the junction the AT/Carter-Moriah Trail climbs, first gradually, then more steeply, past treeline to the summit of Carter Dome (4832 ft.), at 13.8 mi. A cairn and the remains of a fire tower mark the summit, which has more excellent vistas.

Some of the alpine shrubs found here can provide nourishment to the patient. Low sweet blueberry has narrow leaves with fine teeth, and mountain cranberry has red berries and thick, waxy leaves. The urn-shaped fruits borne on both shrubs in August are edible, but the blueberries are far tastier. Labrador tea, another perennial shrub found here, has clusters of white flowers in June and thick evergreen leaves with woolly undersides that can be steeped into a weak tea reputed to treat asthma, colds, stomach aches, rheumatism, and dysentery and used as a topical treatment for burns, stings, poison ivy rash, and leprosy lesions. The krummholz is a great place to find bunchberry, which has whorls of six leaves, four white petal-like bracts, and bunches of red berries in late summer. Native Americans made medicinal teas from the leaves and roots of the plant. The berries are not toxic but taste as if they were.

A short distance west of the summit of Carter Dome, Rainbow Trail leads left (south) 2.5 mi. to Wild River Trail. The AT continues down to a cairn where it turns left and then begins its descent into Carter Notch. At 14.2 mi. a side path leads right to a

Continued on p. 162

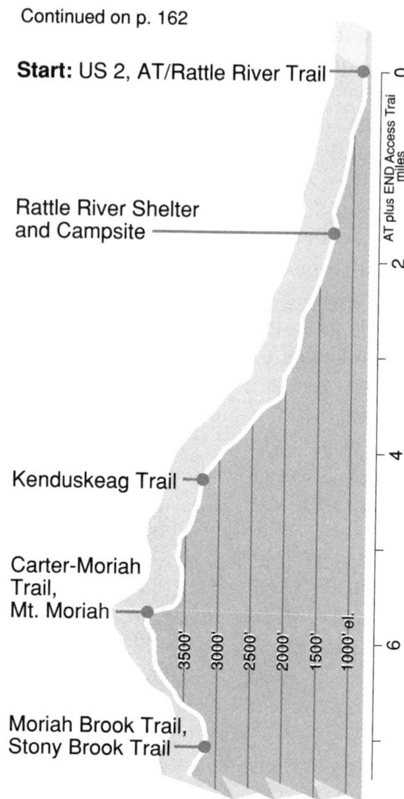

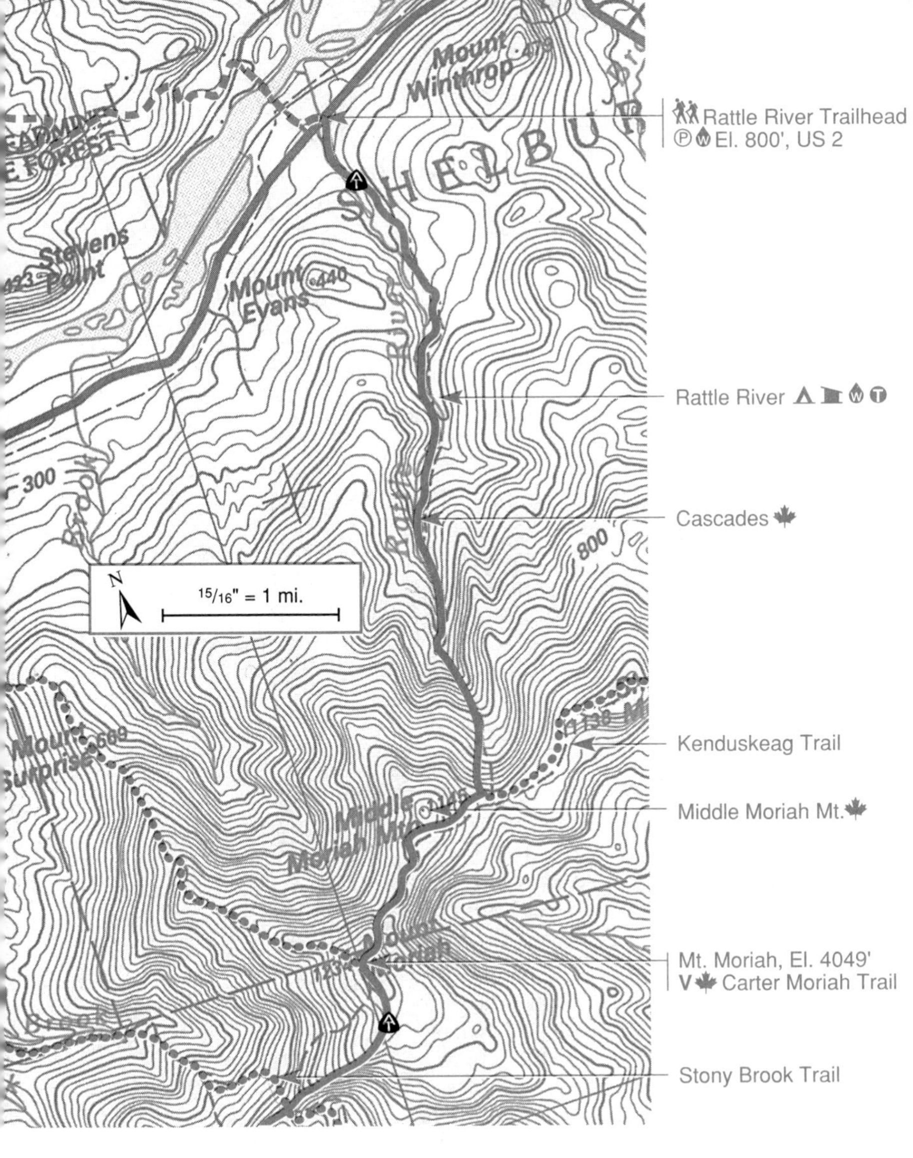

Mount Winthrop
Stevens Point
Mount Evans
Mount Surprise
Middle Moriah Mt.
Mount Moriah
15/16" = 1 mi.
N
Rattle River Trailhead
El. 800', US 2
Rattle River
Cascades
Kenduskeag Trail
Middle Moriah Mt.
Mt. Moriah, El. 4049'
V Carter Moriah Trail
Stony Brook Trail

spring, and what began as a gradual descent becomes a knee-busting 0.8 mi. dive into the wilds of the notch (3388 ft.), with its gothic hanging cliffs, twin tarns, and maze of boulders.

An overnight at Carter Notch Hut, 0.1 mi. west of the AT on Nineteen-Mile Brook Trail (at 15.0 mi.), will allow hikers time to explore this remote and beautiful geologic wonderland. The stone hut, erected in 1914, is the oldest AMC hut still in use and has absorbed much of the character of the backcountry adventurers who prefer it to the posher accommodations of the other huts. The hut has a self-serve kitchen, so bring your own food. Two bunkhouses can sleep a total of forty guests. The hut is open year-round to accommodate winter climbers, skiers, and snowshoers, but from September through May there is only a caretaker on duty. Reservations are strongly recommended. No camping is allowed in Carter Notch.

As you follow Nineteen-Mile Brook Trail 0.1 mi. to the hut, you will pass a pond on your right, which drains into the smaller pond you will pass on your left. A landslide probably dammed the notch to create the ponds. Nearby boulders provide seats and platforms from which to take in the lovely pools. Slides of talus stripe the steep flanks of Carter Dome on the east side of the notch. Cliffs hang above the west side.

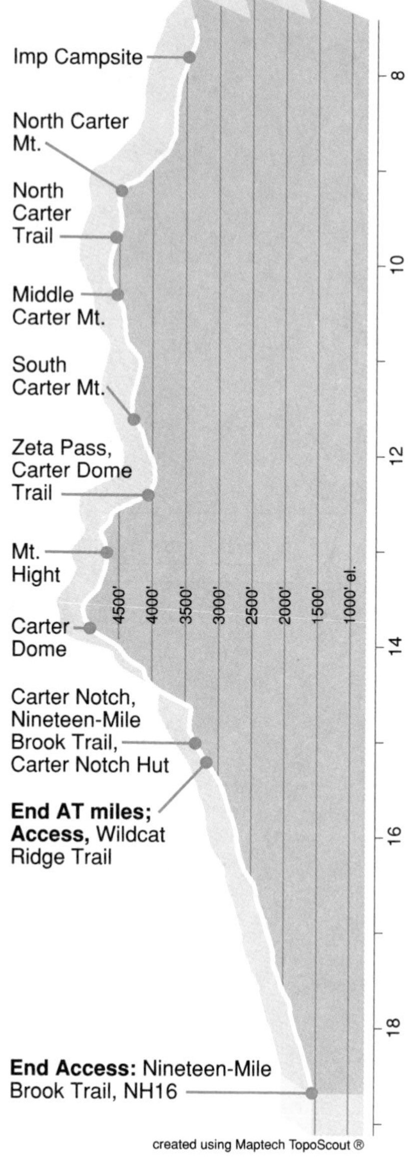

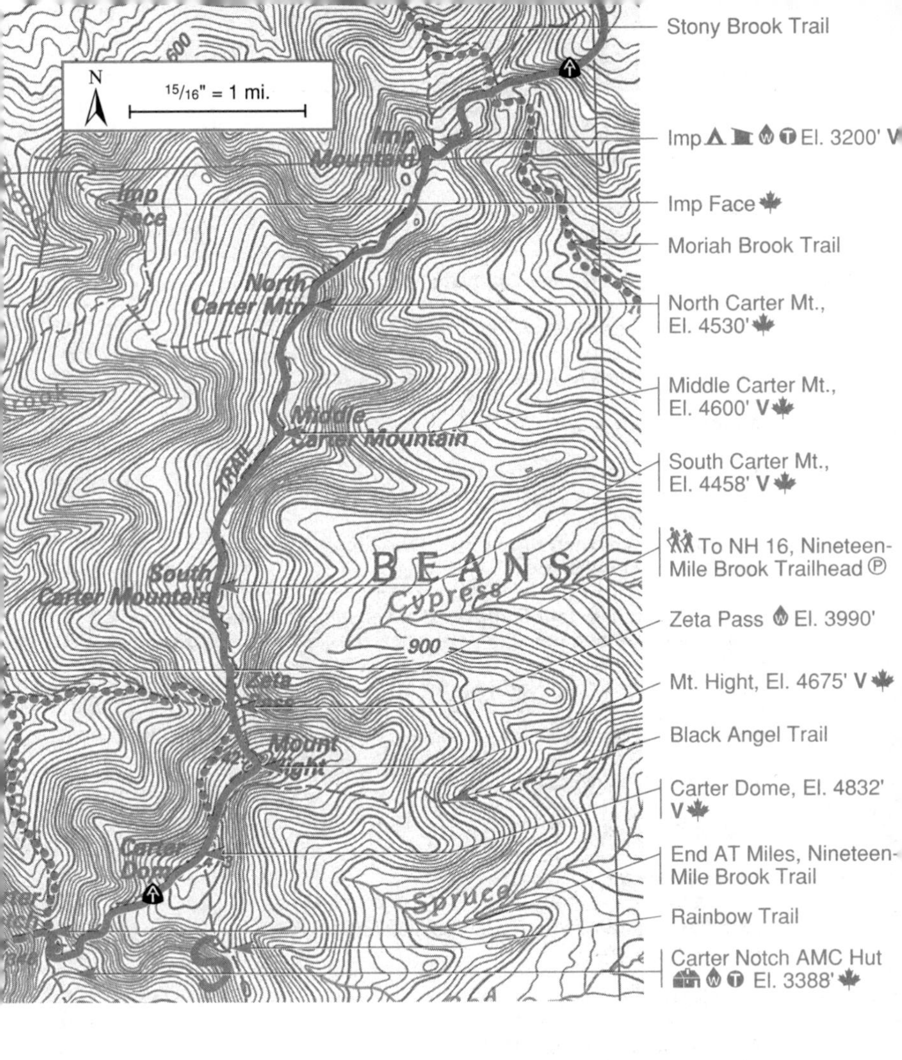
15/16" = 1 mi.
N
Stony Brook Trail
Imp El. 3200' V
Imp Face
Moriah Brook Trail
North Carter Mt.,
El. 4530'
Middle Carter Mt.,
El. 4600' V
South Carter Mt.,
El. 4458' V
To NH 16, Nineteen-Mile Brook Trailhead
Zeta Pass El. 3990'
Mt. Hight, El. 4675' V
Black Angel Trail
Carter Dome, El. 4832' V
End AT Miles, Nineteen-Mile Brook Trail
Rainbow Trail
Carter Notch AMC Hut
El. 3388'
Imp Mountain
Imp Face
North Carter Mtn
Middle Carter Mountain
South Carter Mountain
Zeta Pass
Mount Hight
Carter Dome
TRAIL
BEANS
Cypress
Spruce
900

HIKE #14 Itinerary

Miles N	NORTH	Elev. (ft/m)	Miles S
Total: 18.7 mi. with access trail			
15.2	**Start:** Rattle River trailhead parking area, US 2. Follow AT/Rattle River Trail S.	800/244	0.0
13.5	**Rattle River Shelter** and **Campsite,** water, privy.		1.7
11.5	**Cascade;** trail turns away from river.		3.7
10.9	**Junction:** AT turns R (N) onto **Kenduskeag Trail.**	3300/1006	4.3
10.3	**Middle Moriah Mt.**		4.9
9.6	Junction with **Carter-Moriah Trail;** path 0.1 mi. to summit of **Mt. Moriah,** views. Follow **Carter-Moriah Trail** S.	4049/1234	5.7
8.1	Junctions with **Moriah Brook Trail,** then **Stony Brook Trail** (early exit option).		7.1
7.4	Spur trail 0.1 mi. to **Imp Campsite,** shelter, tent platforms, water, caretaker and fee during peak season; view.	3200/975	7.8
6.1	Steep climb up side of **North Carter Mt.**		9.1
5.7	Summit of **North Carter Mt.** (wooded); views.	4530/1381	9.5
5.5	Junction with **North Carter Trail.**		9.7
4.9	**Middle Carter Mt.**	4600/1402	10.3
3.6	**South Carter Mt.**	4458/1359	11.6
2.8	**Zeta Pass. Carter Dome Trail,** water; trail heads W (early exit option).	3990/1216	12.4
2.2	**Mt. Hight,** views. Very sharp R turn at summit.	4675/1425	13.0
1.8	**Carter DomeTrail** rejoins AT/Carter-Moriah Trail. **Black Angel Trail** heads L. Follow AT/Carter-Moriah Trail.		13.4

(continued on next page)

Miles N		Elev. (ft/m)	Miles S
1.4	Summit of **Carter Dome,** remains of fire tower, views.	4832/1473	13.8
1.0	Side trail to spring; then steep descent into Carter Notch.		14.2
0.2	**Carter Notch;** junction with **Nineteen-Mile Brook Trail.** Turn L 0.1 mi. to **Carter Notch AMC Hut,** self-serve kitchen, bunkhouses, open year-round; no camping. Side trail to the Rampart, views. Follow AT/ Nineteen-Mile Brook Trail W from notch.	3288/1002	15.0
0.0	**End AT miles:** Junction with Wildcat Ridge Trail.	3388/1033	15.2
3.5	Access: Follow **Nineteen-Mile Brook Trail** along brook, steep descent to Pinkham Notch, NH 16, parking, shuttle.	1500/457	3.5

SOUTH

A few hundred yards behind the bunkhouses, a spur trail to the left off Wildcat River Trail leads to the Rampart, a maze of giant boulders similar to Mahoosuc Notch, with caves that hold ice well into summer. At the top of the Rampart an overlook gazes out onto the valley to the south.

A glacier carved the notch between Wildcat Mt. and Carter Dome. Blocks of rock dropped from the notch walls when the glacier retreated. Others were quarried later by freezing water, then fell into the notch.

From the notch, follow the AT/ Nineteen-Mile Brook Trail west, reaching a junction with Wildcat Ridge Trail in 0.2 mi. (at 15.2 mi.). Here you will part company with the AT, which climbs onto Wildcat Mt. Follow Nineteen-Mile Brook Trail, which makes a short, steep drop, then descends gradually along the eastern bank of its lovely namesake brook. At 3.5 mi. the trail reaches the parking area on NH 16 in Pinkham Notch (18.7 mi. from the start); the parking area is served by the AMC shuttle.

HIKE #15

Androscoggin River to Dream Lake

Maps: ATC N.H. and Vt. #1

Route: From Hogan Rd. over Mt. Hayes and Cascade Mt. to Trident Col, then to Page Pond, Dream Lake, and North Rd.

Recommended direction: S to N

Distance: 12.3 mi.; 8.8 mi. on AT

Access trail name & length: Peabody Brook Trail, 3.5 mi.

Elevation +/-: 760 to 2631 to 760 ft.

Effort: Moderate

Day hike: Yes

Overnight backpacking hike: Optional

Duration: 8 to 10 hr.

Early exit option: Mahoosuc Trail, at 3.1 mi.

Natural history features: Birch glades; tundra bogs; little brown bats; glacial tarns; Androscoggin River and river valley

Social history features: Trail commemorating AMC's 100th anniversary

Trailhead access: *Start:* From the junction of US 2 and North Rd. in Shelburne, (3.6 mi. E of Gorham, NH, and 19 mi. W of Bethel, ME), follow North Rd. 0.3 mi. past a power plant and dam to Hogan Rd., on the L where North Rd. curves to the R. Parking at intersection of North Rd. and Hogan Rd. or 0.3 mi. NW where Centennial Trail diverges from Hogan Rd. *End:* N side of North Rd. 0.8 mi. E of Hogan Rd. at a stone house (no parking here). Follow North Rd. 0.3 mi. W to roadside parking at intersection of North Rd. and Leadmine Rd. (overnight not recommended), or 0.8 mi. to Hogan Rd. parking areas.

Camping: Trident Col Tentsite

This hike begins on a trail that was blazed to commemorate the 100th anniversary of the Appalachian Mt. Club in 1976, which, coincidentally, was the bicentennial of the United States; so this part of the AT is a bicentennial trail as well as a centennial trail.

Although Hike #15 is the AT's southern entrance to the fierce Mahoosuc Range, it has little in common with the punishing, rocky battlegrounds that define the rest of the range. Its infrequent steep climbs are broken up by long flat sections through expansive glades of bleach-white paper birch trees. Spring arrives a little earlier in this part of the Mahoosucs, which is nestled in the elbow formed by the Androscoggin River's turn to the east. Lower elevations and better drainage remove heavy snows sooner and keep the footing drier than in the rest of the range. When the surrounding peaks of the Carter-Moriah and Presidential ranges are still snowcapped, the Centennial Trail is often lined with the first flowers of spring.

Park for this hike on Hogan Rd.,

either at its intersection with North Rd. in Shelburne or 0.3 mi. up the dirt road in a parking area on the left. Be careful not to block the road, which is often traveled by heavy logging equipment.

Walk directly across the road from the parking area and 100 ft. up a logging road to a trail sign and register. Both day and overnight hikers should develop the habit of recording their plans in these registers. It takes only a minute, and it can prevent a lot of anxiety. The AT/Centennial Trail forks left from the logging road and climbs past an AT survey plate in the trail, then passes to the left of a 20-ft. crag where the trail flattens out and swings left to the first of several outlooks over the Androscoggin River valley. The overlooks on the Centennial Trail provide not only a view over the valley but also an overview of the geology, history, environment, and economy of Coos County. On a clear day you will be able to see the smoke from the paper mills upriver. You will probably be able to smell them too.

When the glaciers retreated more than 10,000 years ago, the notch they carved here was filled by a series of lakes connected by rivers. Sediment eventually filled the lakes, creating a valley 0.5 mi. wide and 7.5 mi. long—one of the most fertile in New Hampshire.

Early white settlers believed the Androscoggin to be the most powerful river on the continent. By the 1970s the river had developed a different reputation: it was considered to be one of the most polluted rivers in North America. Lumps of sludge the size of rowboats floated in the water, and fumes from the river would peel the paint off nearby buildings.

Today the Androscoggin has staged a recovery as dramatic as that of any river in America. Thousands of largemouth and smallmouth bass make this the best bass fishing river in Maine. Brown trout and rainbow trout are also abundant. While the river's filthy reputation has made many fishermen slow to return, kingfishers and osprey have proved far less skeptical. They are commonly seen diving for fish in the river north of Berlin. New Hampshire's only pair of nesting bald eagles live on Lake Umbagog, the headwaters of the Androscoggin.

This river's fantastic recovery, however, wasn't painless and is not complete. Since the first logs were floated down the Androscoggin more than 200 years ago, logging, paper milling, and the manufacture of wood products have been at the heart of the economy of Coos County. The industries also created most of the pollution. While the Clean Water Act of 1972 helped to revive the river, it also placed a heavy burden on industries already in decline.

In 1989 the Appalachian Mt. Club, hoping to aid further the recovery of the river, intervened in the Federal Energy Regulatory Commission's process of relicensing several dams

David Emblidge

Black bear foraging

operated on the Androscoggin by Crown Vantage pulp and paper mill, the area's largest employer. The AMC hoped to ensure public access to the river, encourage riverfront conservation, guarantee water releases for whitewater boating, and protect the fish. Their efforts backfired.

Local residents and businessmen saw the club as a representative of elitist outsiders and environmental extremists determined to undermine the economic health of the region. They circulated petitions to persuade the forest service to withhold renewals of AMC's permits to operate huts and visitor centers in the White Mts. In 1994 the AMC withdrew from the relicensing process for dams in Berlin and Gorham and developed a fifteen-principle Operating Philosophy for community-based conservation.

The AMC's relationship with the mill towns has not fully recovered, and neither has the river. Mercury, dioxin, PCBs, and overflow sewage are still found in the water. It's wise to limit consumption of fish caught in the Androscoggin and to avoid swimming in the river between Lewiston and the Brunswick dam.

From the last viewpoint over the valley, the AT climbs gradually back to the right up rocky ramps to another level section. Then at 0.7 mi. it drops into a sag and crosses two small brooks, which are the last chance for water in dry years.

The drumrolls of woodpeckers often accompany hikers on this section as they climb along the left edge of a wooded plateau. Spruce trees along the trail are decorated with dozens of holes drilled by the birds in their search for insects and sap. Oblong holes 1 to 3 in. in diameter are the work of pileated woodpeckers, which eat carpenter ants. Although rarely seen, pileated woodpeckers are easy to identify by their large size and distinctive red crest. Horizontal rows of small holes are left by yellow-bellied sapsuckers, which have a red cap, black and white ladder pattern on the back, and of course, a yellow belly. Downy and hairy woodpeckers, the varieties most commonly seen in these woods, have a white streak on the

Black Bear

Who is the black bear *(Ursus americanus)* frequenting New England woods—and gardens—more and more often these days? This bear is wild and shouldn't be toyed with. He (or she) is not an actor in costume for the U.S. Forest Service, nor a cartoon character from children's TV, nor a huge, aggressive beast likely to eat your dog for a snack. Nonetheless, if provoked, frightened, or unduly hungry, black bears can be dangerous. They weigh 200 to 300 lb., and upright, the male is a good 5 ft. tall.

Male bears may roam hundreds of miles, crisscrossing their territory in search of mates. Generally the black bear likes to feed at night, but don't be surprised to see a daytime wanderer. Being abroad in daylight, however, doesn't mean a bear wants to give you a photo opportunity, especially if she is a mother with her cubs. Steer clear.

A dry summer can reduce the supply of berries, chokecherries, and skunk cabbage in the woods (staples in a bear's warm-weather diet), inducing bears to forage more widely.

The best way to see bears up close, unless they accidentally wander into your path, is through a telephoto lens or binoculars. Do not chase a bear: she can turn on you and give you chase at 30 mph.

Two land-use factors play a part in the upsurge of the New England bear population: farmland is dwindling rapidly (often returning to forest), while suburban development spreads ever more deeply into forested land. New Hampshire is estimated to have between 2500 and 3000 black bears.

Hiking with a group is fun, but the collective impact of human scent and footstep noise may keep wildlife out of your way. In the Smoky Mts. of North Carolina and Tennessee, the Green Mts. of Vermont, the White Mts. of New Hampshire, and throughout Maine, however, bear sightings are common despite the hiker foot traffic (and sometimes because of unprotected food and improperly disposed-of garbage). In fact, black bears appear from time to time in all fourteen AT states.

If the bruins come visiting, don't feed them, especially not with garbage. A dependent bear can grow frustrated when the easy supply disappears and then may become a nuisance or a danger. The best thing to do with bears is to admire them in respectful stillness. If a bear appears intent on harming you or your pets, clanging a few pots and pans together should quickly send the curious beast up a tree or back into the cover of his homeland woods.

—David Emblidge and Michael Kodas

back and a red patch on the back of the head. The small bill and short stature of the downy distinguish it from the hairy.

Shortly after the riddled trees, the trail cuts left to a series of lookouts at the edge of the plateau. Before you are the Carter-Moriah Range, the Northern Presidential Range, and the western Androscroggin Valley. During one late-May hike, the AT/Centennial Trail was warm and dry, but the overlook showed us that the Presidentials were still covered with snow.

From the last of the overlooks the trail climbs somewhat steeply up stone steps to the north, then ascends more gradually to the east. At a series of open ledges at about 1500 ft., the trail follows cairns to views of the eastern Androscoggin Valley rolling into Maine, with the Carter-Moriah range across the valley. Then, at 1.6 mi., the trail turns left and descends into the woods.

Here the AT crosses through a forest as diverse as any in the White Mts., but it is the sprawling glades of paper birch, like the Shelburne Birches Memorial Forest that borders US 2 near the start of the hike, that give these mountains their magic. As the trail heads to the top of Mt. Hayes and Cascade Mt., the ghostly trees become gradually larger and more mature. Paper birch thrive in moist upland soils and in old clearcuts. They often grow in nearly pure stands, like those found here. The Anasagunticook Indians, who lived along the Androscoggin River, stretched the stripped bark of the paper birch over frames of northern white cedar to make their lightweight canoes. Before the Androscoggin was dammed, these canoes were the only boat that could navigate amid the river's cascades and waterfalls. Today paper birch, which is also known as canoe birch and white birch, is used to make popsicle sticks, clothespins, toothpicks, and pulp. If you want to bring home some birch-bark souvenirs, take them only from fallen logs or from the ground. Bark stripped from living trees leaves an unsightly black scar. In the shade of the birches, dozens of dogtooth violets (a.k.a trout lilies) sprout like rolled pieces of purple paper stuck in the ground, maturing into plants with distinctive mottled leaves and nodding yellow flowers. Where the trail becomes more moist, alpine marsh violets bloom in white and lavender.

After the first birch glades, the AT/ Centennial Trail climbs a ramp of glacier-scarred schist onto Mt. Hayes. At the top of the long, gradual climb, a cairn marks a turn to the left where the footpath leads across a heath to the 2555-ft. eastern summit of Mt. Hayes at 2.8 mi., the view encompasses the Northern Presidentials in the southwest and North Carter Mt., Imp Mt., and Mt. Moriah in the south and southeast.

From Hayes's eastern summit the trail turns right, crosses open ledges, and descends to the northwest. It turns again to the right and climbs through an area where birch bark covers the ground like confetti, then climbs again past a glacial erratic with a trail blaze on it. At 3.1 mi. there is a sign marking the junction where Centennial Trail ends at Mahoosuc Trail, which the AT now follows to the right. (To the left, Mahoosuc Trail leads 0.2 mi. to the true summit of Mt. Hayes, and then 3.3 mi. to NH 16 and Gorham, to provide an early exit and day hike alternative.)

The AT/Mahoosuc Trail descends gradually into a col, then crosses a brook and continues past an improvised campsite, finally climbing up the flat blocks of schist that armor the side of Cascade Mt. At 5.0 mi. the trail reaches the top of Cascade Mt., 2631 ft., where views from the ridgeline show the ski trails of Wildcat Mt. in the south and the timber harvest in the woods below.

The descent into Trident Pass begins on steep slabs, then makes a strenuous plunge down a rocky gully. Near the bottom of the pass, at 6.1 mi., a blue-blazed spur trail leads 175 yd. through the gully on the left to Trident Col Tentsite. Wooden platforms for four tents are spread out nicely in the spruce, fir, and birch woods of the col, and crags in the east and west enclose the lovely, secluded camping area. A spur trail marked by two cairns leads to an outlook atop the eastern cliff.

The site has a composting privy, water nearby, and resident insect exterminators: a cave just south of here, near Leadmine Brook, is filled with thousands of little brown bats. On summer nights you will see the bats darting through the air as they hunt insects, navigating with their ultrasonic cries. Their wings are thin membranes that extend between long fingers. They are most easily recognized by their distinctive flight, which is far more agile than that of most birds.

From the spur trail to the tent sites, the AT/Mahoosuc Trail descends gradually and crosses several two-plank bog bridges as it swings to the right, eventually reaching a slab with views over acres of birches that cover the side of the mountain. The trail descends to the right here, following two small, easily missed cairns to a short, steep drop. The AT crosses a brook, steps onto a logging road, crosses another brook, then forks to the left off the road at a junction that you might pass if you are not watching for it. After crossing a series of small ridges and gullies, at 7.4 mi. the AT/Mahoosuc Trail reaches the outlet of Page Pond, a beautiful woods pond that is crossed on a beaver dam on the right, which is marked by cairns and an AT sign nailed to a tree. Prints often visible in the mud and/or snow along the bank show that this is a popular swimming hole for moose. Dawn and dusk are the best times to see beaver and moose, and with Trident Col Tentsite only a mile away, a wildlife viewing trip to Page Pond is remarkably convenient.

At a muddy sag west of the pond, the AT/Mahoousuc Trail begins a steep climb over rocky steps. After a horseshoe turn to the left, the trail reaches a sign marking Wocket Ledge, at 7.7 mi., then continues to climb gradually past it. The back side of Wocket Ledge often holds knee-deep snow until late spring, so be prepared for a slog during the descent. Gaiters are a good idea—or bring extra-long socks and tuck in your pants legs.

At the bottom of the descent from the ledge, a long, gradual climb reaches the magnificent glacial tarn of Dream Lake at 8.8 mi. The trail crosses the inlet on bog bridges, then reaches the junction with Peabody Brook Trail. Like many of the brooks in the Androscoggin Valley, the Peabody is named for a once-prominent family in Shelburne. An orchestra of ducks on Dream Lake often distracts trampers from the trail beside the tarn, which is so soggy in spring that many of its bog bridges are afloat. A walking stick may prove helpful here.

From here, Hike #15 leaves the AT, turning right and following Peabody Brook Trail for 3.5 mi. as it descends back to North Rd. in Shelburne. (The AT/Mahoosuc Trail turns left at Dream Lake and continues on to Gentian Pond Campsite in 2.2 mi.; see Hike #16.)

Below the lake Peabody Trail follows the left side of the brook as it descends in steep, rocky spurts. After dropping down wooden stairs, the trail crosses the brook, then recrosses it somewhat lower. At 2.2 mi. down Peabody Trail, a spur trail on the right

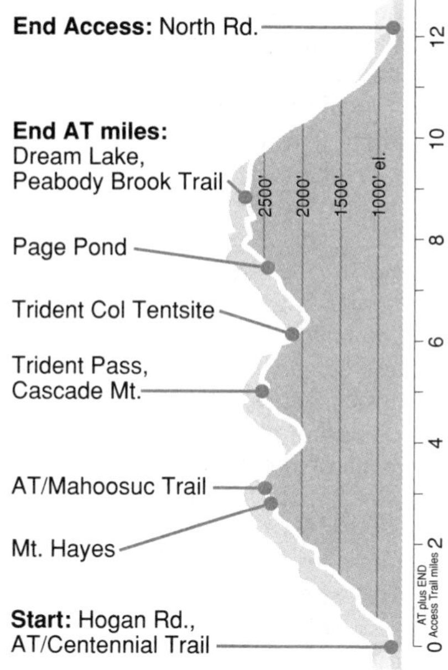

created using Maptech TopoScout ®

leads 0.3 mi. to Giant Falls, a magnificent series of falls and cascades that you can hear from the trail when they are flooded in the spring. After crossing the brook, the trail heads left on a woods road, then veers to the right on another road and reaches the trailhead between two houses on North Rd. at 3.5 mi. (12.3 mi. overall). The Leadmine Rd. parking area is 0.3 mi. to the right, and the Hogan Rd. parking areas, where we started out, are 0.3 and 0.5 mi. farther.

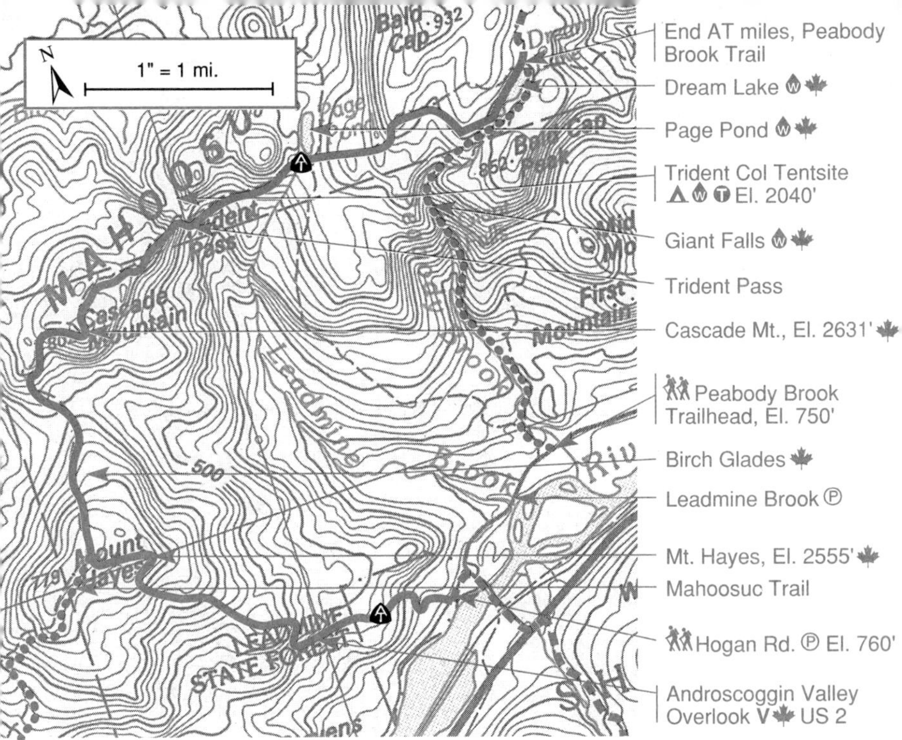

N
1" = 1 mi.
End AT miles, Peabody Brook Trail
Dream Lake
Page Pond
Trident Col Tentsite El. 2040'
Giant Falls
Trident Pass
Cascade Mt., El. 2631'
Peabody Brook Trailhead, El. 750'
Birch Glades
Leadmine Brook Ⓟ
Mt. Hayes, El. 2555'
Mahoosuc Trail
Hogan Rd. Ⓟ El. 760'
Androscoggin Valley Overlook V US 2

HIKE #15 Itinerary

Miles N	NORTH	Elev. (ft/m)	Miles S
Total: 12.3 mi. with access trail			
3.5	Access: **Peabody Brook Trail** S to North Rd.		3.5
8.8	**End AT miles: Dream Lake,** junction with Peabody Brook Trail.		0.0
7.7	**Wocket Ledge.**		1.1
7.4	**Page Pond.**		1.7
6.1	Spur trail 175 yd. to **Trident Col Tentsite,** privy, water.	2404/733	2.7
5.0	**Cascade Mt.,** views. Then steep descent into **Trident Pass.**	2631/802	3.8
3.1	Junction. Turn R (N) onto **AT/Mahoosuc Trail.** (Turn L (W) for early exit option, 3.5 mi. to NH 16.)		5.7
2.8	Eastern summit, **Mt. Hayes,** views.	2555/779	6.0
1.6	AT turns L (W) away from viewpoints and heads into paper birch glades.		7.2
0.7	Sag and two brooks, water.		8.1
0.0	**Start: Hogan Rd.** parking. Follow logging road to trail sign and register, then **AT/Centennial Trail.** Climb to series of overlooks.	760/232	8.8

SOUTH

HIKE #16

Dream Lake, Gentian Pond, and Mt. Success

Maps: ATC N.H. and Vt. #1

Route: From North Rd., Shelburne, to Dream Lake, Gentian Pond Campsite, and Mt. Success, down to Success Pond Rd.

Recommended direction: S to N

Distance: 11.7 mi.; 5.6 mi. on AT

Access trails name & length: Peabody Brook Trail, 3.1 mi.; Success Trail, 3.0 mi.

Elevation +/-: 760 to 3565 to 1600 ft.

Effort: Very strenuous

Day hike: Optional

Overnight backpacking hike: Yes

Duration: 9 to 12 hr.

Early exit option: Austin Brook Trail, at 5.3 mi.

Natural history features: Giant Falls; Dream Lake; Gentian Pond; Mt. Success; moose habitat; gentians; heaths; tundra bogs

Social history features: Airplane crash on Mt. Success

Trailhead access: *Start:* From the junction of US 2 and North Rd. (3.6 mi. E of Gorham, NH, and 19 mi. W of Bethel, ME), follow North Rd. 0.3 mi. past a power plant and dam to Hogan Rd., on the L where North Rd. curves to the R. Park at intersection of North Rd. and Hogan Rd. or 0.3 mi. NW where the Centennial Trail diverges from Hogan Rd. Additional roadside parking (not recommended for overnight visitors) 0.3 mi. N at the intersection of North Rd. and Leadmine Rd. Peabody Brook trailhead is on North Rd. 0.6 mi. E of Hogan Rd and 0.3 mi. E of Leadmine Rd. *End:* From Gorham, take NH 16 4.5 mi. N. Cross Cleveland Bridge over Androscoggin River. Follow Unity St. L, then R at 0.8 mi. across railroad tracks, where it becomes Hutchins St. After another 0.8 mi. turn L and pass James River mill yard. Turn R on unmarked street, follow this 0.2 mi., and then turn L onto Success Pond Rd. Drive 5.4 mi. to (poorly marked) trailhead on R. *Note:* Success Pond Rd. is one of the most difficult access routes in the region to find and follow. The road itself is often muddy and rutted, and the trailheads are often marked with only a small AMC trail sign or not marked at all. Carry the AMC Carter-Mahoosuc map, the MATC *Appalachian Trail in Maine,* and/or the DeLorme Maine road atlas.

Camping: Gentian Pond Campsite

The beatific names of the landmarks on Hike #16 might seem to counter the Mahoosuc Range's forbidding reputation, but in fact, getting from Dream Lake to Mt. Success requires perseverance. An overnight amid cliffs and cascades in the idylllic shelter at Gentian Pond is ample reward for the hard work.

The hike begins at Peabody Brook Trail, which steps off from North Rd. in Shelburne, NH. Compared to nearby Gorham and Berlin, Shelburne hardly seems a town at all. For more than 30 years this quiet hamlet has worked to maintain its rural nature. The 1996 revision to its 1982 master plan states that "the highest priorities of the town are the preservation of natural beauty, keeping intact the rural nature of the town, [and] guarding against the loss of open space."

The drive to protect the rural nature of Shelburne and the Androscoggin valley isn't just local. In 1994 Indiana flatlanders Larry Ely and Jennifer Lawson purchased 130 acres of the once grand Whitney Farm to prevent their development. The tract includes 1685-ft. First Mountain, visible from Peabody Brook Trail. The new owners plan to manage the First Mountain Forest as a wildlife habitat and recreation area for hikers and cross-country skiers and will allow timber harvesting only when it contributes to the overall health of the forest. They hope to restore an orange-blazed 1917 AMC trail that climbs along the eastern border of the property to views above Joe's Ledges.

From the North Rd. trailhead, proceed along a logging road to the left of a residence, pass a gate, and follow Peabody Brook northward. At 0.8 mi. Peabody Brook Trail forks to the right and begins to climb gradually alongside the brook. As you look back into the Androscoggin valley, it's easy to understand why the town fathers and visiting midwesterners put such a high priority on protecting the rural nature of the town.

In *The White Hills: Their Legends, Landscape, and Poetry* (1864), a seminal book on the White Mts., Thomas Starr King describes the view from nearby Whitney Knoll: "How grand and complete is the landscape that stretches before us as we look up the river seven or eight miles.... Seen in the afternoon light, the Androscoggin and its meadows look more lovely than on any portion of the road between Bethel and Gorham, and more fascinating than any piece of river scenery it has ever been our fortune to look upon in the mountain region."

Peabody Brook Trail climbs moderately, and at 1.2 mi. reaches a spur trail that leads left 0.3 mi. to Giant Falls, where a half mile of cascades roar when the brook is flooded with meltwater in the spring.

At 1.5 mi. the trail arrives at a short set of wooden steps, just slightly past a southerly view of Mt. Washington and Mt. Adams. The climbs here are none too steep, but the path is often quite muddy, which may slow your progress. In 1997 and 1998 Peabody Brook Trail and five other side trails in the Mahoosucs received significant improvements and repairs when the AMC and landowner Mead Paper teamed up in an unusual coalition of environmentalists and businesspeople to split the $14,000 cost of the trail work.

The trail crosses back and forth over the east branch of Peabody Brook and then levels out before it reaches Dream Lake, on the left, and Dryad Falls Trail, on the right, at 3.0 mi. At 3.1 mi. it reaches Mahoosuc Trail, where our AT mileage count begins.

The AT/Mahoosuc Trail bears right onto a logging road, then crosses the lake's inlet. Dream Lake is a popular dining spot for moose, especially at the breakfast and dinner hours—just after dawn and just before sunset. Watch the muddy trail for cloven hoof prints 5 to 7 in. long, and approach the lake quietly if you see any. Near the junction of the Peabody and Mahoosuc trails there are good overlooks from which to scan the lakeshore for these largest members of the deer family, which crave the succulent aquatic vegetation found in ponds, lakes, swamps, and bogs. Tooth marks and areas of stripped bark on maple trees identify one of the moose's favorite winter meals.

You will often hear the ducks before you see them on Dream Lake. American black ducks, ring-necked ducks, and on rare occasions, common mergansers can be found paddling along here.

On wet days, the section of the AT/Mahoosuc Trail north of Dream Lake might seem more like a stream as water rolls down the footpath past teetering bog bridges. At a marshy meadow, many of the dozens of bog bridges sink into the flooded path. The bogs here are more delicate than they appear, so stay on the bridges whether they keep your feet above water or not.

The forest here is an unusually diverse mixture of sugar maple, paper birch, yellow birch, beech, red spruce, balsam fir, and small aspen. Stands of red oak cover steep drainage slopes on the nearby mountains. Slabs of schist exposed by the pulled-up roots of blown-down trees reveal the deep grooves cut by the glacier that carved the valley. A variety of large round metamorphic rocks deposited by the glacier have been polished by the eons of rain and runoff.

At 1.5 mi. you might feel the AT/Mahoosuc Trail is something of a tease when it arrives at the appropriately named Moss Pond, rather than Gentian Pond. The trail follows the rocky north shore to a logging road along the outlet brook as boulders rise and overhang the path dramatically. Don't let your eagerness to get to the campsite keep you from enjoying this pond's namesakes, which create a lush carpet over the ground, trees, and rocks: bog haircap moss, which stands taller than other mosses and has gray threads on its stems; big redstem moss, with obvious red stems; and green peat moss, which has star-shaped heads. The route crosses the brook and descends to the right, away from the logging road and toward Gentian Pond through an area of blowdowns. As the AT/Mahoosuc Trail reaches another stream and begins the final, gradual climb to

Gentian Pond, you will suddenly find yourself flanked by a horseshoe of large cliffs. The trail follows the southwest bank of the pond and at 2.2 mi. reaches Gentian Pond Campsite, 500 ft. after crossing a small brook that provides the site's water.

To the right, the AMC's Gentian Pond Campsite looks out over the beautiful bluff-walled pond. Cascades from the pond's outlet into Austin Brook fall directly below the campsite and, although they cannot be seen from the shelter, provide a gorgeous soundscape. To the left, the shelter enjoys a view over the Androscoggin valley and Shelburne.

In 1781 St. Francis Indians, on a raid from Canada, killed Peter Poor, one of the town's early residents, before camping near Gentian Pond, where their war cries terrorized the town through the night. A monument marking poor Peter's grave can be reached from North Rd. in Shelburne on a footpath that follows the east bank of Mill Brook south.

The present shelter was built by the AMC in 1974 and accommodates fourteen. A stool hewn from the same spruce trees as the walls provides a lift to the upper bunk and a seat for the cook. However, the "Throne"—an experimental solar-powered privy—has been replaced with a more traditional model.

Be diligent in your search for the flowers that the pond is named after —they are not always easy to find. The flower of the closed gentian has five blue petals that are pressed together at their tips, forming a capsule. The flowers sit atop opposite oval leaves on 1- to 2-ft.-tall stems. Narrow-leaved gentians are similar to closed gentians aside from, obviously, their slender leaves. A stand of gentians swaying in the breeze along a pond's edge or a woods road is a delight to hikers but a challenge to bees, which must pry open the closed petals to reach the nectar inside.

From the shelter, blue-blazed Austin Brook Trail descends to the right and reaches North Rd. in 3.2 mi. to provide the hike's best early exit option.

Between Gentian Pond and Mt. Success, the AT/Mahoosuc Trail becomes increasingly rugged. It climbs steeply away from Gentian Pond over slabs, levels out through a thick glade of conifers, then steepens again as it heads northeast. After another flat cruise, the trail climbs sharply up blocky steps to an area of open ledges, then descends in spurts. At 3.6 mi. it skips across a rocky brook, then makes an arduous crossing of the stubble of boulders on Mt. Success's cheek. It's easy to lose your way here, especially during foliage season when fallen leaves can camouflage the blazed rocks.

From the Mt. Success boulder field, the AT climbs in steep drives, broken by traverses to the left that pass and cross several small brooks—many of which pour down the path, forcing hikers to apply their boot soles with both force and care to keep from slipping in the racing water on the steep slabs of gneiss.

From the top of a hump, the trail drops into a series of bogs where, during a rainy period, the bridges may float on the mire and drop you shin-deep into muddy water. Although the bridges can't keep your feet dry when the Mahoosucs flood, they still protect this delicate and unique environment from damage caused by hikers' boots.

The AT crosses several alpine heaths and tundra bogs as it climbs to the flatter upper reaches of Mt. Success. The open heaths spread out among dwarfed black spruce trees and are filled with Labrador tea, which blooms in June with clusters of white flowers atop thick evergreen leaves with woolly undersides, and sheep laurel, which has pink flowers partway up the leaf-crowned stems. Woods herbalists must be careful not to the confuse the shrubs: Labrador tea is used to brew a medicinal tea, but sheep laurel is toxic. The tundra bogs are also filled with bog laurel, which has pink flowers and evergreen leaves with white undersides, as well as cloudberry, also known as baked-apple berry due to its yellow fruit, and small cranberries, which spread out over several varieties of sphagnum moss.

The soil of heaths and bogs is composed of peat—partially decomposed plants and animals—which accumulates in wetlands. Peatland soils are mineral-poor, which limits the types of plantlife they can support. Bogs are usually located in depressions or basins that collect rainwater or are fed by a spring or small stream. Heaths are areas where the peat has accumulated to the point where it has completely filled a bog.

At 5.0 mi. the AT/Mahoosuc Trail arrives at the USGS plate marking the summit of Mt. Success, 3565 ft. Mt. Success is named for the New Hampshire township to the west. In 1954 a DC3 crashed on the mountain, and remnants of its wreckage can still be found approximately 0.3 mi. southwest of the summit. A trail once led from the summit to the crash site, but it has long become overgrown. You may see some of its faded blazes if you search for the plane. In *Our Last Backpack,* Daniel Doan describes visiting the site during his traverse of the Mahoosuc Range twelve years after the crash: "I stared at the wreckage of the great bird crumpled here in the wilderness. The feeling of a recent accident came strongly. I had the illusion that the people, the living and the dead, had only just left the scene."

From the summit block, the AT/Mahoosuc Trail descends steeply over slick rock and roots, passes a bog where moose prints can often be found in the sphagnum moss, then climbs steeply through a notch in the crag.

At 5.6 mi. the AT/Mahoosuc Trail reaches its junction with Success Trail. This hike leaves the AT here and follows Success Trail west to Success Pond Rd. (The AT continues on Mahoosuc Trail to Carlo Col Campsite in 2.1 mi. at the Carlo Col Trail—

where the AT miles of our Hike #17 begin; we omit the 2.1 mi. of AT from here to there.).

Carefully follow Success Trail as it descends gradually through a gully with a small brook in it to another brook at an abandoned logging camp. Here the trail climbs over a ridge, then descends. If there is any life left in your legs, and light left in the day, consider following a spur trail at 0.8 mi. down Success Trail—it leads left to gorgeous views of Mt. Madison and the Northern Presidential Range. After 0.3 mi. the spur trail rejoins Success Trail, which descends steeply, eventually becoming a logging road and reaching Success Pond Rd. in 3.0 mi., for a grand total of 11.7 mi.

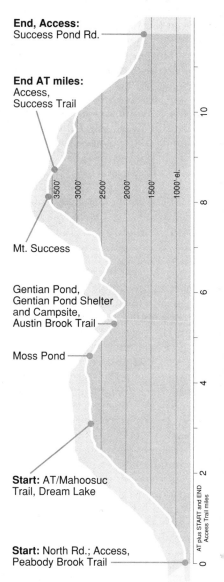

End, Access: Success Pond Rd.

End AT miles: Access, Success Trail

Mt. Success

Gentian Pond, Gentian Pond Shelter and Campsite, Austin Brook Trail

Moss Pond

Start: AT/Mahoosuc Trail, Dream Lake

Start: North Rd.; Access, Peabody Brook Trail

3500' 3000' 2500' 2000' 1500' 1000' el.

0 2 4 6 8 10

AT plus START and END Access Trail miles

created using Maptech TopoScout ®

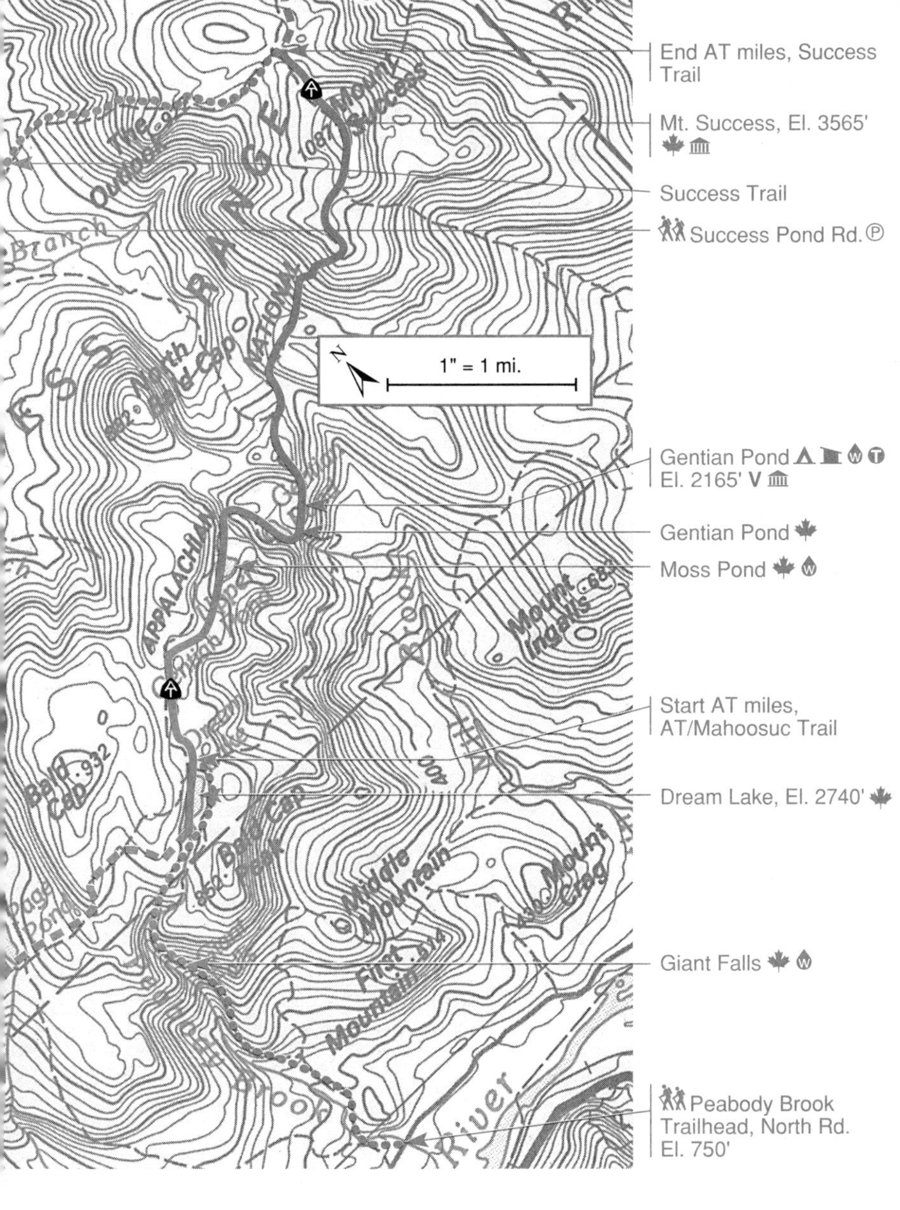

End AT miles, Success Trail
Mt. Success, El. 3565'
Success Trail
Success Pond Rd. Ⓟ
1" = 1 mi.
Gentian Pond
El. 2165' V
Gentian Pond
Moss Pond
Start AT miles, AT/Mahoosuc Trail
Dream Lake, El. 2740'
Giant Falls
Peabody Brook Trailhead, North Rd. El. 750'
Mount Success
Bald Cap
Middle Mountain
Mount Ingalls
Mount Crag
River
Branch

HIKE #16 Itinerary

Miles N	NORTH	Elev. (ft/m)	Miles S
Total: 11.7 mi. with access trails			
3.0	Access: Descend **Success Trail** W to **Success Pond Rd.,** parking.	1600/487	3.0
5.6	**End AT miles:** Junction with **Success Trail.**		0.0
5.0	**Mt. Success;** airplane crash site 0.3 mi. SW.	3565/1087	0.6
3.6	**Brook crossing,** then climb.		2.0
2.2	**Gentian Pond** and **Gentian Pond Shelter and Campsite,** water, privy, views. **Austin Brook Trail** heads R (S) to North Rd. (early exit option).	2165/660	3.4
1.5	**Moss Pond.**		4.1
0.0	**Start AT miles:** Junction with **AT/Mahoosuc Trail** at **Dream Lake,** El. approx. 2700′.		5.6
3.1	Access: **Peabody Brook Trail,** from parking on North Rd., follow N along brook. Spur trail to **Giant Falls** at 1.2 mi.	760/232	0.0

SOUTH

HIKE #17

Carlo Col and Goose Eye Mt.

Maps: ATC N.H. & Vt. #1

Route: From Success Pond Rd. up Carlo Col Trail to AT/Mahoosuc Trail, over Mt. Carlo, Goose Eye Mt., and Fulling Mill Mt. to Mahoosuc Notch, then Mahoosuc Notch Trail to Success Pond Rd.

Recommended direction: S to N

Distance: 11.0 mi.; 5.9 mi. on AT

Access trails name & length: Carlo Col Trail, 2.6 mi.; Mahoosuc Notch Trail, 2.5 mi.

Elevation +/-: 1620 to 3854 to 1620 ft.

Effort: Very strenuous

Day hike: Shorter day-hike options

Overnight backpacking hike: Yes

Early exit option: Goose Eye Trail, at 1.8 mi.

Natural history features: Rugged geology of Carlo Col and Mahoosuc Notch; bald summit of Goose Eye Mt.; tundra bogs; alpine heaths

Trailhead access: *Start:* From Gorham, take NH 16 4.5 mi. N. Cross Cleveland Bridge over Androscoggin River. Follow Unity St. L, then R at 0.8 mi. across railroad tracks, where it becomes Hutchins St. After another 0.8 mi. turn L and pass James River mill yard. Turn R on unmarked street, follow this 0.2 mi., and then turn L onto Success Pond Rd. Go about 6.0 mi. to a logging road that leads to Carlo Col Trail and parking.
End: From parking at Carlo Col Trail, drive 2.8 mi. N to a spur road that diverges to the R and runs 0.3 mi. to a small parking area at base of Mahoosuc Notch Trail. *Note:* For Success Pond Rd. details, see Trailhead Access, Hike #16.

Camping: Carlo Col Shelter; Full Goose Shelter

The Mahoosuc Range's reputation for having some of the most rugged and remote terrain on the AT keeps many hikers at bay. The adventurers who do visit these forebidding and fantastic mountains usually hike the AT's entire 31-mi. route from Shelburne, NH, to Grafton Notch, ME, in an expedition that can last from 3 days to a week.

This mountain range, however, is not reserved for the long-distance crowd. The heart of the Mahoosucs—the rocky wreckage of Carlo Col, the open heaths and summit vistas of Goose Eye Mt., and even Mahoosuc Notch, the most famed mile of the range and perhaps of the entire AT—can be visited with a single overnight or, believe it or not, in a day hike.

The Carlo Col and Goose Eye trails, which merge near Success Pond Rd., provide a convenient, moderately difficult approach to the AT that might make you feel as if you are sneaking into these mighty mountains without paying your dues. Joining these two trails are 1.8 mi. of the AT/Mahoosuc Trail's most dramatic terrain. A loop of the three trails (which works equally well going N – S or S – N) allows visits to Carlo Col and Goose Eye Mt. as part of a 7.5-mi. round-trip that is quite manageable in a day. Day hikers can visit Mahoosuc Notch on Mahoosuc Notch Trail, at the northern end of Hike #17 (see Hike #18).

Backpackers in this part of the Mahoosucs have several options for breaking up their hike. A stay at Carlo Col Shelter allows overnight visitors to take their time on the 5.9 mi. between the Carlo Col and Mahoosuc Notch trails. Full Goose Shelter, on the north side of Goose Eye Mt., provides the range's easiest access to Mahoosuc Notch, allowing plenty of time for a pack-free excursion into the Notch and back. The route from Success Pond Rd. up Carlo Col Trail to the AT/Mahoosuc Trail and back down Mahoosuc Notch Trail is 11.3 mi. long; it can be shortened to 9.0 mi. by taking Goose Eye Trail up to the AT.

Both access trails begin their climb into the Mahoosucs on the same path. From the parking area, follow Carlo Col / Goose Eye trails onto a broad logging road. After about 100 yd., Goose Eye Trail drops off to the left while Carlo Col Trail continues on the logging road. Hike #17 follows Carlo Col Trail here.

The trail begins its climb into the Mahoosucs amid a rich hardwood forest. Maple, American beech, and birch are still the dominant species here, but white pine, aspen, red oak, and hemlock are common as well. Watch the smooth gray trunks of beech trees for the claw marks of black bears, which climb the trees in search of tasty beechnuts.

From the split of the two access trails, Carlo Col Trail follows the generally flat logging road until it reaches a log yard at 0.8 mi., where the trail turns left and crosses a large brook (which can be hazardous in wet weather). It climbs gradually alongside the brook, then at approximately 1.1 mi. cuts left onto a steeper road, then curls back to the right. Follow the trail carefully as it crosses two tributaries to the main brook, about 0.3 mi. apart. Carlo Col Trail steps from New Hampshire into Maine near the crossing of the second tributary. Maine immediately tries to send its visitors back by increasing the angle of the slope.

The forest here is mostly made up of red spruce and balsam fir, trees that flourish in the moist, acidic soils found at higher elevations.

The trail climbs steeply and curves left to follow the brook to Carlo Col Shelter, at 2.3 mi. There are four tent platforms here, along with space for fourteen inside the cozy log-walled shelter. The stream you've been following may be your last chance for water before reaching Full Goose Shelter, so fill up here. If the weather is cold or wet, this will be your best-sheltered lunch spot. However, if the

Predatory Squirrels

The red squirrel is probably the most common mammal encountered by a hiker in New Hampshire or Maine. Surprisingly, the squirrel is an able and efficient predator. A number of normally herbaceous animals—muskrats, voles, lemmings—may grow antagonistic toward each other, even turning cannibalistic, when their populations increase beyond what available habitat can support. Squirrels, however, have long been suspected of more routine sanguinary habits.

Red squirrels, for example, have been accused of preying on eggs and fledgling songbirds, a practice denied by the squirrels' defenders. Other accounts suggest that red squirrels may occasionally attack and kill gray squirrels, and they have been reported to kill cottontail rabbits. A southern flying squirrel, placed in a roomy aviary, killed and ate a yellow bellied sapsucker that was placed in with it, although the two animals were not crowded. A Baxter State Park ranger told us about watching a chipmunk kill a fledgling robin and drag it into the brush. In the south, fox squirrels were found to be the primary predator of tree-nesting ducks.

The most conclusive blow to the squirrel's reputation comes from a study published in *Natural History* (Mar. 1993). Newborn snowshoe hares (called leverets) were tagged in the Canadian Yukon. Mother hares vigorously chased away red squirrels. Researchers expected the most predation would be from the usually named culprits: bobcat, lynx, coyote, foxes and avian predators such as great horned owls, northern goshawks, and red-tailed hawks.

Only about one-third of the leverets survived over two weeks. The typical predators accounted for less than 5% of the leverets killed. Instead, the young hares were found dragged up into trees and in middens—piles of cones on the ground left by squirrels. Others showed up in the burrows of Arctic ground squirrels. When the carcasses were tallied, red and ground squirrels accounted for more than three quarters of the leverets killed.

—Andrew Weegar

weather is clear, head up to the crags west of the col, where several ledges provide far more beautiful places to spread out your picnic.

From the shelter, Carlo Col Trail climbs 0.3 mi. to its junction with the AT/Mahoosuc Trail, which it reaches in the small box ravine of Carlo Col at 2.6 mi. This hike heads north here, but first drop your pack at the trail junction and head to the right to explore some of the most dramatic geology in the range, only a few hundred feet to the west: crags and boulders rise out of the depths of the col like the ruins of a pillaged castle. Hair-raising hand-over-hand climbs lead past apartment-size caves amid the mountain's debris to a ledge that provides an excellent lunch stop in good weather. In midsummer, blueberry bushes between the rocky ledges and the AT's crossing of the Maine/New Hampshire border, 0.5 mi. south of the trail junction, will provide dessert for your picnic. A round-trip to the border is well worth the extra mile of walking.

The granite of the dramatic col was torn apart about 12,000 years ago by a sheet of ice more than a mile thick. Large chips of mica—mirrorlike flakes of rock—are abundant amid the schists, granites, and gneisses of the Mahoosucs, and you'll see plenty of them here.

After exploring Carlo Col, return to the junction and retrieve your pack (our AT mileage count begins at this point). Then follow the AT/Mahoosuc Trail steeply to the east on your way to Mt. Carlo, which is believed to be named after the dog of a tourist who frequented the region. A series of climbs pass dozens of blown-down spruce trees, many of which have been cut to allow the trail through, while others must be climbed over to reach the steep ledges approaching the summit. At 0.4 mi. the AT/ Mahoosuc Trail reaches the slabby summit of Mt. Carlo (3565 ft.), with its excellent vistas. Then, at a cairn, the trail turns left and descends across bog bridges to a short, rocky climb up and left.

At the top of our climb, a startled spruce grouse whirred from the woods and landed on the trail in front of us. A diet of pine needles and evergreen buds gives the flesh of these birds a cedarlike flavor that is unappealing to predators, permitting them a tamer lifestyle than their cousins, the ruffed grouse. Their lack of fear inspires the nickname "fool hen" and makes federal protection necessary. The brown chicken-like birds often prefer to travel on foot. For the next 100 ft. we had an unexpected hiking partner as the bird waddled up the trail in front of us before flying back into the woods.

Descending from the lower knob of Mt. Carlo, the AT/Mahoosuc Trail crosses a boggy heath toward Goose Eye Mt., which rises in the northeast. The trail descends through a glade of waist-high spruce trees before making a series of rocky descents, broken up by flat sections and bog crossings. From the bottom of the sag, at 1.0 mi., the trail turns 90 degrees to the left on bog bridges in front of a large block of schist, then climbs slanting cracks in the outcrop. The trail continues to ascend over ledges and slabs past dwarf spruces, Labrador tea, and bog laurel shrubs, which show scars from the boots that have used the vegetation for traction when the rock is slick with water. After dropping into another bog, the AT continues its thrilling and strenuous ascent over slick ledges that seem to teeter over the evergeens below. At the top of the knoll, the trail drops down bog bridges and steps into another sag, then begins to climb

Goose Eye Mt. in earnest on a steep, narrow, rocky ridgeline.

Take your time here, as the ascent is a fun but tricky rock climb and is particularly hazardous in wet weather. The trail passes to the right of a large vertical inside corner in a cliff wall that will tempt the boulderers in the group, then scrambles to a set of wooden steps.

The AT's relentlessly challenging route through the Mahoosucs can be credited to four legendary AMC trailblazers who for two decades led a crusade to connect trails throughout the White Mts. into a unified system. Paul R. Jenks, Charles W. Blood, Nathaniel L. Goodrich, and Karl P. Harrington cut the trail between Old Speck and Gentian Pond in a series of "trail sprees" between 1918 and 1921. By 1926 they had completed the section between Gentian Pond and Gorham to create a 27-mi. trip connecting Grafton Notch with the Androscoggin River valley. They also cut side trails in the Mahoosucs, including Mahoosuc Notch Trail and Success Trail.

At 1.8 mi. the AT/Mahoosuc Trail reaches its junction with Goose Eye Trail. Whether you are taking this shorcut down or are continuing on, follow Goose Eye Trail 0.1 mi. to the left (west) onto the rocky open summit of the west peak of Goose Eye Mt. (3854 ft.), which offers what many Mahoosuc connoisseurs believe are the best views in the range.

Mt. Washington, the Presidential Range, and the Carter-Moriah Range rise in the distant southwest above Mt. Carlo and Mt. Success in the foreground. To the northeast, Old Speck marks the end of the Mahoosuc Range (see Hike #19). The view of Berlin, on the Androscoggin River in the west, will attract hikers eager to return to civilization and likewise repel those enjoying the Mahoosucs' isolated ambiance.

The most likely explanation for this mountain's unusual name is that it evolved from "goose high"—a reference to the peak's height compared with the altitude of the birds migrating from Rangely Lakes. In October be prepared to duck for geese as you cross its three summits.

From its junction with Goose Eye Trail, the AT/Mahoosuc Trail makes a pleasant ridge run over slabs and scrub to the east. At 2.1 mi., the south fork of the Wright Trail descends 2.5 mi. east to its northern branch and 1.5 mi. farther to Sunday River Rd. Immediately after the junction the AT makes a steep, rocky climb to the open east peak of Goose Eye Mt. (3794 ft.), where the path makes a slow 90-degree curve at 2.2 mi. Quartz blocks atop the cairns here are whiter than the trail blazes painted on the slabs. Both lead to the north side of the summit, which is covered with the snowy crystals.

The AT plunges from the summit over slabs so treacherously steep, smooth, and slick you may be forced to descend in a crab crawl that will leave you wishing you had boot soles on the heels of your hands.

At the bottom of the descent, at 2.3 mi., the northern fork of Wright Trail descends 1.5 mi. east to the south fork. Here the AT drops into the marshy sag, climbs over a knob, then drops onto a large subalpine heath pocked with tundra bogs. This spooky moor high in the ominous Mahoosucs makes it easy to see why Stephen King sets so many of his macabre novels in Maine. The valley falling away to the west—Success Township, NH—only makes the scene seem more remote. The next heath bald crossed by the AT appears close, but recedes into the distance as you walk toward it. Before reaching it, the path drops into a ravine where water can often be found, then climbs back onto the tundralike heath.

Labrador tea, which has thick evergreen leaves with wooly undersides and small white flowers in June, and bog laurel, which has shiny green leaves with white undersides and pink flowers in June and July, are the dominant species on the heaths of the Mahoosucs. Black crowberry, which shows black berries atop an evergreen mat, and bog bilberry, which has round, toothless blue leaves and blue berries, bloom here in late spring and early summer. A variety of grasslike plants such as Bigelow's sedge, cotton sedge, and highland rush are found on the heaths along with reindeer lichen, Iceland lichen, and several types of sphagnum mosses.

Most of these plants would normally have difficuly surviving at this low elevation, but the Mahoosucs provide an unusual cooling system to keep them from withering in the summer heat. Below the moss lies peat—the partially decomposed remains of plants, and, to some degree, animals—which freezes into lenses more than 12 in. thick. The sphagnum insulates the peat, which stays frozen through the summer growing season and in turn cools the root systems of the plants that grow above it, allowing tundra species to survive at a lower altitude and a higher temperature than their habitat in the Presidential Range.

The heath fades into bogland in areas where rainwater collects in depressions and kettle holes carved by the Wisconsin Glacier into the bedrock. The soils in bogs are also made up of peat. Organic material decomposes slowly in water, and since the water in a bog isn't moving, the peat accumulates and the water eventually becomes oxygen-poor and dark. The bogs are highly acidic and low in nutrients, so only a few plants can thrive in them. Bog laurel, hare's-tale cotton grass, deer's-hair sedge, bog sedge, and sundew can be found in and around the bogs. Wren's-egg cranberries thrive in areas where water pools, and baked apple berry, or cloudberry, a plant seldom seen outside Alaska in the U.S., is common here. In Finland the red and yellow berries of cloudberry are harvested to make a liqueur.

The heath balds and tundra bogs atop Mahoousuc, Goose Eye, and Carlo mountains are designated as critical areas by the Maine State Planning Office to help protect the unusual and delicate vegetation found on them.

At 3.4 mi. the path climbs to the north peak of Goose Eye Mt. (3680 ft.), where it might appear to vanish. Ignore the ledges drawing you to the left, and watch for easily missed cairns, then a pair of blazes on a rock, that lead to the right to another harrowingly steep and rocky descent eastward.

At 3.8 mi. the AT/Mahoosuc Trail drops below the northern treeline of Goose Eye Mt. and descends into a tight maze of spruce and fir trees. Shoulder-width corridors through the dense woods and shin-deep mud in the footpath can make for slow going as the trail descends to the north.

Near the bottom of a depression at 4.4 mi., a ladder on the right climbs to the top of a large ledge, atop which is Full Goose Shelter, which has its own legend of the fowl: When the moon wanted to attend a party, the plaque inside the shelter notes, a goose volunteered to cover for it. Hikers that night saw a full goose rather than a full moon.

The long, open faced shelter has space for twelve, while platforms outside will hold four tents. A side trail leads to water 250 ft. southeast of the shelter.

During a very wet hike through the Mahoosucs in early October, two thru-hikers joined us, Conrad the Caterpillar and Okeepa, in Full Goose Shelter. Overnight the rain turned to snow and the temperature dropped to the low 20s. We awoke to find our clothes, wet from the night before, now frozen stiff. Icy wool socks had the weight and density of two-by-fours, hiking pants stood up on their own, and, worst of all, our boots were covered with an inch of ice inside and out. After carefully thawing our clothes over camp stoves for nearly 2 hours, Conrad the Caterpillar smiled and sang out the phrase that had become his hiking mantra: "You've got to suffer to hike the AT. It's going to be a great day!"

The northbound AT/Mahoosuc Trail turns left at the shelter, descends briefly, then begins a moderately steep climb up Fulling Mill Mt. The trail climbs out of the trees about halfway up the mountain and reaches its bald South Peak, approximately 3395 ft., at 4.9 mi. The AT turns left near the top, then crosses a heath before beginning a steepening descent through the trees toward the head of Mahoosuc Notch.

At 5.9 mi., near the bottom of the descent, the AT/Mahoosuc Trail reaches a junction at the western end of Mahoosuc Notch. Here the Mahoosuc Notch Trail descends to the west, reaching Success Pond Rd. in 2.5 mi., while the AT turns sharp right and charges into the Notch. If you have fine weather and a few hours to spare, consider following the AT in. You will have to return by retracing your route, so you can stash your pack here, which will ease your climbing and crawling considerably. (See Hike #18 for details of the AT's route through Mahoosuc Notch.)

At the trail junction, Hike #17 departs the AT and descends moderately to the west on the Mahoosuc Notch Trail, which follows the Bull Branch of the Sunday River flowing out from the Notch. Hikers can thank the AMC and Mead Paper, two organizations that have not historically been allies, for the quality of the footpath here. In 1997 and 1998 Mead, the landowner here, and the AMC split the $14,000 bill for improvements and repairs to six badly eroded trails in the Mahoosucs, inlcuding the Notch Trail, Goose Eye Trail, and Speck Pond Trail. Earlier cooperative arrangements between the AMC and the Brown Company and the James River Company replaced decaying shelters, constructed tent platforms, and installed steps and water bars on the trails of the Mahoosucs. The muddy but mellow footpath curves to the right near a fork in the brook and eventually crosses the brook. Soon the trail steps onto logging roads that descend gradually back into the hardwoods beside the lazy brook. At 2.2 mi. from the AT, the trail turns sharp right onto a spur road that leads to a parking area in 0.3 mi., for a total hike of 11.0 mi. The spur road continues another 0.3 mi. past the parking area to Success Pond Rd.

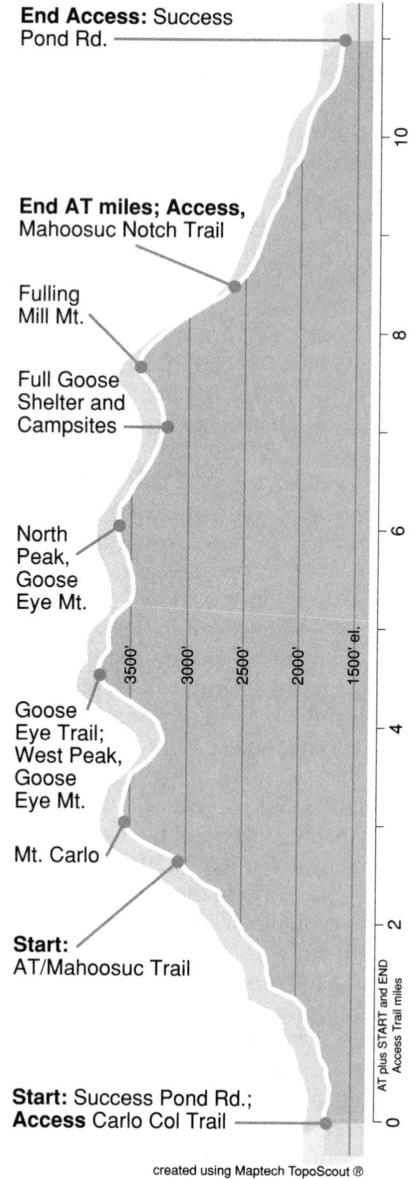

Mahoosuc Notch El. 2500'
End AT miles, Notch Trail
Full Goose
Notch Trailhead, Success Pond Rd. Ⓟ El. 1575'
North Peak, Goose Eye Mt., El. 3675'
West Peak, Goose Eye Mt., El. 3854' V Goose Eye Trail
Carlo Col/Goose Eye Trailhead, Success Pond Rd. Ⓟ El. 1620'
Mt. Carlo, El. 3565'
Carlo Col
Start AT miles, Carlo Col Trail
ME/NH State Line
7/8" = 1 mi.
N
Fulling Mill Mountain
South Peak
Mahoosuc
North Peak
Goose Eye Mountain
Mount Carlo
Carlo Col
OXFORD CO
COOS CO
GOOSE EYE TRAIL
SCENIC

HIKE #17 Itinerary

Miles N	NORTH	Elev. (ft/m)	Miles S
Total: 11.0 mi. with access trails			
2.5	Access: **Mahoosuc Notch Trail** to **Success Pond Rd.,** parking.	1620/494	2.5
5.9	**End AT miles:** Turn W on Mahoosuc Notch Trail.		0.0
4.9	**Fulling Mill Mt.**	3395/1035	1.0
4.4	**Full Goose Shelter and Campsites,** tent sites.		1.5
3.8	Treeline on **Goose Eye Mt.**		2.1
3.4	North peak of **Goose Eye Mt.**	3680/1122	2.5
2.3	North fork of **Wright Trail.**		3.6
2.1	South fork of **Wright Trail.**		3.8
1.8	**Goose Eye Trail,** early exit option at **West Peak, Goose Eye Mt.**	3854/1175	4.1
0.4	**Mt. Carlo.**	3565/1087	5.5
0.0	**Start AT miles:** Junction with AT/Mahoosuc Trail. Follow AT N.		5.9
2.6	Access: **Carlo Col Trail** from Success Pond Rd., parking. Pass **Carlo Col Shelter and Campsite** at 2.3 mi.	1620/494	2.6

SOUTH

HIKE #18

Mahoosuc Notch

Maps: ATC N.H. and Vt. #1

Route: From Success Pond Rd. up Notch Trail to AT/Mahoosuc Trail, through Mahoosuc Notch, over Mahoosuc Arm, to Speck Pond, then down Speck Pond Trail to Success Pond Rd.

Recommended direction: S to N

Distance: 9.4 mi.; 3.6 mi. on AT

Access trails name & length: Mahoosuc Notch Trail, 2.5 mi.; Speck Pond Trail, 3.3 mi.

Elevation +/-: 1575 to 3765 to 1620 ft.

Effort: Very strenuous

Day hike: Yes

Overnight backpacking hike: Optional

Duration: Dayhike – 10 to 12 hr.

Early exit option: None

Natural history features: Boulder-filled glacial valley; pond filling glacial hollow

Social history feature: Lucia & Marion Pychowska, first explorers of the Notch

Trailhead access: *Start:* From Gorham, take NH 16 4.5 mi. N. Cross Cleveland Bridge over Androscoggin River. Follow Unity St. L, then R at 0.8 mi. across railroad tracks, where it becomes Hutchins St. After another 0.8 mi. turn L and pass James River mill yard. Turn R on unmarked street, follow this 0.2 mi., and then turn L onto Success Pond Rd. Go 10.9 mi. to a side road on R, which leads 0.3 mi. to Notch Trail parking.

End: From parking at Notch Trail, return to Success Pond Rd., turn R and drive 1.5 mi. N to a fork in road. Take R fork and continue 0.8 mi. to Speck Pond trailhead. *Note:* For Success Pond Rd. details, see Trailhead Access, Hike #16.

Camping: Speck Pond Shelter and Campsite

Is Mahoosuc Notch really the "Toughest Mile of the AT?" Although selecting just one of the 2150-odd miles of the AT might seem impossibly subjective, every AT hiker will eventually hear the reputation of Mahoosuc Notch. Tales of this underworld inspire northbound hikers to hole up at the nearest shelter (Full Goose Shelter, 1.5 mi. south of the Notch) like knights preparing to enter a dragon's lair. Most of these hikers find that their battle with this monstrous notch is not, however, the "toughest mile" of their hikes on the AT. In fact, many find it to be one of the most enjoyable. A few, upon climbing out of this natural obstacle course, will take off their backpacks, turn around, and dive right back in to continue their explorations of its fascinating wonderland of caves and crevices.

Glaciers cut this steep-walled valley between Fulling Mill Mt. and Mahoosuc Mt. After the river of ice

Michael Kodas

Squeezing through Mahoosuc Notch

retreated, winter freezes quarried huge blocks of rock from the cliffs, and the blocks tumbled into the notch below, filling it with the house-size chunks of schist that have given this piece of the AT its reputation for ruggedness and put it on the National Register of Natural Landmarks. Hikers here must climb over, crawl under, and jump between these huge slabs and boulders. Many remove their backpacks and drag them in order to pass through the tightest squeezes. Some of the caves hold ice well into summer, and snow often makes the notch impassable even in June. The gurgling of a small stream, the Bull Branch of the Sunday River, buried beneath the rubble, enhances the notch's air of mystery.

For many northbound hikers, the Notch is the climax of a traverse of the entire Mahoosuc Range—a final challenge to their already taxed muscles. Hike #18, on the other hand, lets the less ambitious (and those who don't have a week to spare) sneak in a back door to the AT's wild ride through Mahoosuc Notch. The hike's route continues on to the summit of Mahoosuc Arm, one of the range's rugged peaks, and to Speck Pond, a high mountain glacial tarn and home to a beautiful campsite. From here the route leads back to Success Pond Rd., 2 mi. north of the starting point.

Although this 9.4-mi. hike is well within the range of a fit day hiker, an overnight at Speck Pond Campsite will allow time to explore both Mahoosuc Notch and Speck Pond at a comfortable pace. (Day hikers looking for a shorter walk can make a 7.0-mi. round-trip in and out on Mahoosuc Notch Trail.)

Whether you plan an overnight or a single day's adventure, approach Mahoosuc Notch with the sturdy waterproof footwear, warm clothing, map, first-aid kit, flashlight, food, and water that its reputation demands. Most important, head into this hike armed with plenty of time. Although the notch is only a mile long, it usually takes 2 hours or more to pass through, and those intimidated or enchanted by the rocky labyrinth might spend the better part of a day there.

From the parking area, Mahoosuc Notch Trail follows the spur road 0.3 mi. farther across bridges over Shelter Brook, then, at a marked junction, turns left onto a logging road that climbs gently along the lazy brook. Most of the difficulties of this trail are provided by the perpetually muddy footing, although some of these may be alleviated by significant improvements and repairs made through the cooperative efforts of the AMC and Mead Paper, which owns the land. The grade gradually increases during the next 2.2 mi., but it never hints at the challenges to come.

Mahoosuc Notch Trail crosses the brook near a fork, curves gradually to the right, follows another fork in the brook to the left for 0.3 mi., then climbs out of the valley to its junction with the AT/Mahoosuc Trail at 2.5 mi.

Turn left onto the northbound AT at the junction (where our mileage count begins). With your first few strides on the AT, the gentle valley is transformed into a rock-walled chamber. The soaring 800-ft. cliffs of Fulling Mill Mt., on the right, and Mahoosuc Mt., on the left, will have you gazing skyward in amazement —until the city of rock that has fallen from their sides forces you to watch where you're putting your feet. The AT/Mahoosuc Trail jogs right and drops steeply into a passage that opens amid the otherwise impassible jumble of rock into the narrow boulder-filled notch. If you're lucky, you'll meet a southbound hiker who'll reassure you with the obligatory "It's not that bad." Believe it anyway, take a deep breath, and drop into the blocky cavern that will lead to the hike of your life.

For the next mile the AT/Mahoosuc Trail climbs over, crawls under, squeezes between, slides down, and jumps among the huge rocks. Blazes and arrows are painted on the boulders to mark the route, and some of the most difficult sections offer the option of going over or under an obstacle—others appear to provide no way to pass at all. Even on a bright day, much of the notch is dark and filled with spooky shadows. For the sake of both safety and fun, it's important to take your time here. Slabs are often wet, smaller rocks are occasionally loose, deep holes are sometimes hidden, and slick ice can be found in the deepest caves even in the summer. Many of the ascents border on actual rock climbing, with the risk of serious falls. Partners should be prepared to spot each other, reach out hands for pull-ups, and pass packs between one another.

The rocky scrambles through Mahoosuc Notch and the rugged climbs atop Goose Eye Mt. and Carlo Col might make you wonder which hardy woodsmen were the first to explore these formidable mountains. Most are surprised to learn that the first thorough investigations of the Mahoosuc Range were not made by men at all. The flamboyant mother-and-daughter team of Lucia and Marian Pychowska, two of the leading members of the Randolph, New Hampshire hiking circle, made extensive explorations of the Mahoosuc Range in the late 1870s. In 1879 both Pychowkas presented papers detailing their investigations to the AMC. Marian Pychowska would later produce the first detailed map of the Northern Presidential Range.

Halfway through the notch the difficulties ease briefly as the AT becomes walkable for a few hundred feet before again dropping into another rocky playscape. A rich variety of mosses, rock lichens, and moisture-loving ferns cling to the stones. Small spruce, birch, and beech trees growing on the rocks hint at their stability. The trees might provide an occasional handhold or foothold, but beware of stepping on the moss, which may give way into a hole in the rocks. Dead trees and fallen timber create snags that add to the difficulties.

At 1.1 mi. the AT/Mahoosuc Trail climbs out of the last of the boulder caverns and turns sharp left just as it arrives at a clearing along Bull Branch, a convenient and beautiful lunch site. The old fire rings here indicate that some hikers have developed more than a lunchtime relationship with the clearing. If you carefully search the woods on the east side of the notch, you may find an unusual 250-year-old stand of yellow birch.

From the notch side of the clearing, follow the AT/Mahoosuc Trail uphill to the north (the trail may be difficult to find—look for a giant boulder on the right). The path climbs sidehill up the eastern flank of Mahoosuc Mt. and through the valley between Mahoosuc Mt. and Mahoosuc Arm, then swings right to cross a brook. If

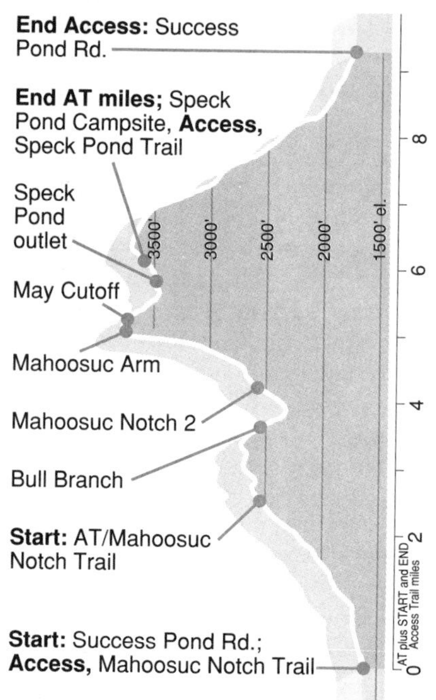

created using Maptech TopoScout ®

you like, follow the brook upstream to the left for approximately 0.3 mi. to Mahoosuc Notch Two, a miniature version of the original.

From the brook crossing the AT/Mahoosuc Trail steepens dramatically as it climbs over slick slabs and sheer ledges on a rough footpath up the southwest slope of Mahoosuc Arm. At 2.7 mi. the trail climbs onto flat ledges near the summit of Mahoosuc Arm (3765 ft.), which looks off to Old Speck and northeastern Maine. (The May Cutoff veers left off the AT/Mahoosuc Trail at 2.8 mi., passes over

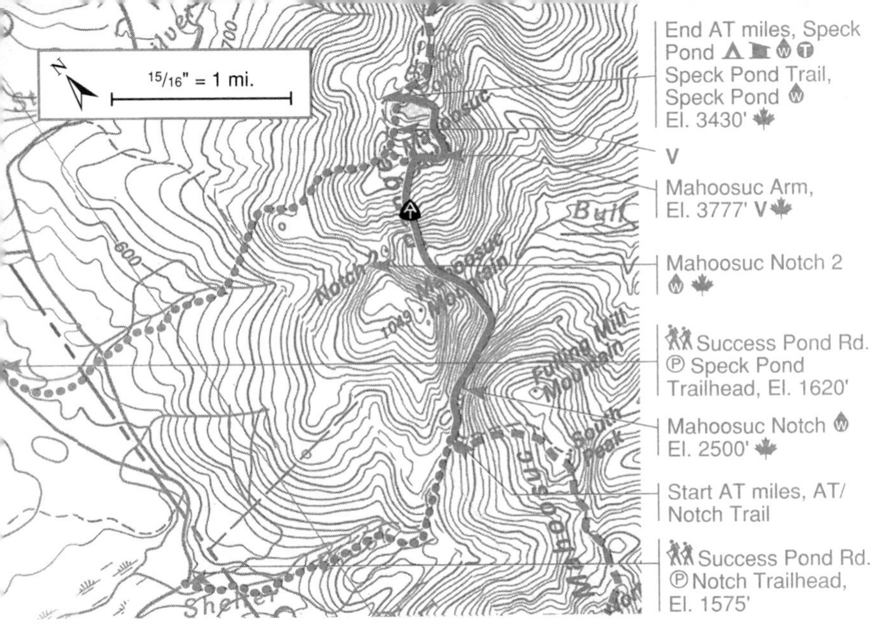

the mountain's summit, and in 0.3 mi. intersects Speck Pond Trail.)

At the May Cutoff the AT turns right, then makes a long left-curving descent of the summit plateau and finally plunges steeply to Speck Pond, a gorgeous glacial tarn surrounded by thick spruce-fir forests in the hollow between Mahoosuc Arm and Old Speck Mt.

The AT/Mahoosuc Trail steps across the outlet of the pond, then follows the eastern bank to a trail junction where the AMC's Speck Pond Campsite is situated, at 3.6 mi. Its shelter holds ten guests, and there are five tent platforms nearby and a privy. During the summer, a fee is charged and an AMC caretaker is present. Water is available from a nearby spring or the pond. Speck Pond is the only AMC facility out of radio range. The caretakers must climb to the top of Mahoosuc Arm each morning to make their regular transmissions to Pinkham Notch.

This scenic tarn, at 3430 ft. the highest pond in the state, is nestled in a rich forest. The AT/Mahoosuc Trail, Speck Pond Trail, and May Cutoff form a 1.7-mi. loop that circles the pond and climbs back to the summit of Mahoosuc Arm. Look for carnivorous plants, such as sundew and pitcher plant, along the shore, and watch for yellow-rumped warblers, black-throated green warblers, white-throated sparrows, and dark-eyed juncoes in the trees. Bear and moose also live in the area.

From the Speck Pond Campsite, Hike #18 leaves the AT/Mahoosuc Trail and follows Speck Pond Trail, which is considerably more difficult than the Notch Trail access route, for 3.3 mi. Be sure to leave time in your plans for this final leg of the trip. Speck Pond Trail initially climbs steeply from the campsite to a stunning overlook of the pond. Then, 0.5 mi. from the pond and 6.6 mi. into the hike, the May Cutoff diverges to the left to the summit of Mahoosuc Arm. Continue on Speck Pond Trail as it descends in several steep pitches to a small brook, which the trail follows to the right during the final 1.4 mi. to Success Pond Rd.

Those who didn't leave a second car at the Speck Pond trailhead will need to walk 0.8 mi. down the road from the trailhead to its junction with Success Pond Rd., then turn left and continue 0.5 mi. to another spur road that leads 0.3 mi. to the Mahoosuc Notch Trail parking area.

HIKE #18 Itinerary

Miles N	NORTH	Elev. (ft/m)	Miles S
Total: 9.4 mi. with access trails			
3.3	Access: **Speck Pond Trail** to Success Pond Rd., parking.	1620/494	3.3
3.6	**End AT miles: Speck Pond Campsite,** shelter, water, fee and caretaker in summer.		0.0
3.3	Outlet of **Speck Pond.**	3430/1045	0.3
2.8	**May Cutoff** leads 0.3 mi. over summit to Speck Pond Trail.		0.8
2.7	Summit of **Mahoosuc Arm, views.**	3765/1148	0.9
1.7	Brook leads to **Mahoosuc Notch Two.**		1.9
1.1	Clearing, Bull Branch, picnic site.		2.5
0.0	**Start AT miles:** Junction with **AT/Mahoosuc Notch Trail.** Turn L onto AT. "Most Difficult" mile begins; boulders and slabs for 1.0 mi.	2500/762	3.6
2.5	Access: From **Success Pond Rd.,** parking, follow **Mahoosuc Notch Trail** along Shelter Brook.	1575/480	2.5

HIKE #19

Old Speck

Maps: ATC N.H. and Vt. #1, Me. #7
Route: Circuit hike from Grafton Notch to summit of Old Speck and back to Grafton Notch
Recommended direction: N to S
Distance: 7.6 mi. (8.4 mi. with loop trails); 5.6 mi. on AT
Access trail names & length: Mahoosuc Trail, 0.3 mi.; East Spur Trail, 1.0 mi. and Link Trail, 0.3 mi. (optional); Eyebrow Trail, 1.2 mi. (optional)
Elevation +/-: 1500 to 4180 to 1500 ft.
Effort: Strenuous
Day hike: Yes
Overnight backpacking hike: Optional
Duration: 8 to 10 hr.
Early exit option: None
Natural history features: Highest peak in Mahoosuc Range; cliff-edge walks on Eyebrow Trail; Cascade Falls
Other features: Old Speck fire tower
Trailhead access: *Start and End:* Grafton Notch State Park, on ME 26, 12 mi. NW of US 2, 18 mi. NW of Bethel, and 7.5 mi. SE of Upton. Park in hikers' parking area on W side of road.
Camping: Speck Pond Shelter and Campsite

You might expect the name "Old Speck" to be attached to a friendly grizzled dog rather than to the highest peak of the ferocious Mahoosuc Range, and in some ways Old Speck, Maine's third-highest peak, *is* friendlier than the rest of the range. The AT is generally in better condition and easier to follow here than in the more remote wilds of the Mahoosucs, and many hikers find that having their car only 3.8 mi. away from the summit of Old Speck encourages them to take up the mountain's invitation for further exploration.

Beware, however, of Old Speck's bite, for its trails are steep, rocky, and often slick.

From the north side of the Grafton Notch parking area, head west on the AT/Old Speck Trail. The path climbs gently into the woods, and at 0.1 mi. reaches a junction with Eyebrow Trail, which heads right, traverses the top of the Eyebrow, an 800-ft. cliff, then rejoins the AT/Old Speck Trail 1.1 mi. farther on. You'll be coming back this way, so save this dramatic optional loop for the return trip.

From the junction, the AT/Old Speck Trail continues to climb gradually through the forest of beech, birch, and occasional sugar maples. The trail crosses a brook, then follows it and begins to climb a series of long steepening switchbacks up the southern side of the Eyebrow.

Near the top of the switchbacks, the trail skirts the falls of Cascade Brook, which is bordered by lush ferns, mosses, and small birch trees. At 1.1 mi. the AT heads right and crosses a brook that is the last reliable source of water this side of Old Speck. At 1.2 mi. Eyebrow Trail rejoins the AT/Old Speck Trail. The AT/Old Speck Trail cuts left here and climbs to the crest of North Ridge at 1.5 mi., then follows the ridge to the southwest. The North Ridge quickly carries the AT into the higher-elevation forest of spruce and fir trees. Gray jays, spruce grouse, and boreal chickadees—alpine birds that are rare elsewhere in Maine—are common in the woods here. The boreal owl, another species that is rare in this region, is suspected to live in the spruce forests on the west side of the mountain.

The AT swings to the left, and at 3.0 mi. crosses a col; you've now climbed about 1800 ft. Then the trail climbs south up the ridgeline, reaching Link Trail, on the left, at 3.1 mi. From this junction the AT continues up the ridge and at 3.4 mi. climbs steeply onto the summit ridge, where it joins Mahoosuc Trail at 3.5 mi.

This day hike departs from the AT here, but many ambitious hikers can't resist the temptation to continue on the AT for 1.1 mi. to Speck Pond, one of the loveliest tarns in Maine, and the highest. That detour, however, will add at least 2.2 mi. (more if you go exploring) of steep walking to the day's tally and should be taken only by those with time and energy to spare (see Hike #18 for a description of Speck Pond). Backpackers could spend the night at Speck Pond Campsite, then retrace their steps to Grafton Notch (a round-trip of 9.2 mi.). Another option is to shuttle a car to Success Pond Rd., then exit the Mahoosucs on Speck Pond Trail (7.9 mi. total) or follow the AT over Mahoosuc Arm and through fabulous Mahoosuc Notch to Mahoosuc Notch Trail, which also leads to Success Pond Rd. (10.7 mi. total). See Hike #18.

Those who choose not to visit the pond will stop worrying about what they're missing during the mellow stroll to the enchanting summit of Old Speck. From the junction of Mahoosuc and Old Speck trails, Mahoosuc Trail leaves the AT and climbs gradually 0.3 mi. east to the summit. The subalpine summit of Old Speck has an unusual mix of characteristics from both lower and higher elevations. Some of the spruce and fir trees scattered along the ridgeline have been gnarled and stunted by wind and ice, but others still stand straight. Between the trees are small heaths where Labrador tea, Bigelow's sedge, black crowberry, mountain cranberry, and the occasional blueberry bush can be found. The forests that descend westward to Speck Pond are pocketed with stands of old-growth spruce.

The observation tower atop the summit of Old Speck is now closed, but the views from ground level at the clearing are spectacular enough.

At your feet are Speck Pond, just west of southwest, and Mahoosuc Notch, just south of southwest. Above them rise the peaks of the Mahoosuc, Presidential, and Franconia ranges. The northern horizon is serrated by Mt. Saddle, Mt. Magantic, and Mt. Gosford, all more than 50 mi. away in Québec.

The overlook also offers some insight into the name of the mountain. Two other peaks—one due south and another east by southeast—are called Speckled Mt., a popular name for mountains whose sides are spotted with rocky ledges and cliffs. Locals becan calling this peak "Old Speck" to distinguish it from the other Speckled mountains in the region.

Finally, glances to both north and south from the summmit provide an interesting perspective on the Androscoggin River. The large lake that spreads out in the valley just west of due north is Lake Umbagog, the source of the Androscoggin. The river bends around the New Hampshire side of the Mahoosucs, then heads east across Maine to Merrymeeting Bay, near Brunswick, on the Atlantic. You can see the river in the the southeast, just left of the Sunday River ski area. When you've taken it all in, retrace your steps to the AT or follow the East Spur down to the Link Trail.

Many hikers will want to head back down Mahoosuc Trail to Old Speck Trail, reversing their route for a straightforward return to Grafton Notch. In that case, retrace your route on the AT/Old Speck Trail north to the upper junction with Eyebrow Trail at 6.4 mi. At that point you can decide whether you want to follow Eyebrow Trail for this hike's second optional addition. Both loops are described below.

The AT/Old Speck Trail reaches the parking area on ME 26 at 7.6 mi. (8.4 if you took both loops; 9.8 if you also went to Speck Pond and the summit). If there is some daylight to spare, consider visiting Screw Auger Falls Gorge, Mother Walker Falls Gorge, or Moose Cave Gorge, all of which are located on ME 26 in Grafton Notch State Park, south of the AT.

Old Speck Loop

Those shopping for a wilder return should consider following East Spur and Link trails down from the summit of Old Speck. The two side trails combine for a strenuous and scenic trip, meeting Old Speck Trail in 1.3 mi. This steep and obscure path is both strenuous to hike and difficult to follow, so allow plenty of time for this short adventure, and avoid it with novice hikers or in wet weather.

East Spur Trail follows blue blazes 30 yd. north of the summit of Old Speck and descends to the northeast through scrub, past the first of countless vistas over the mountains of Maine—including Saddleback, which the AT crosses 34 miles to the northeast (see Hike #24). The trail here slaloms through dwarf balsam firs and glacier-strewn boulders covered

Salamanders Rule

In a truly democratic Appalachian forest, where votes depended on weight (biomass) and ecological importance, salamanders would rule. Salamanders? Yes, those shy, slippery little critters that come out only when there's more water in the air than air and otherwise stay under rocks.

Salamanders eat insects, insect larvae (especially mosquitoes and gnats), worms, spiders, and other goodies, and, in turn, feed snakes, birds, fish, mammals, bigger spiders, frogs, and other predators. Most salamanders taste pretty good to predators such as water snakes, snapping turtles, many fish, and many birds and mammals. They escape (or delay) predation by fleeing or hiding. A few unsporting types, such as the red-spotted newt, have poisonous skin with warning colors and hike boldly along the trails like little orange dinosaurs. Look for other salamanders under rocks or logs, sunning in the spray zones of waterfalls, or dancing in forest ponds before the ice has even melted. (They can't sing like frogs, so they dance to attract mates.)

Salamanders exploit both water and dry-land habitats—an advantage of the amphibious lifestyle. They are active when there are plenty of insects and sleep when there are not. More kinds of salamanders live in the Appalachians than anywhere else in the world because these ancient mountains provide so many forested habitats and an abundance of water and food. Many salamanders are lungless and get oxygen through their skins and by pumping air into their mouths. Studies of salamanders provide information on forest health, evolution of species, regeneration, embryological development, animal behavior, and the workings of vertebrate nervous systems, including our own.

We humans, who use so much energy to maintain a constant body temperature, think of warm bloodedness as an advanced condition. However, salamanders, who were here long before we arrived, outweigh us in the ecosystem, do not pollute or build strip malls, and will probably outlast us, if we don't destroy their habitats along with our own.

—Doris Gove

with a rich variety of lichens, including map lichen, rusty rock lichen, target lichen, and reindeer lichen. Below you stretches Grafton Notch, which was probably the outlet for a lake that formed between the Mahoosuc Range and the retreating glacier. The glacier and its runoff left a gap with a flat floor and steep walls that are spotted with the sheer cliffs that gave Old Speck its name. Water continues to carve Grafton Notch at sites like Screw Auger Falls Gorge, just off ME 26 south of the AT, where the

Bear River has cut fantastic twists and bowls through the granite.

The show continues as East Spur Trail curves to the right and plunges over open ledges with exceptional views and precarious descents, passing a huge peaked boulder on the right as it drops into woods of spruce and firs. The path crosses more open ledges with plenty of views, then begins a long swing to the left over the ridgeline and descends steeply to the west, crossing a brook and meeting Link Trail at the site of an old fire warden's cabin, 1.0 mi. below the summit of Old Speck and 4.8 mi. into the hike. (Be careful to avoid the abandoned fire warden's trail, once a link in the AT, which can be seen dropping to the north here, down a ravine to ME 26.) Follow Link Trail, which fortunately is well marked with blue blazes as it climbs steeply 0.3 mi. west to rejoin the AT/Old Speck Trail.

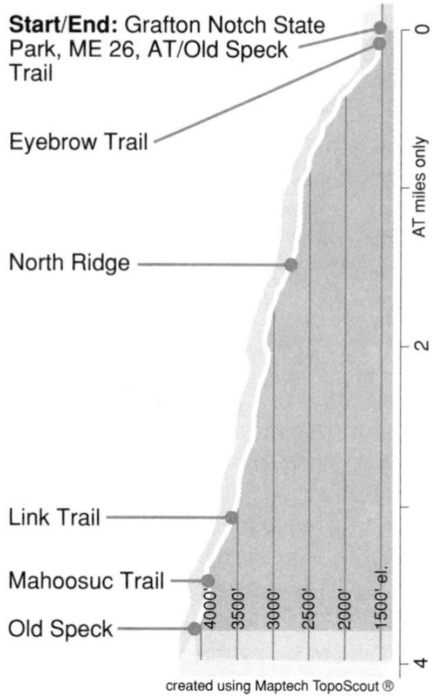

Eyebrow Trail

The Eyebrow Trail detour rejoins the AT/Old Speck Trail 0.1 mi. from the ME 26 parking lot, making this rock face the perfect capstone for your hike on Old Speck. The 1.2-mi. trail, which traverses the largest of the ledges that speckle Old Speck, is far better marked and somewhat easier to hike than East Spur Trail, but the rock scrambles are hazardous in wet or icy weather. The towering cliff provides excellent views of the north end of Grafton Notch and spectacular perches from which to watch for birds riding the thermal updrafts.

From the AT/Old Speck Trail, turn left (northeast) onto Eyebrow Trail, which runs level for 0.1 mi. to the first outlook atop the majestic 800-ft. cliff. From here the trail climbs slightly, then descends at a moderate grade along the top of the cliff, with head-

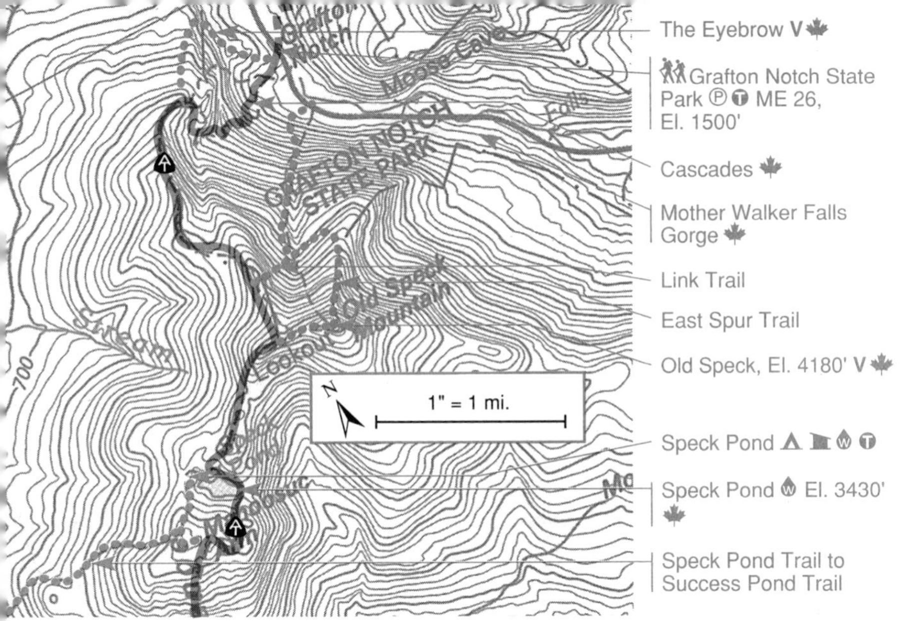

The Eyebrow V

Grafton Notch State Park Ⓟ ME 26, El. 1500'

Cascades

Mother Walker Falls Gorge

Link Trail

East Spur Trail

Old Speck, El. 4180' V

1" = 1 mi.

Speck Pond

Speck Pond El. 3430'

Speck Pond Trail to Success Pond Trail

turning overlooks, until it turns right and descends, then turns left at a spur trail to another outlook. After crossing a difficult talus slide of rocks broken loose from the crags above, Eyebrow Trail reaches the base of the cliff, where it turns left and rejoins the AT/Old Speck Trail at 8.3 mi.

HIKE #19 Itinerary

Miles N	Circuit Hike	Elev. (ft/m)	Miles S
Total: 7.6 mi. round-trip; 8.4 mi. with both loop trails			
	Start: Old Speck parking area in **Grafton Notch State Park,** ME 26. Head W on **AT/Old Speck Trail.**	1500/457	0.0
	Lower junction with **Eyebrow Trail.**		0.1
	Cross brook.		1.1
	Upper junction with **Eyebrow Trail.**		1.2
	Crest of **North Ridge.**		1.5
	Col.		3.0
	Junction with **Link Trail.**		3.1
	Junction of **Mahoosuc Trail** and **Old Speck Trail.** Follow Mahoosuc Trail E off AT.		3.5
	Summit of **Old Speck,** views. (**Optional:** Follow East Spur Trail, then Link Trail, for strenuous 1.3-mi. loop back to AT.)	4180/1274	3.8
	Reverse direction. Go north. Read from bottom up.		
7.6	**End:** Old Speck parking area in **Grafton Notch State Park,** ME 26.	1500/457	
7.5	Lower junction with **Eyebrow Trail**		
6.5	Cross brook.		
6.4	Upper junction with **Eyebrow Trail.** (**Optional:** Follow Eyebrow Trail for 1.2-mi. loop back to AT.)		
6.1	Crest of **North Ridge.**		
4.6	Col.		
4.5	Junction with **Link Trail.**		
4.1	Junction of **Mahoosuc Trail** and **Old Speck Trail.**		

Circuit Hike

HIKE # 20

Baldpate Mt.

Maps: Maine AT Club, #7
Route: From ME 26 at Grafton Notch to West Baldpate and East Baldpate Mts. and return
Recommended direction: S to N
Distance: 8 mi. round trip
Elevation +/-: 1500 to 3812 to 1500 ft.
Effort: Strenuous
Day hike: Yes
Overnight backpacking hike: Optional
Duration: 5 to 6 hr.
Natural history features: Table Rock; exposed alpine areas
Trailhead access: From Bethel drive 6 mi. N on US 2, then 12 mi. farther N on ME 26 to AT parking on W side of ME 26. AT trailhead is 0.1 mi. N.
Camping: Baldpate Lean-to

Capt. Farrar's 1880 guidebook to the Rangeley region mentions a blazed path up Baldpate but states clearly that "if you have not considerable experience in woodcraft, the chances are ten to one you will lose it." Much has changed since Farrar's day, and the trail through Baldpate is popular and well marked, making it a good choice for strong hikers looking for a pleasant day hike.

Baldpate Mt. is in western Oxford County, roughly 7 mi. east of Grafton Notch and the beautiful state park by the same name. The parking lot for the Baldpate hike is on the west side of ME 26 in Grafton Notch, under the imposing cliffs of the Eyebrow on Old Speck (see Hike #19).

The trail up Baldpate heads east from ME 26, traveling first through a low marshy area and crossing a log footbridge over the headwaters of the Bear River. A few minutes beyond the brook, at 0.1 mi., the first of several side trails leading to Table Rock leaves on the right. In season, the hooded flowers of jack in the pulpit grow along the trail here, although you might miss them if you don't look carefully. More noticeable are the imposing yellow birch along this section of the trail, some of them more than 30 in. in diameter. If you are not familiar with this species, look at the branches at the top, which retain their characteristic smooth bark; the bark on the trunk of old trees separates into thick scaly plates. The cambium layer of young twigs of yellow birch has a pleasant wintergreen scent, and can be chewed or used for tea.

Beyond the first junction with the Table Rock trail, the AT leads uphill, steeply at times, through mixed woods dotted with mature red spruce. At 0.8 mi., the upper end of the Table Rock Loop meets the trail

The White-Throated Sparrow

In *Don Quixote,* Cervantes wrote, "One swallow never makes a summer." Along the length of the AT in New Hampshire and Maine, however, one white-throated sparrow does make a spring. The bravado of other earlier-arriving species fades when a late-season storm shows that winter hasn't quite departed, but the first *Sam-peabody-peabody-peabody* of the white-throated sparrow means spring is here to stay. A member of the finch family, these sparrows are small and dully camouflaged in brown and gray. They thrive on seeds.

The white-throated sparrow loves to sing. When we were camped on the summit of Baldpate one night, a male sparrow sang past dusk and straight through the night.

"This was the prevailing bird in the northern part of Maine," wrote Thoreau after one of his several trips to Maine in the mid-1800s. "The forest generally was alive with them at this season, and they were proportionally numerous and musical about Bangor. Their simple *ah te-te-te, te-te-te, te-te-te,* so sharp and piercing, was as distinct to the ear as the passage of a spark of fire shot into the darkness of the forest would be to the eye."

—Andrew Weegar

on the right. At the end of this hike, you will be retracing your steps through here: If there is time on the way back, the trail to Table Rock, scrambling over giant boulders part of the way, makes a fine side trip. Table Rock, an enormous overhanging cliff face, juts out over the valley and offers fine views of Old Speck. The Table Rock trail is a 1.5-mile loop; if you decide to take it, it will add roughly .75 mi. to your hike.

Continuing north on the AT beyond the second intersection with the Table Rock trail, the trail winds through mature forest before joining with an old tote road for a time. At 2.3 mi. the trail reaches a small brook in an open area of softwoods. Many of the trees in this area, particularly the mature balsam fir, show heavy damage from spruce budworm—which, despite its name, is more a pest of fir than of spruce. A short side trail on the right leads at 2.3 mi. to the Baldpate Lean-to, completed in 1995. Baldpate Lean-to is roomy, but its setting looks more like a clear-cut logging area than a wilderness site. There is no long- distance view.

From the stream, the AT heads steeply uphill for 0.8 mi. The forest here is made up of young spruce and fir. After cresting a rocky knoll, the trail emerges onto the partially open West Peak of Baldpate at 3.1 mi.

Covered in krummholz, West Peak offers views that take in the White Mts. of New Hampshire to the west and a broad sweep of Maine. The two peaks of Baldpate are bare massifs of slate, schist, and gneiss that run from the southwest to the northeast. If you climb on a clear day, however, don't linger on the West Peak. It is just under 1.0 mi. from here to the more open summit of East Peak, which offers outstanding views in every direction.

Between West and East Peaks, the trail drops roughly 240 ft. into a marshy saddle, with a boardwalk of split fir logs over the wet areas. The col between the two peaks is mostly a low growth of black spruce and balsam fir, with an understory of pale laurel, alpine bilberry, and Labrador tea.

The bilberry is a member of the heath family and is also called bog bilberry. Look for a low, branching plant (under 24 in.) with blue-green toothless leaves (turning purple come fall). Its flowers are white to pink; its berries are blue, but not the sweet kind you'd want to eat. Labrador tea is a cousin from the heath family. This shrubby alpine plant is usually found in or near a bog. Its leaves are evergreen, fuzzy beneath, fragrant if you crush them, and rather thick. The flowers, only 0.3 in. wide, are white and bloom in clusters, like mountain laurel.

There are great slabs of lichen-encrusted ledge here as well. Many of the lichen are of the "map" variety, forming imaginary "continents" as they grow, ever so slowly (like the continents), usually green-yellow in color. What some guidebooks refer to as a canyon in the saddle (at 3.7 mi.) is actually a deep fissure in the rock.

Rising again from the sag, the AT scales bare rock on giant natural steps and ramps to reach East Peak. This is easy, rewarding, and exciting climbing, though you'll want to come prepared for exposure to the elements. There's no place to hide on this side of the mountain.

The panorama from East Peak of Baldpate is stunning, with views extending 360° to Umbagog Lake and the western Maine mountains as well as to the Whites in New Hampshire on western horizon. Bring binoculars and a compass.

If you arrive at the summit of Baldpate on a cloudy day, there is some solace. From late spring to early fall, the summits and the col between the two peaks are an excellent place to listen for the song of Bicknell's thrush, a close relative of the robin found only in the alpine areas of New England. The thrush gives a quick *wee-yew* call when it is startled, but its song is more extended and is best described as flutelike. Although the Bicknell's sings at dawn or dusk, it often sings all day long on an overcast day.

On one trip to Baldpate, we found the summit shrouded in mist. Every few minutes a window would open up, allowing a tunnel-like view of the western Maine countryside. At many places along the trail, bright orange slugs were crawling on the bare rock. This species of slugs—the same ones you might see in your garden if you live anywhere in the Northeast—is an exotic introduced from Europe, and their arrival this far into the woods is a major accomplishment. Slugs, not an especially agile species, disperse only as far as they can crawl. It's something for any hiker who has made it this far to ponder: The summit of Baldpate is a long crawl for an inch-long slug.

Carry on across the east summit for a few minutes. The views improve, and the rocks and lichens are beautiful.

When you're ready for the return trip, reverse direction and follow the AT south to Grafton Notch and ME 26, enjoying the side trip to Table Rock if time allows. (The Table Rock trail appears on your left about 1.5 mi. beyond the Baldpate Lean-to spur trail.) From Table Rock, follow the loop side trail, returning to the AT at a junction only 0.1 mi. from the highway.

Hikers heading north on the AT from Baldpate will descend somewhat to the top of Little Baldpate Mt. at 4.5 mi. and shortly step below treeline for the duration of the hike. Frye Notch Lean-to comes up at 5.8 mi., as does Frye Brook. The trail then crosses Surplus Mt. at 6.3 mi. and nearly 3.0 mi. farther on passes through Dunn Notch, where there is a ford across the West Branch of the Ellis River. On the north side of the stream a short trail brings you to a waterfall at the upper gorge. Close by the AT crossing, but downstream, are two handsome waterfalls.

From the ford, hikers have a choice of paths to the AT trailhead at East B Hill Rd.: follow either the AT itself or take the Cascade Trail on the south side of the river. Either way, you will arrive at the trailhead and parking (10.1 mi. via AT; 10.4 mi. via Cascade Trail). From here it is 8.0 mi. south to Andover.

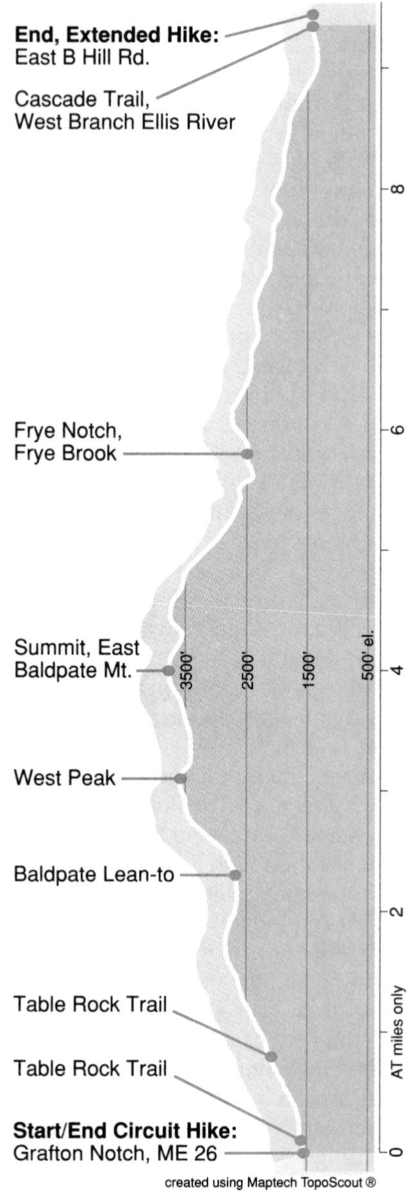

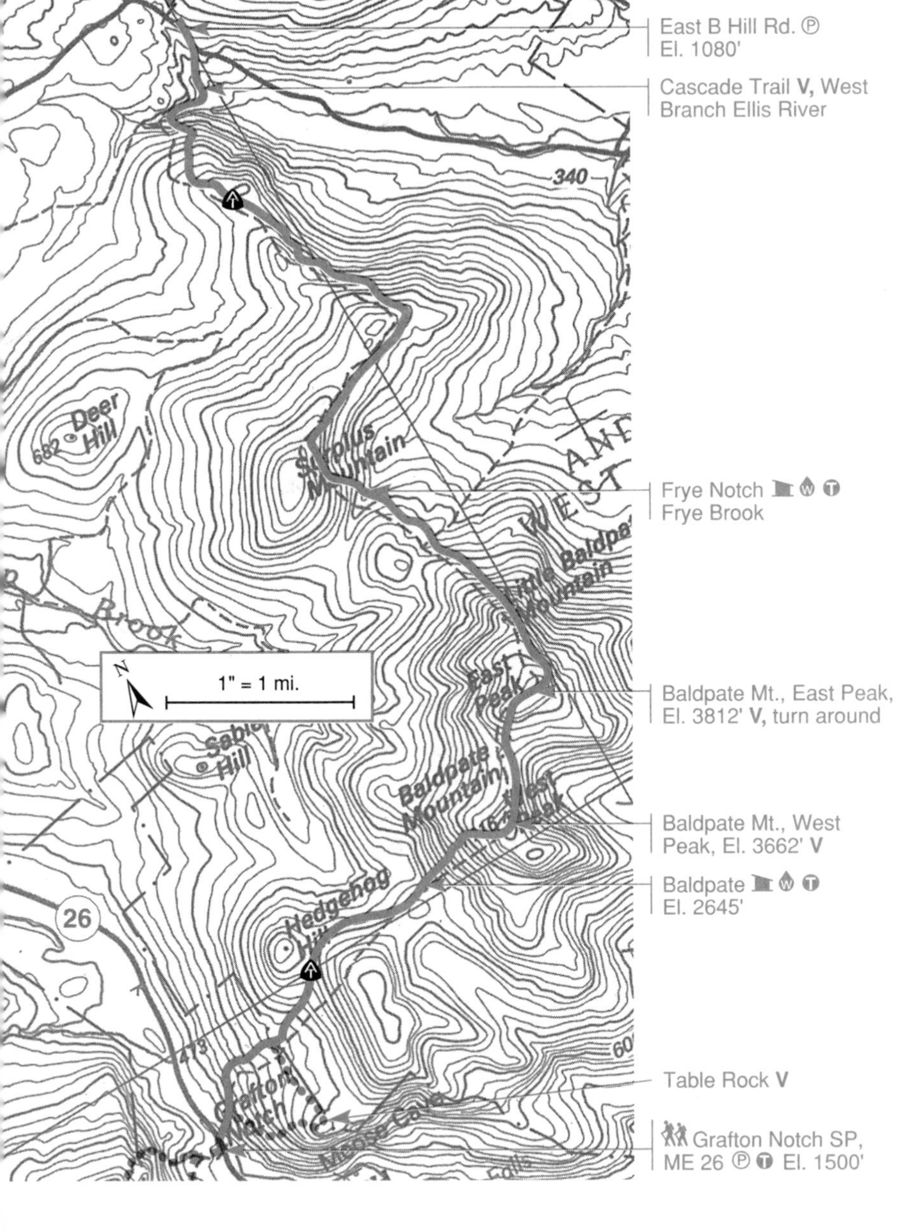
East B Hill Rd. Ⓟ
El. 1080'
Cascade Trail V, West
Branch Ellis River
340
Deer
Hill
682
Frye Notch
Frye Brook
Little Baldpate
Mountain
Brook
1" = 1 mi.
East
Peak
Baldpate Mt., East Peak,
El. 3812' V, turn around
Sable
Hill
Baldpate
Mountain
Baldpate Mt., West
Peak, El. 3662' V
Baldpate
El. 2645'
26
Hedgehog
Hill
Table Rock V
Grafton Notch SP,
ME 26 Ⓟ El. 1500'

HIKE#20 Itinerary

Miles N	Circuit Hike	Elev. (ft/m)	Miles S
	Sag between east and west peaks of Baldpate Mt.		4.3
	West Peak, Baldpate Mt. views.	3662/1116	4.9
	Brook; spur trail to **Baldpate Lean-to.**	2645/806	5.7
	Junction with upper branch of **Table Rock Trail.**		7.2
	Junction with lower branch of **Table Rock Trail.**		7.9
	Grafton Notch, ME 26, parking.	1500/457	8.0
	Reverse direction. Go south. Read from top down.		
4.0	**End, day circuit hike:** Summit, **East Baldpate Mt.,** panorama.	3812/1162	
3.7	Sag between east and west peaks of Baldpate Mt.		
3.1	**West Peak, Baldpate Mt.,** views.	3662/1116	
2.3	Brook; spur trail to **Baldpate Lean-to.**	2645/806	
0.8	Junction with upper branch of **Table Rock Trail.**		
0.1	Junction with lower branch of **Table Rock Trail.**		
0.0	**Start: Grafton Notch, ME 26,** parking.	1500/457	

Circuit Hike

HIKE #21

Wyman Mt. to Moody Mt.

Maps: Maine AT Club, #7
Route: From East B Hill Rd. to Wyman Mt., to Hall Mt., to Sawyer Notch, to Moody Mt., to South Arm Rd.
Recommended direction: S to N
Distance: 10.1 mi.
Elevation +/-: 1080 to 2945 to 1428 ft.
Effort: Strenuous
Day hike: Yes
Overnight backpacking hike: Optional
Duration: 6 to 7 hr.
Early exit option: Sawyer Notch Road, 7.4 mi.
Natural history features: Sawyer Notch, Moody Cliffs
Trailhead access: *Start:* East B Hill Rd., 8 mi. W of Andover, 5 mi. E of ME 26 near Upton; parking (overnight) on S side of road. *End:* South Arm Road, 8.3 mi. N of Andover; parking on N side.
Camping: Hall Mt. Lean-to

In 1978 the Maine Appalachian Trail Club relocated much of this section of the AT, transforming what most considered a mediocre stretch of the trail into an enjoyable and challenging hike. The trail now crosses over the top of a range of low but rugged mountains. Like Baldpate (see Hike #20) and the Mahoosuc Range to the south and west, this section of trail winds up and over mountains and down into ravines and notches, roller-coaster-style. Because the low mountain summits here are wooded, this hike is recommended primarily as a very good forest walk. Hike #21 does have good alpine views off some side trails, but this is generally an immersion into a woody, mountainous wilderness.

The trail begins on the north side of East B Hill Rd. The first 1.8 mi. ascend gradually up several small ridges, winding through a mixed forest of maple, birch, oak, spruce, and fir. (Typically, hardwoods favor warmer south-facing slopes, while conifers, which range all the way to eastern Canada and have adapted to cold and snow, dominate north-facing slopes.) The AT weaves a serpentine path around a streambed before descending steeply to Surplus Pond, where a rustic camp fronts this quiet body of water. It's hard not to romanticize a quaint place like this, imagining sitting before a roaring fire sipping cocoa after a long day of tromping through the woods and mountains.

Putting daydreams aside, ford Burroughs Brook and cross an old camp road (a spring is located some 200 ft. off the trail), as well as a gravel road, and begin a 2.8-mi. climb up the southern shoulder of Wyman Mt.

Glenn Scherer

Hobblebush

Along this long flank of the mountain, deciduous trees are eventually subsumed by fir and spruce trees. On top of Wyman (2,945 ft.), a short side trail, approximately 4.7 mi. into the hike, offers great southerly views to the leafy village of Andover, to oval Ellis Pond, and to the blue mountain silhouettes of the Mahoosuc Range.

Descending steeply from the summit into a ravine, you may start to notice thin pieces of rock that look like shards of broken glass. This is the familiar mica, a minor mineral component of granite, which forms much of the bedrock of the mountains that the AT crosses. Though mica is strong and flexible, it is bonded together weakly, which causes the mineral to split easily into very thin flakes. Mica's role in northern New England geology is noted in several White Mt. hikes also.

The trail continues down into the ravine for approximately 0.3 mi. before rising moderately through an impressive stand of white birch, also known as paper or canoe birch. Native Americans used these beautiful native trees to construct their lightweight birch-bark canoes by stretching the stripped bark over cedar frames, sewing it with thread from tamarack roots, and sealing the seams with pine or balsam fir resin. Don't be tempted, however, to strip bark off a living tree. It leaves ugly black scars. Instead, gather souvenirs from fallen logs.

At 6.0 mi., between the two peaks of Hall Mt., the trail reaches the Hall Mt. Lean-to, which accommodates six and has water and a privy. A 200-yd. side trail leads to a superb overlook toward the cliffs of Moody Mt. in the northeast, and beyond to Old Blue and Elephant Mts. This area is called the Gun Sight, so labeled because erosion has created a narrow slit in what was probably one huge rock—a slit that, yes, resembles a gun sight. So stop here and take aim at the spectacular views across Sawyer Notch.

The trail descends 1500 ft. in just 1.4 mi. down Hall Mt., over a rugged path of roots and rocks. At approximately 6.6 mi., a short side trail leads to another viewpoint of Moody Cliffs and Sawyer Notch. The trail levels off at the floor of Sawyer Notch, at 7.4 mi. crossing a gravel road, that leads back to Andover. (You can park a second car at the end of Sawyer Notch Rd., approximately 6 mi. from Andover, and walk the remaining 2 mi. on this gravel road to the car for an early exit.)

Sawyer Brook (1100 ft.) is a nice spot to take a lunch break, or at least an extended rest, as the toughest part of Hike #21 is yet to come. Sitting on a rock in the shade of the trees that line the brook, dwarfed by the sheer walls of the notch, you can contemplate the history of this spectacular piece of geology. Approximately 15,000 years ago, geologists say that water from the melting glacier, as well as collected sediment, coursed through the low passes between the mountains, carving out these steep U-shaped valleys. This topographic phenomenon is seen at Black Brook Notch, located at the northern end of this hike and in Grafton Notch (Hike #19).

The trail rises steeply out of Sawyer Notch, climbing up a narrow, woodsy path on the slope of Moody Mt., circling around the cliffs through a thick canopy of poplar, maple, and birch—some growing out at bizarre angles due to the radical pitch of the slope. The AT gains 1100 ft. in less than 0.9 mi. here. This is clearly the lung-searing portion of the hike—like a natural Stairmaster.

But sweet are the rewards for the hardworking hiker. At 8.3 mi. the trail levels off and arrives, at approximately 2400 ft., at a spur trail just before the summit of Moody Mt. This overlook above open ledges offers superb views to the south and west of a valley blanketed by trees. The village of Andover is ringed by the crenellated lines of the Mahoosuc Range. White Cap, Puzzle, and Plumbago are just a few of the mountains in the southwest that can be identified with a compass and a map. Sipping water for relief after the climb, watch for hawks riding the crests of a steady wind over the valley.

The trail then traverses the wooded summit of Moody Mt. (2440 ft.) before gradually descending into the saddle that separates Moody and

Sawyer Mts. at 9.0 mi. It then drops steeply down the slope of Sawyer. At roughly 9.5 mi., the AT passes exposed rocky cliffs and offers wonderful views down into Black Brook Notch. The trail reaches the floor of the notch at 10.0 mi., crossing Black Brook (1428 ft.) before ending at South Arm Rd.

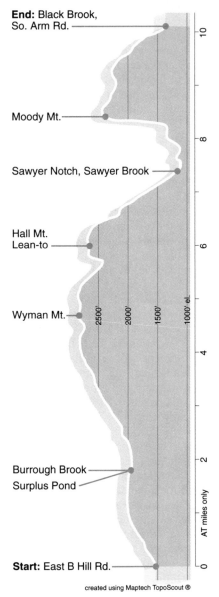

End: Black Brook, So. Arm Rd.

Moody Mt.

Sawyer Notch, Sawyer Brook

Hall Mt. Lean-to

Wyman Mt.

Burrough Brook

Surplus Pond

Start: East B Hill Rd.

2500'
2000'
1500'
1000' el.

0
2
4
6
8
10
AT miles only

created using Maptech TopoScout ®

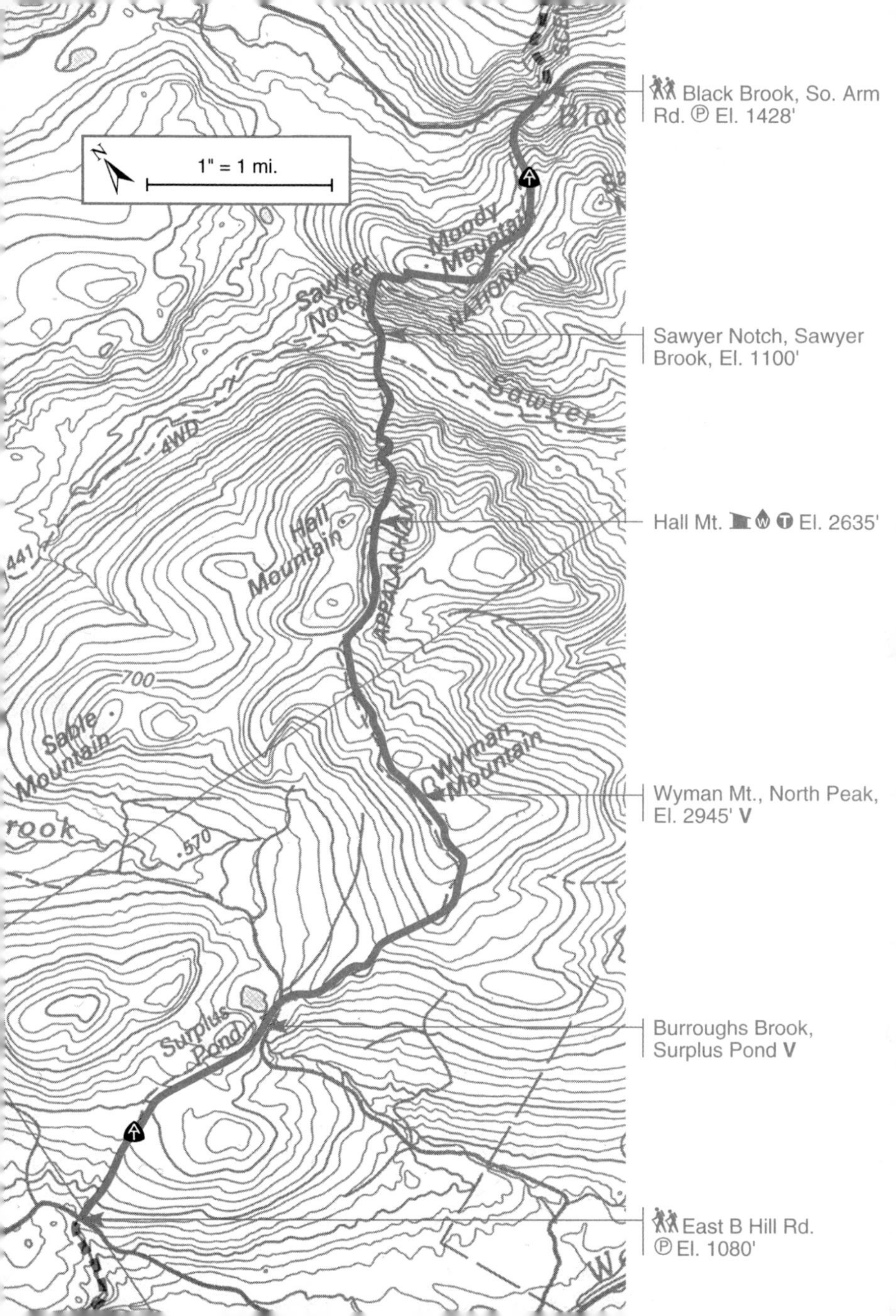

1" = 1 mi.
N
Black Brook, So. Arm Rd. Ⓟ El. 1428'
Sawyer Notch, Sawyer Brook, El. 1100'
Hall Mt. El. 2635'
Wyman Mt., North Peak, El. 2945' V
Burroughs Brook, Surplus Pond V
East B Hill Rd. Ⓟ El. 1080'
Moody Mountain
Sawyer Notch
NATIONAL
Sawyer
4WD
Hall Mountain
APPALACHIAN
700
Sable Mountain
Wyman Mountain
570
Surplus Pond

HIKE #21 Itinerary

Miles N	NORTH	Elev. (ft/m)	Miles S
10.1	**Black Brook. End: South Arm Rd.,** parking.	1428/435	0.0
9.6	**Sawyer Mt.,** N shoulder.		0.5
9.0	Saddle between Sawyer and Moody Mts.		1.1
8.3	**Moody Mt.** spur trail to views.	2400/732	1.8
7.4	**Sawyer Notch, Sawyer Brook,** gravel road (early exit option)	1100/335	2.7
6.0	**Hall Mt. Lean-to,** water, privy. Spur trail to overlook at N peak.	2635/803	4.1
4.7	**Wyman Mt.,** side trail to view.	2945/898	5.4
1.8	**Surplus Pond.** Ford **Burroughs Brook.**		8.3
0.0	**Start: East B Hill Rd.** parking. Enter forest, go N on AT toward Surplus Pond.	1080/329	10.1

SOUTH

HIKE #22

Old Blue, Elephant, and Bemis Mts.

Maps: Maine AT Club, #7

Route: From South Arm Rd. to summit of Old Blue, to old-growth forest and return; or continue to Elephant Mt., Bemis Mt., Bemis Stream, and ME 17

Recommended direction: S to N

Distance: Circuit day hike 8.6 mi.; backpacking trip, 13.3 mi.

Elevation +/-: 1400 to 3600 to 2900 to 3592 to 1500 to 2250 ft.

Effort: Strenuous

Day hike: Optional

Overnight backpacking hike: Optional

Duration: Day hike 6 hr.; backpacking trip 8 to 10 hr.

Early exit option: None

Natural history features: Old-growth red spruce

Trailhead access: *Start:* Take US 2 to ME 5 in Rumford Point; follow ME 5 to Andover; turn R and drive 8.5 mi. on South Arm Rd. to trail crossing in Black Brook Notch. *End:* From Rumford follow ME 17 N for 26 mi. to AT trailhead; from Oquossoc, follow ME 17 S 11 mi. Parking 0.5 mi. S of trailhead.

Camping: Bemis Mt. Lean-to

Hike #22 offers two options: a day hike over the summit of Old Blue and back, or a longer (possibly overnight) hike continuing from Old Blue over Elephant and Bemis Mts.

Day Hike

The hike up Old Blue Mt. has much to recommend it: impressive hardwood forests, fine views from the open summit (3600 ft.), and an old-growth red spruce forest on the saddle between Old Blue and Elephant Mts., with individual trees dating back into the 1600s. The 8.3 mi. make a strenuous day hike on a round-trip route.

Until 1979, when the route up Old Blue was blazed by the outing club from Bates College, the AT followed Clearwater Brook Trail (now closed), skirting the summit of Old Blue altogether. Old Blue remained trailless and probably saw more visits from hunters than from hikers.

From South Arm Rd., the present route of the AT climbs very steeply up the walls of Black Brook Notch, gaining 900 ft. before reaching the top of Black Brook Cliffs at 0.6 mi. There are fine views toward Sawyer and Moody Mts. to the southwest. Beyond Ellis Pond, what looks like a half-inflated balloon is the remains of the Andover Telstar Tracking Station. On July 11, 1962, this station sent the first transatlantic TV transmission across the ocean to France; the image showed the U.S. flag flut-

Flyrod Crosby

At the end of the last century and into the 20th, the Richardsons and the other lakes of the Rangeley Chain were part of a grand tradition of sporting camps that catered to tourists and anglers. The greatest promoter of the area was Cornelia Thurza Crosby, who wrote under the *nom de plume* of Flyrod Crosby. Crosby's newspaper articles on the Maine woods earned the attention of the head of the Maine Central Railroad, who hired her as a full-time publicist. Crosby stole the show at the 1895 Sportsman's Show in Madison Square Garden, where she arranged to have a log cabin built in the hall, complete with a life-size stuffed moose. Soon Crosby was demonstrating her skill with a fly rod and a rifle at fairs around the country. She appeared on stage with Annie Oakley and Buffalo Bill Cody. In 1898 Crosby added another accomplishment: she shot the last caribou legally killed in the state, near Square Lake in Aroostook County. Her writing and performing attracted so many people to the Rangeley region that it increased the demand for backwoods guides. Soon the state stepped in, declaring that guides must be licensed and registered with the state. In honor of her accomplishments, Maine's Commissioner of Fish and Wildlife made Crosby Registered Maine Guide Number One. Flyrod Crosby died in 1946 at the age of 93.

—Andrew Weegar

tering against the station, called "Radome." Thirteen stories high and made of nylon, the dome was an occasional target for hunters, and at least once Radome personnel themselves purposefully shot the dome to deflate it and keep it from collapsing under the weight of a winter blizzard.

Continuing on from Black Brook Cliffs, the trail levels off for a time, then climbs at a gentler grade through mixed woods. Generally here, the AT meanders under magnificent mature hardwood forest, mainly yellow birch and sugar maple. Because of the hardwoods, Old Blue is an excellent hike to plan for mid- to late September, when autumn foliage is at its peak. At the same time, the hike is also rewarding in late May and early June, when warblers are migrating and spring wildflowers are in bloom. Flowers along the trail here include the white spikes of Canada mayflower and starflower, with the higher shoots of sarsaparilla, false Solomon's seal, and the occasional red trillium.

In several places, the trail cuts through dense thickets of hobblebush, named for its tendency to trip you up. With small "horns" flanking each leaf, the plant is also called "witches hobble." If you hike along this section in springtime, take a careful look at the hobblebush's white "flowers." The showy petals are actually not part of the flower at all, but are modified leaves; the pale yellow flowers are nondescript.

At 2.3 mi., the trail reaches the base of Old Blue, then ascends steeply for another half mile to the peak at 2.8 mi. The summit of Old Blue, 3600 ft., is a large expanse of bare ledge clad with low spruce krummholz and shrub growth of laurel and Labrador tea. The view from the summit takes in an area from Old Speck to Elephant Mt. and north to the Richardson Lakes. Hiking has a long history in this area, and an 1892 account said that Mt. Blue afforded excellent views for anyone who "scaled its cliffs."

From the summit of Old Blue, the trail drops sharply into a valley between Old Blue and Bemis Mts. The ground is often soggy underfoot here in the shade of fir and spruce, and the trees grow noticeably larger as you continue on, reaching a cathedral forest of old-growth red spruce at 4.3 mi. The beginning of this forest is marked by Clearwater Brook Trail (now closed) on the left.

This old-growth forest is at an elevation between 2880 and 3000 ft. Red spruce is a long-lived tree, and some of the specimens here date back into the 1600s. This stand has regenerated with new growth emerging periodically under the canopy, rather than being replaced all at once by a new generation following a fire, windstorm, or harvest. The spruce is grouped in several distinct age categories of roughly 60, 140, 160, and 280 years.

Balsam fir are also scattered throughout this forest. Fir is a more short-lived species, and the fir component here is relatively young, with most of the trees well under 100 years. Much of the regeneration that you see around you here is balsam fir and spruce from 1 to 2 ft. high. Spruce seedlings can survive for years at relatively small size, waiting for light to enter and "release" them for growth; one small spruce seedling here was found to be 13 years old.

Dwarfed by the spruce, there is also some hardwood in this stand—for the most part an occasional white birch or mountain ash. Flowering plants here are similar to what you have seen on the hike thus far, demonstrating the adaptability of many of these plants: Canada mayflower, wood sorrel, clintonia, goldthread, and twinflower.

The day hike now reverses direction to hike back (south) up and over old Blue, reaching the trailhead at South Arm Rd. in 8.6 mi. total.

Backpacking Hike

Backpackers continuing northward will pass the following way points en route to ME 17: From the old-growth forest, up modestly to forested Elephant Mt., then, after another dip and rise, the junction with Bemis Stream Trail at 6.0 mi. This side trail leads 6.1

mi. northeast to ME 17, following the valley and the shoulders of the mountains and avoiding any climbs over the tops, arriving at ME 17 at a point 0.6 mi. south of the AT trailhead. Although it's not a shorter route, in bad weather you may want to take Bemis Stream Trail to avoid exposure on the mountaintops.

Bemis Mt. has several peaks, referred to on the ATC maps by numbers. Heading north, Bemis Mt. proper comes first, at 7.0 mi. and 3592 ft., virtually the same height as Old Blue; then "third peak" at 8.3 mi. (3115 ft.); Bemis Mt. Lean-to, with a nearby spring, at 8.7 mi. (2790 ft.); then the Bemis Range with "second peak" at 10.2 mi. (2915 ft.); and "first peak" at 11.1 mi. (2604 ft.). Next comes a precipitous drop of about 1000 ft. spread over 1.0 mi. to a former railroad bed at 12.3 mi. and Bemis Stream at 12.5 mi.; and finally a climb back up to the state highway (ME 17) at 13.3 mi. (2250 ft.).

Overall, Hike #22 is ambitious as either a day hike or a backpacking trip, with the fine reward of a visit to giant old trees along the way. On this trip, you will have walked not only through space but also through time —hundreds of years of it.

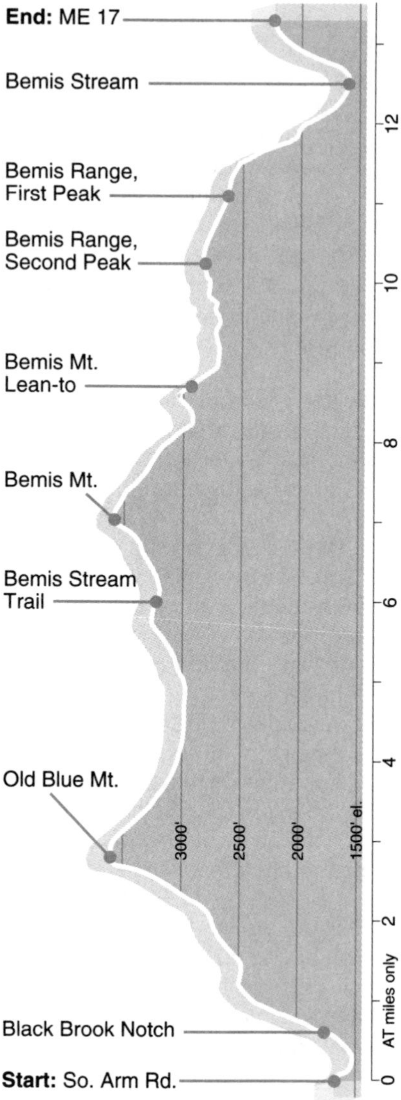

End: ME 17
Bemis Stream
Bemis Range, First Peak
Bemis Range, Second Peak
Bemis Mt. Lean-to
Bemis Mt.
Bemis Stream Trail
Old Blue Mt.
Black Brook Notch
Start: So. Arm Rd.
3000'
2500'
2000'
1500' el.
0
2
4
6
8
10
12
AT miles only
created using Maptech TopoScout ®

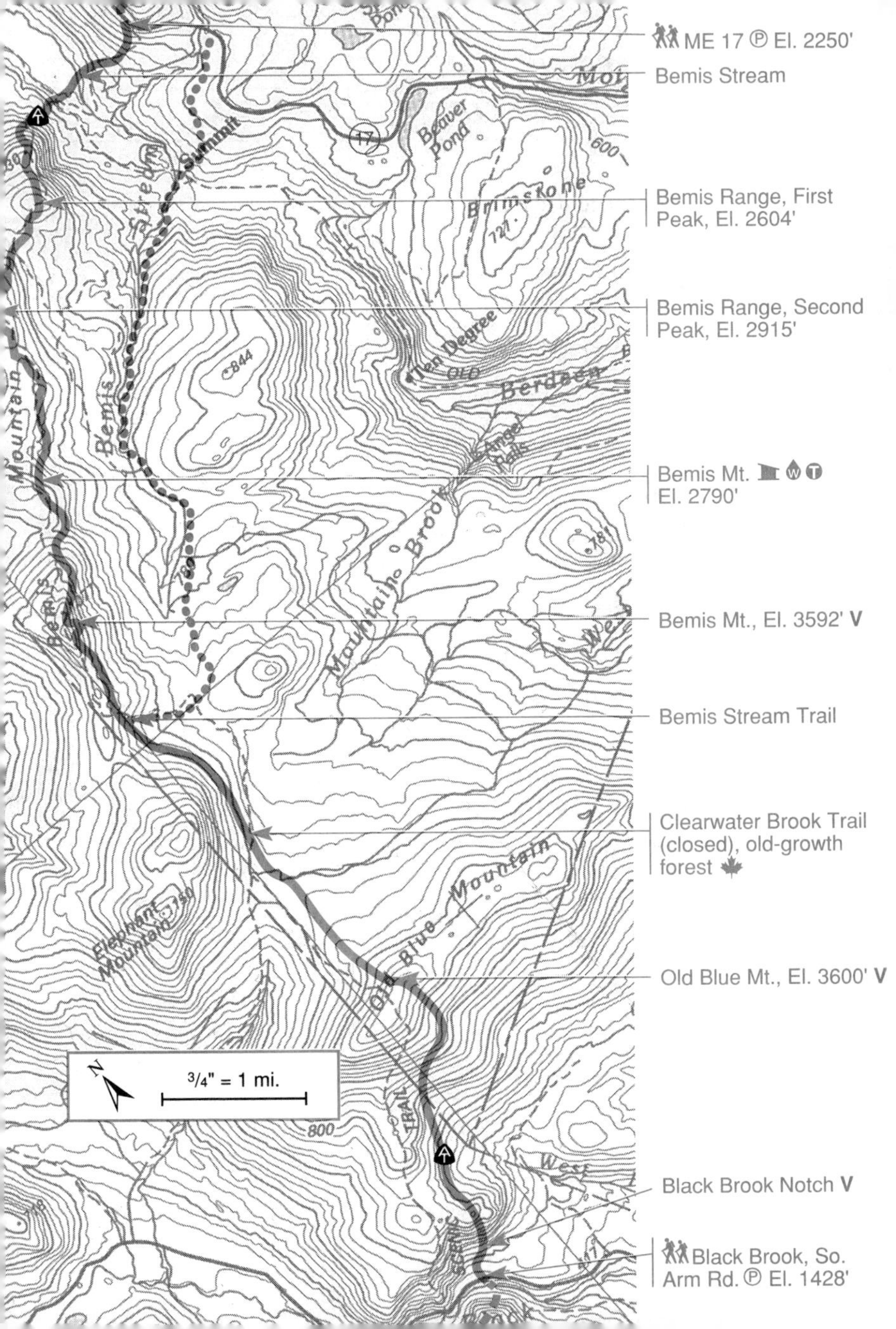
ME 17 Ⓟ El. 2250'
Bemis Stream
Bemis Range, First Peak, El. 2604'
Bemis Range, Second Peak, El. 2915'
Bemis Mt. El. 2790'
Bemis Mt., El. 3592' V
Bemis Stream Trail
Clearwater Brook Trail (closed), old-growth forest
Old Blue Mt., El. 3600' V
Black Brook Notch V
Black Brook, So. Arm Rd. Ⓟ El. 1428'
3/4" = 1 mi.
N
Beaver Pond
Brimstone
Ten Degree
Berdeen
Angel Falls
Mountain Brook
Bemis
Bemis Stream
Mountain
Elephant Mountain
Old Blue Mountain
Summit
TRAIL
West
800
600

HIKE #22 Itinerary

Miles N	NORTH	Elev. (ft/m)	Miles S
13.3	**End: ME 17,** parking.	2250/686	0.0
12.5	**Bemis Stream,** ford at island.		0.8
12.3	Dirt road.		1.0
11.1	**Bemis Range,** first peak, cairn.	2604/794	2.2
10.2	**Bemis Range,** second peak, exposed ledge, views.	2915/888	3.1
8.7	**Bemis Mt. Lean-to,** water, privy.	2790/850	4.6
8.3	**Bemis Mt.,** third peak.	3115/949	5.0
7.0	**Bemis Mt.,** views.	3592/1095	6.3
6.0	Junction with **Bemis Stream Trail,** 6.1 mi. to ME 17 (0.6 mi. S of AT trailhead); bad-weather option.		7.3
4.8	Shoulder of **Elephant Mt.**		8.5
	Reverse direction for day hike		
4.3	Col, **old-growth forest.**	2900/884	9.0
2.8	Summit of **Old Blue Mt.,** views.	3600/1095	10.5
0.6	**Black Brook Cliffs,** view.		12.7
0.0	**Start: South Arm Rd.,** overnight parking. Cross **Black Brook.**	1428/435	13.3

SOUTH

HIKE #23

Sabbath Day Pond

Maps: Maine AT Club, #6
Route: ME 17 to Four Ponds, to South Pond, to ME 4
Recommended direction: S to N
Distance: 13.1 mi.
Elevation +/-: 2250 to 2970 to 1600 ft.
Effort: Moderate
Day hike: Yes
Overnight backpacking hike: Optional
Duration: 7.5 hr.
Early exit option: None
Natural history features: Ponds; boreal bog
Trailhead access: *Start:* ME 17, 26 mi. N of Rumford, 11 mi. S of Oquossoc; overnight parking 0.5 mi. S of trailhead. *End:* ME 4, 9 mi. S of Rangeley, 12 mi. N of Phillips; overnight parking S side of road.
Camping: Sabbath Day Pond Lean-to; Little Swift River Pond Campsite

This hike offers a comparatively easy walk over gentle, wooded terrain, weaving around five lovely remote ponds. The trail leaves ME 17 at approximately 2250 ft. and heads up a steep, rocky path toward Spruce Mt. Look back to the south and west for terrific views of the Upper Richardson and Mooselookmeguntic (Abenaki for "moose feeding among trees") lakes and of Beemis, Elephant, and Old Blue Mts. (see Hike #22). At 0.8 mi., the trail crosses over the wooded summit of Spruce Mt. (2530 ft.) before gradually descending through a mixed forest to Moxie Pond at 1.6 mi., the first of the five ponds. "Moxie" is an Abenaki word for "bog-colored waters," and is a hint of things to come. Much of this hike crosses swampy, wet areas. Who hasn't groaned when a boot is sucked into the slurpy soup of a boggy section of a trail? Hint: Bring an extra pair of socks.

In this stretch of conifers, you may encounter the gray jay, a fluffy bird that looks like a giant chickadee. This bird, which has a whitish face with a dark gray crown, is generally tame and quiet, as opposed to the noisy behavior of most jays. Some may even eat trail mix out of a hiker's hand.

The trail now climbs slowly up a long wooded ridge to Bates Ledge, which features great views of Long Pond, just below the summit of Four Ponds Mt., so named because it overlooks the interconnected ponds of Moxie, Long, Round, and Sabbath Day. After the ledge, the trail drops steeply to Long Pond, where there is a beautiful sandy beach at 3.4 mi., a good spot for a rest break and, weather permitting, a soothing swim. The trail then continues over gentle terrain to Sabbath Day Pond Lean-to at Sabbath Day Pond, at 3.7 mi. The lean-to accommodates eight and has a privy; water is taken from the pond. Fragments of granite litter the campsite, a reminder of the ancient process of glaciation, one of the forces that formed the ponds along this hike. In general, geologists believe that weaknesses in the bedrock eroded away, causing depressions in the rock that then filled with water. Later the glacier, as well as moving bodies of water, deposited sediment that contributed to a damming of the ponds.

The trail next rises up and over a small knob to reach the old Houghton fire road at 4.2 mi., and then climbs steeply up a ridge that passes from deciduous trees to conifers. The trail passes under a power line at 5.4 mi. and continues climbing another 0.5 mi. to the unnamed high point of this hike at 2928 ft. This vista features good views to the north and east of the low hills on the south of the Saddleback Range (see Hike #24).

The AT gradually descends a rolling ridgeline to Little Swift River Pond Campsite at Little Swift River Pond at 8.3 mi. This site features the usual AT amenities: improved tentsites, privy, and water from a spring. It also has an added, tempting attraction—a canoe and paddle rest on the bank of the quiet pond. Take a paddle around the peaceful pond rimmed by trees and think of it as cross-training.

The hike continues its descent to Chandler Mill Stream, the outlet of a large boreal bog, at 9.5 mi. Bogs, which are common along the AT, generally form in a depression that was scooped out of the rock by a glacier. A bog characteristically has a thick floating mat of living and dead organic matter that aids the development of flora such as mosses, sedges, and sphagnum. This flora enhances the floating mat until it eventually covers the surface of the water—thus most of the water is out of sight below the vegetation. The acidity of a bog contributes to the development of plant species like sundew and pitcher plants, which have adapted to survive in a nutrient-poor environment.

From the bog the trail gradually climbs over a small ridge of conifers before descending to the west shore of South Pond at 11.0 mi. The pond features great views of Saddleback Mt. (4120 ft.). This is also good place to spot a moose, whose large oval fecal pellets litter this section of the trail. Moose, which have heavy, brown bodies with humped shoulders and a thick trunklike muzzle, enter these small shallow ponds to feed on water plants and to escape insects.

Hike #23 then continues along easy terrain in a mixed forest of hardwoods and softwoods, crossing two small streams before coming (at 12.0 mi.) to the top of a steep slope with good views over to Saddleback. The AT next drops down a steep ridge, passing through stands of fir and birch and cedar before ending at the parking lot on the south side of ME 4.

Short-Tailed-Shrew, Handmaid of Death

Hikers on the AT in Maine can be thankful for at least one thing beyond scenery and moose: Maine is the only state along the trail that has no poisonous snakes. Nor do we have spiders venomous enough to threaten death.

Maine does have at least one creature, however, with a poison more toxic than cobra venom. What's more, it is probably the most common mammal along the length of the trail. It's the short-tailed shrew.

To a casual eye, shrews look like moles or small rodents. They are neither, but belong to the family Soricidae. Shrews have tiny eyes that are concealed, or nearly concealed, by soft, short fur, and they have no visible ears. Their fur is usually a dull slate color; like a mole's, it lacks a definite direction and can't be rubbed the wrong way, a feature that aids them in tunneling in the forest duff. Voles have larger, noticeable eyes and barely visible ears; their much longer fur is a dark brown streaked with black or silver.

The short-tailed shrew is one of at least six species of shrew in Maine. It may be the world's only poisonous mammal, although an African shrew is also suspect. The Roman naturalist Pliny the Elder claimed the same for a shrew in Italy, noting that "the bite of the shrewmouse is venomous"—though the shrews that survive there now have no venom. Since Pliny also noted that "in whatever country it exists, the shrew always dies immediately if it goes across the rut made by a wheel," perhaps we can take his account with a grain of salt.

Short-tailed shrews secrete a venom from glands located between their lower incisors; mixed with saliva, this penetrates wounds in the shrews' prey. This simple delivery system limits the size of the prey, although it is effective enough to help the shrew feed on mice, one of their most common prey. In one experiment one seventh of the amount of poison produced by an average shrew was enough to kill a 3-pound rabbit.

It is unlikely a shrew could deliver enough poison to kill a human being, although the 19th-century biologist Charles Maynard described the alarming effect of being bitten on the finger by a captive shrew: "The burning sensation predominated in the immediate vicinity of the wounds greatly intensified, accompanied by shooting pains, radiating in all directions from the punctures, and in half an hour they had reached as high as the elbow.... I could not use my left hand without suffering great pain for three days, nor did the swelling abate much before that time."

Do you need to worry about being bitten by a shrew? Probably not. These excitable animals are among the shyest along the trail, and it is unlikely you will ever see one. If you do, be thankful you're not a rabbit.

—Andrew Weegar

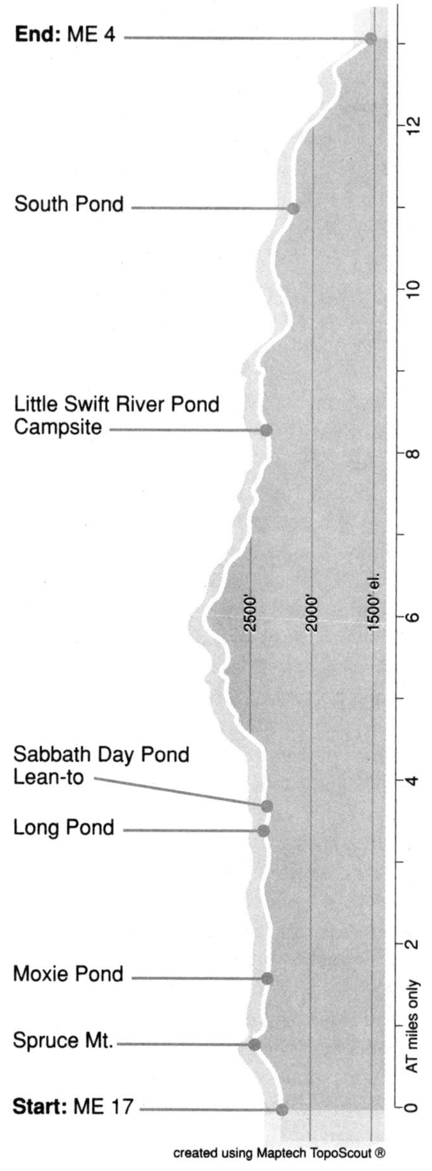
End: ME 4
South Pond
Little Swift River Pond Campsite
Sabbath Day Pond Lean-to
Long Pond
Moxie Pond
Spruce Mt.
Start: ME 17
2500'
2000'
1500' el.
0
2
4
6
8
10
12
AT miles only
created using Maptech TopoScout ®

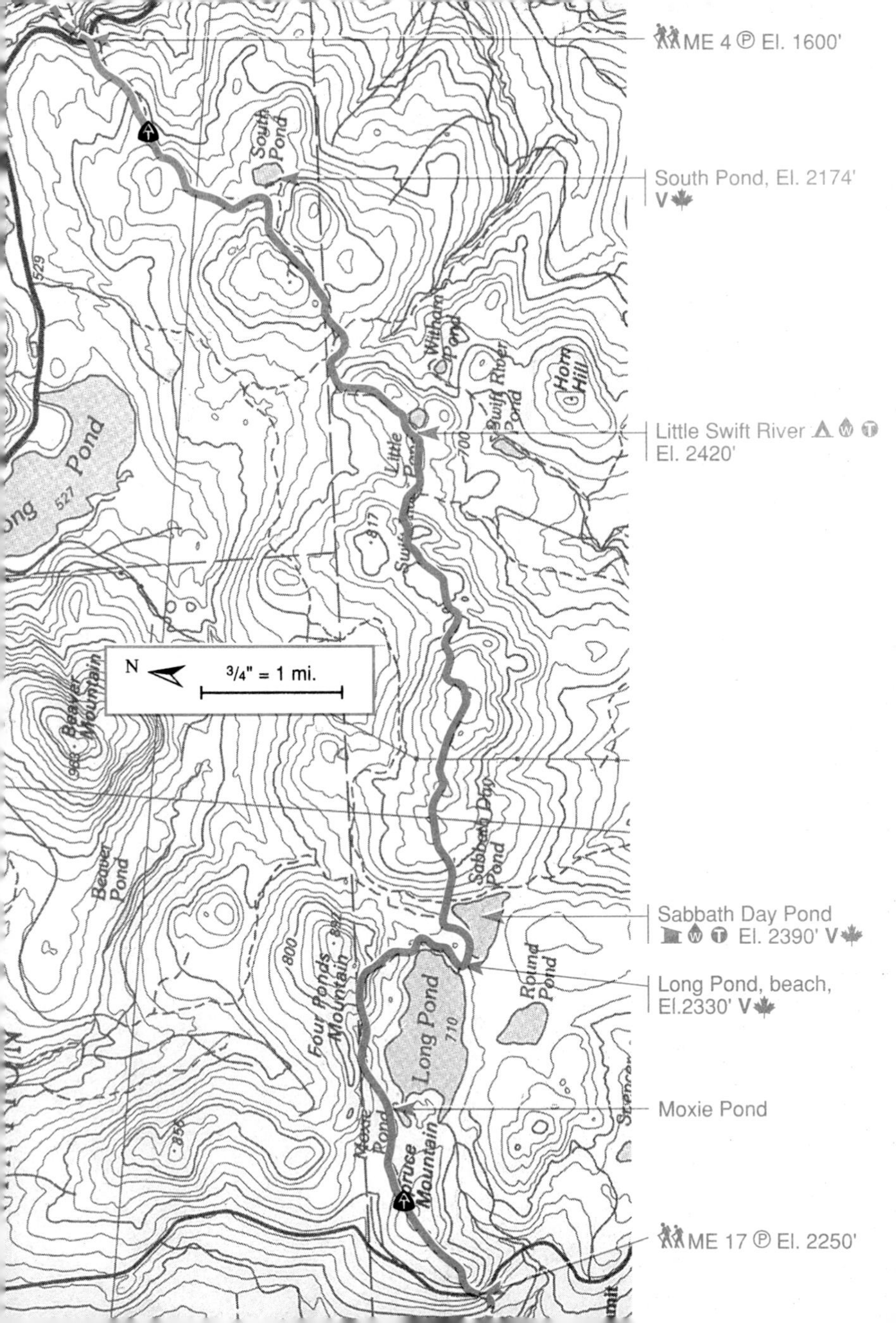

ME 4 Ⓟ El. 1600'
South Pond, El. 2174'
V
Little Swift River
El. 2420'
Sabbath Day Pond
El. 2390' V
Long Pond, beach,
El.2330' V
Moxie Pond
ME 17 Ⓟ El. 2250'
N
3/4" = 1 mi.
South Pond
Witham Pond
Swift River Pond
Horn Hill
Little Swift River Pond
Long Pond
Beaver Mountain
Beaver Pond
Sabbath Day Pond
Four Ponds Mountain
Round Pond
Long Pond
Moxie Pond
Spruce Mountain

HIKE #23 Itinerary

Miles N	NORTH	Elev. (ft/m)	Miles S
13.1	**End: ME 4,** overnight parking.	1600/488	0.0
12.0	Overlook to NE.		1.1
11.0	**South Pond.**	2174/663	2.1
9.5	**Chandler Mill Stream.**		3.6
8.3	**Little Swift River Pond Campsite** at LSR Pond, water, privy.	2420/738	4.8
5.9	High point of hike.	2938/896	7.2
3.7	**Sabbath Day Pond Lean-to** at **Sabbath Day Pond,** water, privy.	2390/729	9.4
3.4	**Long Pond,** beach.	2330/710	9.7
2.7	**Bates Ledge,** view.		10.4
1.6	**Moxie Pond.**		11.5
0.8	Summit of **Spruce Mt.,** no view.	2530/771	12.3
0.0	**Start: ME 17,** parking.	2250/686	13.1

SOUTH

HIKE #24

Saddleback Mt. and Mt. Abraham

Maps: Maine AT Club, #6

Route: From ME 4 to Ethel and Eddy ponds, to Saddleback Mt. and The Horn, and return; or continue to Saddleback Jr., Poplar Ridge, Orbeton Stream, Lone Mt., Spaulding Mt., Carrabassett River, and Caribou Valley Rd.

Recommended direction: S to N

Distance: Circuit hike, 14.6 mi.; backpacking trip, 23.9 mi.

Elevation +/-: 1600 ft. to 4120 ft. to 4041 ft. to 3655 ft. to 1500 ft. to 3988 ft. to 2200 ft.

Effort: Very strenuous

Day hike: Optional (circuit hike)

Overnight backpacking hike: Optional

Duration: Day hike, 9 to 10 hr.; backpacking trip, 15 to 17 hr.

Early exit option: None

Natural history features: Numerous small ponds; long alpine ridge; Piazza Rock; slab caves; bogs

Trailhead access: *Start:* From Farmington follow ME 4 for 30 mi. N to AT trailhead, or from Rangeley go 9 mi. S on ME 4; parking on N side of road. *End:* From Farmington follow ME 27 about 40 mi. to the Sugarloaf ski area, then proceed approximately 1 more mi. to Caribou Valley Rd. (unmarked dirt road off S side of highway). Take Caribou Valley Rd. 4.3 mi. to AT trailhead. *Note:* Caribou Valley Rd. may be impassable in wet seasons.

Camping: Piazza Rock Lean-to, Poplar Ridge Lean-to; Spaulding Mtn. Lean-to

The Saddleback Mt. hike offers some of the finest alpine scenery in the state, and the summit provides a stunning panoramic view of the mountains and lake country of western Maine. Saddleback—named for its profile when viewed from Rangeley—is made up of two peaks above 4000 ft.: Saddleback (4120) and the Horn (4041). The peaks are connected by a 1.6 mi. ridge. A delight on warm days, significant portions of this summit ridge are above treeline, and hikers should be well prepared for worsening weather, high winds, and dangers of exposure. These AT miles are known as the most strenuous in Maine after Mt. Katahdin and the Mahoosucs.

Hikers can approach this area in a number of ways. It's possible to do a day hike up the AT to the summit of Saddleback, returning by the same route. However, the magnificent scenery, the long area above treeline, and the relative isolation of this country also make this a fine choice for a 3-day backpacking trip for well-prepared hikers in good shape. Hikers interested in this option will find

Glenn Scherer

Pileated woodpecker excavations

a number of trails to choose from between Saddleback and ME 27, with side trails leading up Mt. Abraham and Sugarloaf off the AT; hikers can either shuttle a car to ME 27 or hitchhike back around.

Day Hike

A day hike up Saddleback starts at the AT crossing on ME 4. From here, the trail leads north 0.1 mi. to a footbridge over the Sandy River. At 0.7 mi., it crosses a gravel road, leads through mixed woods to cross an old logging road at 1.5 mi., then crosses an inlet brook to Sandy River Pond at 1.7 mi. Just south of the brook, a side trail leads a few hundred yards to Piazza Rock, an enormous granite slab protruding from a cliff.

Immediately north of the brook a side trail leads to Piazza Rock Lean-to. The lean-to accommodates 8 people, with several tentsites available as well. There is a privy, and water nearby.

Continuing north on the AT, a side trail at 2.0 mi. leads to a series of talus caves in the slope below a set of cliffs. "Talus" generally suggests rock debris, often the result of rock breakup caused by freezing and thawing of water in crevices.

At 2.7 mi., the trail skirts along the shore of Ethel Pond, crossing over a thick mat of sphagnum moss and passing through aromatic stands of balsam fir. There are two kinds of sphagnum moss: big red peat moss and green peat moss. AMC's *Field Guide to New England Alpine Summits* notes that the green variety is the more common one, found in all plant zones right up to elevations where the krummholz grows. The plant is characterized by long branches and star-shaped heads. The red variety is most likely to be seen in lowland or alpine bogs. The balsam fir that lends such a sweet aroma to the forest is most often seen as a dwarf or in mats spreading across the ground. The cones stand straight up, with short needles sporting a whitish stripe beneath.

Just after crossing over Saddleback Stream at 3.1 mi., the trail skirts the east side of Mud Pond, a small open bog pond. This entire section of the trail abounds in moose. Keep an eye out and give any moose near the trail a wide berth. (See Hike #34 for more about moose.)

At 3.7 mi. the trail crosses the outlet from Moose and Deer Pond. Stock up from running water here: Last chance for 5.8 mi. Then the trail continues through a series of boggy areas to an overlook above Eddy Pond. From this point, the trail skirts the east shore of the pond. Though the bottom is mucky, 9-acre Eddy Pond can be a good spot for a swim on a hot day. If you're a birder, the fir stubs that surround the trail from Ethel to Eddy ponds are a good spot to look for black-backed woodpeckers, a rare northern species that prefers dead and damaged trees. Saddleback is also a good spot to see the foolishly tame spruce grouse.

There are brook trout in Eddy Pond. Both ponds have a good population of sticklebacks, small predaceous fish, and it's possible to spend an afternoon here with small children as they try to coax sticklebacks into a Sierra cup.

At just under 4.0 mi. the trail crosses another logging road, and then it begins to gain elevation. The AT reaches treeline on Saddleback's southern slope at 4.7 mi. Like Baldpate and other areas with an extensive borderland between forest and alpine habitat, Saddleback is an excellent place to look and listen for the Bicknell's thrush from late spring to fall.

From treeline, it is 1.0 mi. across mostly bare rock to the open summit of Saddleback. The bedrock of the Appalachians in Maine is primarily granite intrusions, metamorphosed in some areas by great heat and pressure of ancient, massive underground forces. The geology of the Rangeley region shows more variation than elsewhere, with siltstone, slate, and igneous rocks all making up the rock underfoot. Though studying the rock on Saddleback can be fascinating, it is easy to end up on your rear end while you're doing it: The rock is slippery in wet weather, particularly early and late in the season.

As you hike above treeline, there are fine views behind you, especially of the northern Sandy River valley. Approaching the summit, these views open up in all directions to include the Rangeley region and the western Maine mountains. The distinctive profile of Mt. Washington in New Hampshire is visible to the south, along with Old Speck, and Mt. Abraham looms to the east. Beyond Abraham, Katahdin is visible on a clear day.

For hikers who have the time, the energy, and the weather on their side, the 1.6 mi. of open ridge leading to the treeless summit of The Horn (4041 ft., at 7.3 mi.) is a stunning hike.

The ridge consists mostly of boulder fields and slabs and ledges. This is a long day hike (14.6 mi. round-trip), and if you continue to the Horn, make sure you're leaving enough time to get back to your car before dark. It is important to stay on the trail anywhere above treeline. The alpine environment in Maine offers a habitat similar to Labrador, and hosts a number of rare species. Maine has only 1524 acres of arctic-alpine plant communities statewide, with 207 of those acres around you here on Saddleback.

The northwest slope of Saddleback is now home to the Saddleback ski area.

The long alpine area on Saddleback has a fine example of black spruce krummholz. In many areas, the trees are deformed, battered stubs, often with all but the crown torn and abraded by winter ice action. This erosion of the tree's tissue is particularly severe just above the normal snowpack. Rime ice forms another hazard: particles of water condense and freeze on the foliage, where they are ripped off by wind. In some areas, trees in the alpine zone lose a quarter of their foliage this way.

Some species, particularly black spruce, have developed an evolutionary response to this stress, growing completely prostrate and thus finding maximum protection under the snow. Although black spruce and balsam fir are the two primary species in the krummholz zone, other trees can supplement these communities: Here

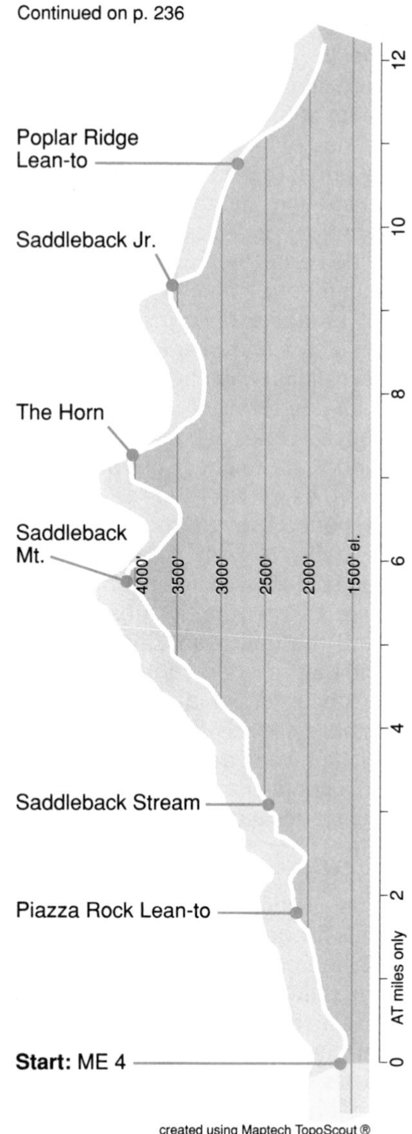

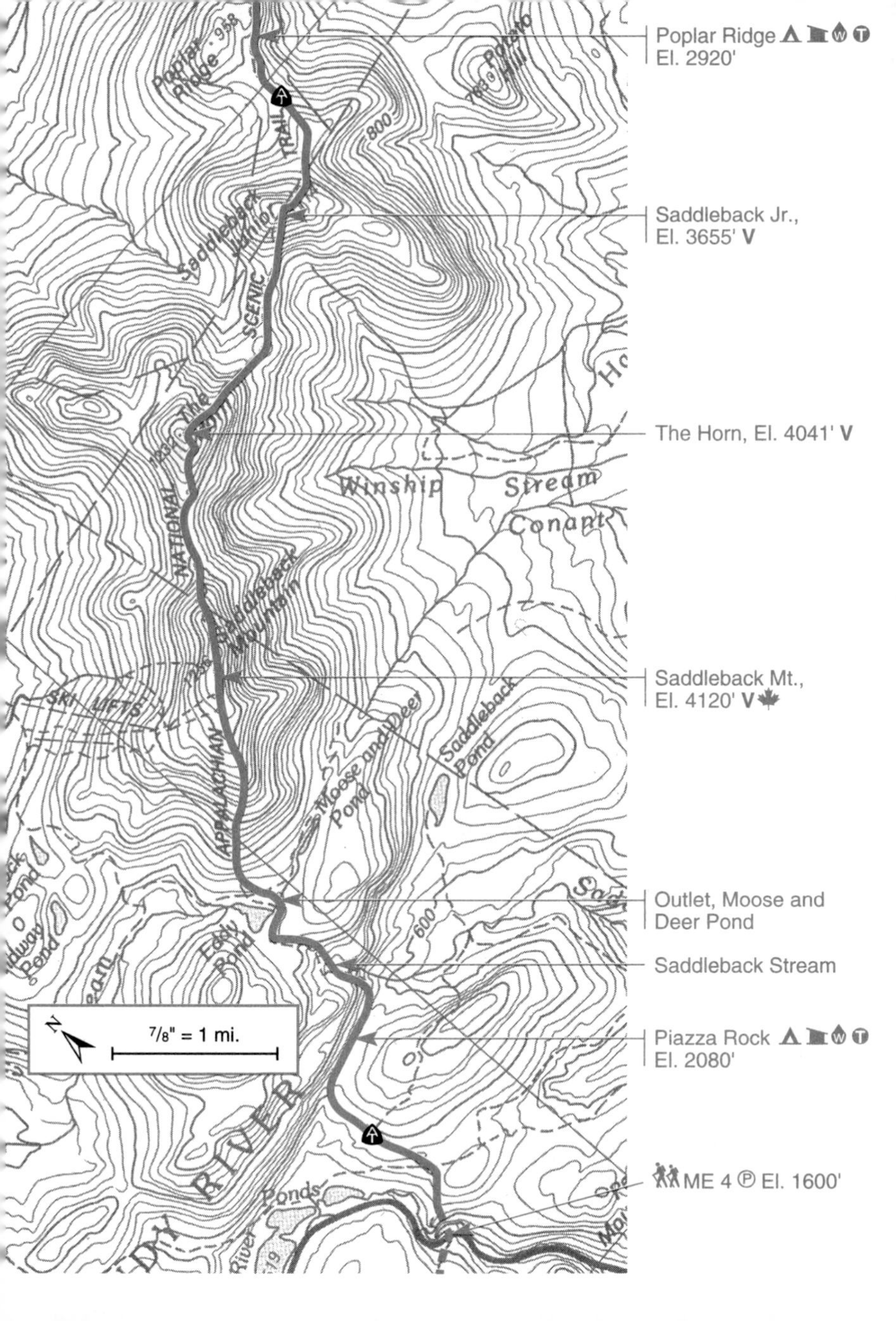

Poplar Ridge
El. 2920'
Saddleback Jr.,
El. 3655' V
The Horn, El. 4041' V
Saddleback Mt.,
El. 4120' V
Outlet, Moose and
Deer Pond
Saddleback Stream
Piazza Rock
El. 2080'
ME 4 Ⓟ El. 1600'
7/8" = 1 mi.
N
Poplar Ridge
Potato Hill
800
TRAIL
Saddleback Junior
SCENIC
The Horn
NATIONAL
APPALACHIAN
Winship Stream
Conant
Saddleback Mountain
SKI LIFTS
Moose and Deer Pond
Saddleback Pond
Eddy Pond
600
RIVER
River Ponds

on Saddleback, a close inspection will find larch and speckled alder among the stunted plants. Other species that thrive below can also be found here. In places the rocks bristle with Labrador tea (an alpine plant) and with the shaggy growth of reindeer lichen.

The day hike finishes with a return to ME 4 on the same route.

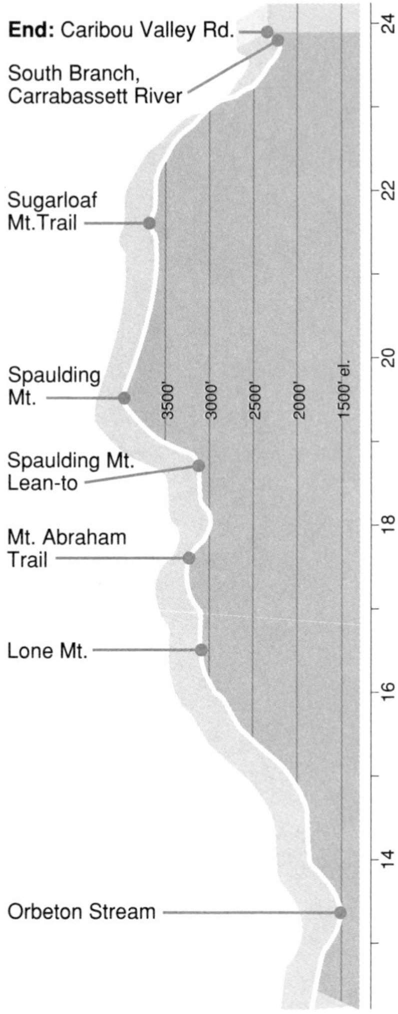

Backpacking Hike

Hikers who carry on northward will pass the following way points en route to Caribou Valley Rd. First, Saddleback Junior (3655 ft., at 9.3 mi.), another open summit; then Poplar Ridge Lean-to at 10.7 mi.; next, the top of Poplar Ridge (ledges, 3120 ft.) at 11.2 mi.; followed by a steep descent to a ford at Orbeton Stream at 13.4 mi.; back up to the top of Lone Mt. (partially clear, 3280 ft.) at 16.5 mi.; and then Mt. Abraham Trail at 17.6 mi, leading to the peak (4043 ft.) in just under 2 mi.

Continuing on the AT, Spaulding Mt. Lean-to is just off the trail at 18.7 mi. The AT comes within 0.1 mi. of the forested top of Spaulding Mt. (3988 ft.) at 19.5 mi. Sugarloaf Mt. Trail appears at 21.6 mi. (it's 0.6 mi. to the top, at 4237 ft., and the views are definitely worth the effort). Only Katahdin reaches higher into the sky among Maine's mountains. At 23.8 mi. the AT crosses the South Branch of the Carrabassett River (a ford). And the backpacking hike ends at 23.9 mi., Caribou Valley Rd., at a point 4.3 mi. south of ME 27.

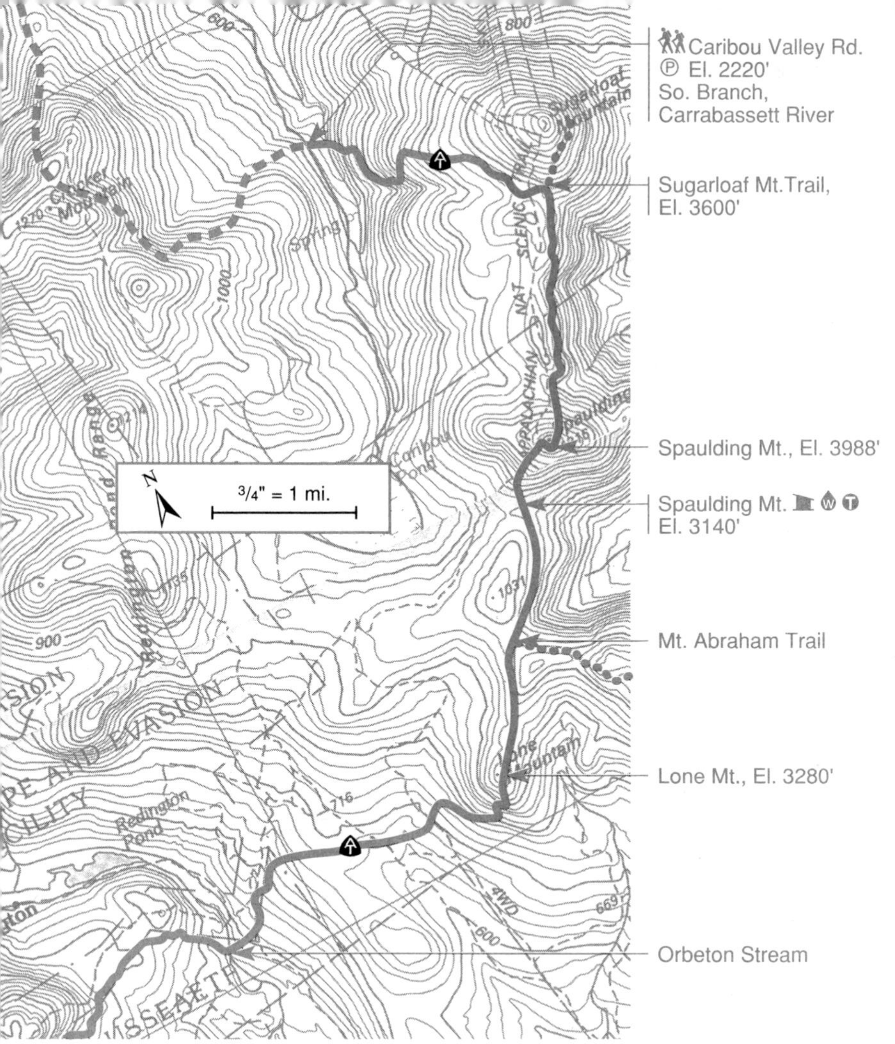
Caribou Valley Rd.
Ⓟ El. 2220'
So. Branch,
Carrabassett River
Sugarloaf Mt. Trail,
El. 3600'
Spaulding Mt., El. 3988'
Spaulding Mt.
El. 3140'
Mt. Abraham Trail
Lone Mt., El. 3280'
Orbeton Stream
3/4" = 1 mi.
N
Sugarloaf Mountain
Crocker Mountain
Spring
Caribou Pond
APPALACHIAN NAT. SCENIC TRAIL
Spaulding
Redington
Redington Pond
Lone Mountain
4WD

HIKE #24 Itinerary

Miles N	NORTH	Elev. (ft/m)	Miles S
23.9	**End: Caribou Valley Rd.** (unpaved), 4.3 mi. S of ME 27.	2200/677	0.0
23.8	**South Branch, Carrabassett River,** ford.		0.1
21.6	**Sugarloaf Mt. Trail,** 0.6 mi. to peak (4237 ft., second highest in Maine), views.	3600/1097	2.3
19.5	Reach AT's high point on **Spaulding Mt.** Spur trail (0.1 mi.) to forested peak.	3988/1216	4.4
18.7	**Spaulding Mt. Lean-to,** water, privy.	3140/957	5.2
17.6	**Mt. Abraham Trail,** 1.7 mi. to summit (4043 ft.), views.		6.3
16.5	Summit, **Lone Mt.**	3280/1000	7.4
15.4	Logging road near Perham Stream.		8.5
13.4	**Orbeton Stream** (ford) at base of deep valley.		10.5
11.2	**Poplar Ridge.**	3120/951	12.7
10.7	**Poplar Ridge Lean-to** and campsite; water, privy.	2920/890	13.2
9.3	Summit, **Saddleback Junior,** panorama.	3655/1114	14.6
	Reverse for day hike		

Itinerary continued

HIKE #24 Itinerary *continues on previous page.*

Miles N		Elev. (ft/m)	Miles S
7.3	Summit, **The Horn,** panorama.	4041/1232	16.6
6.3	Sag between Saddleback and The Horn.		17.6
5.7	Summit, **Saddleback Mt.,** view.	4120/1256	18.2
4.7	Reach treeline and exposed rocky path, Saddleback Mt.		19.2
4.0	Cross logging road.		19.9
3.7	Cross outlet from **Moose and Deer Pond;** water.		20.2
3.2	**Mud Pond** (bog).		20.7
3.1	Cross **Saddleback Stream.**		20.8
2.7	**Ethel Pond.**		21.2
2.0	Spur trail to talus caves.		21.9
1.8	**Piazza Rock Lean-to.** Short side trail to **Piazza Rock,** view.	2080/634	22.1
1.5	Logging road, then cross brook.		22.4
0.7	Dirt road.		23.2
0.1	**Sandy River** footbridge.		23.8
0.0	**Start: ME 4,** 9 mi. N of Rangeley, 12 mi. S of Phillips; parking.	1600/488	23.9

SOUTH

HIKE #25

Crocker Mt.

Maps: Maine AT Club, #6
Route: From Caribou Valley Rd. to South and North Crocker, to ME 27
Recommended direction: S to N
Distance: 8.3 mi.
Elevation +/-: 2220 to 4228 to 1400 ft.
Effort: Strenuous
Day hike: Yes
Overnight backpacking hike: Optional
Duration: 6 hr.
Natural history features: Crocker cirque
Trailhead access: *Start:* From Stratton, drive 5 mi. S on ME 27 to Caribou Valley Rd., about 1 mi. N of turn-off to Sugarloaf ski area; AT is 4.3 mi. S on Caribou Valley Rd., with parking on the side of the road. *End:* ME 27, 5 mi. S of Stratton, overnight parking on S side.
Camping: Crocker Cirque Campsite.

Crocker Mt., with two distinct peaks, is at the northern end of a succession of mountains that constitute the most strenuous hiking on the AT in Maine, along with Katahdin and the Mahoosucs. Like Saddleback, Spaulding, and Sugarloaf (see Hike #24), the Crockers features high-elevation hiking with superb views. It's a short, rugged, and rewarding day hike, with a campsite near the southern end for overnighters.

Hike #25 begins 4.3 mi. down Caribou Valley Rd., from the intersection with ME 27. The entrance to this unmarked gravel road is 1 mi. northwest of the access road to Sugarloaf. The condition of the road varies and there are several wooden bridges, so it may not be possible to drive all the way to the trailhead.

The trail starts at roughly 2200 ft. and climbs gradually up a path littered with fragments of granite, passing through an impressive stand of white birch. Walking through this wooded area, you may encounter a ruffed grouse, a crow-size bird that is common in mixed woodlands. It's named for the black feathers on the sides of its neck, which the male raises into a ruff. Also known as a partridge, the bird explodes raucously into flight when flushed, its beating wings sounding like a propeller plane taking off. The bird is sometimes confused with the spruce grouse, a grayish bird that can be found in fir and spruce stands on the AT. The spruce grouse is tame and approachable, thus earning it the nickname "fool hen" (see Hike #24).

At 1.0 mi., the trail reaches the floor of a large glacial cirque. A 0.2-mi. side trail leads to Crocker Cirque Campsite, which has tent platforms, a privy, and water from a brook.

Scoured by a glacier some 25,000 years ago, the cirque is a deep, steep-walled basin forming the blunt end of the valley. A small beaver pond just north of the campsite offers great views of Crocker Mt.'s south and north peaks. Here you see why some call cirques mountainous amphitheaters, as the walls of the two peaks seem to bend around and surround you.

The trail now climbs steeply toward the summit of South Crocker Mt. The AT rises more than 1400 ft. in just 1.1 mi. The views of Sugarloaf, to the west, and of the Bigelows, to the east, along the steep route are terrific. The combination of the steep hiking and the superb vistas gives a double meaning to the term breathtaking.

At 1.3 mi. there is a traverse of a steep rocky area, which is part of an old rock slide. This is a good place to pause and enjoy the rolling, mountainous landscape that surrounds you.

The trail passes near the summit of South Crocker (4010 ft.) at 2.1 mi. (a 150- ft. side trail leads to the true summit). Sugarloaf Mt. (4237 ft.), which is home to a ski resort, towers to the west. Mountains that rise steeply from the valley floor, which means most of the mountains that the AT winds through in Maine, are called "crunch" mountains because they formed from a series of collisions between continental plates beginning some 500 million years ago.

But the peaks of these mountains are not the peaks of those earlier mountains. The Appalachians are thought to have once been as high as the Himalayas are now—nearly 30,000 ft. The peaks we see now were enveloped in the interior of those early mountains, revealed only after millions of years of erosion.

The AT descends about 400 ft. into a saddle between the two Crocker peaks at 2.6 mi., passing through a thick layer of spruce and fir trees, then climbs up a narrow, rocky trail to the peak of North Crocker (4228 ft.) at 3.1 mi. This is a heavily wooded summit, but woods trails, leading both west and east from the summit, offer good views. The one heading west provides a view of the Saddleback Range to the south and East Kennebago to the northwest. The one heading east features great vistas of the Bigelow Range. Hike 0.3 mi. down the east side trail for even better panoramas of the range and of the small town of Stratton.

The trees here, mostly black spruce, are stunted and pruned by blowing ice and snow. Yet this low, distorted canopy of trees, called krummholz, provides protection for a number of species, including mice, shrews, voles, hares, and grouse, as the temperature can be 40 to 60 degrees warmer under the canopy than outside.

From North Crocker Hike #25 then descends into a taller canopy of spruce and fir trees, heading down a steep, narrow footpath lined with granite fragments and mountain cranberry, a creeping evergreen with slender stems and branches and pink or reddish flowers. The trail continues down an incline with limited views of the Bigelow Range before leveling off just before a small stream at 6.2 mi. A traverse of a long, mostly level ridge, through a stand of white birch, comes next, leading to a small knob at 6.9 mi.

The trail then plummets down a ridge starting at approximately 2500 ft., into a mixed forest of hardwoods and softwoods. The trail continues its descent, weaving through a thick canopy of birch, maple, and cedar before reaching the end of the trailhead at approximately 1420 ft.

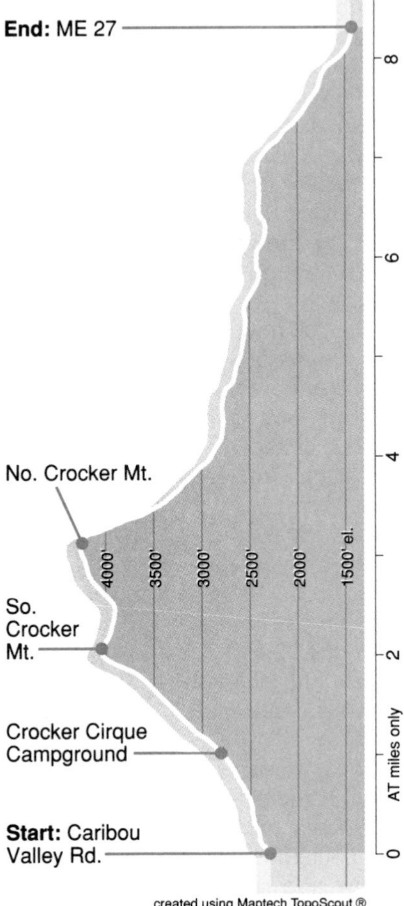

created using Maptech TopoScout ®

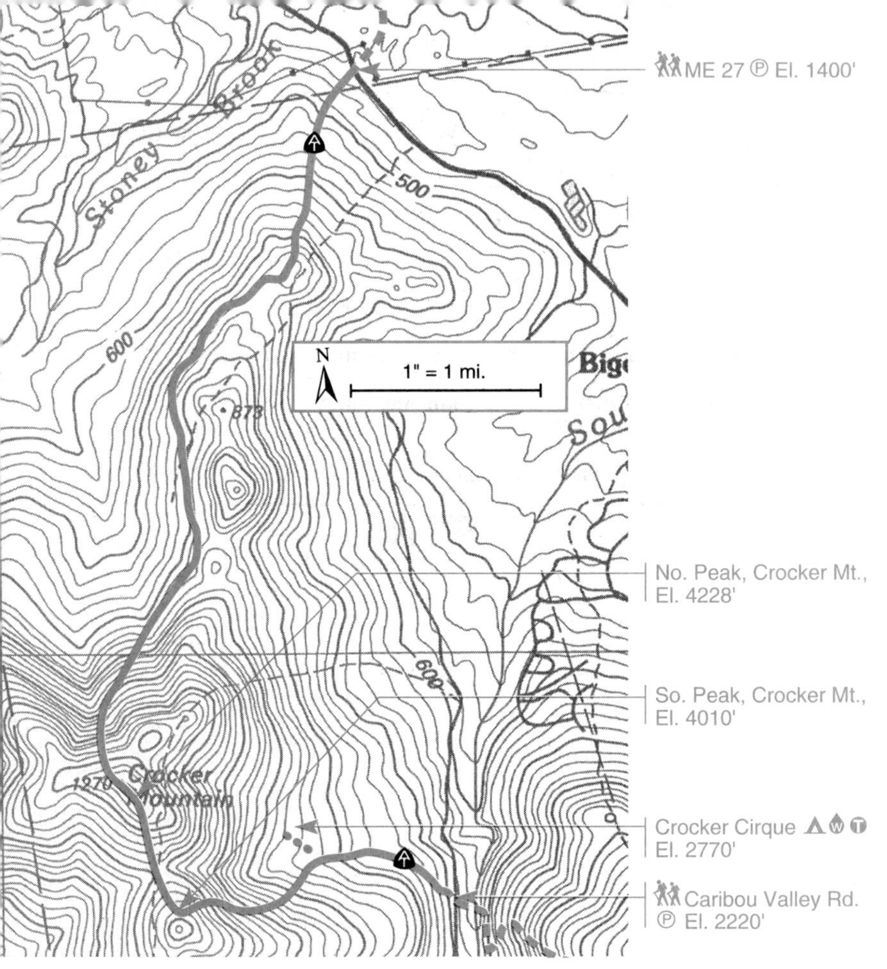
ME 27 Ⓟ El. 1400'
Stoney Brook
500
600
873
1" = 1 mi.
N
Bige
Sou
No. Peak, Crocker Mt., El. 4228'
600
So. Peak, Crocker Mt., El. 4010'
1270
Crocker Mountain
Crocker Cirque
El. 2770'
Caribou Valley Rd. Ⓟ El. 2220'

HIKE #25 Itinerary

Miles N	NORTH	Elev. (ft/m)	Miles S
8.3	**End: ME 27,** parking.	1400/463	0.0
6.9	Ridgetop knob.		1.4
3.1	Summit of **North Crocker Mt.,** views from side trails.	4228/1289	5.2
2.6	Saddle between N and S peaks of **Crocker Mt.**		5.7
2.1	**South Crocker Mt.,** short spur trail to summit, views.	4010/1222	6.2
1.0	Side trail to **Crocker Cirque Campsite,** water, privy, tent platforms.	2770/844	7.3
0.0	**Start: Caribou Valley Rd.,** parking, 4.3 mi. S of ME 27.	2220/677	8.3

SOUTH

HIKE #26

Little Bigelow

Maps: Maine AT Club, # 5

Route: *Day hikes:* 1) Circuit: From Long Falls Dam Rd. to Little Bigelow Mt. and return; 2) From Long Falls Dam Rd. to Little Bigelow Mt. to Safford Brook Trail to East Flagstaff Rd. (two cars required). *Extended backpacking hike:* continue S on AT to Myron Avery Peak, to The Horns, to ME 27

Recommended direction: N to S

Distance: Day hike (circuit): 13.8 mi., all on AT; backpacking trip: 19.1 mi.

Access trail name & miles: Safford Brook Trail, 2.2 mi.

Elevation +/-: 1250 ft. to 3040 ft. to 2250 ft. to 4145 ft. to 3805 ft. to 1400 ft.

Effort: Strenuous

Day hike: Optional

Overnight backpacking hike: Optional

Duration: Day hikes, 7 to 8 hr.; backpacking trip, 12 to 13 hr.

Early exit option: Fire Warden Trail, at 11.1 mi.

Natural history features: Alpine summit ridge; Safford Notch

Social history features: Submerged village of Flagstaff; Benedict Arnold's camp

Trailhead access: *Start:* From North New Portland follow Long Falls Dam Rd. N 19.8 mi. to AT trailhead. (No access from the N.) Roadside parking. *End:* (Day hike on Safford Brook Trail) From junction of Long Falls Dam Rd. and Bog Brook Rd., take Bog Brook Rd., then East Flagstaff Rd., 5.3 mi. to parking at Safford Brook trailhead. (Backpacking trip) From Stratton, at junction of ME 16 and 27, go N on ME 27 for 5.2 mi. to AT. Parking on former road (W side).

Camping: Safford Notch Campsite; Little Bigelow Lean-to

The westernmost peak in the Bigelow Range, Little Bigelow, like its larger neighbor, Bigelow Mt., has some outstanding views of the Flagstaff Lake country and the Dead River. Not particularly difficult or demanding, the Little Bigelow hike can be treacherous in wet weather, as much of it travels over exposed rock. This section of the AT takes you through some remote and rugged country, with outstanding beauty and natural resources. The steep southern slope of Little Bigelow is the site of a rare 20-acre old-growth hardwood forest, made up of beech, yellow birch, and sugar maple.

Park either at the roadside on Long Falls Dam Rd., or for longer term parking in an official lot, on the way north branch off from Long Falls Dam Rd. onto Bog Brook Rd., then East Flagstaff Rd. There is an AT parking lot, just beyond the turnoff onto East Flagstaff Rd. Starting out here shaves 2.3 mi. from the hike's total

Henry Lafleur

Flagstaff Lake

distance (our mileages start at Long Falls Dam Rd.).

From Long Falls Dam Rd., go south on the AT, crossing over a modest ridge at 0.6 mi. Flagstaff Lake's shoreline appears at 1.8 mi., almost at trailside. Bog Brook Rd., then East Flagstaff Rd. (and the parking lot) come up at 2.3 mi. Now the AT leads uphill through second growth hardwood, with some impressive northern white cedar hereabouts.

The trail follows the brook for a time, then leaves it after half a mile and climbs along a beech ridge. Some of the trees through here show the deep pockmarks left in the bark by beech blister disease, which will eventually kill them. Trees unmarked by disease may show other scars—left by bears climbing the trees to feed on beechnuts. Little Bigelow Lean-to is off a short spur at 3.8 mi. There is a privy, and water from a nearby spring. At about 4.5 mi., the AT climbs through boulders in a wet ravine in the mountain's side. The trail leaves the ravine to emerge out onto a series of ledges, with fine views of Flagstaff Lake. In late July and August, this a good place for blueberries. The footpath climbs over a series of rocky knolls, reaching the east summit of Little Bigelow (3040 ft.) at 5.5 mi. From here the view extends to the summit of Bigelow Mt., across the valley to Sugarloaf and Crocker Mts., and to the open summit of Mt. Abraham. Carry on to the west summit as well (at 6.9 mi.) for more views.

Now there are several ways to complete this hike. Hikers with one car can reverse direction and return via

Thru-Hiking Lab Report

Hiking in the spring is glorious. But beware: There's a substantial risk that you will catch whatever it is that drives people to hike all the way to Maine. This insidious disease has a long incubation—so long that you may think you have escaped it. Here are some symptoms that may precede the onset:

1. Victims (you or a loved one) start collecting maps and guidebooks.
2. They ask everyone they meet about tents, Gore-Tex, and water filters.
3. They start introducing themselves by a funny new name.
4. They insist on knowing the weight to the nearest gram of everything they buy.
5. They don't like their 100% cotton underwear and socks anymore.
6. They develop an obsessive interest in weather, day length, elevation gains and losses, and how far they can hike in a day.

The most severe form of this syndrome was first described in 1936, but it was rare until the 1960s (among those rare cases: Supreme Court Justice William O. Douglas, who succumbed in 1958). By 1982 there were 1000 cases on record; that number doubled in only seven years. In the 1990s, it became a major epidemic, and thousands come down with it each year. It respects neither age, sex, physical handicap, nor nationality. An 86-year-old got it in 1975, and a 6-year-old got it just five years later. Some people get it several times, and many victims write books about their struggle. Several dogs and at least one cat have also fallen prey to it.

More men than women suffer from it, but, as with many other conditions, women are catching up. The causative agent has not been identified; there is some evidence of a tiny parasite that burrows through brain tissue, engendering major behavioral changes but only minor permanent damage. No remedy has been found; victims harbor the disease the rest of their lives and seem to be highly infectious. However, many victims can lead lives that are surprisingly close to normal—if they can acknowledge their affliction and get the hiking done, either all at once or in sections. Many self-help books are available, and support groups exist in some communities.

— Doris Gove

same route for a 13.8 mi. round-trip—either spending the night at Little Bigelow Lean-to or doing it as a long 1-day hike. Hikers with two cars have two options: the walk down Safford Notch to Flagstaff Lake (described here) or the longer backpacking trip to ME 27 (described briefly at the end of this narrative).

Continue on, descending about 800 ft. to the floor of Safford Notch at 8.7 mi., where a spur leads to the

Safford Notch Campsite. There are tent platforms, water, and a privy here. This area is marked by enormous boulders, some of them the size of a house. Just north of Safford Brook Trail (see below), there is a series of boulder caves. Keep a watchful eye for porcupines if you explore this area: Crawling through one cave, we found ourselves staring one unexpectedly in the eye!

Just beyond the campsite, at 8.8 mi., Safford Brook Trail leads north 2.2 mi. to (unpaved) East Flagstaff Rd., which runs along the shoreline of Flagstaff Lake. From the AT, Safford Brook Trail drops steeply through the Notch for more than a mile. At 1.8 mi., the trail crosses Safford Brook. From this point the trail levels out, joining an old tote road and descending more gently to East Flagstaff Rd. for a total of 11.0 mi. Safford Brook Trail is actually the old Dead River route of the AT, relocated in the 1930s when the Central Maine Power Company announced its plans to create Flagstaff Lake by damming the Dead. More than the trail was relocated: The entire village of Flagstaff was removed. At low water, stone walls and cellar holes still clearly show in the lake bottom. Although the citizens of Flagstaff loudly protested the destruction of their town, the political might of Central Maine Power was too much to fight, and the town was flooded in 1950.

As one of its last official acts, the town of Flagstaff spent $1000 for a "homecoming" celebration on July 3

Continued on p. 250

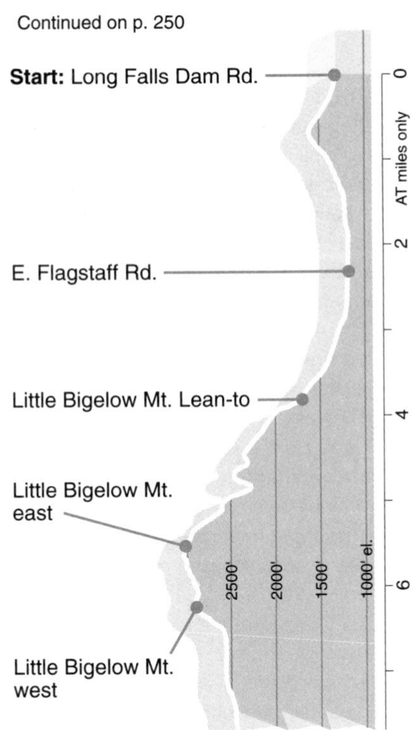

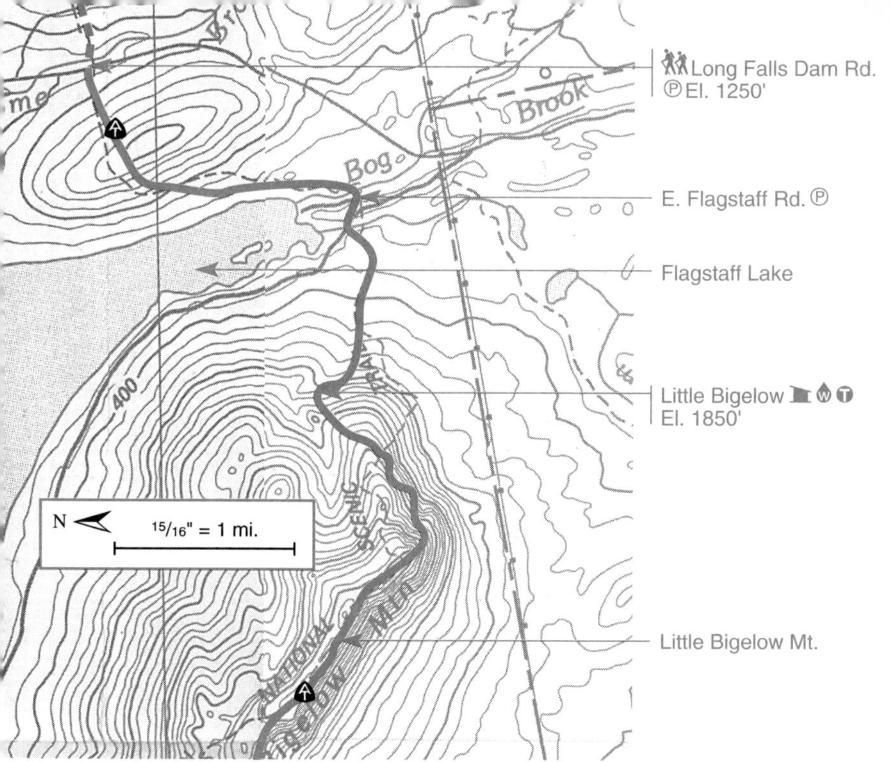
Long Falls Dam Rd.
Ⓟ El. 1250'
E. Flagstaff Rd. Ⓟ
Flagstaff Lake
Little Bigelow
El. 1850'
Little Bigelow Mt.
N
15/16" = 1 mi.
Brook
Bog
400
NATIONAL
SCENIC
Bigelow
Mtn

and 4, 1949. The town hired an orchestra, and hundreds of current and former residents came out for a farewell dance in what remained of the town.

Occasionally other things surface in the lake as well. In 1979 a party of snowmobilers found the remains of an F-120 fighter that had crashed into the lake 20 years earlier. Its rocket launchers were still loaded with explosives.

Flagstaff drew its name from Benedict Arnold's journey through this area on his march to Quebec in 1775 during the Revolutionary War. Arnold arrived at the site of Flagstaff to find that his party had camped there days before, erecting a flagpole. Some of the worst disasters to befall Arnold's party happened here: Near this point, Arnold's men lost much of their materiel and equipment when the river flooded due to what meteorologists now assume was an errant hurricane. "We were awakened by the freshet which came running on us like a torrent, having rose eight feet perpendicular in nine hours, and before we could remove wet all our baggage and forced us from our comfortable habitation," Arnold recorded in his journal.

A second flagpole, erected to commemorate the troops' campsite, was one of the few things left behind after Flagstaff was flooded in 1950. After the lake's waters rose, the pole floated up; and was re-erected at "New Flagstaff" village in Eustis.

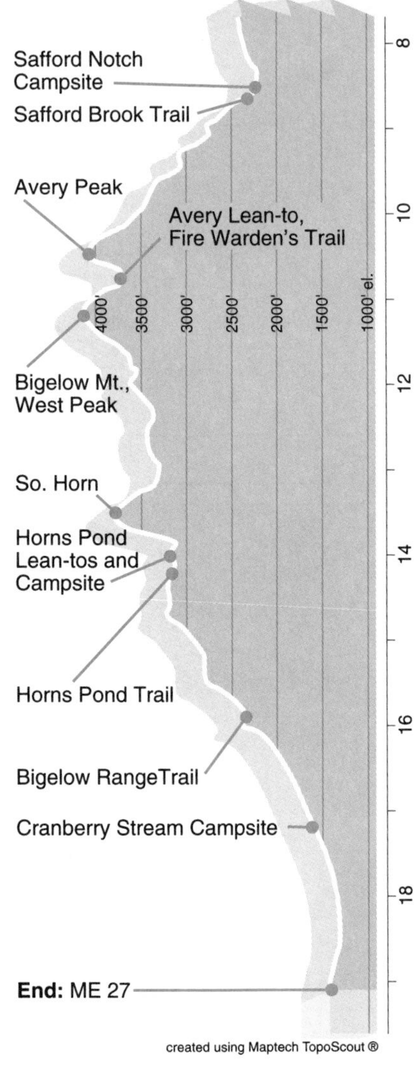

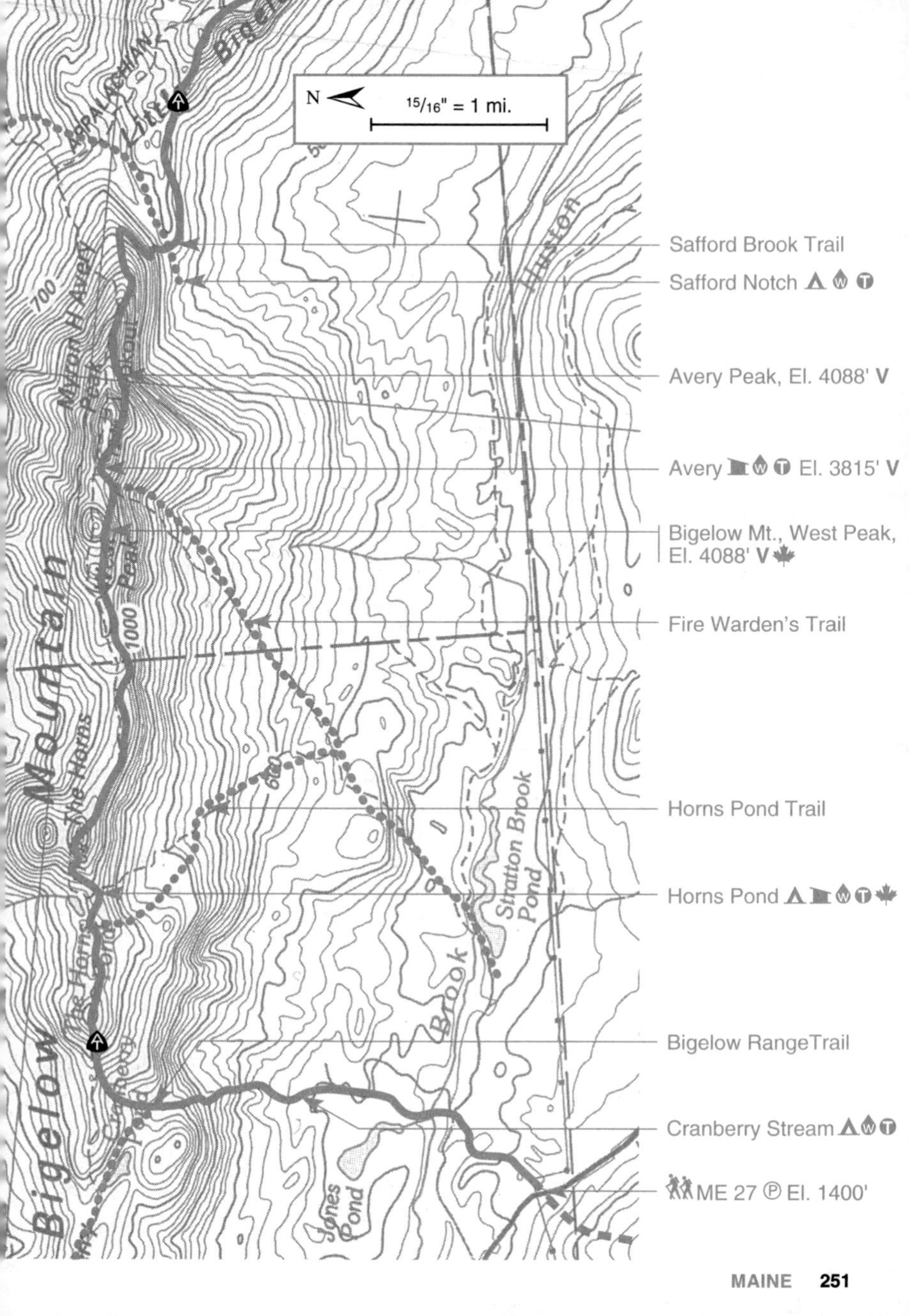

N
15/16" = 1 mi.
Safford Brook Trail
Safford Notch
Avery Peak, El. 4088' V
Avery El. 3815' V
Bigelow Mt., West Peak, El. 4088' V
Fire Warden's Trail
Horns Pond Trail
Horns Pond
Bigelow RangeTrail
Cranberry Stream
ME 27 Ⓟ El. 1400'
Bigelow Mountain
The Horns
Myron H Avery Peak
West Peak
Stratton Brook Pond
Brook
Jones Pond
Huston
APPALACHIAN
1000
700
600

Backpacking

Backpackers who carry on southward will pass the following way points on the Bigelow Range while en route to ME 27: A substantial climb on the AT out of Safford Notch brings you to Avery Peak, the east summit of Bigelow Mt. (4088 ft.), at 10.7 mi. At 11.1 mi. the Myron Avery Lean-to appears. Situated at 3815 ft., this is one of the higher ones on New England's AT.

Myron Avery was a Mainer, an avid hiker, and a go-getter. One of the first chairmen of the young Appalachian Trail Conference in the 1930s, Avery's tenure lasted until 1952. He worked indefatigably for years to push the trail to its completion, Georgia to Maine. He was one of the first people to walk the entire length of the trail, but it took him 16 years to complete his piecemeal journey (1920-1936). He kept detailed notes about trail construction and routing and did a great deal of mapping. An evangelist for a good cause, Avery was sometimes overbearing in his enthusiasm and management style, but his was an unparalleled contribution to creating the Appalachian Trail, making him an equal giant in AT legend beside the trail's visionary founder, Benton MacKaye.

Near Avery Lean-to, Fire Warden's Trail leads 3.8 mi. downhill (south) to Stratton Brook Pond Rd., passing Moose Falls Campsite only 1.0 mi. down the trail.

Continuing on the AT, Bigelow Mt.'s west peak, with good views, comes up at 11.4 mi. (4088 ft.). Another peak, the South Horn, is at 13.5 mi., and a spur to the North Horn and views is at 13.6 mi. There are two lean-tos and tent platforms at the Horns Pond site. At 14.2 mi., Horns Pond Trail descends 3.9 mi. south, joining Fire Warden Trail on its way to Stratton Brook Pond Rd. Bigelow Range Trail comes up at 15.9 mi., leading over Cranberry Peak and down to Stratton Village.

The next official campsite on the AT is Cranberry Stream at 17.2 mi. Stratton Brook Pond Rd. is crossed at 18.3 mi. See itinerary for parking information. And the backpacking hike concludes at ME 27, 19.1 strenuous but rewarding miles from the start.

HIKE #26 Itinerary

Miles N	NORTH	Elev. (ft/m)	Miles S
19.1	**Start: Long Falls Dam Rd.,** roadside parking.	1250/381	0.0
18.5	**Flagstaff Lake,** view.		0.6
18.3	**Stratton Brook Pond Rd.,** parking.		0.8
16.8	**Bog Brook Rd.,** then **East Flagstaff Rd.,** AT parking lot. Go R 0.1 mi., re-enter forest. Parking E of AT.		2.3
15.3	Short spur trail to **Little Bigelow Lean-to;** water, privy.	1850/564	3.8
13.6	E summit of **Little Bigelow Mt.,** views.	3040/927	5.5
12.2	W summit of **Little Bigelow Mt.,** views. Spur trail SW to views.		6.1
	REVERSE direction for circuit hike; return to Start on AT.		6.9
10.4	**Safford Notch.** Spur trail (0.3 mi.) to **Safford Notch Campsite,** water, privy, tent platforms.		8.7
10.3	**Safford Brook Trail** 2.2 mi. N to E Flagstaff Rd., parking. Boulder caves nearby (N) on AT.	2250/686	8.8
8.4	E summit of Bigelow Mt., **Avery Peak,** view.	4088/1246	10.7
8.0	**Myron Avery Lean-to,** view. **Fire Warden's Trail,** (3.8 mi. SW down to Stratton Brook Pond Rd. and **Moose Falls Campsite,** 1.0 mi. from AT); no fires.	3815/1163	11.1
7.7	**Bigelow Mt.,** west peak, panorama.	4088/1246	11.4
5.6	Summit of **South Horn.**	3805/1160	13.5
5.5	Spur trail (0.2 mi.) to **North Horn.**	3792/1156	13.6
5.1	**Horns Pond Lean-tos and Campsite.** Tent platforms, water, privy.	3160/963	14.0

Itinerary continued

HIKE #26 Itinerary *continues on previous page.*

Miles N		Elev. (ft/m)	Miles S
4.9	Junction with **Horns Pond Trail** (3.9 mi. S to Stratton Brook Pond Rd.).		14.2
3.2	Junction with **Bigelow Range Trail** (4.6 mi. W, via Cranberry Peak, to Stratton Village).		15.9
1.9	**Cranberry Stream Campsite,** water, privy.	1700/518	17.2
1.0	**Stratton Brook,** footbridge.		18.1
0.8	Cross **Stratton Brook Pond Rd.** (1.4 mi. W to ME 27, 0.7 mi. E to parking for Fire Warden's Trail and Horns Pond Trail).		18.3
0.0	**End: ME 27.** Parking on W side of hwy.	1400/427	19.1

HIKE #27

Carry Ponds

Maps: Maine AT Club, #5
Route: From Long Falls Dam Rd. to Carry Ponds, to Pierce Pond, across the Kennebec River, to US 201
Recommended direction: S to N
Distance: 17.5 mi.
Elevation +/-: 1250 to 2000 to 540 ft.
Effort: Moderate
Day hike: No
Overnight backpacking hike: Yes
Duration: 9 hr.
Early exit option: None
Natural history features: Carry Ponds; Kennebec River
Social history features: Benedict Arnold's march
Trailhead access: *Start:* From North New Portland, drive 19.8 mi. N on Long Falls Dam Rd. to overnight roadside parking (south side). *End:* US 201, at the N end of Caratunk, 16 mi. N of Bingham and 7.3 mi. S of The Forks; overnight parking up steep incline on E side of road.
Camping: Pierce Pond Lean-to; West Carry Pond Lean-to and campsite

This hike combines beautiful forest scenes with the scene of a dramatic moment in American history. Winding through a series of ponds, along streams and across the Kennebec River, the path also crosses part of the Arnold Trail, the route of the historic march led by Col. Benedict Arnold in 1775.

From the junction of the AT and Long Falls Dam Rd., the trail crosses Jerome Brook on a narrow footbridge. It then winds through a boggy area heavily populated with cedar trees, which thrive in swampy areas. Tea made from the tree's foliage and bark, which is high in vitamin C, saved adventurer Jacques Cartier's crew from scurvy in 1535. It was thus later named *arborvitae,* Latin for "tree of life," and was probably the first North American tree introduced into Europe.

The AT then crosses a gravel road at 0.4 mi. and begins a 1.3-mi. climb up a moderate ridge to the northern shoulder of Roundtop Mt. Look back to the south and west for limited views of broad-shouldered Little Bigelow Mt. The trail passes through a primarily deciduous forest—oak, maple, and birch trees. You may see or hear a hairy woodpecker tap, tap, tapping on the trunk of a tree. Adult birds have a black-and-white striped-head and white spots on the wings; males have a red patch on the nape. Along the AT in forest habitats, you may also see downy woodpeckers, smaller than the hairy with a very

Michael Warren

Backpackers, Kennebec River crossing

small bill, as well as the rarer pileated woodpecker, a crow-size bird that has a distinctive bright red crest and crown. As woodpeckers drill deep into dead trees, they can spear beetles and other bugs that live yearround in the bark. Thus, unlike other insect-eating birds, woodpeckers generally don't need to migrate.

The trail now traverses the shoulder of Roundtop Mt. (2240 ft.) and descends moderately toward West Carry Pond. The AT reaches the southwest corner of the pond at 2.8 mi. and follows the shoreline for 0.7 mi. to reach West Carry Pond Lean-to, which has tentsites, a privy, and water from the pond. The trail then circles around the pond for another 0.7 mi. through a boggy area and woods to reach a short side trail to Arnold Point, which features excellent views of Roundtop Mt. You see the pond in all of its glory—a blue body of water towered over by oval mountains lined by evergreen trees.

Here the AT intersects with the Arnold Trail, which commemorates Benedict Arnold's famous march to Québec (before he switched allegiances). Commissioned by Gen. George Washington to mount a surprise attack on Québec City, which was occupied by the British, Arnold led a detachment of troops from Cambridge, Massachusetts, in mid-September. The flotilla traveled up the Kennebec River to "The Great Carrying Place," the portage between the Kennebec and the Dead rivers used by the Abenakis to avoid rapids on the Dead. In part because of nasty weather, it took the troops six weeks to carry some 200 bateaux (a flat-bottomed boat with a sharply pointed bow and stern), through the swamps, rivers, and bogs of this rugged wilderness. The delay was a major factor in the failure of Arnold's final assault on December 31, 1775.

The AT then leaves Arnold Point and follows Arnold Trail east for approximately 2 mi. past Middle Carry Pond. As you walk through this low, boggy terrain, imagine having to haul a heavy boat loaded with supplies through the muck. At 5.7 mi., the trail crosses Arnold Swamp on an extensive bog bridge.

The trail follows along the top of an esker, a long, narrow, winding ridge of stratified sand and gravel, material deposited in the beds of streams that flowed through tunnels beneath the continental glacier. When the glacial ice melted away, this ridge of water-washed sediment remained where the tunnel had been. Eskers, sometimes called horsebacks, are commonly located adjacent to or in boggy areas.

After 0.1 mi. in the swamp, the AT takes a sharp left turn onto a gravel road, continuing for 0.1 mi. before turning right on another road and crossing Sandy Stream. The trail continues 150 ft. up the road, turning left into the woods. The next 0.8 mi. winds through mixed woods up and over a small knob before crossing the East Carry Pond logging road. Continue another 0.2 mi. to the west shore of East Carry Pond, a small pond rimmed by rocks and ledges. A sandy beach here offers a good opportunity for a lunch break.

The footpath follows the shore of the pond for 0.5 mi. before heading back into the woods. The trail continues on the level for 1.7 mi., reaching a gravel logging road at 9.3 mi.

After crossing the North Branch of the Carrying Place Stream at 10.0 mi., Hike #27 follows a stream, then climbs up and over a leafy saddle between the twin peaks of Bates Ridge at 1500 ft. The trail descends to Pierce Pond Lean-to, with water from the pond, a privy, and a lean-to that accommodates six. The trail continues to a wooden bridge along the edge of Pierce Pond, and features views of Pierce Pond Mt. (2516 ft.), which rises dramatically from the shoreline. At 13.9 mi., the AT reaches a side trail that leads south 0.1 mi. to Harrison's Camps, where the proprietors will call ahead for you to Rivers and Trails, the guide service that ferries hikers across the Kennebec River by canoe. The free ferry service typically runs from May through October. Dates and times of operation are posted at nearby lean-tos and at the crossing. Call 1-888-FLOAT-ME or 207-663-4441 for more information or to make special arrangements. Taking the ferry is important, because fording the river is extremely dangerous due to unpredictable releases of water by a hydro facility upstream. The river is roughly 70 yd. wide, with a current and depth that can change drastically.

The AT then crosses a gravel road at 14.2 mi. The next 3.0 mi., leading to the west bank of the Kennebec, is a terrific stretch of the trail. The narrow needle-lined path parallels Pierce Pond Stream as it heads down to the Kennebec. The AT passes several beaver dams on the stream. Beavers, which are large aquatic rodents, are nature's engineers, building dams—and underwater lodges, their homes—with sticks, logs, and mud.

At 14.7 mi., the trail reaches the first of a series of waterfalls. Waterfalls form from the erosion of the softer parts of the bedrock. As a stream cuts its channel deeper, the soft parts of the bedrock erode easily, but the harder sections of rock remain, blocking the stream and creating a waterfall. Along the Pierce Pond Stream, there is a succession of waterfalls, followed immediately by a pool. There are side trails to see peaceful, lovely waterfalls at 14.9 and 15.2 mi.

The trail crosses Otter Pond Stream, a tributary of Pierce Pond Stream, at 15.3 mi. The AT then descends a wooded ridge, at 15.9 mi., reaching another side trail to a ledge overlooking a waterfall. The footpath then winds through the forest along the lovely, tree-lined stream to the west bank of the Kennebec River, which at approximately 490 ft. is the lowest point on the AT in Maine. The Kennebec River valley was formed in part by the huge weight of the continental ice sheet, which depressed the land, drawing seawater far upstream.

Continued on p. 260

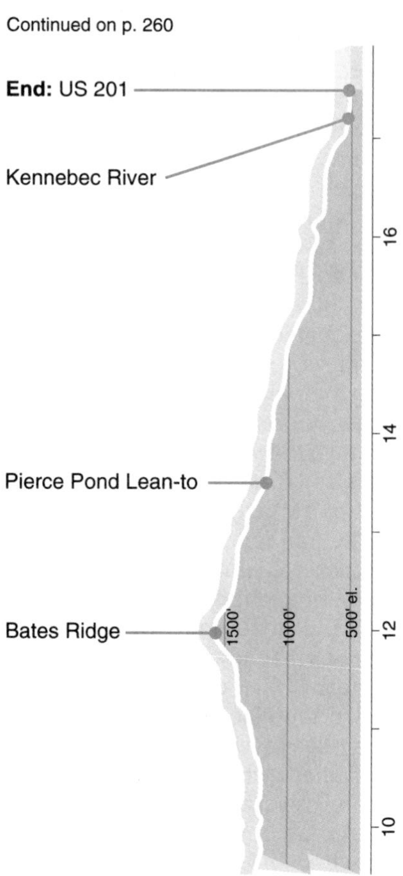

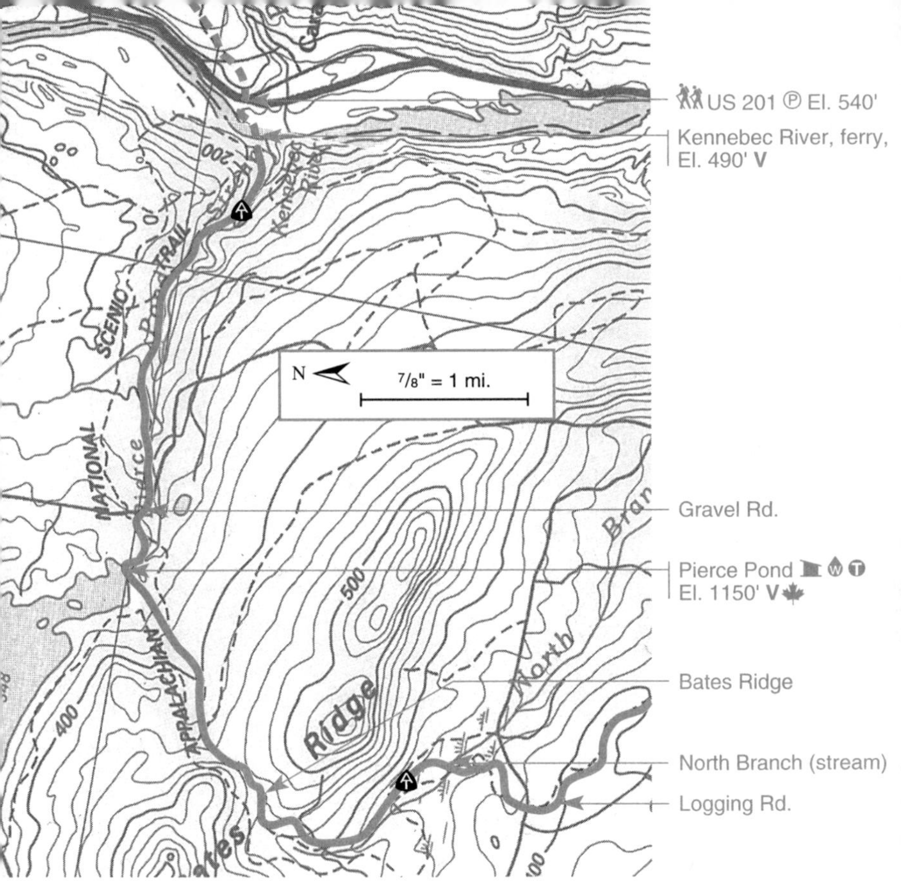

US 201 Ⓟ El. 540'
Kennebec River, ferry, El. 490' V
Gravel Rd.
Pierce Pond
El. 1150' V
Bates Ridge
North Branch (stream)
Logging Rd.
N
7/8" = 1 mi.
APPALACHIAN
NATIONAL
SCENIC
TRAIL
Ridge
North
500
400

Occasionally marine fossils, embedded in silt and clay, are discovered along the riverbanks, evidence of the intrusion of saltwater.

A guide from Rivers and Trails picks you up on the west bank of the Kennebec and ferries you across the swift river in a canoe. The quick journey over water after miles of walking on land is a welcome break. The trail climbs up to US 201, ending Hike #27 at 17.5 mi. Overnight parking is available up a steep incline on the east side of the road. The village of Caratunk, with a general store, post office, and hostel, is 0.3 mi. just to the south, on a branch road of US 201.

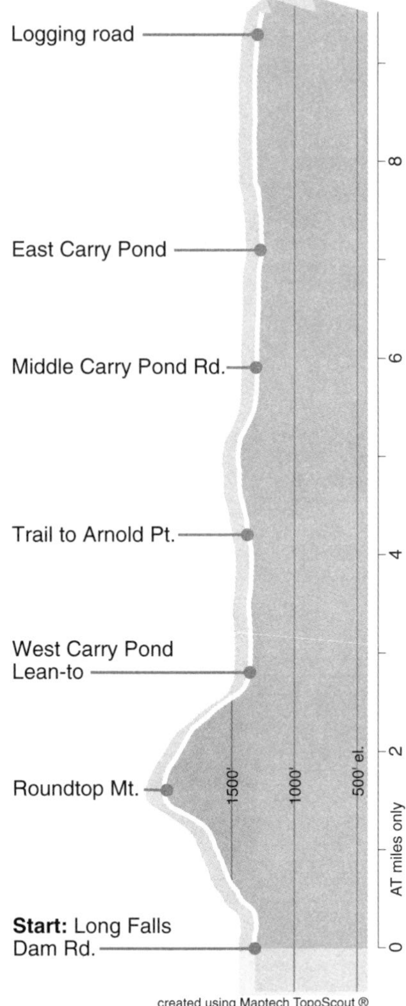

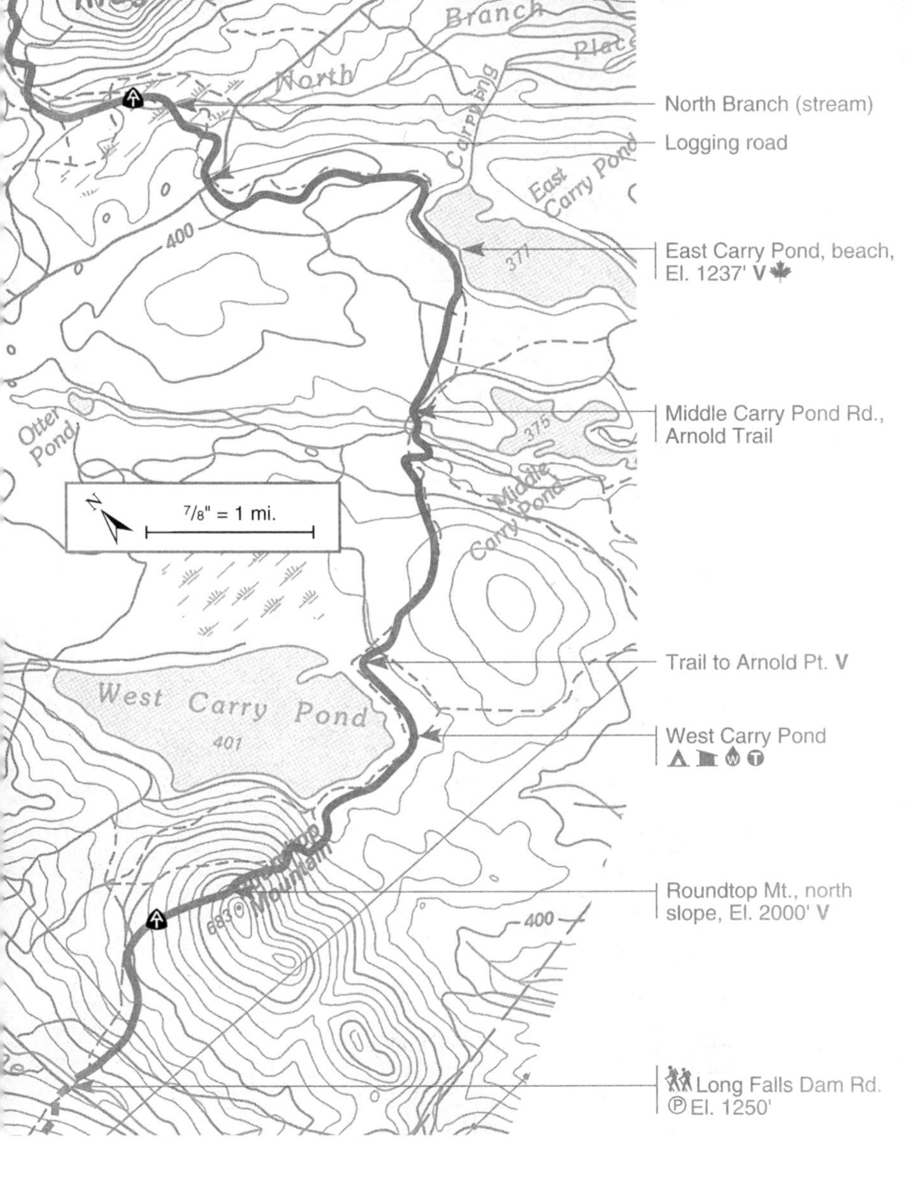
North Branch (stream)
Logging road
East Carry Pond, beach, El. 1237' V
Middle Carry Pond Rd., Arnold Trail
Trail to Arnold Pt. V
West Carry Pond
Roundtop Mt., north slope, El. 2000' V
Long Falls Dam Rd. Ⓟ El. 1250'
7/8" = 1 mi.
N
North
Branch
Carry Pond
East Carry Pond
Otter Pond
Middle Carry Pond
West Carry Pond
Roundtop Mountain
400
377
375
401

HIKE #27 Itinerary

Miles N	NORTH	Elev. (ft/m)	Miles S
17.5	**End: US 201,** Caratunk, parking.	540/165	0.0
17.2	**Kennebec River.** Cross by canoe ferry. Do not ford.	490/149	0.3
15.3	**Otter Pond Stream,** ford.		2.2
14.9	Spur trail to waterfalls, **Pierce Pond Stream.**		2.6
14.2	Dirt road.		3.3
13.9	Side trail to Harrison's Camps; call for canoe ferry service.		3.6
13.7	**Pierce Pond,** wooden dam at outlet.		3.8
13.5	**Pierce Pond Lean-to,** water, privy.	1150/351	4.0
12.0	**Bates Ridge,** saddle.	1500/457	5.5
10.0	**Carrying Place Stream,** North Branch (ford).		7.5
9.3	Logging road.		8.2
7.1	**East Carry Pond,** W shore; trail follows shoreline.	1237/377	10.4
6.1	**Sandy Stream,** bridge at dirt road.		11.4
5.9	**Middle Carry Pond Rd.**		11.6
5.7	Bridge across **Arnold Swamp.**		11.8
4.2	Spur trail to **Arnold Point.** AT follows Arnold Trail.	1317/401	13.3
3.5	**West Carry Pond Lean-to,** water, privy, tentsites.		14.0
2.8	**West Carry Pond,** trail follows shoreline		14.7
1.7	**Roundtop Mt.,** N slope.	2000/610	15.8
0.4	Logging road (gravel).		17.1
0.1	**Jerome Brook,** bridge.		17.4
0.0	**Start: Long Falls Dam Rd.;** head E from trailhead (toward Jerome Brook).	1250/381	17.5

SOUTH

HIKE #28

Pleasant Pond Mt.

Maps: Maine AT Club, #4

Route: (Day hike) From Boise-Cascade Rd. at Pleasant Pond to Pleasant Pond Mt. and return; (extended hike) continue to Moxie Pond

Recommended direction: S to N

Distance: Circuit hike, 3.2 mi.; extended hike, 6.5 mi.

Elevation +/-: 1400 to 2477 to 900 ft.

Effort: Moderate

Day hike: Yes

Overnight backpacking hike: No

Duration: Circuit hike, 2 hr.; to Moxie Pond, 4 to 4.5 hrs.

Early exit option: None

Natural history features: Old-growth spruce-fir forest

Trailhead access: *Start:* From Caratunk, turn R from ME 201 onto the road that loops through the village; turn R again at village store and post office. Road soon becomes unpaved and follows Pleasant Pond Stream for 3.2 mi. to Pleasant Pond. Veer L at pond; follow road 1.8 mi. to AT parking just beyond Boise-Cascade Rd. *End:* From US 201 in Bingham, go 0.8 mi. N on ME 16, then N on dirt road (Scott Paper Co.) at intersection with Cassidy Rd. AT trailhead and parking are 15.9 mi. from Bingham.

Camping: Pleasant Pond Lean-to

Just a few miles south from the start of Hike #28 is the village of Caratunk, frequently visited by long-distance hikers. "Caratunk" is an Indian word for "forbidding or crooked stream," according to the *Appalachian Trail Guide to Maine*, and refers to a falls in the Kennebec River near the site of the present Wyman Dam, which generates power for the New England grid.

The dam buried more than the falls: more than 30 farmhouses had to be moved, along with two cemeteries. Over time, the village had grown to have an axe factory, a gristmill, and a sawmill. Walter York built snowshoes here until the 1980s. But the town's history is inextricably bound with lumbering, particularly with the log drives on the Kennebec. The last log drive in Maine was held on this river in 1976. The long history of the drives is filled with tragic events. In 1893, a young Caratunk man named Austin Moore left a poker game to check on a logjam in the river; his companions heard a yell and went outside in time to see Moore slip from a log and drown. Hikers crossing the Kennebec today must use a (canoe) ferry service rather than attempting to ford the river (see Hike #27).

Butterflies and Mudpuddles

Hiking near the trailhead for Pleasant Pond Mt. on an August afternoon, I saw hundreds of butterflies gathered around a mud puddle, excitedly sipping from the puddle with extended proboscis. Oblivious to my presence, these butterflies let me approach within a few feet.

Lepidopterists refer to this butterfly habit, matter-of-factly enough, as "mud puddling." In Maine, some of the butterflies that most often show this behavior are also the most striking. Compton's tortoiseshell is a rich blend of black, white, and deep oranges and yellows. One of our earliest butterflies, it hibernates as an adult. Emerging in the spring, it often gathers at white birch sap oozing from scars on the trunk, and maple sugarers occasionally find them in their buckets. Tiger swallowtails, one of the largest butterflies in the state, are boldly patterned in yellow and black. White admirals—the species I saw at Pleasant Pond—are black butterflies with a bold white border. In addition to loving mud puddles, they are drawn to carrion and excrement, a habit one researcher delicately calls "nectaring off droppings."

Butterflies are also drawn to the salt in urine and perspiration. Hiking in Baxter State Park one day, I stopped to change my sweaty socks. A mourning cloak butterfly landed on one sock, then moved to my foot, and then spent more than an hour licking perspiration from my feet and legs. Lepidopterists suspect the butterflies may use the mud puddles as a type of "salt lick." Curiously, the "puddling clubs," as congregations are called, are largely made up of bachelor males. The group appears to be a continually changing one composed of new individuals, who stay for several days before disbanding to seek mates. The puddles may be a source of mineral salts needed for reproduction by breeding males.

Much of the stimulus and dynamics of puddling remain poorly understood: Why are some species attracted to puddles and others are not? Are the same areas used repeatedly, or do individuals move from one puddle to another?

You can lure some of these butterflies to your home. A mixture of sugar and beer works well for some species; for others, rotting fruit is attractive; and for others—you may not want to try this one—decaying feces. An attraction for tiger swallowtails is a dish of table salt diluted in water, along with a mounted swallowtail or a hand-colored photocopy from a field guide.

If that fails, hike in Baxter Park until your feet start to blister, then change your socks. —Andrew Weegar

Pleasant Pond Mt. is steep but short and makes for an easy day hike. The trail is wide and simple to follow, though it is eroded in several steep ledgy spots. This is a good winter hike, as the road is plowed to the trailhead parking lot off Boise-Cascade Rd.

From the parking lot, the trail leads north into the woods under a large forked pine, its head destroyed by white pine weevil. Often these pines take on a characteristic bushy shape; lumbermen call them "cabbage" pines. Only 0.3 mi. into the hike, the spur trail to Pleasant Pond Lean-to appears. Water and a privy are here. Stock up on water: there's not much more from here to Moxie Pond. If it's swimming season or if you enjoy sitting for a while by the water, watch for the side trail to the sandy beach at Pleasant Pond at 0.5 mi. Or you might want to save the detour to the beach for the end of the round-trip hike.

Pleasant Pond offers only mediocre fishing. Apparently not much has changed in this regard since the great naturalist John Burroughs visited here in 1881. He described Pleasant Pond as "the only strictly silver lake I ever saw" but went on to say the fish were only in the deepest part of the lake, and then you needed "a letter of introduction to them."

The trail follows along an old tote road, then angles left and crosses a small brook. Though this brook is hardly worth a second thought in summer, imagine leaping across it on snowshoes with a full pack in February, when winter's snows have left it deep as a canyon. One hiker reported following a fisher's tracks as it leapfrogged along the trail through here: in some places the tracks measured a full 64 in. between bounds.

Along this section there are also innumerable blowdown spruce, their root masses thrust up close to the trail. Spruce, and particularly balsam fir, are shallow-rooted and tend to windthrow (uproot). One particularly destructive windstorm northwest of Katahdin blew down over 5000 acres in one day in 1984. Over time, the soil thrust up by these root masses leaves a characteristic hump next to the hollow created when they were pulled from the soil. This "pit and mound" topography is characteristic of old-growth softwood forests in the Northeast.

Hikers along this trail in 1993 reported the progress of a winter wren nesting in one of these root masses. Though the bird flushed every time a hiker passed, it managed to raise a brood.

Leaving the spruce forest, the trail continues up through a stand of large aspen (called poplar or "popple" in Maine), then climbs steeply uphill along open ledges with views of the pond.

The forest through here is mixed woods, with some fine red pine and cedar. Red pine, often called Norway pine, is named not for the country but for the town of Norway, Maine, where the tree was first identified. Cedar is also commonly known as *arborvitae* (as are several other North American and Asian evergreen trees and shrubs of the genus *Thuja*). See Hike #27.

At several places, wire dangles from the trees, the remains of the telephone service to a onetime fire warden's camp at the top of the mountain. Isolated camps like these were provided with phone lines, but the lines were often more of a nuisance than they were worth, as any branch blown down during a storm would ground the line and deaden the connection, requiring a careful inspection of the wire along its whole length until the short was found.

Approaching the top of Pleasant Pond Mt., the trail passes a small spring on the right. Just a few steps beyond, you will see the remains of the old fire warden's cabin. Porcupines have sought refuge here, so the cabin may not be around much longer. Like all rodents, porcupines must chew to keep their teeth honed, and they love to chew anything associated with man, which often carries salt deposits from perspiration.

Near the summit, the trail turns hard right and clambers up over rocky outcrops, following blazes and cairns to the peak. Pleasant Pond Mt. (2477 ft., at 1.6 mi.) has fine views, particularly of the Bigelow Range to the southwest. The summit of Moxie Bald (Hike #29) is visible to the east

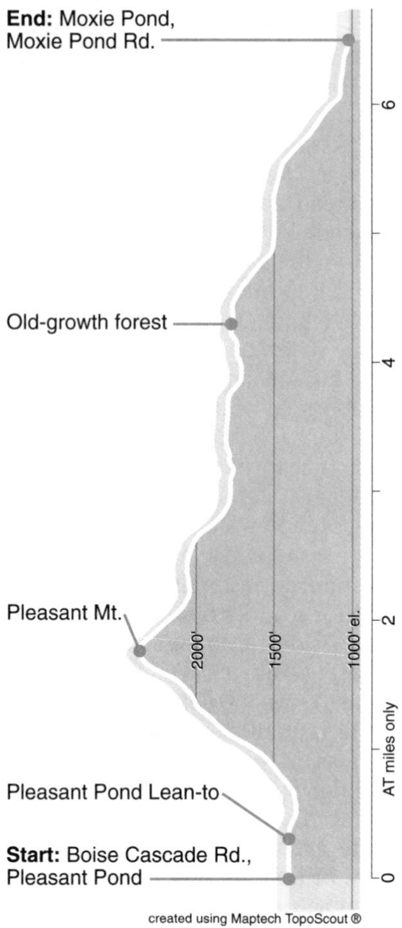

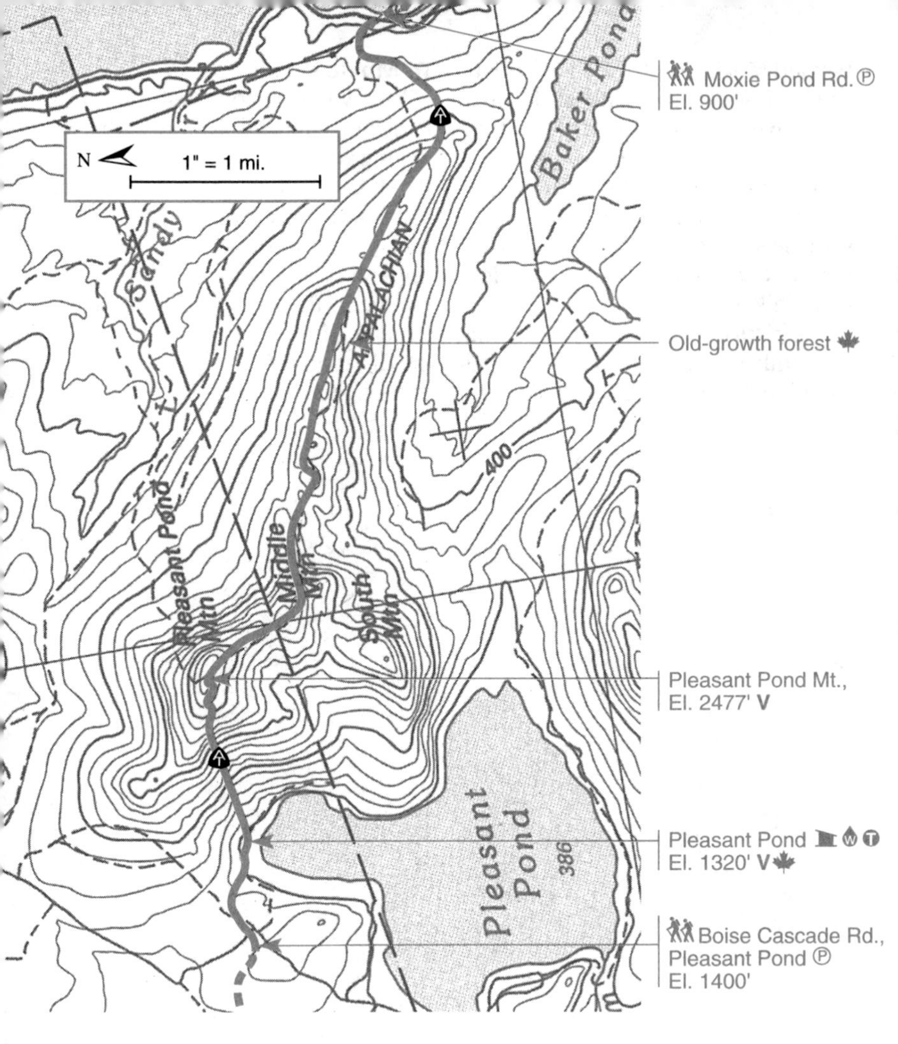
Moxie Pond Rd. Ⓟ
El. 900'
N
1" = 1 mi.
Baker Pond
Sandy
APPALACHIAN
Old-growth forest
400
Pleasant Pond
Middle Mtn
Pleasant Mtn
South Mtn
Pleasant Pond Mt.,
El. 2477' V
Pleasant Pond
386
Pleasant Pond
El. 1320' V
Boise Cascade Rd.,
Pleasant Pond Ⓟ
El. 1400'

beyond Moxie Pond. The long, nubbly ridge of Squaw Mt. (site of the first fire tower in the country, built in 1905) is off to the north.

Linger a while up here and enjoy the views. The top makes a fine lunch spot. Be sure to carry out any litter—yours or some left behind by a forgetful hiker.

The return to the start is a 1.6 mi. downhill walk, with Pleasant Pond awaiting you for a dip if you like.

To Moxie Pond

Hikers who carry on northward from Pleasant Pond Mt. will pass the following way points en route to Moxie Pond: At 4.3 mi. an old-growth section of fir and spruce. At 6.0 mi. a minor brook crossing, followed by a pass under a power line at 6.4 mi. And immediately thereafter, at 6.5 mi., Moxie Pond itself, with hiker parking just off the dirt road the AT crosses before reentering the woods.

Hike #28 Itinerary

Miles N	NORTH	Elev. (ft/m)	Miles S
6.5	**End: Moxie Pond,** unpaved road, parking off W side.	900/274	0.0
6.4	Power line.		0.1
6.0	Brook (stock up on water for next 5.7 mi. S).		0.5
4.3	Old-growth evergreen woods.		2.2
	Reverse direction for circuit hike.		
1.6	Summit of **Pleasant Mt.,** views.	2477/755	4.9
0.5	Spur trail (0.2 mi.) to **Pleasant Pond beach.**		6.0
0.3	Spur trail to **Pleasant Pond Lean-to,** water (stock up for next 5.7 mi. N), privy.	1320/402	6.2
0.0	**Start: Boise-Cascade Rd.,** Pleasant Pond, AT parking lot.	1400/427	6.5
	SOUTH		

HIKE #29

Moxie Bald Mt.

Maps: Maine AT Club, #4

Route: (Day hike) From Moxie Pond to North Peak, Moxie Bald Mt., and return; (extended backpacking hike) continue on to Bald Mt. Pond, to Piscataquis River, to Shirley-Blanchard Rd.

Recommended direction: S to N

Distance: Day hike, 9.6 mi. round-trip; backpacking hike, 18.5 mi.

Elevation: 900 to 2629 to 900 ft.

Effort: Strenuous

Day hike: Yes

Overnight backpacking hike: Optional

Duration: Day hike, 5-6 hr.; backpacking trip, 10 to 11 hr.

Early exit option: None

Natural history features: Blueberries and raspberries in season

Social history features: First views of Katahdin for northbound hikers

Trailhead access: *Start:* From US 201 in Bingham, go 0.8 mi. N on ME 16; then N on dirt road (Scott Paper Co.) at intersection with Cassidy Rd. AT trailhead and parking are 15.9 mi. from Bingham. *End:* From Blanchard go 1.3 mi. N on Shirley-Blanchard Rd. to AT trailhead; parking on W side of road.

Camping: Bald Mt. Brook Lean-to and Campsite; Moxie Bald Lean-to; Horseshoe Canyon Lean-to

The origin of the word "Moxie" is obscure, though it is thought to be an Abenaki word meaning "dark water." Say "Moxie" to a Mainer and he or she will probably think of the soft drink, but the relationship of the drink to the place is unclear.

Some Mainers grew up drinking Moxie in their baby bottles; others can't stand the stuff. Whatever your feelings about the drink, the hike up Moxie Bald is one of the prettiest you'll find.

Even the beginning of this hike is gorgeous, leapfrogging across the rocks at a small rapid on Baker Stream (0.1 mi.). If you are feeling adventurous, or if the water is high, there is a single-cable crossing slightly downstream.

Across the stream, the AT leads through a stand of Balm of Gilead poplar, with an occasional towering white pine. At 0.5 mi., it passes under a power line. Before and after the power line, the AT travels under thick stands of overgrown pole spruce, with dead white birch dotting the forest. The birch were the pioneer species, providing shade for the spruce seedlings that now make up this stand. A decade ago, these spruce would have produced smooth untapered trunks ten ft. high and as thick as a young girl's wrist, ideal for fashioning a canoe pole. In late summer, with rivers too shallow to paddle, a canoeist with a good pole can maneuver his canoe for miles upstream or down. Poling is dying out, and it is a rare thing to see a poler today.

Beyond the spruce, the trail heads through a forest of mature sugar maples, then passes a stand of young hardwoods. This is the type of forest ruffed grouse prefer, and it is common to see them rocket from the underbrush. As you continue on the AT, the hardwoods are more mature, and the trail slabs along a hardwood ridge. From here the trail leads over a low spruce-clad knoll, and at 1.2 mi., it reaches Joe's Hole Brook, named for a legendary fishing guide on Moxie Pond.

Len Clifford

Raccoon

At this point the AT joins an old tote road, climbing gradually through deciduous woods made up of sugar maple, beech, and an occasional yellow birch for about a mile and a half. As you gain elevation, the woods change to a mature forest of black spruce, dotted underneath with wintergreen, partridgeberry, and starflower. The trail continues into a raspberry-filled clearing. One hiker through here reported that when he stopped to pick berries one day, he noticed he had company: a sow bear and two cubs. The bears were as nervous as he was and bolted for the woods when they caught his scent.

Beyond the clearing, the trail crosses Bald Mt. Brook at 2.6 mi., where you'll find Bald Mt. Brook Campsite, and Bald Mt. Brook Lean-to comes up at 2.8 mi. Beyond the brook, the trail leads to another clearing, then into a mature hardwood forest. Leaving this area, the AT hops over another brook, which runs only in the spring. Now the trail begins to climb more abruptly on Moxie Bald and heads through stands of fir and spruce and mixed hardwoods. Leveling off in a forest of low spruce, mountain ash, laurel, and Labrador tea, the trail next rises again over a series of knolls. This rocky area before the summit is referred to by locals as "the devil's doorstep."

At 4.2 mi., the summit bypass trail leads off to the left. This trail skirts to the northwest of the open summit of the mountain and can be taken in poor weather. The AT climbs steeply over a series of ledges to the peak (2629 ft.) at 4.8 mi. A lookout tower on the summit provides views in all directions. Among the highlights: the first views of Katahdin for northbound hikers.

Our day hike ends here, reversing direction and retracing the route back to Moxie Pond. Hikers who want to add some distance to the day hike circuit can continue north on the AT, descending somewhat for 0.3 mi. to the summit bypass trail on Moxie's east side (at 5.1 mi.), which leads back to the bypass trail junction you crossed on your way up. This is one option for the circuit hike. Another is to continue north on the AT to 5.8 mi. and the spur trail (0.7 mi.) up to the North Peak of Moxie Bald. Extending to here makes the circuit a 13.0-mi. affair. Be sure to allow plenty of time (and water and food) for the return trip.

In late July and early August, there is a good incentive to take the side trail up to the North Peak: The open summit is covered with blueberries, and low wet spots along this section of the trail yield wild cranberries.

Older maps and references to Moxie Bald refer to it as Bald Mt. Because it is one of any number of "Bald Mountains" in the state, it is now generally referred to as Moxie Bald. The great naturalist John Burroughs, friend of John Muir and Theodore Roosevelt, hiked Moxie Bald in 1881. Burroughs was impressed by the mountain's large exposed granite crown and the stunning views it afforded over Maine's vast wilderness of lakes and forest. Caribou, deer, and

Continued on p. 274

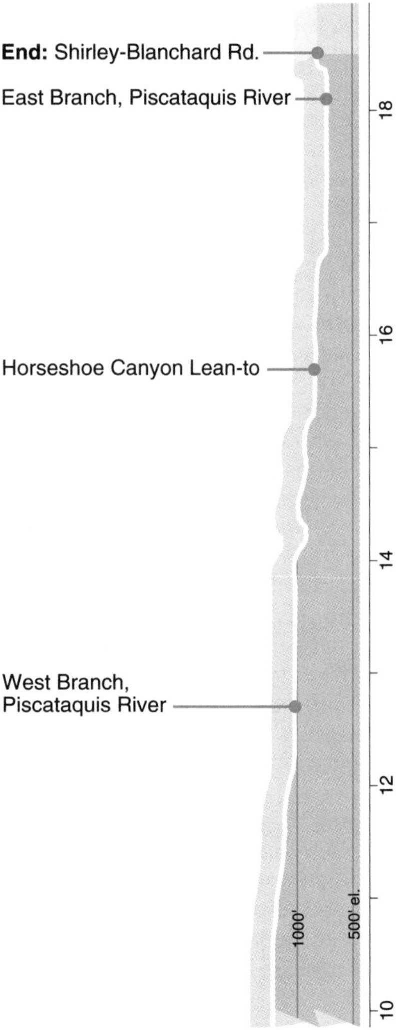

End: Shirley-Blanchard Rd.
East Branch, Piscataquis River
Horseshoe Canyon Lean-to
West Branch,
Piscataquis River
1000'
500' el.
18
16
14
12
10

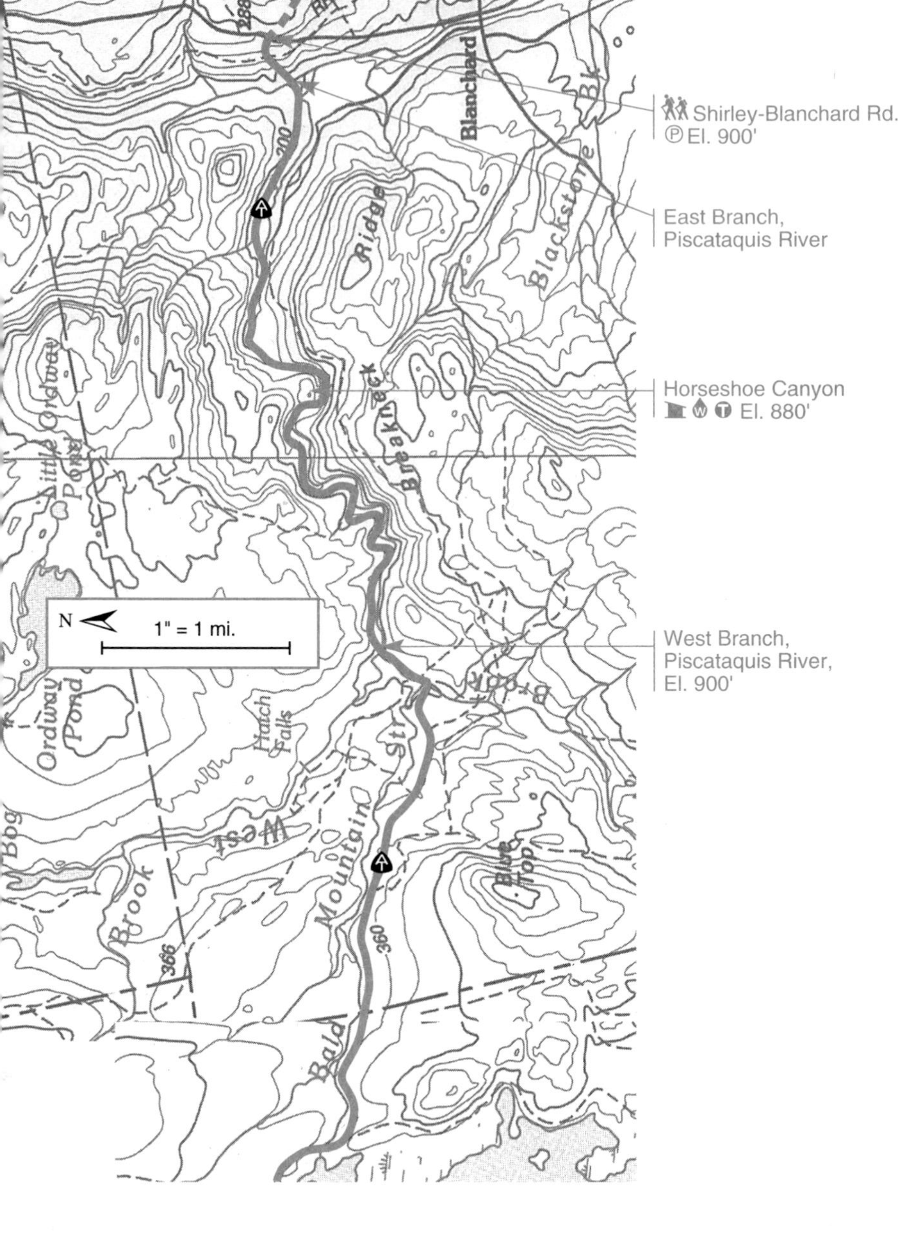
Shirley-Blanchard Rd.
El. 900'
East Branch,
Piscataquis River
Horseshoe Canyon
El. 880'
West Branch,
Piscataquis River,
El. 900'
N
1" = 1 mi.
Blanchard
Ridge
Blackstone
Breakneck
Little Ordway Pond
Ordway Pond
Hatch Falls
West
Brook
Mountain
Bald
Blue Top
288
300
360
366
RR

bear were plentiful in the 1880s, but the caribou are gone from Maine in our time.

Backpacking trip

Backpackers who carry on northward will pass the following way points en route to Shirley-Blanchard Rd.: Moxie Bald Lean-to at 6.9 mi., with water and privy. Bald Mt. Stream comes up at 9.0 mi., and the next water is at Marble Brook (12.4 mi.), where there is also an old dirt road. Shortly thereafter, at 12.7 mi., a potentially difficult and dangerous ford is necessary near the junction of the West Branch of the Piscataquis River and Bald Mt. Stream. "Piscataquis" means "at the river branch" according to *The Appalachian Trail Guide to Maine*. Exercise caution, use a walking stick, and reserve a dry pair of socks! The next shelter is Horseshoe Canyon Lean-to at 15.7 mi., where there is water and a privy. The Piscataquis River appears again, East Branch this time, and another ford, at 18.1 mi. A former railroad bed intersects the AT at 18.4 mi., and the hike concludes just beyond it at 18.5 mi., Shirley-Blanchard Rd., where there is an AT parking lot.

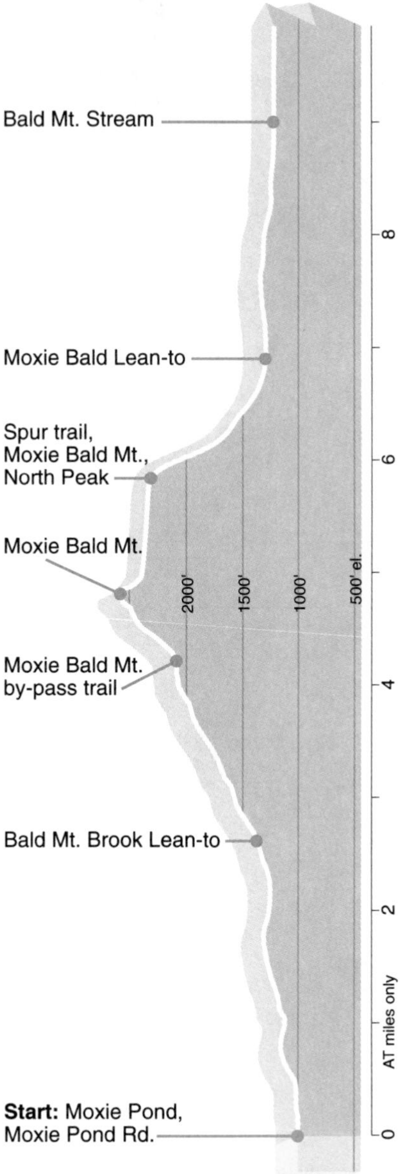

Bald Mt. Stream

Moxie Bald Lean-to

Spur trail, Moxie Bald Mt., North Peak

Moxie Bald Mt.

Moxie Bald Mt. by-pass trail

Bald Mt. Brook Lean-to

Start: Moxie Pond, Moxie Pond Rd.

2000' 1500' 1000' 500' el.

0 2 4 6 8

AT miles only

created using Maptech TopoScout ®

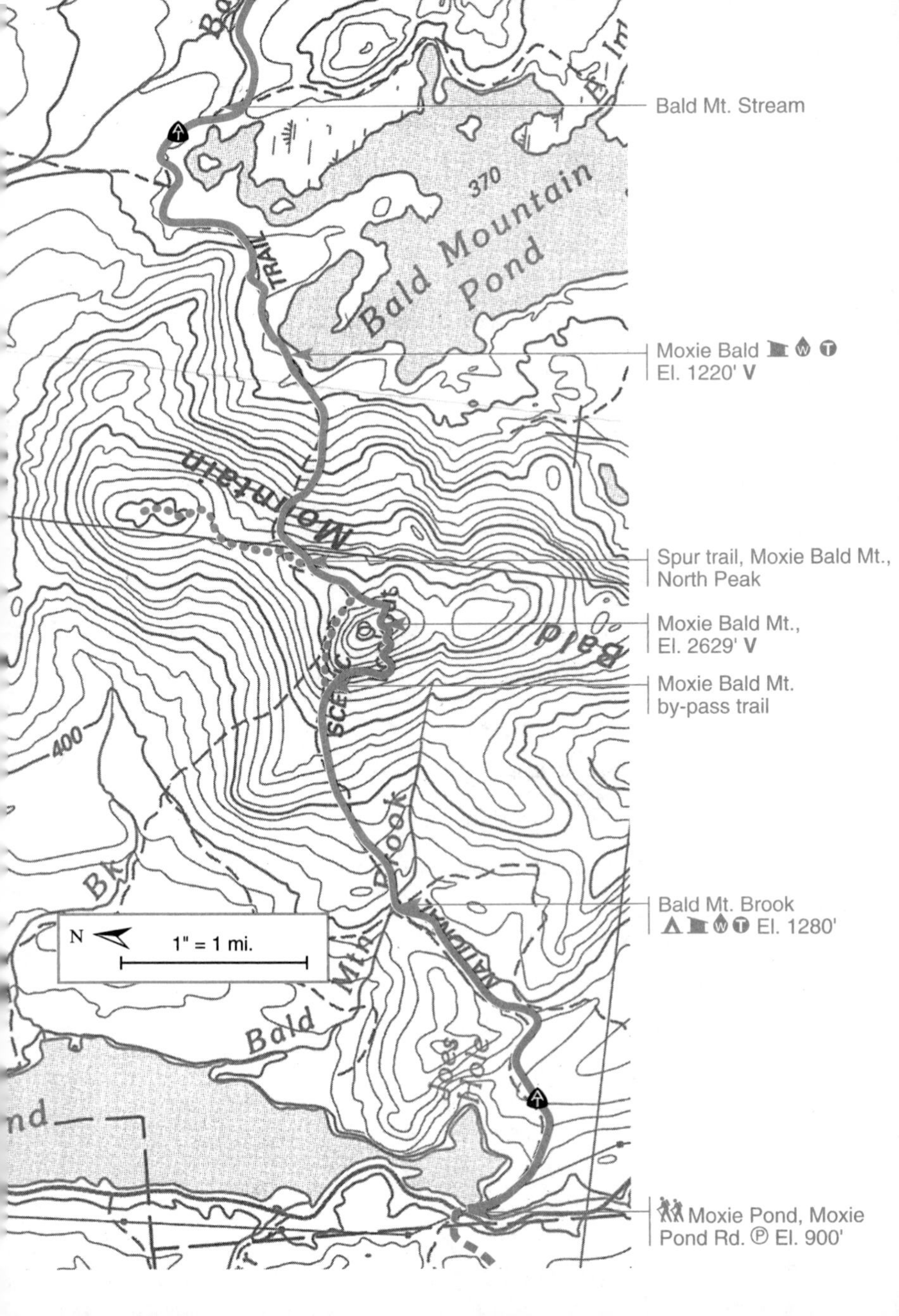

Bald Mt. Stream
370
Bald Mountain Pond
TRAIL
Moxie Bald
El. 1220' V
Mountain
Spur trail, Moxie Bald Mt., North Peak
Moxie Bald Mt., El. 2629' V
Bald
Moxie Bald Mt. by-pass trail
SCENIC
400
Brook
Bk
Bald Mt. Brook
El. 1280'
N
1" = 1 mi.
Bald Mtn
NATIONAL
Bald
Joes Hole
nd
Moxie Pond, Moxie Pond Rd. Ⓟ El. 900'

HIKE #29 Itinerary

Miles N	NORTH	Elev. (ft/m)	Miles S
18.5	**End: Shirley-Blanchard Rd.** (paved). AT parking lot, W side of road (0.1 mi. S).	900/274	0.0
18.4	Former Bangor & Aroostook Railroad bed.		0.1
18.1	**East Branch, Piscataquis River,** ford.		0.4
15.7	Spur trail to **Horseshoe Canyon Lean-to,** water, privy.	880/268	2.8
12.7	**West Branch, Piscataquis River** and **Bald Mt. Stream.** Potentially difficult fords.	900/274	5.8
12.4	**Marble Brook;** cross rough, unpaved road.		6.1
9.0	**Bald Mt. Stream.**		9.5
8.4	Dirt road.		10.1
6.9	**Moxie Bald Lean-to,** water, privy.	1220/372	11.6
5.8	Spur trail (0.7 mi.) to **North Peak,** Moxie Bald Mt.; views from ledges.		12.7
5.1	Moxie Bald Mt. bypass trail (0.5 mi.). Spring, S of clearing below cliff.		13.4
	Reverse direction for day hike.		
4.8	Summit of **Moxie Bald Mt.,** lookout tower, views.	2629/801	13.7
4.2	Moxie Bald Mt. bypass trail (0.5 mi.).		
2.8	Spur trail (0.1 mi.) to **Bald Mountain Brook Lean-to,** water, privy.	1280/390	15.7
2.6	**Bald Mt. Brook Campsite,** Bald Mt. Brook.		15.9
1.2	**Joe's Hole Brook.**		17.3
0.5	Power line.		18.0
0.1	Cross **Baker Stream.**		18.4
0.0	**Start: Moxie Pond,** unpaved road, parking off W side.	900/274	18.5

SOUTH

HIKE #30

Buck Hill

Maps: Maine AT Club, #4
Route: From Shirley-Blanchard Rd. to Buck Hill to ME 15
Recommended direction: S to N
Distance: 6.3 mi.
Elevation +/-: 900 to 1380 to 1220 ft.
Effort: Easy
Day hike: Yes
Overnight backpacking hike: No
Duration: 3 hr.
Early exit option: At 3.0 mi. (0.3 mi to Pleasant St.)
Natural history features: Monson slate
Trailhead access: *Start:* Shirley-Blanchard Rd., 1.3 mi. N of Blanchard; parking 0.1 mi. S on W side of road. *End:* ME 15, 11.0 mi. S of Greenville, 3.5 mi. N of Monson; overnight parking.

Hike #30 is a short but enjoyable day hike just outside the town of Monson. Though it offers no major views, it's a fine walk through the woods.

From the trailhead on the Shirley-Blanchard Rd., the trail rises up under a thick canopy of trees, including several superb stands of eastern white pine, the largest conifer in the Northeast, with a straight trunk and a crown of horizontal branches. The pine is the state tree of Maine, and its tall straight trunks were sought after for ships masts during colonial times.

The AT passes by an old farm field, now planted with a number of conifers, including the native white spruce, whose bluish-green foliage sometimes resembles the Colorado blue spruce. White spruce is commonly harvested for lumber. Deer, rabbits, and grouse browse its foliage in the winter.

At 1.5 mi., the trail crosses a logging road, then continues through the forest before skirting the west side of Lake Hebron. At 3.0 mi., the AT reaches a side trail that leads 0.3 mi. to a parking area on the north side of the lake, an early exit option. The lake has no public access close to the AT. There are no views from the trail, and the lake has a dense population of summer camps and year-round homes. There are, however, good lake views if you walk Pleasant St. into Monson (1.7 mi.).

The next 1.1 mi. leads under a heavy canopy of trees, up and over the east shoulder of Buck Hill. The trail climbs moderately through a dense cover of alder, beech, and maple. The AT continues its gradual ascent, narrowing as it enters a stand of young beech trees, located under a canopy of older and taller oaks and maples. Sugar maples are a pop-

Terry Karkos

Wild iris

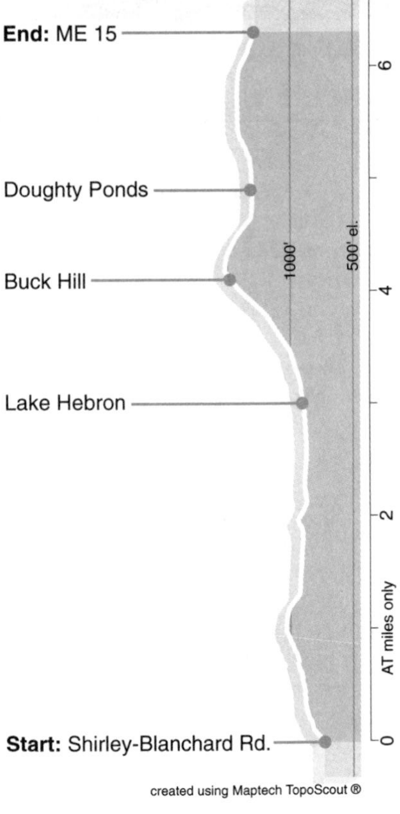

ular tree, harvested as wood for furniture and flooring. And the boiled concentrated sap is used to make maple syrup, a process taught to the colonists by the native Indians. In late fall, walking through this stand of trees, with their red and yellow and brown leaves falling, is like walking through a colorful snowstorm.

The AT reaches the east shoulder of Buck Hill at 4.1 mi. and approximately 1380 ft., where there are limited views of Monson Pond to the east, The trail then descends gradually to a side trail to one of the two Doughty Ponds at 4.9 mi. The 0.1-mi.-long pond is ringed by deadwood and a selection of hard and soft woods—a good place for a waterside picnic.

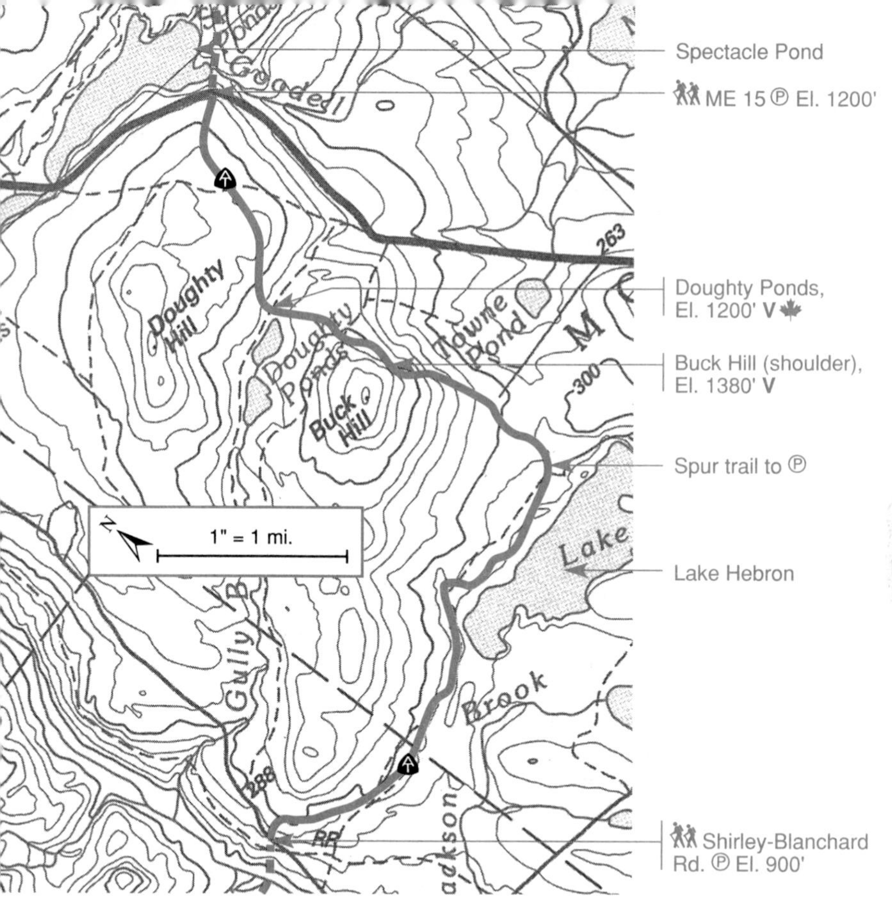

Spectacle Pond
ME 15 Ⓟ El. 1200'
Doughty Ponds, El. 1200' V
Buck Hill (shoulder), El. 1380' V
Spur trail to Ⓟ
Lake Hebron
Shirley-Blanchard Rd. Ⓟ El. 900'
Doughty Hill
Doughty Ponds
Buck Hill
Towne Pond
Gully B
Brook
Lake
263
300
288
RR
1" = 1 mi.
N

HIKE #30 Itinerary

Miles N	NORTH	Elev. (ft/m)	Miles S
6.3	**End: ME 15,** overnight parking.	1200/366	0.0
4.9	Spur trail to **Doughty Ponds.**	1200/366	1.4
4.1	**Buck Hill,** high point.	1380/421	2.2
3.0	**Lake Hebron,** Spur trail 0.3 mi. to parking, early exit option.		3.3
1.5	Logging road.		4.8
0.0	**Start: Shirley-Blanchard Rd.,** parking.	900/274	6.3

SOUTH

The trail then crosses over a stream, passes through a thicket of cedar and alder trees, and then slabs along the east shoulder of Doughty Hill, reaching an elevation of about 1360 ft. Here you will begin to see chunks of a black rock called Silurian slate. This distinctive fine-grained slate, also known as Monson slate, was mined from the late 19th to the early 20th century, primarily for use as roofing. The Black Monson slate marks the memorial at John F. Kennedy's grave site at Arlington National Cemetery.

Now the AT descends moderately to ME 15 and the trailhead parking area. Monson, which has a general store, laundromat, and restaurants, is 3.5 mi. south on ME 15. The town (pop. 750) is a key resupply point for thru-hikers because it stands at the southern end of the 100 Mile Wilderness, a stretch of the AT with no towns or services and barely a road crossing (see Hikes #31-#36).

HIKE #31

Monson Slate Hills

Maps: Maine AT Club, #3

Route: From ME 15 over Leeman Brook, past North Pond and Little Wilson Falls, over Big Wilson Cliff to Big Wilson Stream, to Long Pond Tote Rd.

Recommended direction: S to N

Distance: 14.2 mi.

Elevation +/-: 1200 to 1265 to 600 ft.

Effort: Moderate to strenuous

Day hike: No

Overnight backpacking hike: Yes

Duration: 10 hr.

Early exit option: None

Natural history features: Monson slate; tallest waterfall on AT

Social history features: Slate quarrying; Iron Road Railroad line

Trailhead access: *Start:* Drive 3.5 mi. N of Monson on ME 15; overnight parking lot. *End:* Follow ME 15 for about 0.5 mi. N of Monson. Turn R on Elliotsville Rd., continue to Big Wilson Stream bridge, cross and fork L, and arrive at Bodfish Farm site, 11.8 mi. from Monson. Turn L onto Long Pond Stream Tote Rd. (sometimes accessible by high-clearance vehicles, but not in wet spring weather) and drive 1.6 mi. to the trailhead (overnight parking along the road).

Camping: Leeman Brook Lean-To; Wilson Valley Lean-To

About the 100 Mile Wilderness

At the AT trailhead on the east side of ME 15, just 3.5 mi. north of the town of Monson, a wooden sign offers a stern warning:

CAUTION. There are no places to obtain supplies or help until you reach Abol Bridge—100 miles north. You should not attempt this section unless you carry a minimum of ten days' supplies. Do not underestimate the difficulty of this section. Good hiking! — *M.A.T.C.*

This sign marks the start of Maine's legendary 100 Mile Wilderness, some of the most remote country along the AT's entire 2150-mi. length. The region's glacially carved topography includes jagged slate hills, the rugged Barren-Chairback Range, White Cap Mt. (3654 ft.), and the 50-mi.-wide expanse of the Lake Country, an area where moose easily outnumber people. High ledges in the Wilderness offer breathtaking views of the vast Maine woods. Northern hardwood and spruce-fir forest stretches away in emerald green sheets, spreading over hundreds of unpaved, unsettled square miles.

You won't find a single fast-food joint, store, or gas station between Monson and Abol Bridge. But hikers

Best Damn B&B on the AT

Rural hospitality is legendary along the Appalachian Trail, and one source of that reputation can be found at Shaw's Boarding House, 3.5 miles south of the trail in Monson, Maine. Here Keith and Pat Shaw run a B & B where northbounders prepare for the final push toward Mt. Katahdin and southbounders recoup after the rigors of the 100 Mile Wilderness.

Let the cholesterol-squeamish beware! Instant oatmeal and freeze-dried foods are forgotten when the Shaws serve their standard 4 x 4 breakfast of four eggs, four strips of bacon, four sausage links, four syrup-soaked blueberry pancakes, heaps of hash browns, donuts, milk, and coffee.

Keith Shaw unknowingly began preparing for his role as AT innkeeper by picking blueberries on the slopes of Mt. Katahdin as a boy. "We used to hurry like hell to get our pails full so we could run all over that mountain!" he declares. In his twenties, Shaw drove stock cars, training himself for wild-and-woolly AT shuttle trips along gravel roads plied by fast-moving logging trucks. A later job milking 110 cows a day readied him for the nonstop demands of running a hiker B & B.

Then, in 1977, a chance meeting with an AT thru-hiker led to the opening of Shaws' home to walkers. Word quickly spread, and within weeks he was receiving twenty AT guests a night. Backpacking legend Ed Garvey then clued Shaw in to the possibilities of the new enterprise. "Garvey told me, Keith, you know this trail's gonna be a goin' thing. You get set up for em, you build up yer business, and you'll be here as long as the trail stays open.'"

Keith Shaw built it and they did come: Over 1000 hikers per summer and over 20,000 in the last 20 years. Today Keith and Pat Shaw are trail celebrities, written up in *Backpacker* magazine and pictured in *National Geographic*. "Hell, we're even on the Internet!" Shaw explodes with a wry grin. Just don't mention the competition.

should realize that these seemingly wild lands are not true wilderness. They are what Maine Yankees call "working forest." This country has been heavily used, and sometimes abused, by man since the 1700s. Its mountains have been mined for iron, quarried for slate, logged for paper pulpwood and construction lumber, hunted for deer, moose, and bear. Its lakes and rivers have been repeatedly explored by canoe and float plane.

While many hikers choose to tackle the entire 100 mi. in one backpacking trip (Hikes #31 through #36), it's possible to use logging roads and car shuttles to divide the Wilderness into smaller overnight and day trips. These logging roads, and their many forks, can be confusing. Carry the

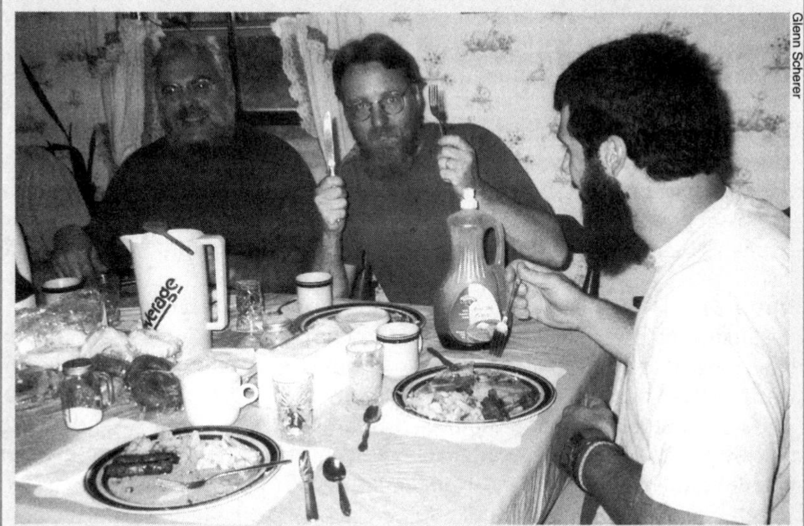

Shaw's 4 x 4 breakfast

A casual remark about Monson's Pie Lady (a rival B & B) sends Shaw into a frenzy, though it seems there's enough business for all.

There's no better snapshot of the hiking community than at Shaw's. In the bunkhouse, hikers lay out their pack contents, trying to cut weight. On the patio, they animatedly debate the virtues of various boots, stoves, tents and walking sticks. Best of all, they retell their outdoor adventures. If you're hiking nearby in Maine on the AT, stop by and have a listen. —Glenn Scherer

MATC map (listed at the beginning of each hike) and/or the DeLorme Maine Road Atlas. (See "Useful Information.") These roads are often cooperatively managed by large paper companies plus smaller property owners. For maps, road conditions, and hiker use fees (avg. $7.00/person/day if entering by car; free to hikers entering on foot), contact North Maine Woods, Box 421, Ashland ME 04732 (207-435-6213). Logging road conditions vary drastically. Some are impassable in wet weather, lack bridges, or may be in disrepair. Some areas and access roads in the 100 Mile Wilderness are managed by the Maine Bureau of Parks and Lands, whose staff can often provide information about road crossings. (Call

207-287-3061 for the telephone numbers of local offices.) A four-wheel-drive vehicle is recommended. Despite the remoteness of the 100 Mile Wilderness, it is still important to purify all spring, stream, or pond water. Agricultural runoff may not be a problem here, but upstream animals —such as beaver—definitely are.

Hike #31

This first walk in the 100 Mile Wilderness covers its southernmost 14.2 mi., where the AT passes over a portion of the Monson Slate Hills. It features many small ponds, the AT's highest waterfall, and fine views of the Barren-Chairback Range. While map contour lines display seemingly insignificant elevation gain and loss, this hike is strenuous. There are many brief but steep ups-and-downs over slate outcrops. The southern starting point of the hike is easily reached by car, but the north end, at Long Pond Tote Rd., is accessible only by high-clearance vehicles. If necessary, park your car near the left turn onto Long Pond Stream Tote Rd.—adding another 1.6 mi. to the hike total.

As soon as the trail leaves ME 15, road noise is swallowed up in the silence of a beautiful northern hardwood forest. Sugar maple and beech predominate, with a scattering of small balsam and spruce in the understory. The forest floor is covered with striped maple saplings; clintonia, a pretty member of the lily family; bunchberry, a showy white wildflower belonging to the dogwood family; and trillium, offering a spectacular flower display in late spring.

The walking is easy and relatively level at first, as the trail skirts to the east of Spectacle Pond (0.1 mi.), then passes Bell Pond (1.0 mi.) and Lily Pond (2.0 mi.). But it becomes progressively more rugged. The greatest challenge is stepping clear of the heaps of moose droppings. Moose regard the AT in Maine as their personal nighttime highway, and hikers should never set up camp on or directly next to the path. One AT thru-hiker who did so awoke at dawn to find a moose nearly trampling her tent.

Birders will enjoy this stretch of trail; we spotted three woodpeckers playing in the high branches of a sugar maple. The small downy and the larger hairy woodpecker are both common in these northern hardwood forests. Look for evidence of the pileated woodpecker's insect excavations: large deep cavities drilled into standing dead trees.

The trail descends to Leeman Brook at 3.5 mi., a fern-filled slate grotto with a fast-moving stream cascading through its depths. A quick crossing of the stream and a 20-ft. hand-over-hand climb bring you up to the Leeman Brook Lean-To, perched on a rock slab above the stream. Because this shelter, which accommodates six, is close to ME 15, it is easy to reach before dark—a bonus for weekend hikers who get a late start on Friday evening. It is the prettier of the two shelter locations on this hike, and a great place to spend your first night in the Wilderness.

Just in front of the lean-to is a tall northern white cedar. These water-loving trees are found near New England streams, lakes, ponds, and within swamps. They give off a sweet scent that adds to the pleasant setting of the Leeman Brook Lean-To.

Shelter water comes from the stream (purify as always), and the privy is about 0.1 mi. further up the trail. The glass toilet paper cozy and privy wallpapering (with its deer-and-mounted-horseman motif) add a humorous touch of class.

The trail now ascends and descends an increasingly more rugged series of undulating slate ridges. At the crest of each sharply etched slate outcrop grows a profusion of lichen and mosses. Especially noticeable are wide mats of reindeer lichen, with their tiny twisted antler-like "branches." In the 100- to 200-ft. deep valleys between the ridges of slate lie secluded ponds, streams, and bogs cloaked in forest.

North Pond (3.8 mi.), with its boulder- and tree-covered islands, invites a swim. This is just one of the many watery blue-green gems created along this stretch of trail when the glaciers scoured out Maine's landscape just 12,000 years ago. Mud Pond, at 5.2 mi., is somewhat less inviting. At about 6.0 mi. the trail passes a glacial erratic the size of a midsize automobile, more evidence of the power of the Ice Age.

The trail ascends and descends Bear Pond Ledge (with limited views) and at 6.6 mi. arrives at the top of Little Wilson Falls, one of the highest waterfall on the entire AT. The wild and beautiful cascade plummets 60 ft., rushing through a narrow 300-yd.-long ravine. Exposed rock strata are tipped vertically, with the up-tilted slate layers breaking away in jagged angular blocks and smooth sheets. This fine-grained dark-black Silurian (aka Monson) slate was formed out of mud washed from islands and deposited at the bottom of ancient oceans. Hikers quickly learn that this stone is treacherous when soaked with rain: the rock's smooth surfaces are extremely slippery, and its sharp edges cut like a razor.

Turning right, the AT descends steeply along precipitous slate ledges and over tangled tree roots to the bottom of the falls, then crosses Little Wilson Stream, an easy rock hop in dry weather but a potentially difficult fording in wetter seasons. Watch out for that wet slate! There are good pools for swimming here. This ravine is filled with the pungent scent of balsam fir.

A steady climb through young beech trees leads to a 200-yd.-long beaver dam at 7.1 mi., over which the AT passes on bog bridges. The beavers' cutting of trees, building of ponds, and resulting opening of the forest canopy has transformed the landscape here, creating a mini ecosystem where water-loving plants such as heal-all and turtlehead grow.

Heal-all, with its dense cluster of purple flowers around a single spike, was once used as a cure for throat ailments. Turtlehead is named for its cluster of tortoise-head-shaped white flowers.

Opposite the dam, the AT briefly follows a logging tote road, then turns right and climbs steeply through a beech forest to a set of open slate ledges. The cliffs are topped by white pine and blueberry bushes (you can feast on the fruits of your labor in early August). From the ledges there are spectacular views of the surrounding Monson Slate Hills and of the distant sawtooth summits of the Barren-Chairback Range. The highest vista is reached at 7.5 mi., where the trail abruptly turns to the left and climbs higher, though it offers no more views. The AT soon begins descending into a dark spruce-fir forest.

As you pass from the beech forest above the beaver dam into the spruce-fir forest beyond the ledges, notice which habitats have asserted themselves in which locations. In this case, the northern hardwood forest of beech and maple has colonized the deeper soils and warmer south-facing slope well above Little Wilson Falls, while the spruce-fir forest occupies the shallow soils and cooler north-facing mountainside. Both conifers and deciduous trees are capitalizing on their species advantages in these locations. Conifers do well in shallow, nutrient poor soils. They are also built to handle the cold: their sap works as a natural antifreeze,

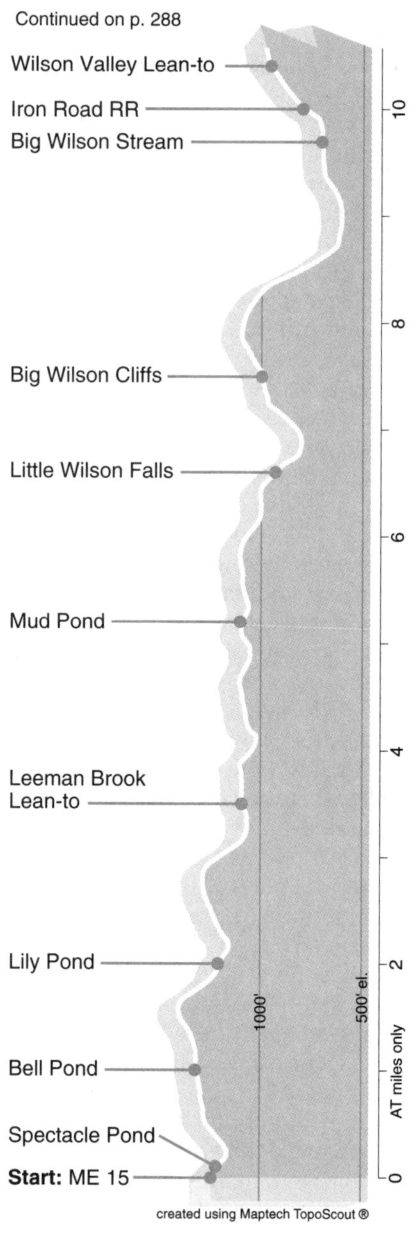

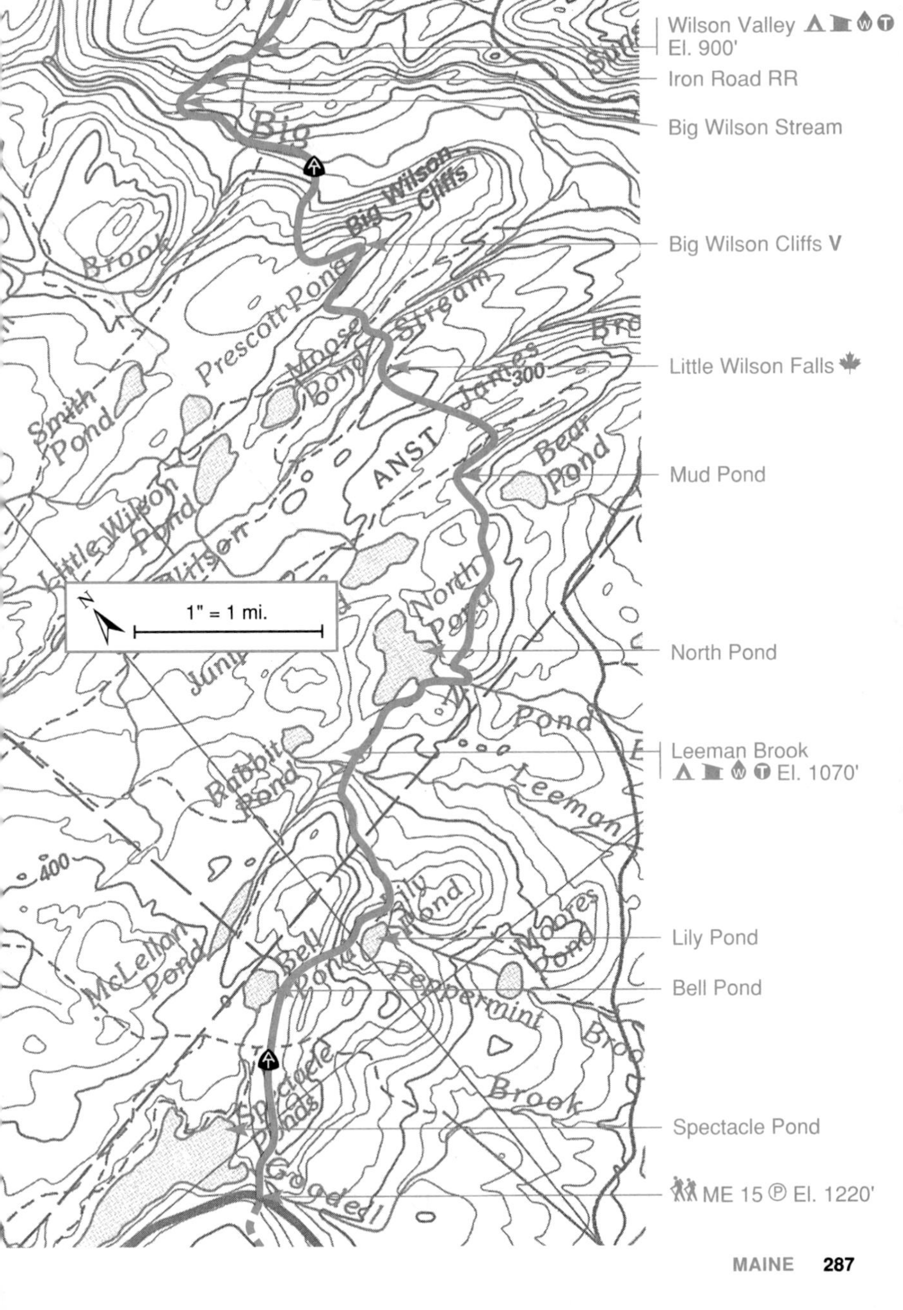
Wilson Valley
El. 900'
Iron Road RR
Big Wilson Stream
Big Wilson Cliffs V
Little Wilson Falls
Mud Pond
North Pond
Leeman Brook
El. 1070'
Lily Pond
Bell Pond
Spectacle Pond
ME 15 Ⓟ El. 1220'
1" = 1 mi.
N
Big Wilson Cliffs
Prescott Pond
Moose Pond
Stream
James
ANST
Bear Pond
Smith Pond
Little Wilson Pond
North Pond
Rabbit Pond
Leeman
Lily Pond
Moores Pond
McLellan Pond
Bell Pond
Peppermint
Brook
Spectacle Ponds
Goodell

good to –80°F. The trees also hold their needles all winter long, so they get a head start in springtime. Deciduous trees need deeper, richer soils. They grow best on sunny slopes, where their millions of broad leaves make ideal solar collectors; they absorb vast quantities of energy during the brief Maine growing season and store it for use throughout the winter and into the following spring.

Descending slowly through spruce-fir forest, the trail passes over a soft bed of conifer needles interspersed with an ankle-twisting tangle of tree roots. In the dark silence of the conifer forest, the solitude of the 100 Mile Wilderness becomes complete. As the trail descends it reaches the richer soils of the Big Wilson Valley near the base of the hillside, and beech trees again take over.

At 9.1 mi. the AT reaches the bottom of the narrow valley and follows the dirt Big Wilson Tote Rd. The next 0.6 mi. is a pleasant level road walk, giving sweet relief from the previous miles of jagged slate and rooty treadway.

Big Wilson Stream, a wild expanse of water and rock, parallels the road. Erosive forces have sculpted potholes and perfect backpacker seats in the streamside bedrock. This is also the ultimate rock-skipping stream in the 100 Mile Wilderness—giving weary hikers an excuse to pause for a while and send flat, smooth stones skipping across the river's quiet pools (12 skips is the record to beat). The stream supports a plant community of beech,

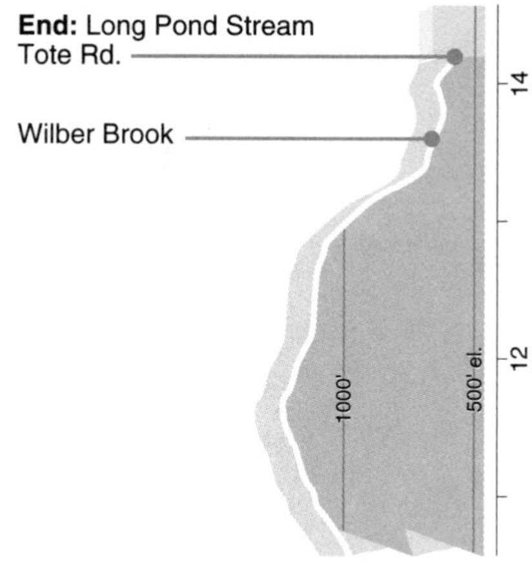

white pine, sugar maple, and bigtooth aspen. A few impressive hemlocks also rise in wide pillars above the fern-covered forest floor.

The gentle road walk passes by far too quickly. At 9.7 mi. hikers must leave the road and ford Big Wilson Stream (watch closely for the turn blaze). This is a challenging but possible rock hop in dry times. Wetter times demand the removal of boots and the donning of sandals (don't try fording in bare feet). Always release your pack belt as a safety precaution

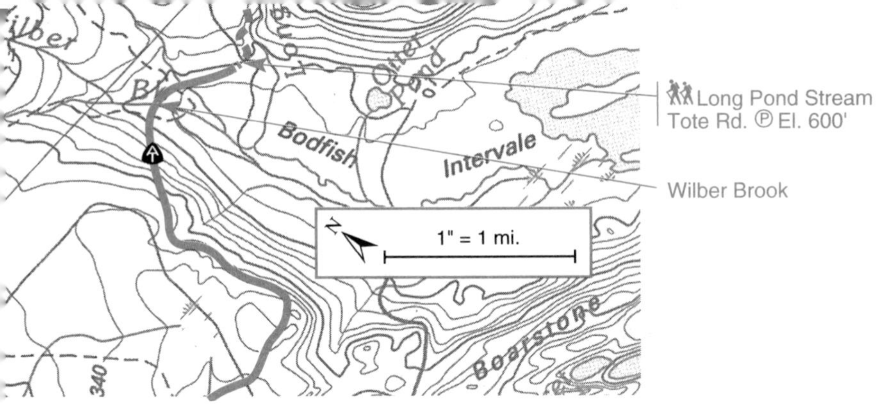

when fording a stream. A walking stick can be a real help.

There is a bridge crossing 1.5 mi. downstream; use this during very high water or flood times.

The climb away from Big Wilson Stream is the steepest of the hike so far: 200 ft. in 0.3 mi. up the side. This south-facing ridge is covered in beech and sugar maple, although a few massive eastern hemlocks also wear AT blazes. The trail crosses the Iron Road Railway at 10.0 mi. Its shiny rails reveal this to be a very active line (watch for fast-moving trains). Built in 1889, it is the only active railroad intersected by the AT in all of Maine, a state that was once crisscrossed by wide- and narrow-gauge logging railways.

The steepness of the ascent lessens beyond the railroad tracks, and at 10.4 mi. a short blue-blazed side trail leads to the Wilson Valley Lean-To, sitting in a small forest clearing. There is a spring and a privy. This shelter, which holds six people, provides a good overnight stopping place before hiking the final 3.8 mi. to the Long Pond Tote Rd. Late-night trains rumbling by on the Iron Road Railroad may shock you awake and offer a loud reminder that civilization is not quite so far away as these wild roads lead you to believe.

Leaving the shelter, the trail rises through deciduous forest for 1.2 mi. until it reaches open ledges (1265 ft.), offering good views of Barren Mt.

At 11.7 mi., the AT begins a steady 600-ft. descent through northern hardwood forest. Beech trees again predominate. Beechnuts are a choice food of red squirrels and bears. Beeches are unusual in that they reproduce in two ways: they sprout from the seeds in the nuts, and they also clone themselves by producing sprouts from their roots—an ideal technique for colonizing prime locations on moist, sunny hillsides.

The trail crosses Wilber Brook at 13.6 mi. and Vaughan Stream at 13.7 mi. This second stream, a good place to take a food or water break and soak your feet, plunges over a small (by Maine standards) 20-ft. waterfall just beyond the trail crossing. Both of these streams may require fording in high water.

At 14.2 mi. the AT intersects the Long Pond Tote Road, which leads to the site of Bodfish Farm. This pleasant valley, called the Bodfish Intervale, once formed part of an ancient lake bed, and its sediments offered better-than-average farmland to Samuel G. Bodfish, the first white settler, who came to the area in 1823.

HIKE #31 Itinerary

Miles N	NORTH	Elev. (ft/m)	Miles S
14.2	**End: Long Pond Tote Rd.,** overnight parking.	600/183	0.0
13.6	**Wilber Brook** then Vaughan Stream; small waterfall.		0.6
11.6	Ledges, views.	1265/386	2.6
10.4	Side trail to **Wilson Valley Lean-to** and campsite; water, privy.	1000/305	3.8
10.0	Cross **Iron Road Railway** tracks.		4.2
9.7	Ford **Big Wilson Stream;** alternate crossing by bridge 1.5 mi. downstream.		4.5
9.1	**Big Wilson Tote Rd.,** unpaved; follow road 0.6 mi.		5.1
7.5	**Big Wilson Cliffs,** ledges, views.		6.7
7.1	Beaver dam, bog bridges.		7.1
6.6	**Little Wilson Falls.**		7.6
5.2	**Mud Pond.**		9.0
3.8	**North Pond,** swimming hole.		10.4
3.5	**Leeman Brook; Leeman Brook Lean-to** and campsite; water, privy.	1070/326	10.7
2.0	**Lily Pond.**		12.2
1.0	**Bell Pond.**		13.2
0.1	**Spectacle Pond.**		14.1
0.0	**Start: ME 15,** 3.5 mi. N of Monson; overnight parking.	1200/366	14.2

SOUTH

HIKE #32

Barren-Chairback Range

Maps: Maine AT Club, #3
Route: From Long Pond Stream over Barren, Fourth, Third, Columbus, and Chairback Mts. to the West Branch of the Pleasant River
Recommended direction: S to N
Distance: 16.2 mi.
Elevation +/-: 600 to 2670 to 650 ft.
Effort: Strenuous
Day hike: No
Overnight backpacking hike: Yes
Duration: 12 hr.
Early exit option: None
Natural history features: Slugundy Gorge, Barren Slide, Barren Ledges, Cloud Pond, Fourth Mt. bog, E Chairback Pond
Trailhead access: *Start:* Follow ME 15 for about 0.5 mi. N of Monson. Turn R on Elliotsville Rd., continue to Big Wilson Stream bridge, cross and fork L, and arrive at Bodfish Farm site, 11.8 mi. from Monson. Turn L onto Long Pond Stream Tote Rd. (sometimes accessible by high-clearance vehicles) and drive 1.6 mi. to the trailhead (overnight parking along the road). *End:* Drive 25.6 mi. S from Millinocket on ME 11, or 5.5 mi. N from Brownville Junction. Turn W at sign for Katahdin Iron Works, and follow gravel road for 6.8 mi. to Katahdin Iron Works gate (pay fee). Continue W, cross West Branch of Pleasant River, and turn R. Fork L on main haul road at 3.0 mi., and drive 3.7 mi. to Gulf Hagas parking area (6.7 mi. from the iron works).
Camping: Long Pond Stream Lean-To; Cloud Pond Lean-To; Chairback Gap Lean-To

The Barren-Chairback Range rises to just 2670 ft. at its highest point, making it one of the lower mountain chains crossed by the AT in Maine. But this little range makes up in ruggedness what it lacks in altitude. In just 16.2 mi., the trail crosses five major summits, ascending and descending a total of nearly 4000 vertical feet. This is a challenging backpack trip over tough terrain that repeatedly rewards hikers with panoramic vistas of the Maine woods and, on a clear day, gives distant glimpses of Katahdin's granite summit.

This range is remote, and there are no practical early exit opportunities or resupply points over the length of the hike. See Hike #31 for information about the 100 Mile Wilderness.

The walk begins where the AT crosses the Long Pond Tote Rd. Turn right (east) and follow the trail into an open hardwood forest of sugar maple and beech trees. At 0.1 mi. the

AT crosses Long Pond Stream, notable for the boxcar-size boulders around which the waters must force their way. Normally knee-deep, Long Pond Stream can be treacherous in flood times. A walking stick and sandals help in the fording. Also, unbuckle your pack belt and loosen the shoulder straps to allow for a quick escape from your gear should you fall into the water. On the far bank, the AT turns immediately left, paralleling the stream.

A side trail at 0.8 mi. leads left for 150 yd. to one of this hike's highlights, Slugundy Gorge: a narrow ravine cut into slate bedrock. Here Long Pond Stream surges around immense boulders, cascades over waterfalls, and churns down chutes into swimmable pools. Fine sprigs of purple harebell provide subtle accents of color on the fern-covered slate slopes. These bell-like flowers bloom singly or in delicate clusters from threadlike stalks, rising out of jagged cracks in the slate.

Just 0.1 mi. past the Slugundy Gorge side trail, the AT intercepts a second side trail, leading left to Long Pond Stream Lean-To. This shelter serves as a good base camp from which to explore Slugundy Gorge's topography. It is also a convenient overnight staging place for those beginning this backpacking trip late on a summer evening. Water comes from the stream, and there is a privy.

Now the real work begins, as the AT ascends Barren Mt. The 1000-ft. climb over the next 1.1 mi. is relentlessly steep, though the treadway is well maintained for such a remote area. The remarkable trees lining the path provide a useful diversion from the uphill grind. The mature forest includes beech, yellow birch, hemlock, and sugar maples. Some of the maples here have grown to over 3-ft. in diameter, and their highly shade-tolerant progeny grow in the dark shadows of these giants. These monster trees may live for up to 300 years.

A sharp-eyed hiker may spot a snowshoe hare on the AT in these deciduous woods. This large hare is common in Maine, but it is well camouflaged; turning brown in summer and white in winter. Its large padded, powerful hind feet can propel it through the forest in 12-ft. bounds at 30 mph. The hare is usually shy, since it is the favorite fare of weasel, fox, mink, owl, hawk, and bobcat.

At 2.0 mi. a side trail leads right 250 ft. to a sight not to be missed where the Barren Slide falls away in a frightful jumble of house-sized boulders, fractured cliffs, and jagged crevices —looking as if a giant had ripped out the entire shoulder of Barren Mt. The Slide also offers a quintessential Maine vista over mountains, lakes, and forest.

Just 0.2 mi. farther up the AT, another side trail leads right a short distance to a second spectacular view from Barren Ledges. The waters of Lake Onawa, dotted with small islands, lie far below. "Onawa" is Chippewa for "awaken," and any hiker viewing this panorama is likely to feel revived. At the outlet of Lake Onawa is the Onawa Viaduct, the tallest railroad trestle east of the Rockies. A train wreck near here in December 1919 killed 20 people and injured 50 more. The line is still active, though today the Iron Road Railway offers only freight service.

A closer look at the far-reaching scenery reminds walkers that these lands are not as wild as they first appear. Small light-green areas form a patchwork of forest clear cuts: islands of industry where trees have been harvested for pulpwood, lumber, and other uses. Widespread use of heavy equipment, such as mechanized fellerbunchers and whole-tree harvesters has led to heated controversy over clear cutting. In 1996 Maine voters rejected a ban on clear- cutting proposed by the Green Party, but in response to public pressure, the state's major forest landowners have agreed to limit the practice to less than 1 percent of their ownership per year.

The trail leaves Barren Ledges behind and levels off for more than a mile, winding through blueberry bushes and passing along the northwestern shoulder of Barren Mt. The AT begins its final climb to the summit at 3.2 mi.

The very steep 750-ft. climb up the cone of Barren Mt. has been made far easier in recent years by the Maine FORCE, volunteer and professional trail builders recruited by the Maine AT Club and the Appalachian Trail Conference. The stonework is some of the finest to be found on the East Coast. Two hundred forty massive rock steps, plus stone-lined rock drains, check dams, and water bars, protect the silty slopes from erosion and make the hiking experience more enjoyable. They replace an old trail route that had eroded until it was a hip-deep trench.

As the AT rises above 2000 ft., the deciduous forest gives way to spruce and fir. The conifers (mostly balsam fir, and red, black, and white spruce) are superbly adapted to the cold climate and thin, rocky, nutrient-poor soils of these inhospitable ridgetops. They also grow well in the boggy hollows found between the summits.

At 4.0 mi., the trail crosses the open top of Barren Mt. (2670 ft.). A fire tower, built in 1950, is closed to the public and should not be climbed by hikers. Views are just as good from the ground. Look for Big and Little Spencer Mts. to the north, and the other peaks of the Barren-Chairback Range to the east.

A rugged 0.9-mi. descent brings walkers to a side trail that leads to the right, downhill and over bog bridges to Cloud Pond Lean-To. Cloud Pond, a little gem, is a glacial tarn (scooped out by the ice) sitting within a shallow cirque (a semicircular basin) also carved by the Wisconsin Glacier more than 15,000 years ago. Similar glacial tarns and cirques are found on this hike at West

Chairback Pond (10.1 mi.) and East Chairback Pond (14.5 mi.).

The shelter and its surrounding campsites overlook the pond, which is a great place to watch the sunrise or sunset. This area is empty of people throughout most of the year. Winter snows come early and stay late, and black flies keep hikers away from April through July. But in August, the hordes of insects are replaced by masses of hikers who overflow the available campsites. Stay on trail, and avoid trampling the delicate mountain landscape. Water for campers comes from Cloud Pond, and there is a privy.

From Cloud Pond onward the AT descends and ascends over the jagged sawteeth of the Barren-Chairback Range, traversing Fourth Mt. (2378 ft.), Third Mt. (2069 ft.), Columbus Mt. (2432 ft.), and Chairback Mt. (2219 ft.).

There are great views from open ledges at 8.3 mi., atop Monument Cliff on Third Mt. at 8.8 mi., from ledges near the summit of Columbus Mt. at 11.4 mi., and on the open summit of Chairback Mt. at 12.3 mi. Hikers looking northward will be rewarded by distant views of Mt. Katahdin.

The spruce-fir forest continues to dominate the ridges and saddles of the Barren-Chairback range. Beginners trying to identify these trees should remember that balsams are "flat, friendly firs." Their needles are soft to the touch and unrounded. Spruce needles are short and sharp-pointed (prickly to the touch), and are diamond-shaped in cross section. Another difference: spruce cones grow downward, whereas balsam fir cones grow upward. All cones found on the ground are spruce cones, since fir cones fall apart on the trees, leaving only central spines standing upright on branches. The acidic layers of brown needles covering the ground prevent a great many other species from growing here, though many lichens, mosses, and ferns manage to find their niche in the spruce-fir forest.

One of the most interesting habitats in the entire range comes in the saddle between Barren Mt. and Fourth Mt., at 6.6 mi. This bog is home to two carnivorous plants: the tiny sundew and the larger pitcher plant. Acidic bogs are notoriously lacking in plant nutrients, so the carnivorous plants supplement their meager diets with nitrogen-providing insects (see "Carnivorous Plants" in Hike #34).

While it's only 6.9 mi. between Cloud Pond Lean-To (4.9 mi.) and Chairback Gap Lean-To (11.8 mi.), this is extremely difficult terrain, and hikers are advised not to push for big miles. For those planning to stay at Chairback Gap Lean-To during dry times, it's important to note that this shelter's spring is intermittent. It's best to stock up on water at the outlet of West Chairback Pond (10.1 mi.). Chairback Gap Lean-To has a privy.

One of the boldest of the northern forest's inhabitants is likely to pay a visit as you prepare dinner at Chairback Gap Lean-To. The Canada jay (also known as the Gray jay) is a joyful, energetic bird that descends on hikers with a variety of jaunty coos, trills, whistles, and screams. But the bird has ulterior motives behind its friendly behavior. It will happily accept hiker handouts, and just as happily make off with a mouthful of unattended gorp, soap, tobacco, or matches. The bird is as hardy as it is larcenous. It spends the winter in the Maine woods, insulating its nest with bits of hair and feather, surviving subzero temperatures, and laying its eggs in March.

Leaving Chairback Lean-To, the AT climbs up over Chairback Mt. at 12.3 mi. and shortly reaches Chairback Cliffs. For a moment the trail appears to dead-end, offering no hope of a route down. The drop over a rock slide looks impossibly precipitous, but closer inspection reveals a well-thought-out descent that is far easier than expected.

At 14.5 mi. there is a side trail leading 0.2 mi. to East Chairback Pond. This sparkling water, with visibility to a water depth of 50 ft., is well worth the trip. Summertime frogs provide a welcoming serenade, and the fishing for brook trout is excellent. Fisherfolk report taking trout with nothing but a bare hook and a small piece of red wool.

From the tarn, the AT descends steeply out of the Barren-Chairback Range and back into deciduous for-

Continued on p. 298

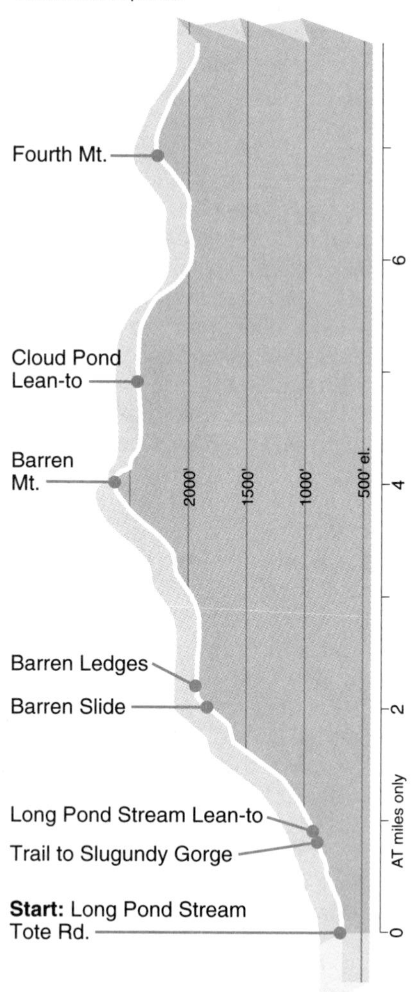

created using Maptech TopoScout ®

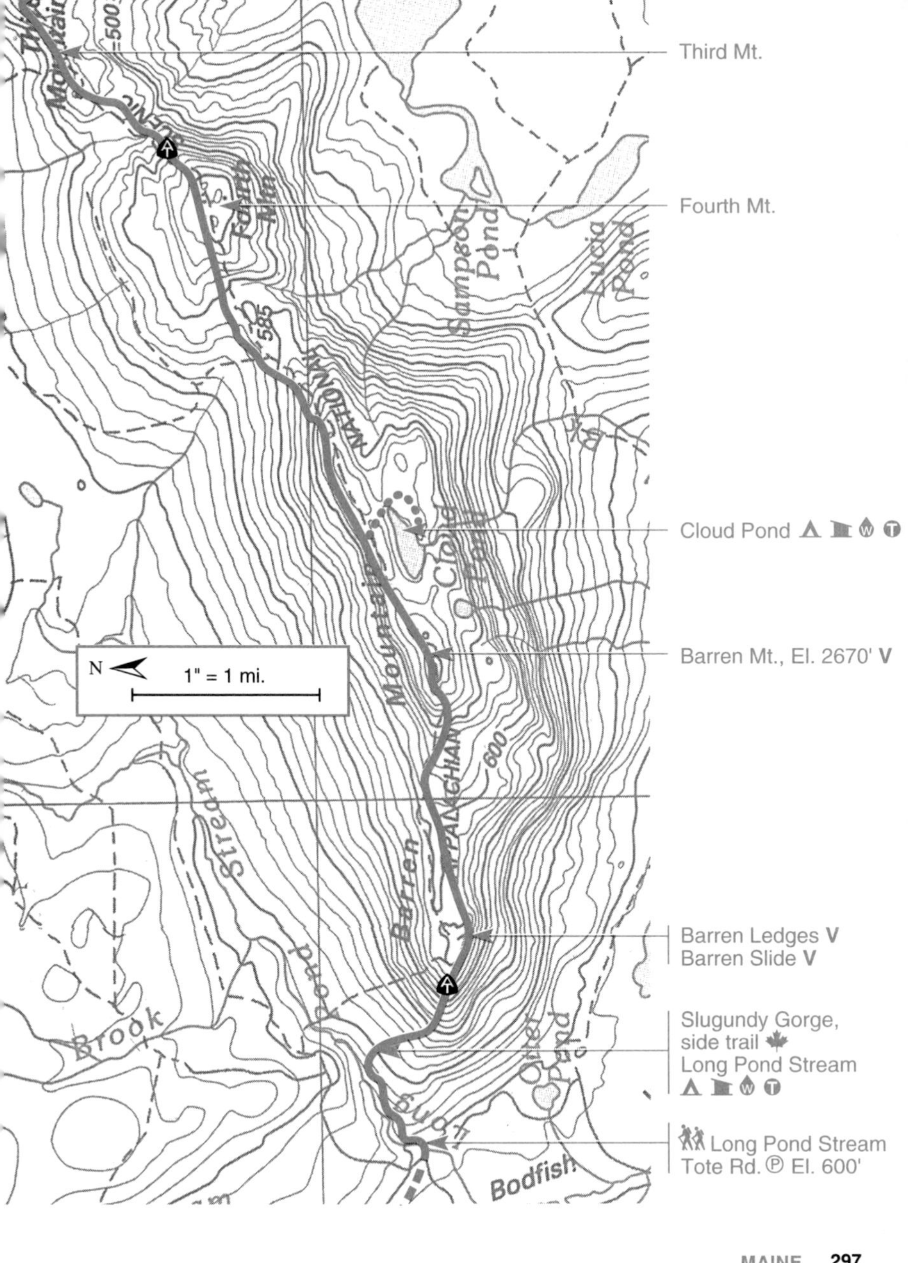
Third Mt.
Fourth Mt.
Cloud Pond
Barren Mt., El. 2670' V
Barren Ledges V
Barren Slide V
Slugundy Gorge, side trail
Long Pond Stream
Long Pond Stream Tote Rd. Ⓟ El. 600'
N
1" = 1 mi.
Sampson Pond
Lucia Pond
Cloud Pond
Barren Mountain
APPALACHIAN
NATIONAL
Fourth Mtn
585
600
500
Stream
Brook
Pond
Long
Bodfish

est. The trail falls for nearly 1000 vertical feet to the main haul road leading to the Katahdin Iron Works (15.7 mi.). After crossing the road, the AT levels out and follows a small stream for 0.5 mi. to its junction with the West Branch of the Pleasant River (16.2 mi.). Here a side trail leads right for 0.2 mi. to the Gulf Hagas trailhead (see sidebar, Hike #33) parking lot along the main haul road.

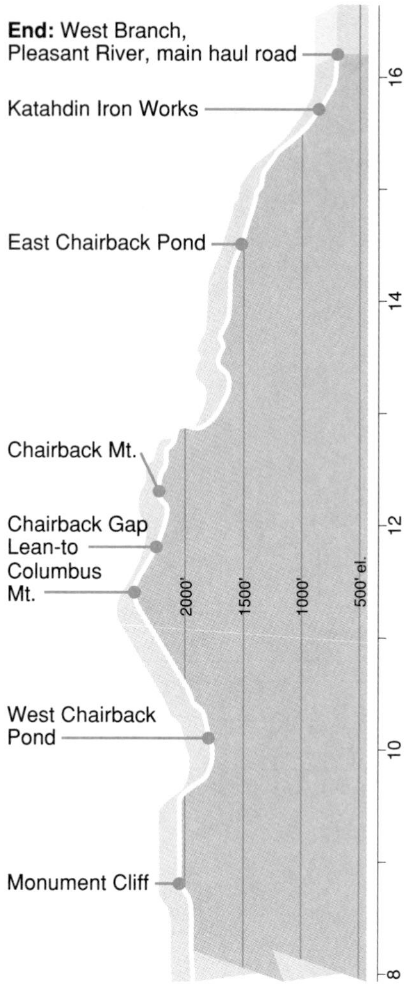

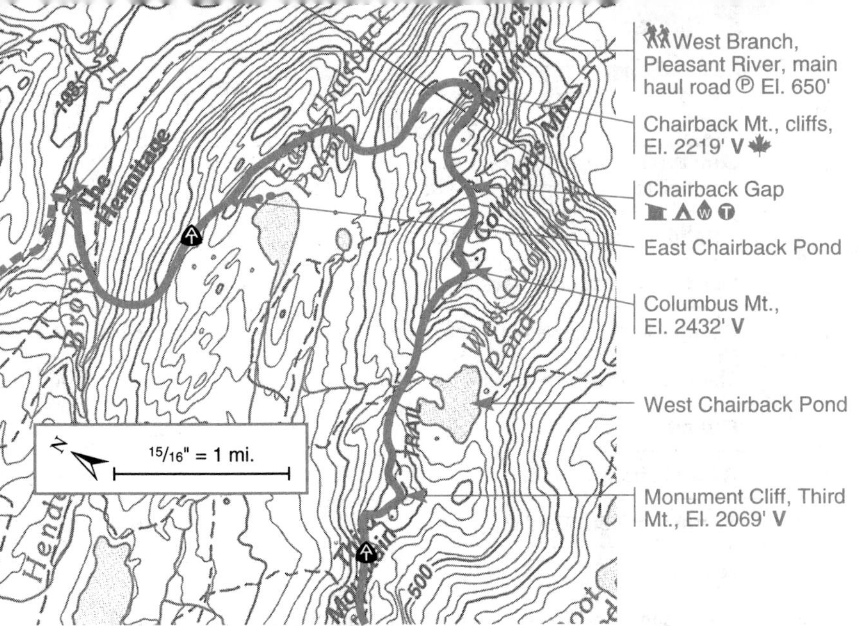

West Branch, Pleasant River, main haul road Ⓟ El. 650'
Chairback Mt., cliffs, El. 2219' V
Chairback Gap
East Chairback Pond
Columbus Mt., El. 2432' V
West Chairback Pond
Monument Cliff, Third Mt., El. 2069' V
15/16" = 1 mi.
N
The Hermitage
Chairback Mountain
Columbus Mtn.
West Chairback Pond
Trail
500

HIKE #32 Itinerary

Miles N	NORTH	Elev. (ft/m)	Miles S
16.2	**End: West Branch, Pleasant River;** main haul road; side trail to **Gulf Hagas trailhead,** overnight parking.	650/198	0.0
15.7	**Katahdin Iron Works;** cross road, follow stream.		0.5
14.5	Side trail to **East Chairback Pond,** fishing.		1.7
12.3	**Chairback Mt.;** views from Chairback Cliffs, 12.4 mi.	2219/676	3.9
11.8	**Chairback Gap Lean-to;** unreliable spring; privy.		4.4
11.4	**Columbus Mt.,** views.	2432/741	4.8
10.1	**West Chairback Pond.**		6.1
8.8	**Monument Cliff,** Third Mt., views.	2069/631	7.4
8.3	Ledges, views.		7.9
6.6	Bog in saddle between Barren Mt. and Fourth Mt.		9.6
4.9	Side trail to **Cloud Pond Lean-to;** water, privy.	2420/738	11.3
4.0	Summit of **Barren Mt.,** views.	2670/814	12.2
2.2	Side trail to **Barren Ledges,** views.		14.0
2.0	Side trail to **Barren Slide,** views.		14.2
0.9	Side trail to **Long Pond Stream Lean-to;** water, privy.	930/283	15.3
0.8	Side trail to **Slugundy Gorge.**		15.4
0.1	Cross **Long Pond Stream,** possible ford.		16.1
0.0	**Start: Long Pond Tote Rd.,** overnight parking. Turn E on AT.	600/183	16.2

SOUTH

HIKE #33

White Cap Mt.

Maps: Maine AT Club, #2

Route: From West Branch of Pleasant River past Gulf Hagas, over White Cap Mt. to the East Branch of Pleasant River, over Little Boardman Mt., and along Cooper Brook to Jo-Mary Rd.

Recommended direction: S to N

Distance: 28.1 mi.

Elevation +/-: 650 to 3644 to 650 ft.

Effort: Strenuous

Day hike: No

Overnight backpacking hike: Yes

Duration: 17 hr.

Early exit option: White Brook Trail at 10.2 mi.; unnamed tote road at 10.9 mi.; Kokadjo-B Pond Rd. (West Branch Ponds Rd.) at 21.2 mi.

Natural history features: The Hermitage, Gulf Hagas waterfalls, White Cap Mt.; glacial ponds; Cooper Brook Falls

Trailhead access: *Start:* Drive 25.6 mi. S from Millinocket on ME 11, or 5.5 mi. N from Brownville Junction. Turn W at sign for Katahdin Iron Works, and follow gravel road for 6.8 mi. to Katahdin Iron Works gate (pay fee). Continue W, crossing West Branch of Pleasant River, and turn R. Fork L on main haul road at 3.0 mi., and drive 3.7 mi. to Gulf Hagas parking area (6.7 mi. from iron works). *End:* Take ME 11 for 13 mi. S of Millinocket or 18 mi. N of Brownville Junction. Turn W on Jo-Mary Rd. From Jo-Mary Check Point gate (pay fee) it is 12 mi. NW to AT at Cooper Brook.

Camping: Carl A. Newhall Lean-To; Tappan Campsite; Logan Brook Lean-To; East Branch Lean-To; Cooper Brook Falls Lean-To

---

White Cap Mt. stands like a great sentinel in the heart of the 100 Mile Wilderness. At 3644 ft., it is the highest peak in the region and the only one to rise into the alpine plant zone. This 28.1-mi. backpacking trip over White Cap's summit offers northbounders their first unobstructed view of Mt. Katahdin. In addition, the hike boasts excellent swimming at Crawford Pond and Cooper Brook Falls. For those wishing to add another 6.5 mi. to their hike plan, Gulf Hagas, dubbed "the Grand Canyon of Maine," makes a fascinating side trip.

All of this walk is within the boundaries of the 210,000-acre Katahdin Ironworks—Jo-Mary Multiple Use Management Forest. This working forest is owned by large paper companies and small property owners, while the AT corridor is managed by the National Park Service. Automobile access is exclusively via logging roads. There are no resupply points along the entire hike route. See Hike #31 for information about the 100 Mile Wilderness.

The hike begins at the West Branch parking area on the Katahdin Iron Works main haul road. Follow the blue-blazed side trail for 0.2 mi., and turn right onto the white-blazed AT. The trail immediately crosses the West Branch of the Pleasant River (no camping). This ford is made easy with a walking stick and sandals. Unbuckle your pack belt and loosen the straps before entering the water. During flood times this stream crossing can be dangerous, though normal levels rarely go above the knees.

Today the river is lined with ferns, hemlocks, beech, and paper birch. Conditions here were not always so idyllic. Discovery of iron in this area by Moses Greenleaf in 1843 led to the construction of the Katahdin Iron Works 2 years later. The stone blast furnace (the ruins of which can be seen 6.7 mi. east of here on the main haul road) operated continuously 24 hours a day until 1890, producing 2000 tons of raw iron each year. The surrounding mountains were denuded of trees to power the operation: 10,000 cords of wood were cut annually to feed the charcoal-hungry furnace, and another 4000 cords were required to propel the ironworks locomotive, the Black Maria. The forest didn't fully recover until late in the 20th century.

If you ford the Pleasant River in the early morning or late evening, leave the AT behind at 0.2 mi. and detour a few hundred yards to the right along Hay Brook Trail. This side trail leads quickly to Pugwash Pond, a popular moose watering hole. (The Hay Brook Trail continues for 0.7 mi. to the Hay Brook parking area.) This is a very beautiful spot, but don't be tempted to camp here. Camping is illegal near the river.

At 0.3 mi., the AT enters the Hermitage, a majestic grove of eastern white pine. Many of these trees are over 120 ft. tall. A Scot named Campbell Young built his cabin, known as "the Hermitage," here in 1890. Others preserved the place as a sportsmen's camp. Now the grove is owned by the Nature Conservancy. A short side trail leads left, deep into the grove, and gives the impression of a walk down the center aisle of a medieval cathedral. On the forest floor striped maple, paper birch, and hemlock saplings stand about like worshipping parishioners, while massive white pine trunks impel hikers to look skyward.

The AT climbs gently now, quickly reentering a northern hardwood forest of sugar maple, beech, and paper birch. Hobblebush, like branched candelabra, cover the forest floor. These viney shrubs are named for their ability to trip up forest walkers. Their large heart-shaped leaves turn a burnished purple.

At 1.3 mi., Gulf Hagas Rim Trail leads left, beginning its exploration of a spectacular river gorge. The Gulf is a 3-mi.-long box canyon carved from slate by the wild cascades and falls

Gulf Hagas: Maine's Grand Canyon

At Gulf Hagas, the West Branch of the Pleasant River drops 500 ft. in a little over 3 mi., cutting a spectacular gorge into solid bedrock. The river pinballs between sheer rock faces and plummets over precipitous waterfalls. The Gulf Hagas Rim Trail hugs the cliff edge above the raging stream and is a highlight of the 100 Mile Wilderness.

AT hikers can add a Gulf Hagas side trip to Hike #33 by turning left onto the Gulf Hagas Rim Trail 1.3 mi. N of the AT's crossing of the West Branch of the Pleasant River.

The Rim Trail immediately crosses Gulf Hagas Brook and enters the Gulf Hagas Nature Reserve, a roughly 2000-acre preserve marked by a bronze plaque imbedded on a fern-covered glacial erratic. The preserve is now part of the protected AT corridor, The unusual name for the gorge (sometimes spelled Hagus) may sound Scottish, but is Native American in origin and means "deep glen."

Just 0.1 mi. farther along, a short side trail leads left from the Rim Trail to Screw Auger Falls on Gulf Hagas Brook. This wild little cascade twists through a water-sculpted ravine, plunging 26 ft. and giving walkers a taste of bigger things to come.

Back on the Gulf Hagas Rim Trail, hikers soon reach a second side trail at 0.7 mi., leading left in 100 yards to Hammond Street Pitch. This waterfall on the Pleasant River was named by 19th century log drivers who thought the cascade's steepness resembled that of a Bangor street.

Now the waterfalls come fast and furious, as the sound of crashing water rises out of the gorge. At the Jaws, the canyon's walls close in, forcing the river through a narrow slot little more than 26 ft. wide. In the 1800s the river poured through an even smaller opening of less than 8 ft., but the Jaws were blasted wider to allow the passage of logs being floated to market. The Rim Trail next makes its way past Buttermilk Falls, with its shimmering pool; Stair Falls, a steplike cascade; and Billings Falls, a sluice deeply etched in bedrock.

At 3.0 mi. the Gulf Hagas Rim Trail continues just beyond the Head of the Gulf and intersects the Pleasant River tote road. This 19th-century logging road intersects with the Gulf Hagas cutoff trail in 0.9 mi., which leads left and in another 1.0 mi. takes walkers back to the AT at a point 0.7 mi. north of where the Gulf Hagas Rim Trail originally left it.

For those planning a backpacking trip from the West Branch of the Pleasant River to the Newhall Lean-to (5.5 mi. on the AT), the Gulf Hagas side trip increases the day's hiking total to 9.9 mi. When choosing this route, remember that the side trail, while it makes relatively minor elevation changes, is very rugged. It also invites walkers to linger at the many vistas. Hikers should allow at least an extra 4 to 5 hours for the side trip. —Glenn Scherer

of the West Branch of the Pleasant River. For a circuit hike of Gulf Hagas, see sidebar.

For the next 3.5 mi., the AT plays tag with Gulf Hagas Brook and grows progressively steeper as it ascends the slope of Gulf Hagas Mt. The path is lined by tall sugar maples, bigtooth aspen, paper birch and an occasional eastern white pine. The understory is a mix composed of striped maple, clintonia, trillium, and the ubiquitous bunchberry. This little four-leafed plant (related to the dogwood tree) will accompany you on the entire hike and will also inform you of your approximate altitude. At 2000 ft., in mid-August, the bunchberry is covered in red berries but at heights above 3,000 ft. it still sports its last summery white flowers.

The trail leaves the deciduous forest behind at about 5.0 mi., entering a spruce-fir forest. At 5.3 mi., an unmarked side trail leads left 50 ft. to a pretty bog with edges lined by rhodora. This showy member of the heath family grows best in acidic soils and blossoms with a vivid display of lavender flowers in late spring. Opposite the bog's small open pool of water, spruce and balsam firs are silhouetted against the sky. They are easy to identify in profile: the balsam fir grows in a tight spire, tapering to a sharp point; spruce grows in a looser, wider pyramidal shape and forms a more rounded crown.

At 5.5 mi. several unmarked side trails lead right to level tentsites. The AT immediately crosses Gulf Hagas Brook, and a blue-blazed side trail goes left to the Carl Newhall Lean-To. The shelter is named for a tireless MATC volunteer who helped clear and blaze the trail throughout Maine from the 1950s to the 1980s. Shelter water comes from Gulf Hagas Brook, and there is a privy.

The solitude of the 100 Mile Wilderness contrasts dramatically with the community life found at AT shelters. Our stay at the Carl Newhall Lean-To was made more musical by Don "Banjo Man" Roak, who strummed a mean backpacking guitar (sounding something like a ukulele).

The trail now begins to climb the chain of peaks that culminate with White Cap Mt. The AT achieves the summits of Gulf Hagas Mt. (2683 ft.) at 6.4 mi., West Peak (3181 ft.) at 8.0 mi., Hay Mt. (3244 ft.) at 9.6 mi., and finally crosses the treeless top of White Cap (3644 ft.) at 11.3 mi. The progressively higher climbs in this range are steep and without switchbacks, though the ascents are mercifully brief. The toughest is the first one of 750 vertical ft. in less than a mile up Gulf Hagas Mt. This climb through spruce-fir forest affords a beautiful cliff-top vista after a little hand-over-hand work.

The Sidney Tappan Campsite (7.3 mi.), named for another dedicated MATC volunteer, is located in a sag between Gulf Hagas Mt. and West Peak. It boasts secluded tentsites, blueberries, and a fine spring. White Brook Trail, at 10.2 mi., and an unnamed tote road at 10.9 mi. lead right down from White Cap Mt. to a logging haul road. This early exit leads back to Katahdin Iron Works in 11.4 mi.

The tallest fir trees on these peaks are dead, rising above the healthy spruce canopy like a ghost forest of naked masts and spars. These fir trees died as a result of a spruce budworm infestation during the 1970s. (The spruce budworm is misnamed since its favorite food is the fir tree!) The epidemic ended naturally in 1985.

The barren, rocky summit of White Cap is encircled by dwarfed and twisted paper birch, black spruce, and balsam fir krummholz, and by a heath community composed of blueberry, black crowberry, Labrador tea, and alpine bilberry bushes. The foundation of the White Cap Fire Tower lies near the summit's rock cairn. The original wooden tower, built in 1906, was replaced by a metal one in 1920, which was then removed in 1982.

Sweeping views from White Cap Mt. survey Maine's Lake Country, a glacially scraped lowland dotted by secluded ponds that mirror sun and sky. Emerald green forest stretches away in all directions, though light-green irregularly shaped patches indicate logging clear cuts. Mt. Katahdin's granite face is silhouetted against the far horizon.

The trail picks its way across the broken rock field of White Cap Mt., descends back through the krummholz, then falls away steeply into a dense conifer forest. Fine rock drains built by volunteers deflect erosive rainwater from the trail. A relentless 1200-ft. descent brings walkers back into deciduous birch forest and to the Logan Brook Lean-To at 12.7 mi. This shelter is right on the trail and overlooks a small creek. There is a privy.

A steady descent along an old logging road passes through a healthy woods of birch, balsam poplars, mountain ash, and sugar, red, and striped maple.

The trail crosses the gravel Kokadjo-B Pond Rd. (West Branch Ponds Rd.) at 14.3 mi. The trail then continues falling into a boggy territory, dotted by moss-draped glacial erratics and dominated by spruce and balsam fir. The AT here is a soft carpet of conifer needles and tangled tree roots, leading to the East Branch Lean-To at 16.3 mi. A short side trail to the East Branch of the Pleasant River provides water for the shelter, and there is a privy.

Another 0.3 mi. along, the AT crosses the East Branch, a boulder-hop in dry August weather, to a far streambank blossoming with the shaggy purple heads of joe-pye weed.

The trail now ascends a shoulder of Big Boardman Mt. The climb is relatively easy and is interrupted by Mountain View Pond, a pretty glacial lake encircled by white pine, northern white cedar, violet-colored pickerelweed, blueberries (ripening in August) and a bumper crop of poison ivy. A side trail to the right at 18.5 mi. leads to a gushing spring—and past Indian cucumber root, a relatively rare plant whose root was once eaten by Native Americans. Ledges in the saddle between Big and Little Boardman Mts, at 19.0 mi., offer great views of White Cap Mt.

The steady descent from Little Boardman Mt. becomes more and more gradual as the trail falls away into Maine's Lake Country, some of the most unusual and magical terrain found anywhere along the AT. This is a vast forested lowland carved out by the last glacial age. Ice-gouged bedrock is covered by a thin, poorly drained layer of soil, containing few nutrients. Sphagnum moss bogs, lakes, ponds, rivers, and creeks make this a wild and water-rich land. The trail in this region alternates between sunny stretches of northern hardwood forest filled with birdsong and the mysteriously silent, sunless reaches of spruce-fir forest.

The trail crosses gravel Kokadjo-B Pond Rd. at 21.2 mi. This is a good early exit opportunity, accessible by automobiles via other logging roads in the Katahdin Ironworks-Jo-Mary Multiple Use Management Forest. The AT then ascends an unusual small ridge (at 21.4 mi.) called an esker, a deposit of gravel and rocky debris that marks the bed of a river that ran beneath the glacier.

Crawford Pond (21.6 mi.) is reached by a short side trail to the left. Its gently sloping sand beach invites swimmers, though, like many Maine ponds, this one must be shared with leeches. Mica particles stirred up by waders' feet turn the

Continued on p. 308

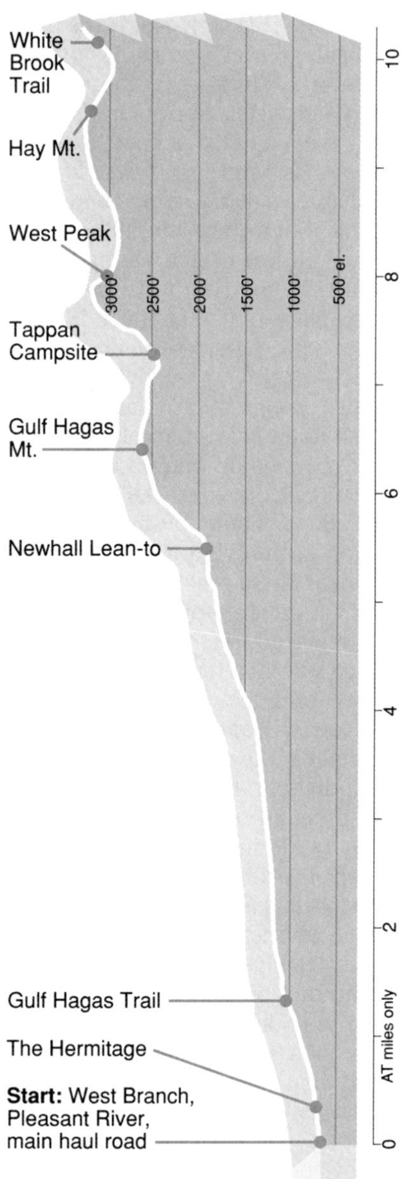

created using Maptech TopoScout ®

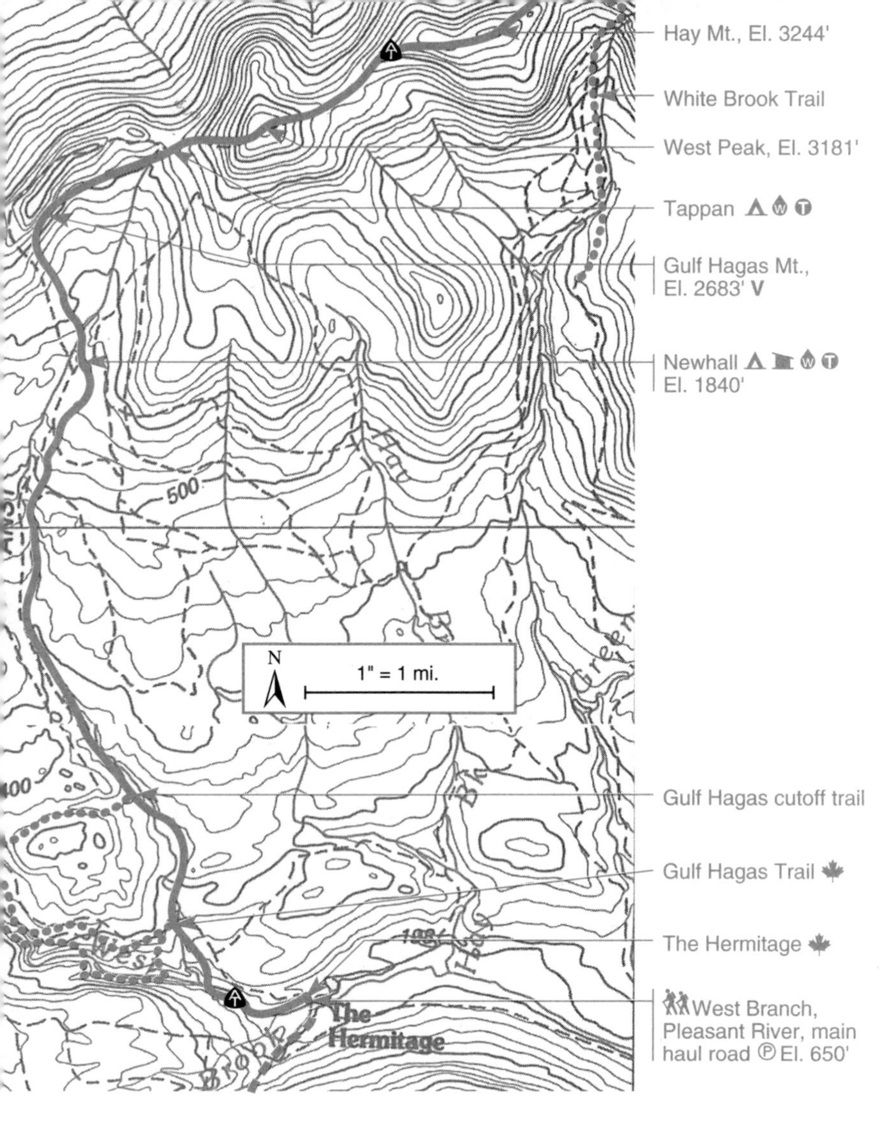
Hay Mt., El. 3244'
White Brook Trail
West Peak, El. 3181'
Tappan
Gulf Hagas Mt., El. 2683' V
Newhall El. 1840'
500
1" = 1 mi.
N
Gulf Hagas cutoff trail
Gulf Hagas Trail
The Hermitage
West Branch, Pleasant River, main haul road Ⓟ El. 650'
The Hermitage

water a shimmering gold. MATC has designated this a no-camping zone.

After crossing the outlet of the pond at 22.1 mi., the AT intercepts a 19th-century tote road, which it follows for the next 9 mi. (into Hike #34). This logging road was once traversed by the Lombard log hauler, a treaded steam locomotive and forerunner to World War I tanks. Today, the racket of modern logging equipment resounds through the forest and reminds hikers that the Maine woods are still a working forest. The tote road parallels Cooper Brook and passes spectacular sugar maples that seem to touch the sky.

See the *Appalachian Trail Guide to Maine*, published by the Maine AT Club, and *Into the Mountains: Stories of New England's Most Celebrated Peaks* from AMC, for a more detailed history of the logging business. The old tote rd. parallels Cooper Brook and passes spectacular sugar maples which seem to touch the sky. Henry David Thoreau, a self-taught expert on the northern forest, wrote colorfully about logging in *The Maine Woods* (1846). The logging drive fascinated him:

> *All winter long the logger goes on piling up the trees which he has trimmed and hauled in some dry ravine at the head of a stream, and then in the spring he stands on the bank and whistles for Rain and Thaw, ready to wring the perspiration out of his shirt to swell the tide,*

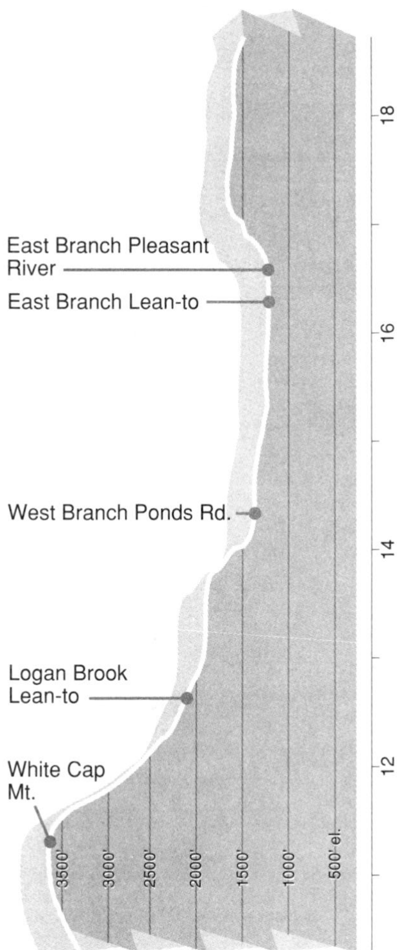

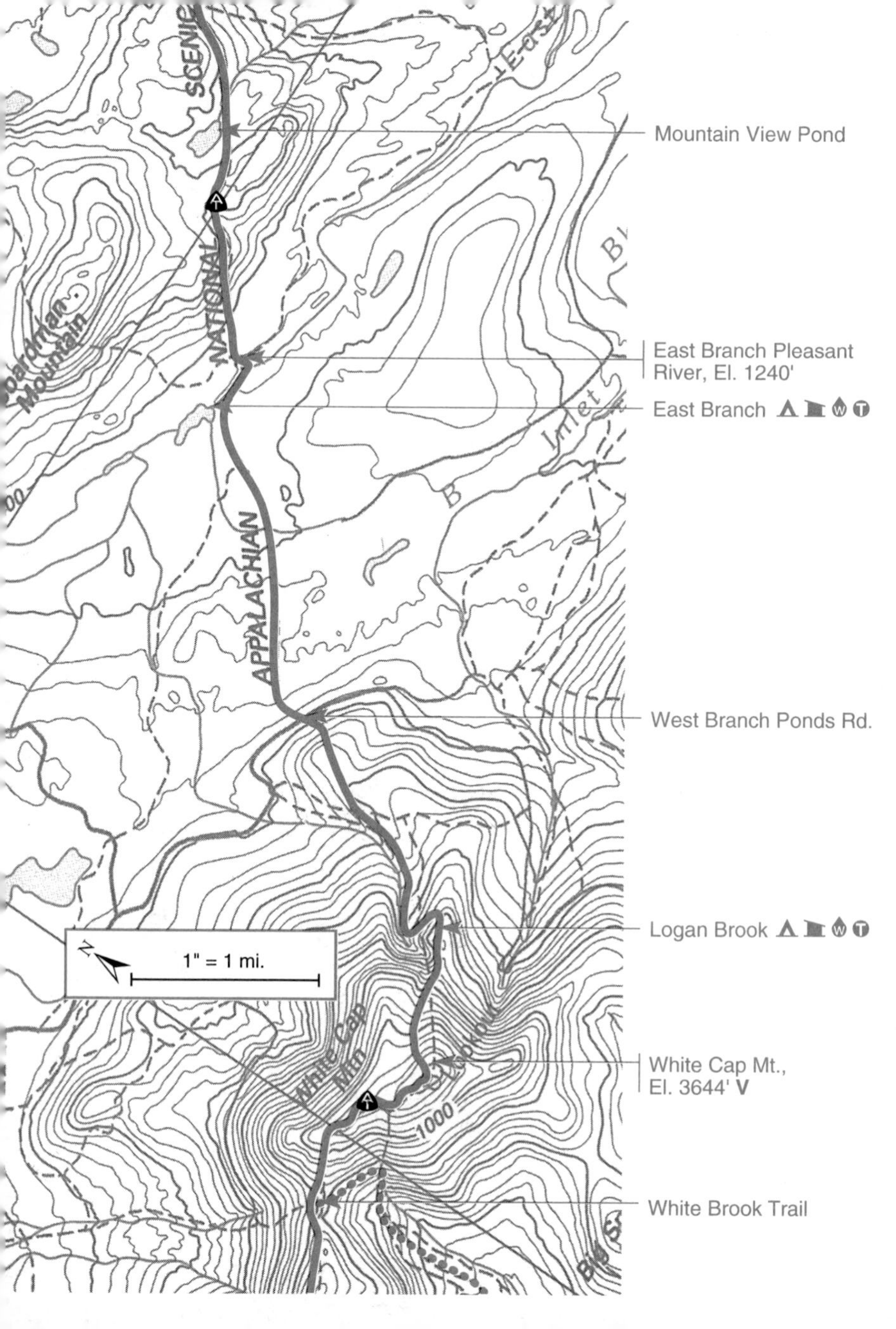

Mountain View Pond
East Branch Pleasant River, El. 1240'
East Branch
West Branch Ponds Rd.
Logan Brook
White Cap Mt., El. 3644' V
White Brook Trail
1" = 1 mi.
N
APPALACHIAN
NATIONAL
SCENIC
Boardman Mountain
White Cap Mtn
Inlet
1000

till suddenly, with a whoop and a halloo from him, shutting his eyes, as if to bid farewell to the existing state of things, a fair proportion of his winter's work goes scrambling down the country, followed by his faithful dogs, Thaw and Rain and Freshet and Wind, the whole pack in full cry, toward the Orono mills. *

At 24.4 mi. the AT arrives at the Cooper Brook Falls Lean-To, arguably the best swimming hole in the 100 Mile Wilderness. A series of rushing cascades offer water slides into a deep, languid pool shaded by northern white cedars, ash, beech, and maple trees. The stream is the drinking-water source, so bathers should avoid soaping up the brook. There is a privy.

The last 3.7 mi. to Jo-Mary Rd. is a flat, friendly walk along the tote road, a relief from the rocks and roots of White Cap Mt. This is an opportunity to stop watching your feet and stare up at the truly huge eastern hemlocks lining the trail. There's good swimming in Cooper Brook as it passes around big boulders here. After playing hide-and-seek with the brook for several miles, at 28.1 mi. the AT arrives at Jo-Mary Rd. (a.k.a. Church Pond Rd.), a main access route into the 100 Mile Wilderness.

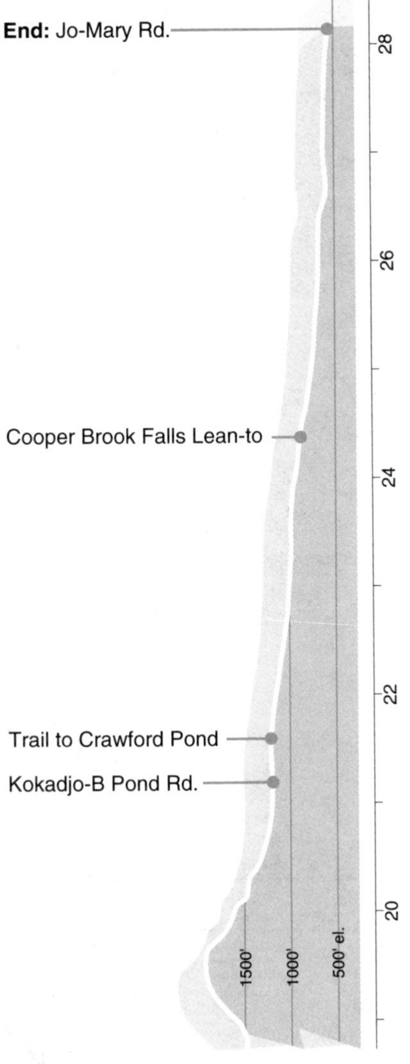

---

*Henry David Thoreau, *The Maine Woods, quoted in Into the Mountains: Stories of New England's Most Celebrated Peaks,* Appalachian Mountain Club, 1995, p. 304.

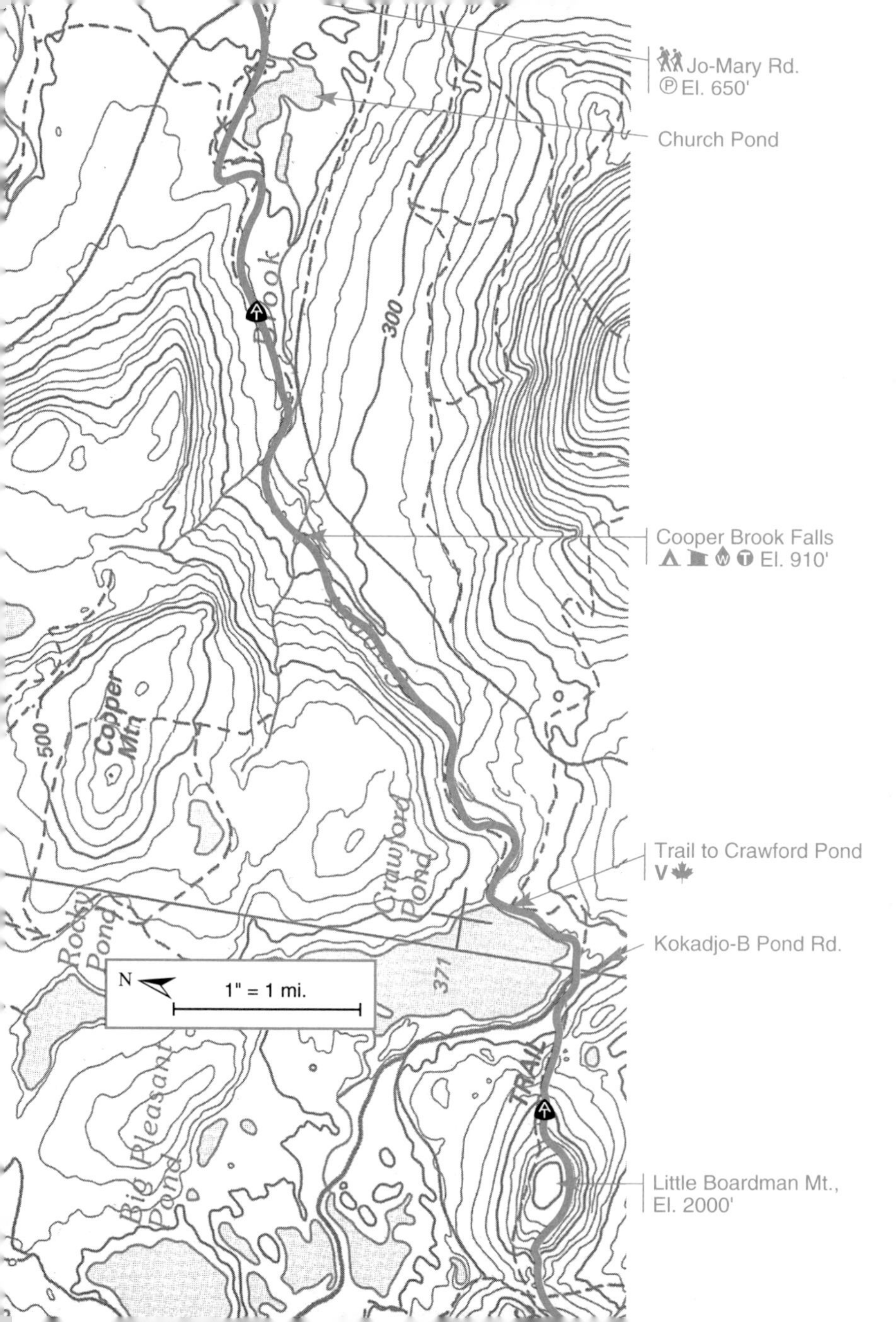

Jo-Mary Rd.
El. 650'
Church Pond
Cooper Brook Falls
El. 910'
Trail to Crawford Pond
V
Kokadjo-B Pond Rd.
Little Boardman Mt.,
El. 2000'
Brook
300
Copper Mtn
500
Crawford Pond
Rocky Pond
371
N
1" = 1 mi.
TRAIL
Big Pleasant Pond

HIKE #33 Itinerary

Miles N	NORTH	Elev. (ft/m)	Miles S
28.1	**End: Jo-Mary Rd.,** overnight parking.	650/198	0.0
24.4	**Cooper Brook Falls Lean-to;** water, privy, cascade, swimming.	910/277	3.7
22.1	Follow old tote road in Cooper Brook valley.		6.0
21.6	Side trail to **Crawford Pond.**		6.5
21.2	Cross **Kokadjo-B Pond Rd.,** early exit option, town.		6.9
19.0	Saddle between **Big and Little Boardman Mts.,** views.		9.1
18.5	Side trail to spring.		9.6
16.6	Cross **East Branch of Pleasant River.**	1240/378	11.5
16.3	**East Branch Lean-to;** water, privy.		11.8
14.3	**Kokadjo-B Pond Rd. (West Branch Ponds Rd.),** unpaved, rough.		13.8
12.7	**Logan Brook Lean-to;** water, privy.		15.4
11.3	Summit of **White Cap Mt.,** views.	3644/1111	16.8
10.2	**White Brook Trail** or unnamed road, at 10.9 mi., early exits back to Katahdin Iron Works (11.4 mi.).		17.9
9.6	**Hay Mt.**	3244	18.5
8.0	**West Peak.**	3181	20.1
7.3	**Tappan Campsite,** water, privy.		20.8
6.4	Summit of **Gulf Hagas Mt.**	2683	21.7
5.5	Side trails to tentsites; then side trail to **Newhall Lean-to,** water, privy.	1840/561	22.6
1.3	**Gulf Hagas Rim Trail** leads L, rejoins AT at 2.0 mi. after 4.4 mi. loop along gorge.		26.8
0.3	**The Hermitage,** white pine forest.		27.8
0.2	**Hay Brook Trail,** side trail to Pugwash Pond.		27.9
0.0	**Start: West Branch, Pleasant River;** main haul road; 0.2 mi. side trail to AT overnight parking.	650/198	28.1

HIKE #34

Southern Lake Country

Maps: Maine AT Club, #2

Route: From Jo-Mary Rd. past Lower Jo-Mary Lake, over Potaywadjo Ridge, around Pemadumcook Lake, to Nahmakanta Stream and Nahmakanta Lake

Recommended direction: S to N

Distance: 14.9 mi.

Elevation +/-: 650 to 900 to 700 ft.

Effort: Moderate to Strenuous

Day hike: No

Overnight backpacking hike: Yes

Duration: 10 hr.

Early exit option: None

Natural history features: Red pine groves at Mud Pond and Lower Jo-Mary Lake; Nahmakanta Stream

Social history features: Antlers campsite (19th-century sportsman camp)

Trailhead access: *Start:* Take ME Rte. 11 for 13 mi. S of Millinocket, or 18 mi. N of Brownville Junction, turning W on Jo-Mary Lake Rd. Shortly, reach Jo-Mary North Maine Woods gate house (register, pay fee, request local map, identify Nahmakanta Stream Rd.). Continue on Jo-Mary Lake Rd. 12 mi. northwest to the AT crossing at Cooper Brook. Roadside parking. En route, stop at Nahmakanta gate house (register, pay fee, confirm road directions). *End:* From starting trailhead (Cooper Brook), continue 12 mi. on gravel roads (concluding with Nahmakanta Stream Rd.) to AT crossing at S end of Nahmakanta Lake. Overnight parking nearby at gravel pit.

Camping: Antlers Campsite; Potaywadjo Spring Lean-To; Nahmakanta Stream Campsite

The northern half of the 100 Mile Wilderness often surprises hikers with its relatively level terrain and its startling beauty. While most of the AT hugs the crests of Appalachian ridges, this walk is through Maine's Lake Country, a rugged lowland etched first by glacial ice and now by flowing water.

When the Wisconsin Glacier (over a mile thick in many places) retreated to the north12,000 years ago, it left in its wake a landscape punctuated by vast lakes, isolated ponds, and bogs, and crisscrossed by rivers and creeks. The remoteness of these Maine woods makes moose and loon sightings commonplace and supports the growth of tall trees and rare wildflowers.

This 14.9-mi. overnight backpacking trip gains only 400 ft. in elevation as it weaves its way along the shores of Lower Jo-Mary and Pemadumcook lakes, passes easily over Potaywadjo Ridge, parallels Nahmakanta

Carnivorous Plants

Along the trail between White Cap and Nahmakanta, the AT passes near a number of small bogs, and a careful hiker can spot two types of carnivorous plants that thrive in this acidic, nutrient-poor environment by supplementing their diet with insects.

The sundew is small enough to pass by—the mature plant is no more than 2 inches across—but is easy to spot once you learn to identify it. The leaves are arranged in a basal rosette, and each leaf sprouts slender filaments topped with a pearl of sticky dew. Neltje Blanchan offered this flowery description in a 1900 book called *Nature's Garden:* "A little fly or gnat, attracted by the bright jewels, alights on a leaf, only to find that clear drops, more sticky than honey, instantly glue his feet, that the pretty reddish hairs about him act like tentacles, reaching inward, to imprison him within their slowly closing embrace.... Here is one of the horrors of the Inquisition operating in this land of liberty before our very eyes! Slowly, surely, the leaf rolls inward, making a temporary stomach; the cruel hairs bind, the glue suffocates and holds him fast. Death alone releases him. And now the leaf's orgy begins."

Surprisingly, the purpose of the pitcher plant's distinct leaves was a mystery unitl the 18th century. Linnaeus thought that the pitchers held the plants over in time of drought. We know now that the pitchers are designed to trap and kill insects—a pitcher plant in the Pacific Northwest is even capable of trapping mice and small birds.

The pitcher of a pitcher plant is ingeniously designed for attracting and trapping prey. A long keel along one edge holds it upright, even when filled with water. Some sources say the color—a purple red coursed with dark purple veins—suggests carrion, and the flared mouth has nectar-releasing glands that attract insects. The odor of the nectar is detectable by humans, and is decribed in *The Carnivorous Plants of the United*

Stream, and ends on the south shore of Nahmakanta Lake. But don't let the gentle topography fool you. In spring and early summer, snowmelt, heavy rains, and black flies make passage difficult. In late summer and early autumn, a gnarly treadway of roots and rocks, plus mud-covered bog bridges may tire even the fittest walkers. See Hike #31 for information about the 100 Mile Wilderness.

From Jo-Mary Rd. the trail heads east, entering the woods beside Cooper Brook and offering easy footing along a 19th century logging tote road. A trailside garden of chest-high ferns, bunchberry, reindeer lichen, and wintergreen creates a varied palette in shades of green. The creeping underground stems of the wintergreen plant allow it to spread out in a wide colonizing mat. When rubbed, the leaves give off a pleasant scent.

States and Canada as both "feline and musty on one hand, and sweet on the other."

Below the opening, thousands of downward pointing hairs, all visible to the naked eye, guide the insect into the pitcher. Farther below, the cells on the walls of the plant are loosely arranged in an overlapping pattern that has been compared to shingles on a roof. These cells are adhesive and easily dislodged, and an insect trying to climb out quickly finds its feet coated with them.

In spite of all of these defenses, a number of animals have learned to form a careful partnership with the plants. A species of biteless mosquito spends its larval stage swimming in the water held in the pitchers; on the macabre side, the larva of a fly (with the appropriate Latin name *Sarcophagi*) feeds on decomposing insects in the plant. Spring peepers have been seen sitting near the entrance of the pitchers, and several species of spider spin their web across the opening. All of the above species do not harm the plant, but the larvae of a certain small moth enters the plant and kills it, using the shriveled pitcher as a shelter for its pupae.

Although Blanchan writes that carnivorous plants depend on insects "for nourishment as men do upon cattle slaughtered in an abbatoir," and wonders if the pitcher plant is more animal than plant, sundew and pitcher plants are photosynthesizing green plants and produce their own energy. Both can survive without killing insects. The insects and invertebrates consumed are thought to provide them with nitrogen, phosphorus, and other minerals lacking in the acidic environment of a peat bog. In a way basic to all plants, however, each of them is dependent on insects to insure the survival of its species. The bladderwort, the sundew, and the pitcher plant grow flowers, attract insects, and send them on their way—unharmed—with a gift of pollen.

—Andrew Weegar

At 1.3 mi., a short side trail leads right for 0.2 mi. to the north shore of secluded Cooper Pond, dammed in the 1800s to provide rushing water for log drives down Cooper Brook. In another 0.2 mi., a second side trail leads right to an intermittent spring.

Cooper Brook now widens out and is lined by the tall straight trunks of bigtooth aspen, eastern white pine, and eastern hemlock. There's much evidence of animal life too: a trailside northern white cedar has been girdled by beaver, passing moose have left heaps of marble-size droppings, and red squirrels frequently scold from the treetops or flit across the path. The ubiquitous red squirrel is at home in northern deciduous and conifer forests, dining with equal enthusiasm on beechnuts, pinecones, berries, fungi, and even birds' eggs and young birds. The squirrels also have a sweet tooth: They harvest maple sugar by biting into the tree's bark and then returning a few days later to sample the oozing sap.

After crossing a gravel logging road at 2.6 mi., the AT turns away from Cooper Brook and continues through a mixed deciduous and conifer forest. A little farther along, a large dead northern white cedar has been drilled and hollowed by a pileated woodpecker. While these shy crow-size birds, with their large red crests (the inspiration for Woody Woodpecker), are rarely seen, the evidence of their ravenous bug-hunger is found throughout these woods.

At a bridge crossing over an outlet to Mud Pond, violet-blue-purple pickerelweed, an aquatic herb, puts on a showy display among the cobbles in late summer. The AT skirts the east end of Mud Pond at 2.9 mi., a setting that is far more picturesque than its name indicates. The pond is lined by the most extensive red pine stand in Maine's AT corridor. The less common red pine can be distinguished from the more common white by counting the needles within the bundles. Red pine needles are bundled in groups of two (equal to the number of points in the letter R), while white pines have needles arranged in bundles of five (equal to the number of points in the letter W).

The trail now moves on through a diverse conifer forest of pine, spruce, and hemlock, then through deciduous woods of beech, maple, and bigtooth aspen, until it arrives at the shore of Lower Jo-Mary Lake, an expansive body of water 4-mi.-long, with an irregular cove-lined shore.

The short side trail leads to the Antlers Campsite at 4.2 mi. This spot is worth exploring, whether you plan to tent here or not. The campsite extends into the lake on a narrow peninsula and was once the location of Potter's Antlers Camp, one of many remote hunting and fishing camps that attracted affluent 19th- and early 20th-century outdoorsmen. The facility closed in 1949, and its last cabins were removed in the 1970s.

Tenting is comfortable here, on a soft bed of pine needles under a canopy of red pine. The trees rise to 60 or 70 ft., with open crowns that look like shaggy green brushes hanging on the end of long red-bark handles. Stars are spectacular over Antlers Campsite after dark. The Milky Way is clearly visible in summer, as is the Andromeda Nebula, a spiral galaxy 2 million light years distant—the farthest object visible to the naked human eye.

The lakeshore invites daytime exploring. Luxurious growths of pickerelweed flourish all summer long. Its triangular leaves and flowering purple spikes grow above water, while its stem grows submerged. Deer are fond of the plant, and Native Americans once roasted the seeds, adding them to cereals and breads.

Another water plant, common pipewort, perfectly resembles its popular name of "hatpin." Its single stem reaches up out of quiet water and is topped by a flower that looks like a tiny button or a white-and-black-speckled nonpareil candy.

Most fascinating of all the plants found at Lower Jo-Mary Lake may be the horned bladderwort, whose flower resembles a child-size yellow rubber rain hat. The plant is carnivorous; its tiny threadlike leaves are covered with minute bladders which attract insects that are then sucked inside the plant.

There's one more landmark at Antlers: the privy. With its glass doorknobs, plastic skylight, elegant windows hung with festively patterned curtains, wicker chair, table, and washbasin, it could be right out of "Out House Beautiful."

Leaving Antlers, the trail hugs the jagged granite-boulder-lined shore of Lower Jo-Mary Lake. Early morning or late evening hikers are likely to hear the weird cries of loons on the mist-covered waters. While awkward on land, loons are ideally suited to water. They are powerful swimmers and divers. Watch for the loon's sudden disappearance from the surface of the lake. These birds are naturally heavy and, like a submarine blowing ballast, can exhale air from their lungs and quickly sink to a desired depth in search of fish. They can also stay underwater for up to 3 minutes.

The trail circles the north shore of Lower Jo-Mary Lake. With its full southern exposure, the woods here resemble those of southern New England. While the expected paper birch, aspen, maple, and beech thrive here, so do ash and even oak trees which are rare in northern Maine.

Michael Warren

Little Wilson Falls

At 5.7 mi. the AT reaches a side trail that leads left and climbs steeply for 1.0 mi. to the open ledges of Potaywadjo Ridge. Another side trail at 5.9 mi. leads right a short distance and offers a last look from the shoreline at Lower Jo-Mary Lake. This sandy swimming beach offers good views back toward Antlers Campsite.

Next comes a 400-ft. climb over a shoulder and through a gap in Potaywadjo Ridge, an easy ascent past the gleaming white trunks of paper birch trees and house-size glacial erratics. "Potaywadjo" means "whale-shaped" in the Penobscot language, a good description of this loaf-shaped ridge.

At 7.7 mi. a short side trail leads right to Potaywadjo Lean-To. While the shelter and privy have nothing unusual to offer, the spring, 15 ft. in diameter, is the largest in the 100 Mile Wilderness. Mark "Rainbow Slick" Erdman nearly met his end here in 1997. The just-married thru-hiker had stooped to fill a pot with water when he heard a shudder and a creak from above. Looking up, he was amazed to see a giant sugar maple toppling toward him. Flinging the pot as he fled, Mark narrowly missed being hit by the tree as it crashed into the center of the spring. "If anyone ever asks you whether a tree falling in the forest makes a sound," Mark quipped for several days afterward, "tell them, Yes. Absolutely, yes!'"

Within 0.4 mi. of the shelter, the trail crosses a very active logging road. Watch for fast-moving logging trucks. Private vehicles do not have access to this road.

At 8.2 mi., the AT fords Twitchell Brook at a point where the creek empties into Pemadumcook Lake, one of the largest lakes along the entire AT. Another 0.1 mi. farther on, a short side trail leads a few yards right to the best view over the lake. If you're very lucky, you may see osprey diving for and catching salmon and trout here. This rocky vantage point

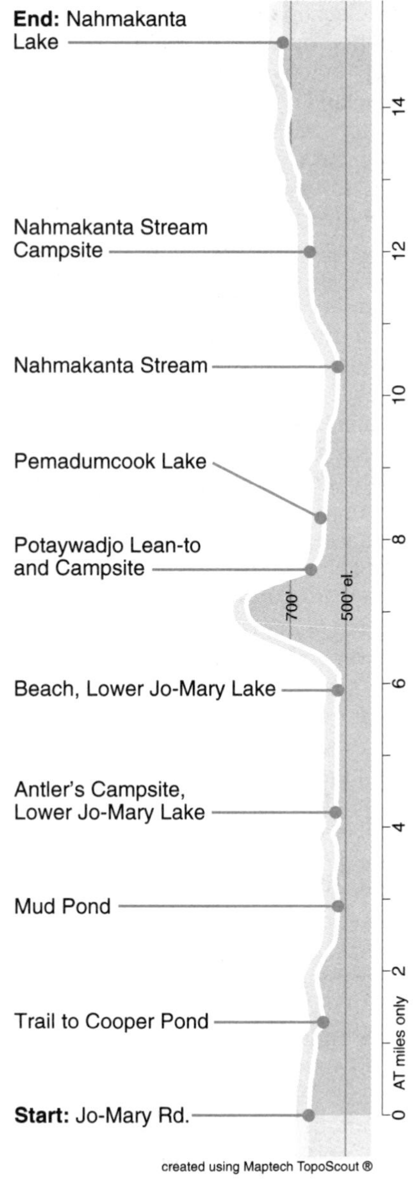

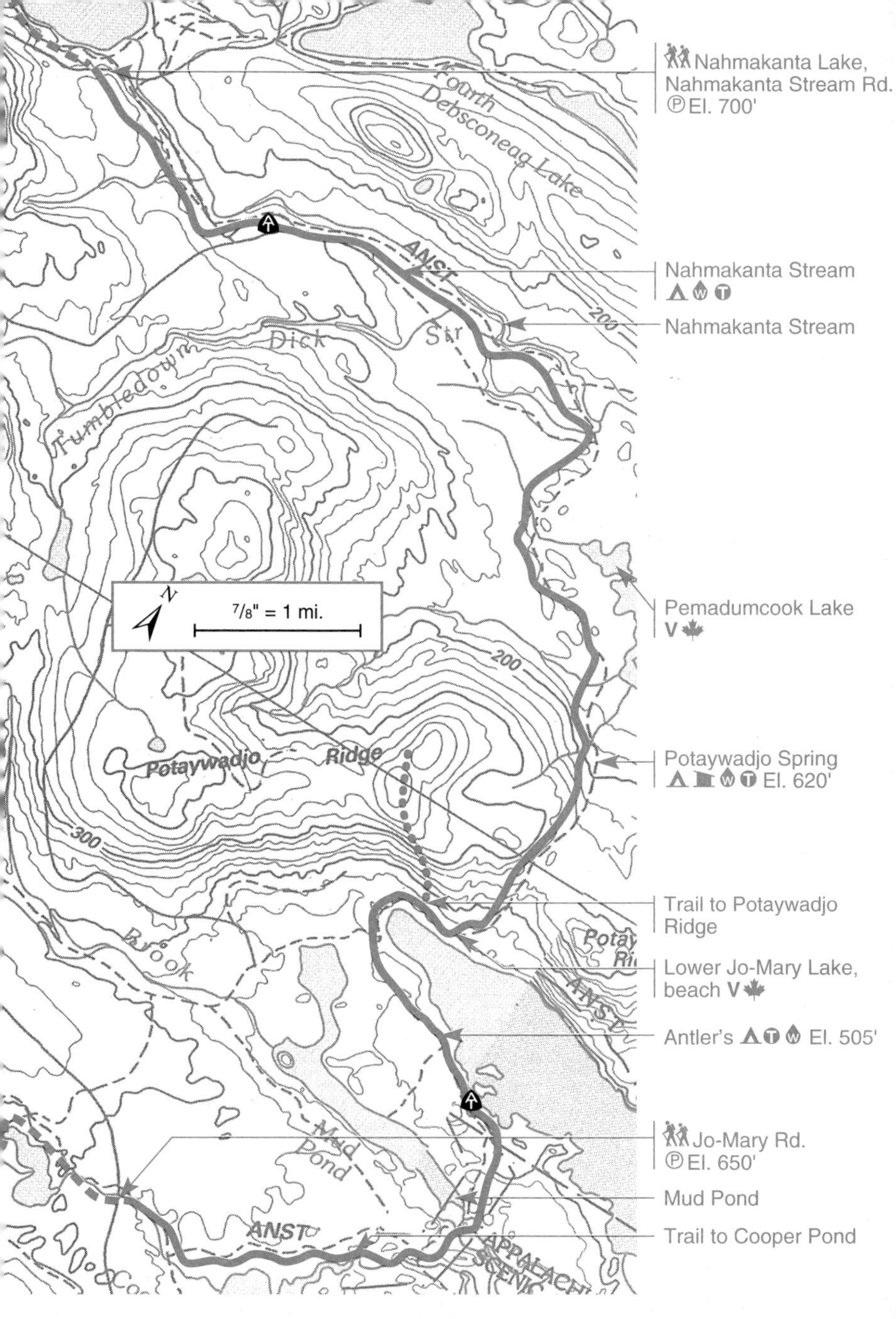

Nahmakanta Lake, Nahmakanta Stream Rd. El. 700'
Nahmakanta Stream
Nahmakanta Stream
Pemadumcook Lake
V
Potaywadjo Spring
El. 620'
Trail to Potaywadjo Ridge
Lower Jo-Mary Lake, beach V
Antler's El. 505'
Jo-Mary Rd.
El. 650'
Mud Pond
Trail to Cooper Pond
Fourth Debsconeag Lake
ANST
Dick
Str
Tumbledown
Potaywadjo
Ridge
Brook
Mud Pond
Appalachian Scenic
200
300
7/8" = 1 mi.
N

also provides a spellbinding view of Mt. Katahdin. On some mornings a tremendous cloud show takes place. Waves of cumulous cloud plowed into the peak and were sliced in two by the mountain's granite knife-edge.

This is the only spot at which the AT actually touches Pemadumcook Lake, so you may want to spend a few extra minutes here to enjoy the unobstructed view. The trail quickly leaves the mostly deciduous forest behind, passing into a northern white cedar swamp on bog bridges. These sweet-scented cedars are also commonly called *arbor vitae*. The swamp also features balsam and spruce, sphagnum moss, and many kinds of ferns. Starflower, goldthread, twinflower, and clintonia commonly bloom in such wetlands.

At 10.3 mi., the AT crosses Mahar Tote Rd., a wide grassy path that leads right for 0.2 mi. to a last view from a northern cove of Pemadumcook Lake. In another 0.1 mi, the trail crosses a tributary of Nahmakanta Stream, a substantial brook that may require fording in high water.

At 10.5 mi., the AT begins to parallel Nahmakanta Stream, a wide river whose smooth flow is repeatedly broken by 10- to 15-ft.-tall glacial erratics, multi-tonned balls and pyramids of stone that create narrow channels through which the stream surges. Smooth fist-size cobbles line the shore.

The next 4.4 mi. are an absolute pleasure. The trail flows alongside the stream, passing beneath immense northern white cedars, eastern white pine, and eastern hemlock. There are also plentiful blueberries (ripening in August). The hemlocks here are truly impressive. Like the white cedar, they produce needles which when brewed make a tea rich in vitamin C (the eastern hemlock is not related to the poison hemlock plant used to execute Socrates). Native Americans made a tea from hemlock bark as a remedy for diarrhea. They also dried and ground the inner hemlock bark for flour, and applied it to wounds to stop bleeding.

At 12.0 mi. the AT passes Nahmakanta Stream Campsite, a fine flat streamside tenting place with a privy. Water comes from the stream. From this point on, the path becomes rougher as it climbs over gnarly roots and traverses swampy stretches on bog bridges. Wood Rat's Spring, at 14.6 mi., is another reliable water source.

At 14.9 mi. the AT comes to Nahmakanta Stream Rd. (gravel) that marks the end of this hike. But before heading home, walk 0.3 mi. farther north along the AT to the edge of Nahmakanta Lake for a fine view. A windblown cobble beach looks northwest along a wide expanse of open water and shoreline toward Nesuntabunt Mt., the trail's next major ridgetop destination.

HIKE #34 Itinerary

Miles N	NORTH	Elev. (ft/m)	Miles S
14.9	**End: Nahmakanta Lake,** Nahmakanta Stream Rd. (gravel logging road), overnight parking.	700/213	0.0
14.6	**Woods Rat's Spring.**		0.3
12.0	**Nahmakanta Stream Campsite,** water, privy.		2.9
10.4	Cross tributary of **Nahmakanta Stream** (ford).		4.5
10.3	Cross **Mahar Tote Rd.,** 0.2 mi. to view.		4.6
8.3	**Pemadumcook Lake,** view.		6.6
8.2	Ford **Twitchell Brook.**		6.7
8.1	Potaywadjo logging road (mileage approx.).		6.8
7.7	**Potaywadjo Lean-to, tentsites,** water, privy.	620/189	7.2
5.9	Side trail to beach, **Lower Jo-Mary Lake.**		9.0
5.7	Side trail (1.0 mi., steep) to Potaywadjo Ridge.		9.2
4.2	Side trail to **Antlers Campsite, Lower Jo-Mary Lake**; privy.	505/154	10.7
2.9	Cross **Mud Pond** outlet on bridge.		12.0
2.6	Cross unpaved logging road.		12.3
1.5	Spring.		13.4
1.3	Side trail to **Cooper Pond.**		13.6
0.0	**Start: Jo-Mary Rd.,** overnight parking.	650/198	14.9

SOUTH

HIKE #35
Central Lake Country

Maps: Maine AT Club, #2 and #1

Route: From Nahmakanta Lake over Nesuntabunt Mt., along Pollywog Stream to Wadleigh Mt. Rd.

Recommended direction: S to N

Distance: 8.3 mi.

Elevation +/-: 700 to 1540 to 650 ft.

Effort: Moderate

Day hike: Yes

Overnight backpacking hike: Optional

Duration: 6 hr.

Early exit option: None

Natural history features: Wildlife at Nahmakanta Lake; old-growth white pine and red spruce on Nesuntabunt Mt.; Crescent Pond and Pollywog Gorge

Social history features: 19th-century log drives

Trailhead access: *Start:* Take ME Rte. 11 for 13 mi. S of Millinocket, or 18 mi. N of Brownville Junction, turning W on Jo-Mary Lake Rd. Shortly, reach Jo-Mary North Maine Woods gate house (register, pay fee, request local map, identify Nahmakanta Stream Rd.). Continue on Jo-Mary Lake Rd. 12 mi. northwest to the AT crossing at Cooper Brook. En route, stop at Nahmakanta gate house (register, pay fee, confirm road directions). Continue 12 mi. on gravel roads (concluding with Nahmakanta Stream Rd.) to AT crossing at S end of Nahmakanta Lake. Overnight parking nearby at gravel pit. Total distance from Jo-Mary gate to starting trailhead about 24 mi. A longer, but free, access route is available from the north via roads from the tiny village of Kokadjo (approx. 18 mi. from Greenville, near First Roach Pond). For route information, contact Maine Bureau of Parks and Lands, P.O. Box 415, Old Town, ME 04468; 407-827-5936. *End:* From starting trailhead, return on Nahmakanta Stream Rd. to Wadleigh Mt. Rd. (also called by some "Jo-Mary Lake Rd."), turn R, follow Wadleigh Mt. Rd. several mi., passing Wadleigh Pond (L), then curving R around northwest side of Nesuntabunt Mt. to AT crossing, and continuing to bridge at Pollywog Stream and AT trailhead. Limited roadside parking. Total distance between start and end trailheads about 8 mi.

Camping: Wadleigh Stream Lean-To

For those who can spend only one day walking in the 100 Mile Wilderness, this 8.3-mi. hike offers a sampler of some of the most beautiful and varied country in the Maine woods. The route includes a walk through old-growth white pine forest and spectacular views of sparkling lakes and the imposing granite face of Mt. Katahdin.

This shuttle hike requires an early start, with one car parked on the gravel road at the south end of Nahmakanta Lake and another at the gravel road bridge crossing of Pollywog Stream. See Hike #31 for information about the 100 Mile Wilderness.

Follow the AT as it leaves Nahmakanta Stream Rd. and heads northwest. In 0.3 mi. a short side trail leads right to the south end of Nahmakanta Lake. This pristine 4.0-mi.-long body of water was created by the uneven grinding of the Wisconsin Glacier more than 12,000 years ago, and by the damming of the valley by glacial till (boulders, gravel, sand, and grit).

The day we hiked here, high winds generated small whitecaps that broke on the rock cobble beach. Because of the stiff breeze, a moose cow and calf swimming across the Nahmakanta Stream outlet didn't detect us. These two seemingly horse-size animals proved to be powerful swimmers, holding their heads high as they plowed through the beating waves.

There are an estimated 20,000-plus moose in Maine, and that number is likely growing. Moose are the largest species of deer in the world, with cows weighing up to 800 pounds and bulls pushing 1,400. Remarkably, they amass this weight from a steady summer diet of aquatic vegetation, with winter meals composed of twigs, buds, and bark browsed from balsam, aspen, birch, cherry, maple, willow, and

Terry Karkos

Ladyslippers

other smaller plants. Generally mellow beasts, protective cows with calves can turn aggressive (and they can move at 35 mph). Like any large animal, moose should be given the right-of-way when met on the trail. The animals we saw turned away from us as soon as they caught our scent. Reaching the lake's far edge, they disappeared into the forest.

For a short distance, the AT passes over granite slabs lapped by Lake Nahmakanta's southwest shore. As the trail quickly rises away from the water it is enclosed by a forest of tall trees. These bigtooth aspen, eastern hemlocks, northern white cedars, and paper birch are some of the largest trees to be found along the AT. Their imposing trunks surprise and amaze, and it's easy to understand why Native Americans held them sacred.

Painted trillium (blooming in early summer) and blueberry bushes line the path as it continues a short, steep, rugged 150-vertical-ft. ascent among white pines and spruce. The trail descends sharply again, reaching the cobbled lakeshore at 1.5 mi. It follows this secluded beach a little way, then begins climbing steeply, this time through spruce and fir.

Rising to about 200 ft. above the lake, the AT passes a place where sphagnum moss and reindeer lichen cascade far down the ridge toward the water's edge. Pixie cup cladonia, a scaly trumpet-shaped lichen; and Labrador tea, with its spicy scented, leathery evergreen leaves, also flourish here. John Eastman writes in *The Book of Swamp and Bog,* that Labrador tea, as its name indicates, make a fine brew. But, he warns, it should only be drunk in small quantities because it contains a toxic chemical, called acetylandromedol, that causes headache, vertigo, and symptoms of intoxication.

The trail emerges onto a rock ledge, giving great views of the lake, before descending sharply back to the shore where a side trail at 2.2 mi. leads to a little spring and a sand beach.

A detour along this crescent-shaped beach, pockmarked with moose tracks (cloven, 7 in. long, spaced 2 to 5 ft. apart), is likely to reward hikers with a great around-the-clock nature show. Loons and grebes glide and skitter across still water, or dive for shiners and small trout at twilight ("Nahmakanta" is an Abenaki term meaning "plenty of fish," a claim that still rings true today). As darkness descends on the lake, waves of bats swoop and dart, gathering insects. At night, owl hoots and coyote howls rise from the surrounding forest. During mid-August, the Perseid meteor shower reaches its maximum after midnight, offering up to fifty shooting stars per hour—highly visible here in deep forest with no interference from human-made light. At dawn, the sun comes up over low ridges on the far shore, the quickly changing scarlet and golden hues enriched by rising lake mist.

For those who want to enjoy Lake Nahmakanta's nature spectacle at all hours of the day and night, camping is possible at Wadleigh Stream Lean-To, an easy 0.4- mi. walk north along the trail. Water is available from Wadleigh Stream, and there is a privy.

The hike between the sand beach and the shelter passes through a fantastic sugar maple grove. Some trees here approach 3 ft. in diameter. New England's maples are, of course, renowned for their maple sugar production. Up to 250 gallons of sap rise in a mature tree on a single spring day, of which 32 or more gallons are required to make a single gallon of refined syrup. Mysteriously, northeastern sugar maples have suffered a decline in recent years. Scientists are perplexed by their failure to flourish and point fingers at global warming, exotic insect invasions, and air pollution as possible causes.

Beyond Wadleigh Lean-To, the trail begins to climb Nesuntabunt Mt., passing from a forest of beech trees into conifers. Spruce and extremely large eastern white pine grow here. Each white pine supports a vast and varied mini-ecosystem. More than eighty species of insect feed on young shoots, twigs, needles and bark. Mice, voles, chipmunks, and red squirrels enjoy the pine seeds. Raccoons climb the trees at midday and rest in safety, high above the forest floor. Hawks and owls prefer the tall trees as nesting places, as do mourning doves, flycatchers, and many types of warblers.

The Maine Appalachian Trail Club is seeking "critical area designation" and protection for a 10-acre stand of old-growth red spruce and white pine on the north slope of Nesuntabunt Mt. Some of these great trees are over 140 years old, with the red spruces averaging 17 in. in diameter and the white pine averaging 23 in.

A 250-ft. elevation gain since leaving the shelter brings hikers past two ledges overlooking Nahmakanta Lake, then near an odd glacial erratic at 3.3 mi. The retreating ice left behind this table-shaped rock, weighing several tons and balanced perfectly atop two larger boulders. The formation could serve as a fine lunchtime rain shelter for one or two hikers.

The trail ascends farther on an increasingly gnarly footpath before descending briefly into a hollow where sugar maple, beech, and birch trees take over. Indian pipe grows in the shadow of these trees. This waxy white plant (shaped, as its name suggests, like an Indian smoking pipe) is saprophytic: it doesn't carry on photosynthesis, but gains nutrients from fungi associated with tree roots.

Soon the AT begins its steep 0.6-mi., 650-ft. final ascent of Nesuntabunt Mt. The trail repeatedly twists left and right, as it seeks out passable chutes between sheer rock cliffs. This stiff climb among stark and fascinating rock formations has been made significantly easier by the installation of over 160 stone steps by the MATC, some exemplary rock work.

The Nesuntabunt summit (1540 ft.), reached at 4.5 mi., is well worth the climb. This sweeping view looks over Nahmakanta Lake, past Rainbow Ledges, and beyond to Mt. Katahdin (5267 ft.). The gray granite slides beneath Katahdin's Howe, Hamlin, Pamola, and Baxter peaks are clearly visible from this vista—just 16 air miles, but still 35 trail miles from the AT's northern terminus. Many northbound thru-hikers stand transfixed at this spot as they realize how close they are to achieving the end of their quest. As one told me, "Thru-hiking the AT is a lot like life. You spend the first half pushing as hard and fast as you can to achieve your goal, then spend the last half savoring every moment and never wanting it all to end."

The 500-ft. descent from Nesuntabunt is less steep than the ascent, and easier on the feet. The conifer-needle-covered trail provides a soft cushion for each falling step. The AT passes by more large red spruce and white pine, goes over another rock ledge with great views of Katahdin and Lake Nahmakanta, then descends more gently among sugar maples and birch trees.

The trail crosses Wadleigh Mountain Rd. (a gravel logging road), at 5.7 mi., then climbs gently through spruce and balsam firs before descending briefly to Crescent Pond. The path hugs the shore of this pretty crescent-moon-shaped glacial tarn, passing first around its east horn (6.3 mi.) and then its west horn (6.9 mi.).

The AT now picks its way among rocks, roots, spruce and fir along the upper lip of Pollywog Gorge. At 7.3 mi. a dead-end side trail leads left 150 ft. to a view of this rocky canyon and the swiftly flowing stream at its bottom.

Today the gorge shelters the rare fragrant fern and even rarer luminous moss. But in the 19th century, this narrow canyon was notorious as a widow-making log- driving stream. Each spring, all across northern Maine, woodsmen would gather stockpiled cut logs and float them down raging rivers swollen with

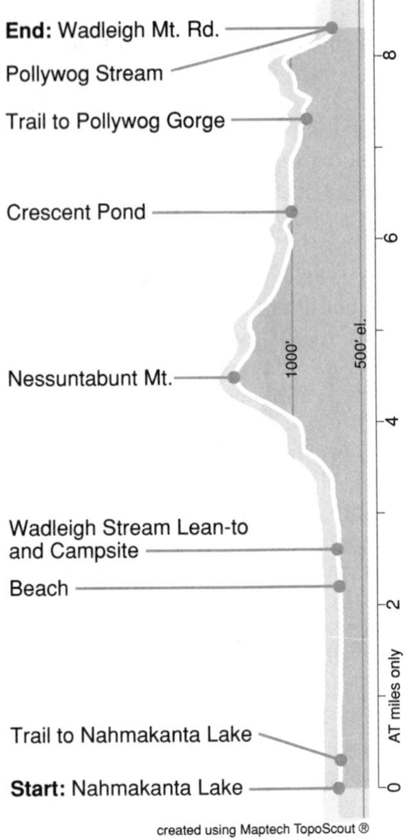

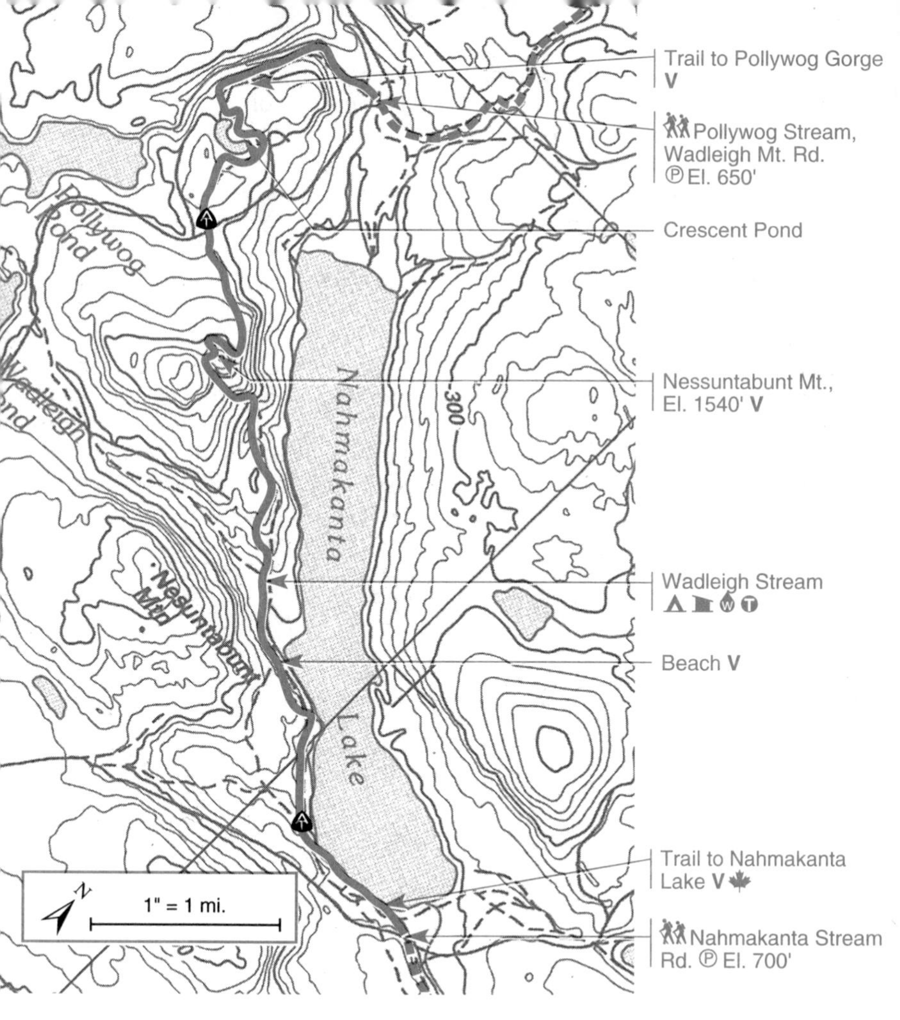
Trail to Pollywog Gorge V
Pollywog Stream, Wadleigh Mt. Rd. Ⓟ El. 650'
Crescent Pond
Pollywog Pond
Wadleigh Pond
Nahmakanta Lake
300
Nessuntabunt Mt., El. 1540' V
Nessuntabunt Mtn
Wadleigh Stream
Beach V
Trail to Nahmakanta Lake V
Nahmakanta Stream Rd. Ⓟ El. 700'
N
1" = 1 mi.

snow melt. Henry David Thoreau, writing in *The Maine Woods*, declared that these hardy men "must be able to navigate a log as if it were a canoe, and be as indifferent to cold and wet as a muskrat." Worse, they had to learn to "walk on floating logs as city boys on sidewalks."

Pollywog Stream, with its treacherous rock-strewn rapids, claimed at least fourteen loggers' lives. The dead were generally buried in a casket made from two pork barrels joined end-to-end, the only grave marker their pair of spiked boots, jammed into a nearby tree. The state of Maine eventually outlawed the dangerous and ecologically destructive river log drives, resulting in the building of the vast network of logging roads that hikers now use to reach remote Maine woods destinations.

The AT sinks steadily down into Pollywog Gorge, and reaching the bottom, follows along the stream on a rocky treadway. The beautiful gorge harbors an awe-inspiring grove of northern white cedars. These aromatic evergreens grow very tall here, spreading their branches and scale-like needles to catch the brief hours of sunlight cast into the deep ravine. Finally the trail reaches the gravel Wadleigh Mountain Rd. and a bridge over Pollywog Stream at 8.3 mi., marking the end of this hike.

HIKE #35 Itinerary

Miles N	NORTH	Elev. (ft/m)	Miles S
8.3	**End:** Wadleigh Mountain Rd. and bridge over **Pollywog Stream**; overnight parking.	650/198	0.0
7.3	Side trail (150 ft.) to **Pollywog Gorge.** View.		1.0
6.9	**Crescent Pond,** west.		1.4
6.3	**Crescent Pond,** east.		2.0
5.7	Cross **Wadleigh Mountain Rd.** (gravel logging road).		2.6
4.5	Summit of **Nesuntabunt Mt.,** view.	1540/469	3.8
3.3	Ledges, large glacial erratic, view.		5.0
2.6	**Wadleigh Stream Lean-to,** water, privy.	685/209	5.7
2.2	Trail at lakeshore, sand beach, views.		6.1
1.5	Trail at lakeshore, then climbs to ledges, views.		6.8
0.3	Side trail to **Nahmakanta Lake,** view.		8.0
0.0	**Start: Nahmakanta Lake,** Nahmakanta Stream Rd. (gravel logging road), overnight parking.	700/213	8.3

SOUTH

HIKE #36

Northern Lake Country

Maps: Maine AT Club, #1

Route: From Pollywog Stream to Rainbow Stream, to Rainbow Deadwaters and Rainbow Lake, over Rainbow Ledges to Abol Bridge

Recommended direction: S to N

Distance: 17.4 mi.

Elevation +/-: 650 to 1480 to 580 ft.

Effort: Moderate

Day hike: No

Overnight backpacking hike: Yes

Duration: 12 hr.

Early exit option: None

Natural history features: Rainbow Stream cascades, Rainbow Deadwaters wildlife, Rainbow Lake

Social history features: 19th-century log drives, Great Fire of 1923

Trailhead access: *Start:* Take ME Rte. 11 for 13 mi. S of Millinocket, or 18 mi. N of Brownville Junction, turning W on Jo-Mary Lake Rd. Shortly, reach Jo-Mary North Maine Woods gate house (register, pay fee, request local map). Continue on Jo-Mary Lake Rd. 12 mi. northwest to the AT crossing at Cooper Brook. En route, stop at Nahmakanta gate house (register, pay fee, confirm road directions). Continue several mi. on gravel Jo-Mary Lake Rd. (also called by some "Wadleigh Mt. Rd."), passing Wadleigh Pond (L), then curving R around northwest side of Nesuntabunt Mt. to AT crossing, and continuing to bridge at Pollywog Stream and AT trailhead. Limited roadside parking. Total distance from Jo-Mary gate is 27 mi. A longer, but free, access route is available from the north via roads from the tiny village of Kokadjo (approx. 18 mi. from Greenville, near First Roach Pond). For route information, contact Maine Bureau of Parks and Lands, P.O. Box 415, Old Town, ME 04468; 407-827-5936. *End:* From Golden Rd. (fee), accessed from ME 11 in Millinocket or from Greenville, drive 20 mi. to overnight parking at Abol Bridge Campground (private parking, reservation required, no phone: write Abol Bridge Campground, Millinocket, ME 04462-0536). Unreserved overnight parking available in public lot (gravel pit) on Golden Rd. at Abol Bridge crossing of West Branch Penobscot River.

Camping: Rainbow Stream Lean-To; Rainbow Spring Campsite; Hurd Brook Lean-To

The northernmost section of the 100 Mile Wilderness traverses a varied landscape of tall trees, placid lakes, and surging streams, where a kaleidoscopic play of sunlight and forest color inspired early explorers in the naming of local features. Here the AT parallels Rainbow Stream and Rainbow Lake, then climbs Rainbow Ledges, a rocky overlook with striking views toward the pot-of-gold-at-the-end-of-the-rainbow: Mt. Katahdin.

No roads cross this 17.5-mi. stretch of trail, and there's no place for backpackers to resupply before reaching Abol Bridge. See Hike #31 for information on the 100 Mile Wilderness.

The hike starts at the bridge over Pollywog Stream. After crossing the stream, the trail turns right (east) and ascends gently through a mixed forest of Eastern white pine, balsam, fir, and spruce. Clintonia, also called bluebeard lily, makes a showy forest floor display with its glossy leaves, delicate drooping yellowish green flowers (ripening in June and July), and dazzling true-blue berries (appearing in July and August).

The AT intercepts and parallels Rainbow Stream at 0.4 mi., and begins ascending along a treadway cut deeply into the steep stream bank. This energetic little river shoots around glacial erratics, roars over sheets of stone, and cascades through chutes and flumes into deep swimmable pools. Beautiful in any season, Rainbow Stream is particularly gorgeous in late September when the sugar maples and paper birches turn a vibrant yellow and drop their leaves into the reflective water.

At 0.7 mi. the trail passes the remains of an old logging dam used to heighten and channel waters for 19th-century log drives. MATC's AT guide describes rugged woodsmen who risked hypothermia, the dangers of runaway logs, dynamite and drowning in their drives of "a river of wood" to market each spring. As you climb along the bank of Rainbow Stream, look for evidence of dynamited ledges and steel drift pins, reminders of the log-driving days.

The trail veers away from and returns to Rainbow Stream several times as it ascends more steeply through a deciduous forest of beech, maple, and birch. Cresting at about 2.0 mi., the AT looks out over a small plateau and the conical silhouettes of a spruce and fir forest.

At 2.4 mi., the AT meets up with Rainbow Stream again and almost immediately arrives at the Rainbow Stream Lean-To. This shelter looks past yellow birches to the river, which descends into fine pools for swimming. Water comes from the stream, and there is a privy.

The shelter register makes poignant reading. With the AT only 30 mi. from its terminus at Mt. Katahdin, many northbound thru-hikers take this opportunity to write notes of farewell to fellow hikers. For these walkers, many of whom have been together for over

5 months, journey's end brings both exhilaration and sadness. In just 2 or 3 days the Dancing Fool, Pogo, and Happy Feet must hang up their trail names, put aside their walking sticks, and don street clothes for their return to the "real" world.

After a precarious log bridge crossing of Rainbow Stream (slippery when wet), the AT arrives at the Rainbow Deadwaters at 2.6 mi., a level section of trail along a calm stretch of open water. If you're fortunate enough to be the first one out of the shelter and to break the trail's early morning cobwebs, you'll be likely to see a moose, half hidden by morning mist, feeding and drinking on the far shore. White pine and northern white cedar line the banks of this quiet stream. Only the clear, gentle call of the black capped chickadee breaks the silence. Look for these little birds as they hang upside down from twigs and branches in a search for insect eggs and larvae.

The AT turns away from the Deadwater at 4.2 mi. and ascends easily through a forest of spruce, sugar maple, and yellow birch. In another 0.2 mi., a side trail to the left leads to the dam at the west end of Rainbow Lake, where there are good views of Mt. Katahdin. The AT continues, passing over a small stream and skirting several swamps where turtlehead flourishes. This white flower is a favorite with bumblebees, who disappear completely inside the flower, then stagger out as if intoxicated by the nectar.

As the trail nears the south shore of Rainbow Lake, the forest becomes predominantly deciduous. Sugar maple and beech trees form the canopy, while tiny shade-tolerant balsam firs and spruce grow up in their shadow. Red maple and bigtooth and quaking aspen soon take over the forest mix, and the conifers disappear altogether.

The quaking aspen, with its distinctive quivering leaves, puts on a fine show here when the wind picks up. The aspen is the most far-flung of tree species in North America, bordering Arctic tundra and thriving in the southern Appalachians. Glacial ice and forest fire explain this wide distribution. Aspens are opportunistic survivors: they can endure –70° F temperatures, their seeds quickly germinate in barren soil, and the roots of a cut or burned tree can sprout hundreds of buds to form a clone. When provided with plenty of light by a retreating glacier or in the aftermath of a wildfire, aspen out-compete almost any plant grown from seed. These pioneering trees support over 500 species of plants and animals, from deer and bear to insects and fungi.

At 6.2 mi., the AT reaches Rainbow Spring Campsite. Grassy tenting areas, a fine spring, a privy, and shore-side views over Rainbow Lake make this an almost ideal overnight stopping place. Sadly, the deafening drone of float planes landing at the private Rainbow Lakes Camp destroys the feeling of pristine wilderness. The noise may also have a damaging ef-

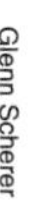

100 Mile Wilderness Feet

fect on the nesting habits of the loons who congregate on the lake. These shy birds, with their evocative, sometimes mournful, sometimes maniacal cry, are among the most ancient of birds. They've inhabited northern waters, unchanged, for 60 million years. Watch the loons and you'll be startled to see them disappear underwater and not reappear for up to 3 minutes. The birds can literally fly submerged, propelling themselves on stubby wings to a depth of up to 180 ft., nabbing small fish, frogs, or crayfish in their watery flight.

At 7.9 mi. the AT reaches a side trail that climbs 500 vertical ft. in 1.1 mi. to the top of Rainbow Mt., which offers good views over the lake. From this point on, the AT gets rootier and rockier as it parallels Rainbow Lake's shore, passes out of deciduous forest into conifers, and winds around several house-size glacial erratics dotted with rock tripe. The trail touches the south end of the lake at 9.6 mi. and passes a second side trail at 9.7 mi. This short trail leads right to Little Beaver Pond (in 0.1 mi.) and Big Beaver Pond (in 0.4 mi.), potentially promising moose-viewing country.

Now the AT begins its steepest climb of the hike, the easy 550-ft. ascent to the top of the Rainbow Ledges at 11.4 mi. This high place has been made magical by fire. Relentless 19th- and early 20th-century logging resulted in huge heaps of slash (treetops and branches not wanted by loggers) scattered across the landscape. This waste became tinder for the Great Fire of 1923, which swept Rainbow Ledges clean of vegetation.

What once was devastation is now a glorious miniature mountaintop garden. At summer's end, golden ferns, dark green mosses, smoky-gray reindeer lichen, reddening blueberry leaves, and tiny bonsai-like eastern white pine saplings create a stunning rainbow effect amid rounded glacial erratics. Through the years, these plants have laid down a thin soil layer for themselves, barely half an inch thick, while the trail, eroded by thousands of vibram-soled boots, passes over a bare slab of gray granite.

Chris "Ms. Direction" Potter, a medical student from Easton, Pennsylvania, declared Rainbow Ledges' blueberry patch the finest in all the 100 Mile Wilderness. She spent a productive hour here gathering ingredients for her "Rainbow Ledges Blueberry Sauce." The simple recipe requires several handfuls of fresh berries and enough water to cover them. Boil until the berries pop, add one-half handful of sugar, stir, and serve with biscuits. The result was tasty enough to entice two thru-hikers to carry Ms. Direction's 15-pound food bag over White Cap Mt.

The big picture from Rainbow Ledges is as striking as is the miniature ridgetop garden. A stunning view looks back over Maine's Lake

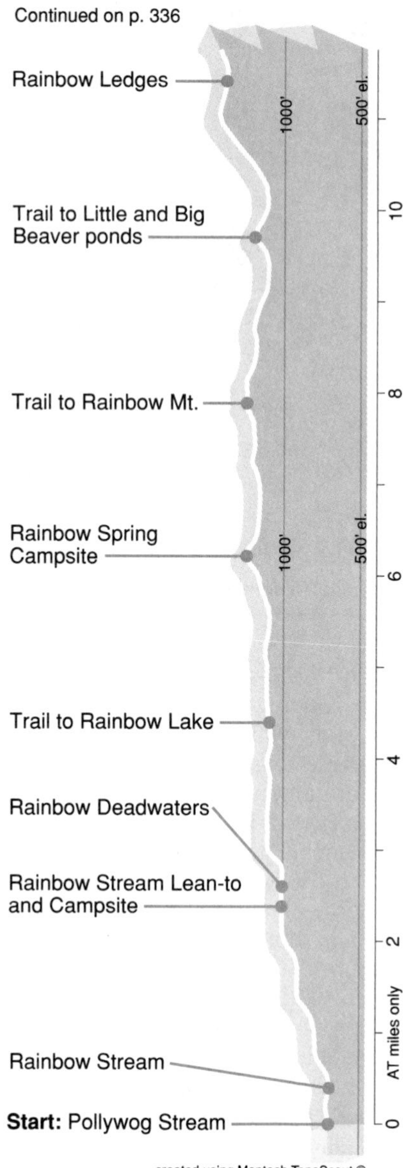

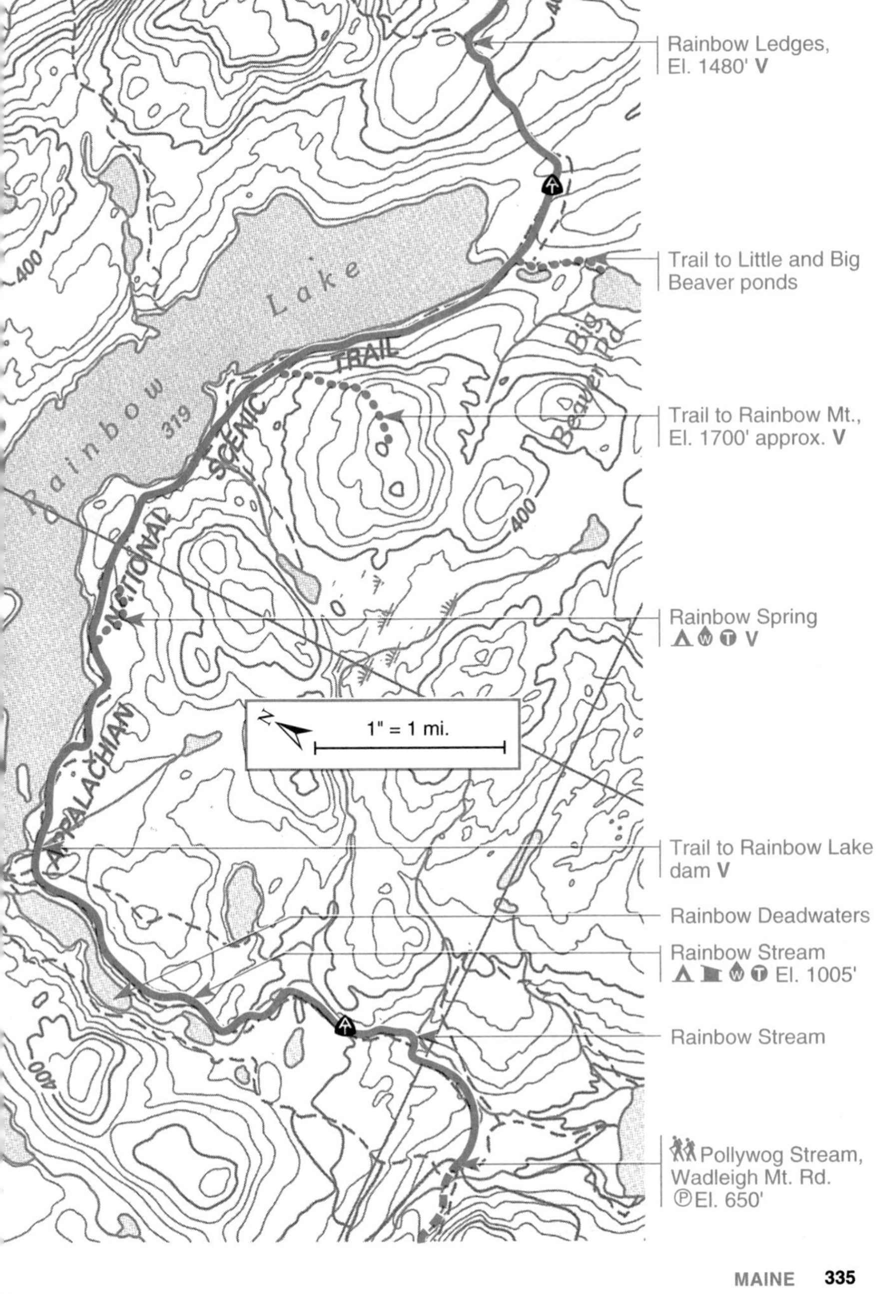
Rainbow Ledges,
El. 1480' V
Trail to Little and Big
Beaver ponds
Trail to Rainbow Mt.,
El. 1700' approx. V
Rainbow Spring
V
Trail to Rainbow Lake
dam V
Rainbow Deadwaters
Rainbow Stream
El. 1005'
Rainbow Stream
Pollywog Stream,
Wadleigh Mt. Rd.
El. 650'
Rainbow Lake
319
APPALACHIAN NATIONAL SCENIC TRAIL
Big Beaver Pd
400
1" = 1 mi.
N

Country and forward to Mt. Katahdin, looming only 21.1 trail miles ahead.

From here the AT descends into a spruce and fir cloaked col, ascends and descends briefly several times, and then, without further views, begins the long, steep, 800-vertical-ft. descent to Hurd Brook. Halfway down the mountain, the spruce and fir forest gives way to beech, red maple, and striped maple.

Hurd Brook Lean-To, at 13.9 mi., sits up on a hillside just beyond Hurd Brook. It is surrounded by trillium, moss-covered boulders, spruce, and fir. Just beyond the shelter's privy is a remarkable, double eastern white pine, its two massive trunks grown together.

Inside the privy is a sign that's hung on every outhouse of the 100 Mile Wilderness: "*Please close the door to this building or porcupines will eat it.*" Along the AT in Vermont and elsewhere, privies and even shelters have been gnawed to ruin. The reason for the wanton destruction is the porcupine's insatiable desire for salt, found in human waste and perspiration, which impregnates the building boards. They also dine on the glue in plywood. The porkie has over 30,000 barbed quills, protecting it from almost all attackers. Its population might explode, except for one predator: the elusive fisher. This house-cat-size relative of the weasel is agile and strong. It grabs the sharp-quilled porkie by its feet, flips it onto its back, and attacks the soft underbelly. So a delicate natural balance has been

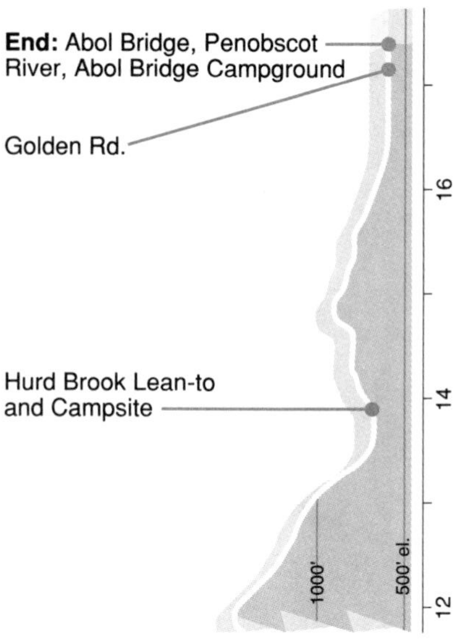

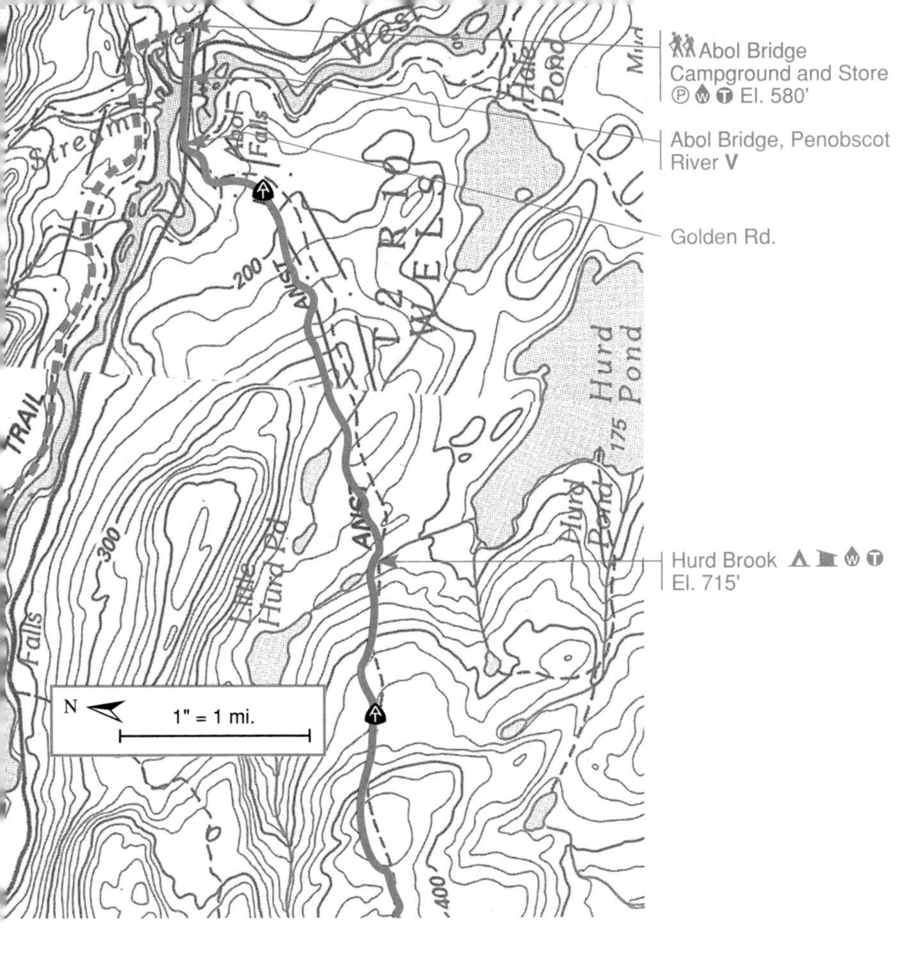
Abol Bridge
Campground and Store
Ⓟ Ⓦ Ⓣ El. 580'
Abol Bridge, Penobscot
River V
Golden Rd.
Hurd Brook
El. 715'
Hurd Pond
Little Hurd Pd
Hurd Pond
Abol Falls
West
Hale Pond
Stream
TRAIL
Falls
200
300
400
175
N
1" = 1 mi.

struck, with the fisher serving as unwitting protector of Maine's privies.

The 3.3-mi. hike from the shelter to the Golden Rd. is an easy, mostly downhill walk that passes repeatedly in and out of northern hardwood forest and spruce-fir forest. Most interesting is the trail's crossing of a large northern white cedar swamp, at 15.2 mi., on bog bridges. These great cedars grow slowly, widening their trunks by a mere inch every ten to twenty growing seasons. Light-weight cedar wood once made ideal Native American canoe frames. Today it is harvested as lumber and the tree's oil is extracted for medicines.

At 17.2 mi. the AT intersects with the Golden Rd. and turns right. For the first time in 100 mi. it passes over pavement and beneath silvery high-voltage electrical transmission towers. Vacationers zoom by, dragging motorboats behind four-wheel-drive vehicles. The short road walk, after so many hours in the woods, makes some hikers feel exposed and wary.

But to most walkers the Golden Rd.'s bridge over the West Branch of the Penobscot River, at 17.4 mi., is a welcome sight, as is the Abol Bridge Campground Store 0.1 mi. farther on, with its famous donuts and fresh-brewed coffee.

The Abol Bridge Campground makes a fine staging area for backpacking trips into Baxter State Park and to Katahdin's summit or for southbound hikes into the 100 Mile Wilderness. The campground is private and has over forty wooded sites. To reserve a site, write to Abol Bridge Campground, P.O. Box 536, Millinocket, ME 04462-0536 (don't call information; the campground has no phone).

Abol Bridge is a fascinating place to linger, especially at twilight. The wide river attracts moose and even eagles, which swoop out of the sky to pluck fish from the flowing waters. In the distance, the stark sunlit summit of Katahdin beckons.

HIKE #36 Itinerary

Miles N	NORTH	Elev. (ft/m)	Miles S
17.4	**End: Abol Bridge,** Penobscot River, Abol Bridge Campground (private), store, overnight parking with campground permission.	580/177	0.0
17.2	Reach **Golden Rd.** (paved), turn R.		0.2
15.2	Cedar swamp.		2.2
13.9	**Hurd Brook Lean-to,** water, privy.	715/218	3.5
11.4	**Rainbow Ledges,** views.	1480/451	6.0
9.7	Side trail (0.1 mi.) to **Little Beaver Pond** and (0.4 mi.) to Big Beaver Pond.		7.7
9.6	South end **Rainbow Lake.**		7.8
7.9	Side trail (1.1 mi.) to **Rainbow Mt.,** approx. 1700′, view.		9.5
6.2	**Rainbow Spring Campsite,** water, privy, views.		11.2
4.4	Side trail to dam at **Rainbow Lake,** views.		13.0
2.6	**Rainbow Deadwaters** to 4.2 mi.		14.8
2.4	**Rainbow Stream Lean-to,** water, privy.	1005/306	15.0
2.0	View.		15.4
0.7	Old logging dam.		16.7
0.4	**Rainbow Stream.**		17.0
0.0	**Start:** Wadleigh Mountain Rd. Bridge over **Pollywog Stream**; limited overnight parking.	650/198	17.4

SOUTH

HIKE #37

Baxter Ponds

Maps: Maine AT Club, #1

Route: From Abol Bridge along the West Branch of the Penobscot River to Nesowadnehunk Stream, to Daicey Pond, Elbow Pond, and Tracy Pond, to Perimeter Rd.

Recommended direction: S to N

Distance: 9.9 mi.

Elevation +/-: 580 to 1120 to 1100 ft.

Effort: Easy to Moderate

Day hike: Yes

Overnight backpacking hike: Optional

Duration: 5 1/4 hr.

Natural history features: Nesowadnehunk Stream and waterfalls; West Branch of Penobscot River; ponds

Social history features: Logging; Percival Baxter

Trailhead access: *Start:* Abol Bridge on Golden Rd., 20 mi. W of Millinocket. *End:* Katahdin Stream Campground on Perimeter Rd., 8.2 mi. from Baxter State Park's Togue Pond Gate

Camping: Abol Bridge Campground (tent sites, store, no phone; write Abol Bridge Campground, Millinocket, ME 04462); Daicey Pond Campground and Katahdin Stream Campground in Baxter State Park (reservations necessary; write Baxter State Park, 64 Balsam Dr., Millinocket, ME 04462, or call 207-723-5140).

This section of the AT is best described as a walk on the water side. Hike #37 winds along a river, then along a stream, and then along the shore of several ponds before reaching the foot of majestic Mt. Katahdin, the northern terminus of the AT. It's a spectacular combination of waterways and forest path.

The hike begins at Abol Bridge. (To reach Golden Rd., cross to the road immediately north of the causeway at Millinocket Lake.) Parking is available between the trailhead and Abol Bridge. After passing the Abol Bridge Campground, which has tentsites on the West Branch of the Penobscot River and is the only private campground on the AT, the trail veers off Golden Rd. at 0.2 mi., and after a sharp left turn at 0.4 mi., continues up a gravel road.

For the next 3.7 mi., the trail parallels the West Branch of the Penobscot River, which was a major thoroughfare for log drives in the late 1800s. Lumberjacks cut the wood in the winter and hauled it over the frozen ground to the river's edge. In the spring, assisted by the fast-moving river current, the lumberjacks "drove," or floated, the logs downstream, feeding about 250 sawmills located just above the city of Bangor. In 1846 those sawmills had an annual capacity of 2 million board feet. In 1872 that

Percival Baxter and His Park

One of the largest wilderness areas in the United States outside of Alaska (over 200,000 acres), Baxter State Park was the brainchild of Maine's governor Percival Baxter. He had a vision of the role the Katahdin region could play as a recreation resource for his state, and he saw how a park would serve the interests of wildlife preservation as well. Working against daunting odds (a recalcitrant legislature, a stubborn logging industry), Baxter lobbied for 30 years and several times personally bought thousands of acres for the park. Eventually Maine adopted Baxter's plan with enthusiasm and stewardship. Typical of the governor's persuasive arguments for the park are the words that follow.

To Maine Sportsmen's Fish and Game Association, January 1921

To most people Mount Katahdin is but a name. To those who have both seen and climbed the Mountain, it is a wonderful reality, and the memories of a trip to its summit remain vivid through the years. At present the great Mountain, weather-beaten by time and scarred by the avalanche, is almost inaccessible, the journey entailing expense, hardship and discomfort. The grandeur of the Mountain, its precipitous slopes, its massive cliffs, unusual formation and wonderful coloring cannot be surpassed or even equalled by any mountain east of the Mississippi river. Katahdin rises abruptly from the plain to the height of 5,273 feet, and, without foothills to detract from its solitary dignity, stands alone, a grim gray tower overlooking the surrounding country for hundreds of miles. It is small wonder that the aboriginal Indians believed it to be the home of the spirits of wind, storm and thunder.

The history of these lands is fascinating. It is a story of intrigue and corruption, where powerful and selfish men often took that to which they had no right, from those too weak to defend themselves and their property. It is a story in which the rights of the people in a princely inheritance were given away or bartered for a song, for the folly of which future generations forever will pay.

To Governor H. A. Hildreth and the Legislature, January 1945

I want pleasant foot-trails built and attractive campsites laid out in the valleys, by the brooks and on the shores of the waters. Sites where simple forest lean-tos and small log cabins are available for those who love nature and are willing to walk and make an effort to get close to nature.

Everything in connection with the Park must be left simple and natural, and must remain as nearly as possible as it was when only the Indians and the animals roamed at will through these areas. I want it made available to persons of moderate means who, with their boys and girls, with their packs of bedding and food, can tramp through the woods, cook a steak and make flapjacks by the lakes and brooks. Every section of this area is beautiful, each in its own way. I do not want it locked up and made inaccessible; I want it used to the fullest extent but in the right, unspoiled way.

Percival Baxter, *Greatest Mountain: Katahdin's Wilderness*. Scrimshaw Press, 1972.

— David Emblidge

capacity had jumped to 225 million board feet. Modern transportation and road construction has made the romantic river drives a relic of history.

After the sharp left turn, the AT heads west through deciduous woods, crossing Abol Stream on a bridge at 0.7 mi. and fording Katahdin Stream at 1.1 mi. The trail continues over fairly flat terrain, crossing first a small brook, dammed by beavers, and then Foss and Knowlton Brook on a footbridge. The path follows along the wide West Branch, lined by towering pine trees. Occasionally a logging truck can be heard rumbling along Golden Rd., which runs along the river on the opposite bank, a reminder of how the transportation of logs has changed.

At 4.1 mi., the footpath reaches Pine Point, at the junction of the West Branch and Nesowadnehunk Stream. To the northwest there are vistas of Nesowadnehunk Falls, running all year. In the mid-1980s, this section of the river was the subject of intense debate over a proposed hydroelectric dam. The proposal was eventually defeated, so instead the West Branch remains a popular place for the flotilla of rafting companies that ride the river down the gorge and over the falls. For information about going on a trip, contact Raft Maine (an association of rafting guides and outfitters), P.O. Box 3, Bethel, ME 04217; 800-723-8633.

Over the next 3.4 mi. the AT parallels Nesowadnehunk Stream for a lovely streamside walk. The trail narrows, and rocks and roots make the going a bit rougher as it rises slowly through the enveloping forest along the boulder-strewn Nesowadnehunk, an Indian word that means "swift stream between mountains." Rising in Nesowadnehunk Lake, on the western edge of Baxter State Park, the stream flows south, separating a western range of mountains dominated by Doubletop and an eastern range dominated by North and South Brother. At 4.5 mi., hikers must ford the lower fork of the stream, which is dangerous at high water. Use a tall walking stick for balance. Sandals or other water shoes may help. At the very least, bring extra socks.

The trail here is littered with granite fragments, remnants of millions of years of erosion. Mt. Katahdin, now roughly 5 to 6 mi. in diameter, is actually the remains of a huge oval-shaped slab of granite thought to have been originally 30 mi. long.

On the tops of large granite boulders, you will occasionally see lichen growing, like a toupee on top of the bald rock. Lichens, which grow in association with algae, from which they obtain nutrition, secrete chemicals powerful enough to slowly break down rocks and create soil, allowing other plants to take root on the otherwise inhospitable surface. As the plants die and break down, humus is formed, encouraging soil buildup.

The AT crosses the boundary of Baxter State Park at 4.8 mi. Baxter was created through the munificence of Gov. Percival Baxter, who

Visiting Baxter State Park

There are two gatehouses to this magnificent state park (one of the largest in the U.S.), and a stop at these ranger stations is required for check-in and to obtain weather and trail condition reports. Arriving from Millinockett, enter at Togue Pond Gate; on the northeast side of the park, enter at Matagamon Gate. Baxter is famous for having few roads and many hiking trails. The Perimeter Rd. links all but two of the nine campgrounds. Camping is by reservation only, by mail or in person (not by telephone). Call for information as much as six months ahead. Traffic flow is strictly limited in order to preserve the wildness and quiet in the campgrounds and on the trails. Rustic cabins are available at some choice sites, such as Daicey Pond. The campground at Chimney Pond, on Katahdin, is unreachable by any road.

Come fully prepared with all supplies —Baxter offers no stores or gas stations. If you're driving up the Maine coast en route to Baxter, you'll probably want to make the ritual stop at L.L. Bean in Freeport (open 24 hr.). And don't expect to find a hot shower in Baxter. For that you'll need to head to a motel near Millinocket.

Moose are plentiful here, so drive carefully in the park. If you see one, give it a *wide* berth. Sandy Stream Pond, near Roaring Brook Campground, is know as prime moose-spotting territory.

Winter use of the park is by permit only; some mountain trails are closed. Warm-weather hiking is regulated too. On some trails, when the trailhead parking lot is full, that's it for the day. The moral: Get there early. There is plenty of sweet lowland hiking in Baxter, but if you're ascending Katahdin or other peaks with above-treeline exposure, be sure to check in with the ranger before going up and to check back in when you're down. Don't put a rescue party at risk by failing to communicate.

These important rules taken care of, Baxter welcomes hikers and campers and canoeists and nature observers with enthusiasm. Once you have seen the charms of this wilderness, you will want to come back many times.

Baxter State Park Headquarters, 64 Balsam Dr., Millinocket, ME 04462; 207-723-5140. — David Emblidge

purchased and donated 5,960 acres in 1931, including much of Mt. Katahdin. Over the years, Baxter, who died in 1969, gave more than 202,000 acres to the state of Maine. All of these gifts were granted with a condition that they "shall ever be kept in its natural wild state." (See "Percival Baxter and His Park.")

The path crosses the upper branch of the Nesowadnehunk at 5.5 mi., and at 5.6 mi. passes a balancing rock (a glacial erratic). The AT then ascends in a mostly fir forest to a series of waterfalls. The trail reaches thundering Big Niagara Falls at 6.5 mi., where there is a large open area of rock overlooking the cascade, an excellent spot to take a rest or a lunch break. From there the AT climbs up to a 100-yd. side trail leading to Little Niagara Falls at 6.6 mi., an area that offers superb views to the east of The Owl, Barren Mt. and Mt. O-J-I, so named because the three rock slides on its southwestern flank suggested these three letters—at least until 1932, when a storm enlarged the slides and changed their shape. Just above Little Niagara Falls is the Toll Dam, formerly used by lumberjacks to control the volume of water for floating logs down the stream to the West Branch.

The AT levels off and widens over the next 1.1 mi., on the way to Daicey Pond. This is an easy, comfortable stroll through the woods, with nice views to the northwest of Doubletop and Squaw's Bosom. Daicey Pond Campground, reached at 7.5 mi., has a ranger station, lean-tos, cabins, and tentsites. Reservations are required, in part because the campground is immensely popular. And for good reason: The massif of Mt. Katahdin towers over this lovely pond. In fact, camping in Baxter State Park demands *early* reservations, especially in July, August, and September (see "Visiting Baxter State Park").

The trail continues along Daicey Pond Rd. for 0.1 mi. before taking a sharp right turn into the woods. The

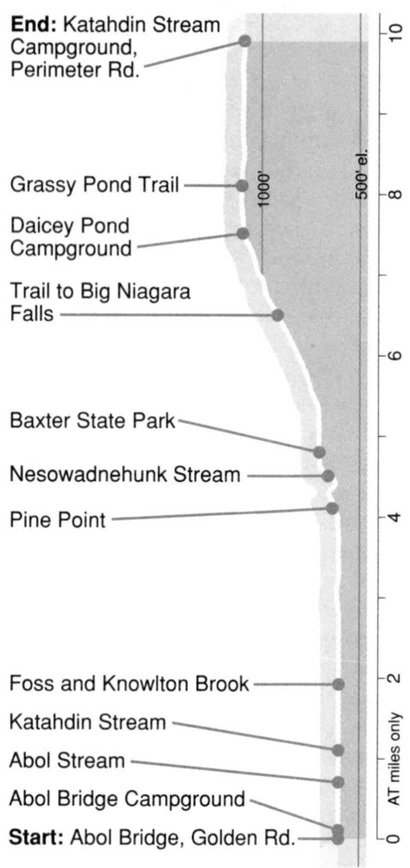

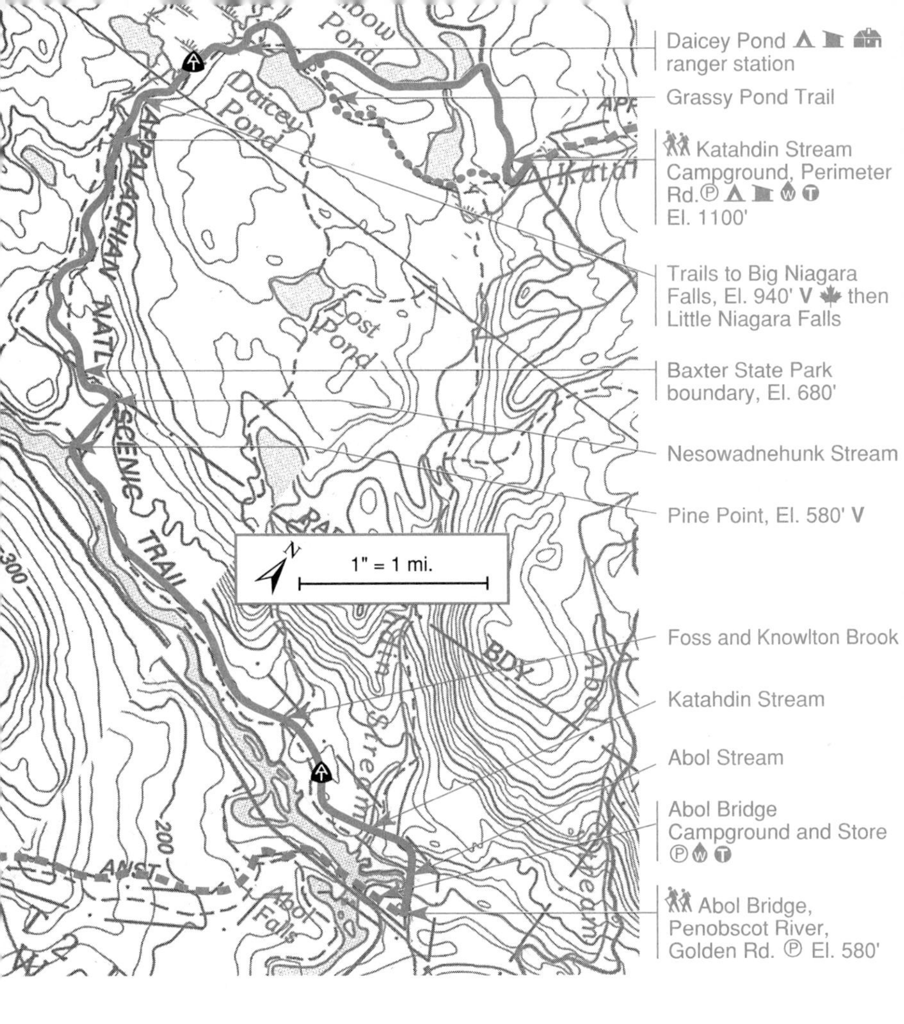
Daicey Pond
ranger station
Grassy Pond Trail
Katahdin Stream Campground, Perimeter Rd.
El. 1100'
Trails to Big Niagara Falls, El. 940' V then Little Niagara Falls
Baxter State Park boundary, El. 680'
Nesowadnehunk Stream
Pine Point, El. 580' V
Foss and Knowlton Brook
Katahdin Stream
Abol Stream
Abol Bridge Campground and Store
Abol Bridge, Penobscot River, Golden Rd. El. 580'
Daicey Pond
Lost Pond
APPALACHIAN NAT'L SCENIC TRAIL
1" = 1 mi.
N
BDY
Abol Falls
ANST
300
200

path then climbs up and over a small knob, now descending to the east side of the pond. The trail passes into the woods again, reaching the junction with Grassy Pond Trail at 8.1 mi. (an alternative, shorter route to Katahdin Stream Campground that avoids the AT's section on the Perimeter Rd., but seeing the ponds along the AT are worth the extra steps). The AT continues over flat terrain to Elbow Pond, so named because, well, it's shaped like an elbow. Tamarack trees grow near the pond's edge. Tamarack is an unusual tree—the only deciduous conifer whose needles turn yellow and drop in autumn. Native Americans sewed pieces of birch bark together with the slender roots of the tamarack to build their canoes.

The AT continues along the shore of Elbow Pond through a softwood forest, passing the outlet to the pond at 8.8 mi. The high point of this hike, approximately 1120 ft., comes at 8.9 mi. when the trail crosses the outlet to Tracy Pond, with views to Doubletop Mt. and Mt. O-J-I to the north.

Shortly after that Perimeter Rd. appears, at 9.1 mi., where the AT turns right and continues along the road until the sharp left turn into Katahdin Stream Campground at 9.8 mi. The campground, which has parking, lean-tos, tentsites, and a bunkhouse, is 0.1 mi. off Perimeter Rd. Here, too, early reservations are advised (see Hike #38).

Day Hike Loop—Grassy Pond Trail

For a short day hike loop, consider the Grassy Pond Trail. Start from the north end of Hike #37 at Katahdin Stream Campground. The trailhead leaves across the Perimeter Rd. and heads west. The trail passes the small remote Grassy Pond. There are remnants of an old lumber camp on the south shore. After 1.5 mi. Grassy Pond Trail reaches the AT (at a point 0.5 mi. north of Daicey Pond—also worth viewing). To return to the start, go north on the AT, reaching Katahdin Stream Campground after a loop walk of about 3.2 mi.

HIKE #37 Itinerary

Miles N	NORTH	Elev. (ft/m)	Miles S
9.9	**End: Katahdin Stream Campground,** 0.1 mi. N of Perimeter Rd.; ranger station, lean-tos, tentsites, water, privy, overnight parking. Park entrance 8.2 mi. SE.	1100/335	0.0
9.1	**Perimeter Rd.,** Baxter State Park. AT turns R onto road.		0.8
8.9	**Tracy Pond** outflow.	1120/341	1.0
8.8	**Elbow Pond** outflow.		1.1
8.1	Junction with **Grassy Pond Trail.**		1.8
7.5	**Daicey Pond Campground,** ranger station, lean-tos, camps, tentsites; reservations necessary.	1060/323	2.4
6.6	Spur trails: W to **Toll Dam,** S (100 yd.) to **Little Niagara Falls,** views.		3.3
6.5	**Big Niagara Falls.**	940/287	3.4
5.5	**Nesowadnehunk Stream,** upper branch, ford.		4.4
4.8	Boundary of **Baxter State Park.**	680/207	5.1
4.5	**Nesowadnehunk Stream,** lower fork, ford.		5.4
4.1	**Pine Point,** views of Nesowadnehunk Falls.	580/177	5.8
1.9	Cross **Foss and Knowlton Brook,** footbridge.		8.0
1.1	Cross **Katahdin Stream,** ford.		8.8
0.7	Cross **Abol Stream,** bridge.		9.2
0.4	Intersection: unpaved and paved roads.		9.5
0.1	**Abol Bridge Campground** and store; reservations necessary.		9.8
0.0	**Start: Abol Bridge,** Golden Rd., park S side of road, W of bridge.	580/177	9.9

SOUTH

HIKE #38

Mt. Katahdin

Maps: Maine AT Club, # 1

Route: From Katahdin Stream Campground to Katahdin Stream and Katahdin Falls, to Thoreau Spring, to summit of Mt. Katahdin, and return

Recommended direction: S to N

Distance: 10.4 mi. circuit hike

Elevation +/-: 1100 to 5267 to 1100 ft.

Effort: Very strenuous

Day hike: Yes

Overnight backpacking hike: No

Duration: 9 to 10 hr.

Early exit option: None

Natural history features: Katahdin Stream Falls; Table Land; alpine environment; Great Basin

Social history features: Baxter State Park; Henry David Thoreau at Katahdin

Trailhead access: *Start and End:* Katahdin Stream Campground, on the Perimeter Rd., 8.2 mi. from Baxter State Park's Togue Pond Gate

Camping: Daicey Pond Campground and Katahdin Stream Campground in Baxter State Park (reservations: Baxter State Park, 64 Balsam Dr., Millinocket, ME 04462; 207-723-5140). Reservations available from Jan. 1; call well in advance. No camping on Mt. Katahdin. Baxter State Park open for overnight use May 15 to Oct. 15; open for day use year-round, although roads are not maintained. No dogs allowed in the park.

Legendary along the AT, the jagged, treeless profile of Mt. Katahdin seems incongruous among other rounded, forested Appalachian peaks. The glaciers never reached high enough to smooth off Katahdin's rugged summit. To the first time visitor, Katahdin seems a mountain more suited to the high Rockies or the snowy netherworld of Patagonia.

Into the Mountains: Stories of New England's Most Celebrated Peaks names Charles Turner and a group of surveyors, in 1804, as the first white men to ascend Katahdin. By this time Lewis and Clark were exploring the West, but the far reaches of northern Maine (part of Massachusetts until 1820) were nearly as unknown as the upper Missouri. Throughout colonial times and the first decades of the Republic, Katahdin was considered inaccessible. This remote, wild mountain's exploration came later than at any other major peak in New England. Katahdin is the only one of the tallest New England mountains that has never had a building on its top or a road to its summit. Although it is considerably lower than Mt. Washington (5267 ft. vs. 6288 ft.), Katahdin is still the sixth highest peak in the New England Appalachians and the tallest in Maine.

Today's Appalachian Trail follows a path blazed up Katahdin's southwestern flank in 1900 by Irving Hunt. A leader in putting the AT on Katahdin's shoulder was a young man named Helon Taylor (in the early 1930s). Taylor went on to become superintendant of Baxter State Park, of which Katahdin is the centerpiece. Credit is due as well to Myron Avery, native Mainer, and 30-year-long president of the Appalachian Trail Conference. Avery authored AMC's first guide to Katahdin.

The top of Katahdin, from about 3500 ft. up, is an alpine environment mostly above treeline. Before you go up, be sure to register at the park ranger's cabin. Make a careful plan for getting back down safely. Check the weather report with the ranger. Be prepared to wait for a better day rather than expose yourself—or a rescue team—to unnecessary risk.

Hike #38 leaves Katahdin Stream Campground on the AT (Hunt Trail), meandering up a slight gradient along the stream for the first few miles. The woods here are young (spruce-fir interspersed with white birch and mountain ash). Enormous boulders of pink Katahdin granite dot the forest. On Katahdin, rocks are mostly gray and pink granite, a mix of quartz, feldspar, and mica. *Underfoot: A Geologic Guide to the Appalachian Trail* explains that it's the greater potassium content in Katahdin's granite feldspar, especially up top, that gives it the pinkish cast. *50 Hikes in the Maine Mountains* also has a good description of Katahdin's complex geology, noting for instance that granite tends to break into consistently sized and shaped boulders.

At 1.0 mi. Owl Trail leaves the AT to the left. If the weather on top of Katahdin (4000 ft. or higher) won't permit a safe ascent, consider this alternative. The trip to The Owl is 2.2 mi. one way, and the open domed summit (3736 ft.) affords wonderful views. Carry water on this hike. However, the top of The Owl is also above treeline. Avoid it too if weather threatens at 3000 ft. or above.

The AT crosses an attractive gorge cut into the granite by Katahdin Stream at 1.1 mi. (a waterfall worth visiting is, nearby off the AT, at 1.2 mi.). Moose signs abound as the AT continues to rise steeply (gaining 1750 ft. over 1.5 mi.). Around 1.7 mi. look for O-Joy Brook (first chance to replenish water supplies if you're coming down the mountain). A mile beyond the brook (at 2.7 mi.), brings you to a small protected space under huge boulders ("The Cave"), the last "shelter" during the ascent. Minutes later, near 3.1 mi. and a group of large boulders, the AT emerges from the forest at treeline. Now the AT follows the Hunt Spur towards Baxter Peak, climbing steeply along an exposed ridge.

The Hunt Spur/AT passes between two granite slabs, at about 3.6 mi. from the start. This is "The Gateway" to

Thoreau at Katahdin

When Henry David Thoreau climbed Mt. Katahdin in 1846, he never made it to the summit (fog), got lost (more fog and clouds), sprained an ankle (fell out of a tree he had climbed to get a view), and wrestled with an unfriendly Nature his Transcendentalist philosophy was unaccustomed to acknowledging. Nonetheless, a remarkable book, *Ktaadn* (later incorporated in *The Maine Woods,* 1864), with keen observations on geology and plant life, backwoodsmen and their ways, and the spiritual side of Nature, was the happy result. Dying from tuberculosis at forty-five, Thoreau's last fevered words were reportedly "moose.... Indian." Thoreau reminds us that the Abenaki god "Pomola" presides atop Katahdin and rarely welcomes visitors with good weather.

At length I entered within the skirts of the cloud which seemed forever drifting over the summit, and yet would never be gone, but was generated out of that pure air as fast as it flowed away; and when, a quarter of a mile farther, I reached the summit of the ridge, which those who have seen in clearer weather say is about five miles long, and contains a thousand acres of table-land, I was deep within the hostile ranks of clouds, and all objects were obscured by them. Now the wind would blow me out a yard of clear sunlight, wherein I stood; then a gray, dawning light was all it could accomplish, the cloud-line ever rising and falling with the wind's intensity. Sometimes it seemed as if the summit would be cleared in a few moments, and smile in sunshine; but what was gained on one side was lost on another. It was like sitting in a chimney and waiting for the smoke to blow away. It was, in fact, a cloud-factory,—these were the cloud-works, and the wind turned them off done from the cool, bare rocks. Occasionally, when the windy columns broke in to me, I caught sight of a dark, damp crag to the right or left; the mist driving ceaselessly between it and me. It reminded me of the creations of the old epic and dramatic poets, of Atlas, Vulcan, the

upper Katahdin, the wide open "Table Land." For a mountain so steep-sided, Katahdin is surprisingly level (a series of flat ledges) in this highest section.

From this point on, the AT and other trails up top are windswept and exposed, with no available shelter. The advice about surviving the alpine environment above treeline in New Hampshire's White Mts. (see Hike #12) applies here as well. Katahdin newcomers especially should read the hikes along the Presidential Range (above treeline) in New Hampshire (Hikes #11 and #12). Grand hiking adventure awaits you on Katahdin's rooftop, but remember: People have died here for lack of proper equipment, food, water, or a sensible plan of escape.

At 4.2 mi., the Hunt Spur/AT reaches a junction at Thoreau Spring, named for the famous writer who

Cyclops, and Prometheus. Such was Caucasus and the rock where Prometheus was bound. Æschylus had no doubt visited such scenery as this. It was vast, Titanic, and such as man never inhabits. Some part of the beholder, even some vital part, seems to escape through the loose grating of his ribs as he ascends. He is more lone than you can imagine. There is less of substantial thought and fair understanding in him than in the plains where men inhabit. His reason is dispersed and shadowy, more thin and subtile, like the air. Vast, Titanic, inhuman Nature has got him at disadvantage, caught him alone, and pilfers him of some of his divine faculty. She does not smile on him as in the plains. She seems to say sternly, Why came ye here before your time. This ground is not prepared for you. Is it not enough that I smile in the valleys? I have never made this soil for thy feet, this air for thy breathing, these rocks for thy neighbors. I cannot pity nor fondle thee here, but forever relentlessly drive thee hence to where I am kind. Why seek me where I have not called thee, and then complain because you find me but a stepmother? Shouldst thou freeze or starve, or shudder thy life away, here is no shrine, nor altar, nor any access to my ear.

"Chaos and ancient Night, I come no spy
With purpose to explore or to disturb
The secrets of your realm, but...
.... as my way
Lies through your spacious empire up to light."

The tops of mountains are among the unfinished parts of the globe, whither it is a slight insult to the gods to climb and pry into their secrets, and try their effect on our humanity. Only daring and insolent men, perchance, go there. Simple races, as savages, do not climb mountains,—their tops are sacred and mysterious tracts never visited by them. Pomola is always angry with those who climb to the summit of Ktaadn.

Henry David Thoreau, *Ktaadn*, 1848; revised as *The Maine Woods*, 1864.

—David Emblidge, Andrew Weegar

climbed to this point in 1846. You may trust Thoreau's philosophy, but don't trust this unreliable spring: Bring your own water. There are superior views here, though, and a good resting place.

From Thoreau Spring, the Hunt Spur/AT continues for 1.0 mi., comfortably gaining another 600+ ft. over ledges, to Baxter Peak, the apex of Katahdin. If the weather is threatening at Thoreau Spring, turn back, using the Hunt Trail/AT to descend. From Thoreau Spring to Baxter Peak, you are fully exposed to the elements.

To return to the start, retrace your steps on the same route or, use Abol Trail from Thoreau Springs.

First step, last step

At 5267 ft., Mt. Katahdin is 13 ft. shy of 1 mile high. Trail builders and thruhikers have remedied that: Baxter Peak is crowned by a massive cairn standing exactly 13 ft. high. The AT trail sign atop Katahdin is a favorite prop in hiker photos: "Here I am at the terminus of the AT." No doubt the best visits to Katahdin are those unclouded by memory or anticipation, visits to the wild mountaintop (or as close as Pamola will let you approach) made with a quiet and appreciative mind, seeing the mountain always as if for the first time, always on its own terms.

Hikers continuing north to Chimney Pond (beyond Baxter Peak) can avoid the summit by following Baxter Peak Cut-off Trail to meet Saddle Trail. Also at Thoreau Spring, Abol Trail intersects the AT. The steepest and most direct hiking trail on the mountain, Abol makes a good choice for ascending the mountain but is a more difficult descent than the AT. Abol's climb begins at Abol Campground, following the scar left by an 1816 landslide. The slide is said to have erased a set of massive cliffs on the south face. For more than a century, this was the most popular route up Katahdin.

Views of and from Katahdin

From The Table Land and Baxter Peak (5267 ft., 5.2 mi. from Katahdin Stream Campground and about 2150 mi. from Springer Mt. in Georgia), the expansive views show why Mt. Katahdin dominates the landscape around Baxter State Park. Visible to northbound hikers from a long distance, the mountain pulls them forward toward the end of the AT. Katahdin is equally familiar to mountain-gazing canoeists on the Allagash River north of Baxter Park and to potato farmers in southern Aroostook County. The mountain takes on a dramatically different appearance from each view. From the West Branch above Abol Deadwater, it is a brooding, flat-topped mesa, often capped in clouds by midmorning even on clear summer days. Downstream, from the great lakes of Pemadumcook and Ambajejus, the profile shows the jagged contours of the Knife Edge (see below). From the north, the mountain stares back with the most dramatic face of all. The Great Basin presents the hiker with an enormous cirque torn from the mountain by the retreating glaciers, with sheer cliffs of more than 2000 ft.

Because Katahdin rises like a monadnock from the lower-elevation surrounding forest, it offers views from the top in all directions. Perhaps the most striking sight is the myriad lakes and ponds, sparkling like cut glass under sunlight, brooding dark and cold under clouds, but always beautiful.

Pamola, the storm-god

Katahdin figures more prominently in Maine legend than any other mountain in the state. The Penobscot Abenaki word "Katahdin" means "highest land" or "preeminent mountain," and the mountain was thought to be home to the storm-god Pamola, a strange creature with the antlers of a moose, the legs and wings of an eagle, the body of a man. To the Abenaki, "Pamola" means "comes flying." Mountaintops were sacred places in the Penobscot religion, not places to go for recreation. Those who challenged the mountain god's domain might suffer bad consequences. In 1804, surveyor Charles Turner's Indian guides reported that they lived in fear of Pamola: they avoided the summit of the mountain.

The Knife Edge

Connecting Pamola (peak) and Chimney Peaks, the mile-long Knife Edge is one of the most celebrated alpine routes east of the Rockies. It was first crossed in 1847 by Marcus Keep, an itinerant preacher and Katahdin guide. At times the Knife Edge narrows to only a few feet, flanked by the precipitous cliffs (dropping 2000 ft.) of the North Basin and the only slightly more gradual drop of the eastern slope. Glaciers on both sides of the ridge (an *arête*) scoured away the mountain's sides, leaving back to back colossal cirques. *50 Hikes in the Maine Mountains* calls this "the most exciting nontechnical traverse in the East." Giant boulders here require careful walking and climbing—not much fun with a full backpack. Hikers are fully exposed, and this trail should never be crossed if the weather looks threatening. See "Alternate routes down the mountain," below.

Opening Katahdin's Wilderness

Until a few decades ago, Katahdin's isolation kept it from attracting the crowds drawn to comparable peaks in the White Mts. Well into the 19th century, only a handful of people—nearly all of them surveyors or geologists—had climbed Katahdin. When Henry David Thoreau climbed the mountain in 1846, the only access was by poling a bateaux up the West Branch of the Penobscot, then hiking the Abol Slide. In 1856 the Maine legislature voted to construct a road from the town of Stacyville to Katahdin and hired a party of surveyors, but the Civil War diverted the legislature's attention, and the project was abandoned. Also in 1856 the American painter Frederick Edwin Church visited Katahdin, sketching and painting the mountain repeatedly. His work took the image of Katahdin into the salons of New York and other cities, spreading the gospel: northern Maine embodied both the sublime and the picturesque that every good Transcendentalist saw in Nature. Church's work was art, but it was also the seed of a recreational marketing phenomenon—wilderness Maine—that carries on to our own time, as this book attests.

By the 1880s, the need for lumber accomplished what the legislature had failed to. Thus began of a network of logging roads extending around the mountain, including the Wassataquoik wilderness north of the mountain. Even then, nature conspired to protect the mountain's

Michael Warren

Daicey Pond with 5,267 ft. Mt. Katahdin on the horizon, Baxter State Park

remoteness: a great forest fire in 1903 put an end to logging around Katahdin.

At roughly the same time, the mountain received its first visit from a young, well-to-do Portland man named Percival Baxter. The son of a former governor and heir to a great merchant fortune, Baxter developed a vision of protecting the mountain in a park. (See "Percival Baxter and His Park.")

Thoreau himself had wondered what kind of men could inhabit terrain such as Katahdin. "I fear bodies," he wrote in his *Maine Woods*. "I tremble to meet them." Today, climbing the mountain has become a very different experience. On a busy summer day, it can seem that there is an endless stream of bodies hiking up the mountain. None of this, however, means that hikers in Baxter State Park have to give up their solitude. While to many visitors the park remains synonymous with Katahdin, there are 47 other mountain peaks in the park, 30 with an elevation over 3000 ft. There are 64 ponds, including Mattagammon Lake, the South Branch ponds, Russell, the Wassataquoiks, Kidney, and Daicey. On even the busiest days on Katahdin, a visitor can hike the surrounding peaks—OJ-I, Doubletop, Mt. Coe, or the Brothers—without seeing a single hiker. On Hunt Trail, hikers who take the spur trail up to The Owl will find views that are the equal of those from Katahdin, and will have the scenery to themselves.

International Appalachian Trail

You've done 2150 miles (Georgia to Maine) and still haven't had enough hiking? Not to worry. The International Appalachian Trail/Sentier International des Appalaches (IAT/SIA) will eventually carry you northward another 700 km./430 mi. (99 mi. in Maine) to the inspiring cliffs of Quebec's Gaspé Peninsula by joining Mt. Katahdin, Mt. Carelton, and Mt. Jacques Cartier, the highest points in Maine, New Brunswick, and Quebec. Trail's end will afford a memorable vista over the Gulf of St. Lawrence, bringing the AT finally to within sight of the sea. Work is underway but it may take some years to complete the IAT. As of 1998 there was more progress and enthusiasm on the Canadian side of the border than in the U.S., although the Appalachian Trail Conference had given its blessing to the project. The traditional thru-hike, Georgia to Maine, will not change its definition. Open sections of the IAT as of '98 included some miles in Mt. Carleton Provincial Park. To join the Maine chapter of IAT/SIA, write to 52 Center St., Portland, ME 04101 or call 207-774-2458.

— David Emblidge

Katahdin above treeline

The Katahdin massif offers some of the most impressive alpine habitat in New England. Its flora and fauna are similar to plants found from Labrador north to the Arctic Circle. A close eye may see sets of pine marten tracks moving through the rocks on lingering snow. Even on the most exposed parts of The Table Land, diapensia grows in small hard knots—if you step on one, it feels as hard as a rock under your feet—and in the more sheltered spots are rhodora, black crowberry, alpine azalea, and cloudberry, with its slightly minty translucent berries. Dwarf and alpine willows poke out in the lee of boulders, and meadowsweet mixes with dwarf alders. The plants are in a great struggle to hold on: mats of black spruce grow in places above treeline, but they reach only a few inches in height before the wind and ice shear them back.

Still, life triumphs. Among the birds you may see in the alpine region are pipits foraging among brown wisps of deer hair sedge, probably flushing quickly when you approach. At Thoreau Spring, you can try an experiment: Put a hand in the water and look at your watch. After 5 seconds you may feel the pulse in your fingertips. In 10 seconds your fingers may be numb and pounding. In 15 the pain may make you yank your hand from the pool. The water looks utterly limpid—surely nothing could live there. But look closer and you may find that the pool is peppered with snow fleas, hopping on the water's surface tension. A whole colony of creatures, alive and well in a hostile zone.

Alternate routes down the mountain

With no camping on top of Katahdin and no shelters near the summit, those who go up must come down in the same day. Baxter State Park advises careful planning for hikes crossing the mountain from one side to another. Camping is permitted *only* at official campgrounds and official backcountry campsites. No bivouacking, please. Some of the alternate routes down from Baxter Peak are among the steepest trails in the eastern U.S. This and the fact that the Knife Edge is treacherous for anyone carrying a full backpack suggests that only experienced hikers should attempt a *backpacking* traverse of Katahdin, and even these hikers face a daunting challenge to start early enough, position two cars, get back to the starting trailhead and hike up, over, and down the mountain to the ending trailhead—*all in one day.* Highly unlikely, except with perfect weather, a long summer day, and a very early start and late conclusion to the hike.

A better plan, if you want to traverse Katahdin, is to make camping reservations for night #1 at the campground or cabin nearest your start (Katahdin Stream Campground for the AT trailhead) and another reservation for night #2 at the end of your hike, where your second can be

Continued on p. 358

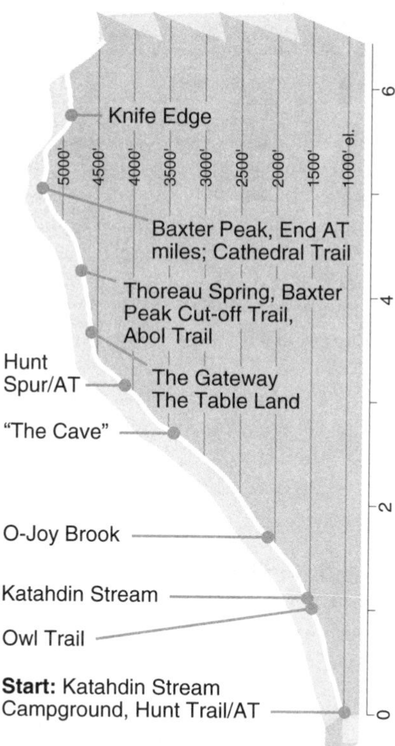

created using Maptech TopoScout ®

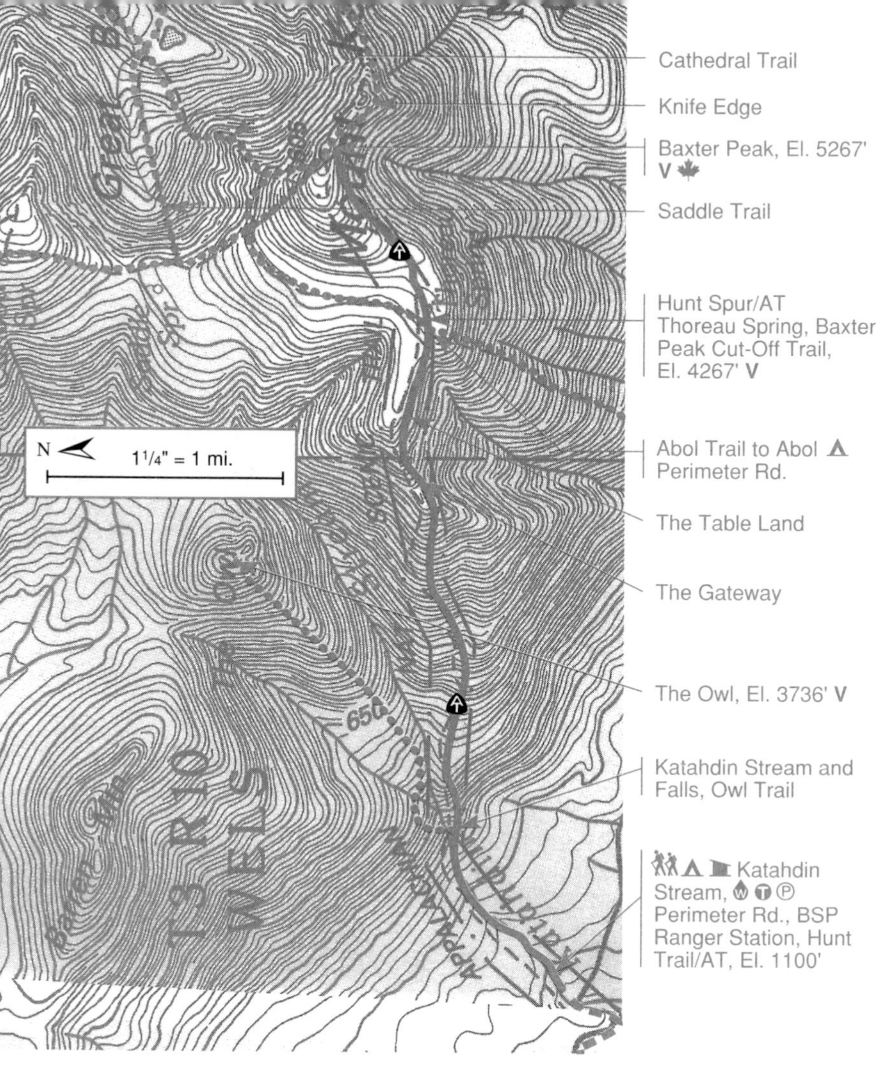
Cathedral Trail
Knife Edge
Baxter Peak, El. 5267'
V
Saddle Trail
Hunt Spur/AT
Thoreau Spring, Baxter
Peak Cut-Off Trail,
El. 4267' V
Abol Trail to Abol
Perimeter Rd.
N
1 1/4" = 1 mi.
The Table Land
The Gateway
The Owl, El. 3736' V
Katahdin Stream and
Falls, Owl Trail
Katahdin
Stream,
Perimeter Rd., BSP
Ranger Station, Hunt
Trail/AT, El. 1100'
T3 R10
WELS

parked. Begin planning in January and reserve no later than early spring.

The most detailed guide for such planning is *Katahdin: A Guide to Baxter State Park and Katahdin* by Stephen Clark (see Bibliography).

These caveats aside, for an alternative to a circuit hike on the Hunt Trail/AT (starting and ending at Katahdin Stream Campground), hikers may choose among the following Katahdin *traverse* routes. In all cases use a detailed topo map (MATC map #1, Stephen Clark's Katahdin topo, or Delorme Co.'s Katahdin topo; see Bibliography). Always inquire with park rangers about trail conditions before starting.

Distances are from Baxter Peak (add 5.2 mi. for hike up from Katahdin Stream Campground to Baxter Peak):

From Baxter Peak, cross **The Knife Edge** (1.1 mi., exposed; cross only in good weather) to Chimney Peak to Pamola (excellent views into South Basin and Chimney Pond), then go down Keep Ridge (exposed, windy) on Helon Taylor Trail (3.2 mi.) to Roaring Brook Campground. Distance: 4.3 mi. Reserve campsite/parking for night #2 at Roaring Brook Campground. It's a 20 mi. drive back to Katahdin Stream Campground.

From Baxter Peak, cross The Table Land and go down Saddle Trail to **Chimney Pond** (2.2 mi.) and down to Roaring Brook Campground (3.3 mi.). Distance: 5.5 mi. See above information about camping and parking.

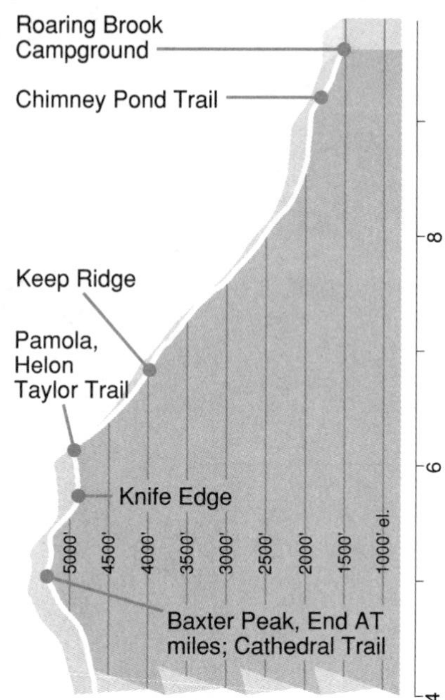

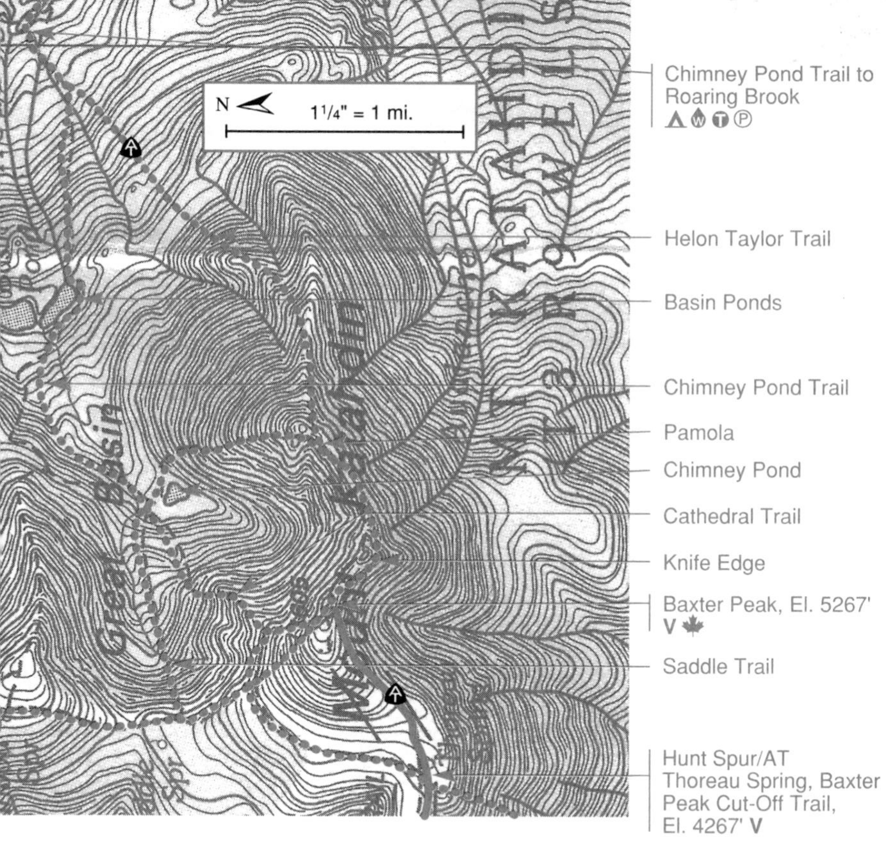

The north side of Katahdin offers longer routes, requiring more driving time to position cars. From Baxter Peak, cross The Table Land, then descend on Northwest Basin Trail down to Davis Pond Lean-to (permission to stay here requires staying the previous night at Chimney Pond or Russell Pond campsite, both by reservation only); from Davis Pond, continue to Russell Pond Campground (where your second car must be parked). Overall, a *rugged* 9.6 mi. from Baxter Peak. The shortest routes out from Russell Pond to the road are Russell Pond Trail or Tracy Trail, both about 7.0 mi. This is not a trip for the inexperienced.

Cathedral Trail: Baxter Park rangers do not recommend this trail as a descent (too steep and exposed). It's a tough, exhilarating climb, however. Call Baxter for advice on day hikes or overnight traverses of Katahdin using Cathedral Trail.

HIKE #38 Itinerary

Miles N	Circuit Hike	Elev. (ft/m)	Miles S
Total: 10.4 mi. round-trip			
5.2	**Baxter Peak,** extraordinary views; highest elev. in Maine; N terminus of AT. Junction of Table Land, Knife Edge, Cathedral trails (alternate routes down). **Return to Start** by same route (10.4 mi. total).	5267/1605	0.0
4.2	**Thoreau Spring** (unreliable); junctions with **Baxter Peak Cut-off Trail** (1.0 mi. N to Saddle Trail summit bypass) and **Abol Trail** (down to Perimeter Rd., parking, 2.0 mi. from Katahdin Stream Campground).	4627/1410	1.0
3.6	**The Gateway.** The Table Land (plateau) begins.		1.6
3.1	Leave Hunt Trail. Follow **Hunt Spur/AT** (begin at treeline near giant boulders) to Baxter Peak. Climb narrow ridge (0.2 mi.) to The Gateway.	3849/1173	1.2
2.7	**"The Cave."**		2.5
1.7	**O-Joy Brook.**		3.5
1.2	Spur trails (N side of AT) to **Katahdin Stream Falls.**	1510 (est.)/460	4.0
1.1	**Katahdin Stream,** bridge. Replenish water; supply scarce ahead.		4.1
1.0	**Owl Trail,** 2.2 mi. to The Owl peak (3736 ft.).		4.2
0.0	**Start & End: Katahdin Stream Campground.** Go N on **Hunt Trail/AT.** Campground: parking, ranger station, lean-tos, tentsites, water, toilets.	1100/335	5.2

Circuit Hike

Useful Information

LIST OF MAPS

US Geological Survey Topographical Maps

Note: USGS maps used in this series are scaled at 1:100,000 (1 cm = 1 km), but in this book we have converted the scale generally to 1"= 1 mi. or a close fraction thereof. The maps listed below are quadrangles covering the area surrounding the named city or other place; approximately 50 mi. E-W and 35 mi. N-S.

Millinocket
Moosehead Lake
Dover-Foxcroft
Skowhegan
Flagstaff Lake
Rumford
Groveton
Lewiston
Mount Washington
Lake Winnipesuakee
Rutland
Claremont

Appalachian Trail Conference: Maps

Note: ATC sells its own 4-color topo hiking maps and some maps published by regional hiking clubs. Together these maps cover the entire AT. Generally these maps are scaled at 1:62,500 (1"= 1 mi.). Maps referred to in this volume are listed here.

Maine AT Club Map 1, Katahdin to South End of Nahmakanta Lake
Maine AT Club Map 2, Nahmakanta Lake to West Branch of the Pleasant River
Maine AT Club Map 3, West Branch of the Pleasant River to Monson
Maine AT Club Map 4, Monson to the Kennebec River
Maine AT Club Map 5, Kennebec River to Maine Highway 27
Maine AT Club Map 6, Maine Highway 27 to Maine Highway 17
Maine AT Club Map 7, Maine Highway 17 to Maine-NH State Line
ATC New Hampshire and Vermont Map 1, Grafton Notch (Maine 26) to Androscoggin Valley (US 2)
ATC New Hampshire and Vermont Map 2, Androscoggin Valley (US 2) to Crawford Notch (US 302)
ATC New Hampshire and Vermont Map 3, Crawford Notch (US 302) to NH 25 (Glencliff)

Many ATC maps are double maps on one sheet (a map on each side); for example, ATC New Hampshire and Vermont Maps 1 & 2 appear on one sheet.

DEGREE OF DIFFICULTY

Definitions

Easy: gentle ups and downs, fairly smooth path, few obstacles

Moderate: elevation gain or loss of up to 1000 feet; narrower, rocky path; some obstacles (for example, brook crossings with no bridge)

Strenuous: elevation gain or loss of more than 1000 feet; steep ups and downs; difficult, challenging path; numerous obstacles; possibly unsuitable for young children or the infirm.

Hikes

EASY

#1, Velvet Rocks
#30, Buck Hill

EASY TO MODERATE

#37, Baxter Ponds

MODERATE

#2, Moose Mt. and Holts Ledge
#3, Smarts Mt. and Mt. Cube
#4, Wachipauka Pond and Webster Slide Mt.
#7, Lonesome Lake and the Basin
#15, Androscoggin River to Dream Lake
#23, Sabbath Day Pond
#27, Carry Ponds
#28, Pleasant Pond Mt.
#35, Central Lake Country
#36, Northern Lake Country

MODERATE TO STRENUOUS

#31, Monson Slate Hills
#34, Southern Lake Country

STRENUOUS

#5, Mt. Moosilauke
#8, Franconia Ridge
#9, The Pemigewasset Wilderness and Zealand Notch
#11, Mt. Washington and the Southern Presidential Range
#19, Old Speck
#20, Baldpate Mt.
#21, Wyman Mt. to Moody Mt.
#22 Old Blue, Elephant, and Bemis Mts.
#25, Crocker Mt.
#26, Little Bigelow
#29, Moxie Bald Mt.
#32, Barren-Chairback Range
#33, White Cap Mt.

VERY STRENUOUS

#6, Kinsman Mt.
#10, Webster Cliff Trail
#12, Northern Presidentials
#13, Wildcat Mt.
#14, Carter Moriah Range
#16, Dream Lake, Gentian Pond, and Mt. Success
#17, Carlo Col and Goose Eye Mt.
#18, Mahoosuc Notch
#24, Saddleback Mt. and Mt. Abraham
#38, Mt. Katahdin

SHELTERS AND CAMPSITES

See page 14 for general notes about shelters and campsites on or close to the AT. We list here the shelters (a.k.a. lean-tos) and named campsites (a.k.a. tentsites) described in this book. When shelters have officially designated tentsites, we indicate "campsite" below. Consult the narrative of each hike for information on unofficial tentsites at some shelters and on shelters that are farther off the AT.

Hike #	Shelter	Campsite	Lodge/Cabin	Name
1	x			Velvet Rocks
2	x			Moose Mt.
	x			Trapper John
3		x	x	Smarts Mt. Tentsite/ fire warden's cabin
	x			Hexacuba
5	x			Jeffers Brook
	x			Beaver Brook
6	x			Eliza Brook
		x		Kinsman Pond
	x			Lonesome Lake Hut
7		x		Lafayette Place Campground
			x	Lonesome Lake Hut
8		x		Lafayette Campground
			x	Greenleaf Hut
9		x		Garfield Ridge
			x	Galehead Hut
		x		Guyot
			x	Zealand Hut
		x		Ethan Pond
10			x	Mitzpah Spring Hut
		x		Nauman Tentsite

continues on next page

Hike #	Shelter	Campsite	Lodge/Cabin	Name
11			x	Mizpah Spring Hut
		x		Nauman Tentsite
			x	Lakes of the Clouds Hut
12	x			Hermit Lake
	x			The Perch
		x		Crag Camp
	x		x	Gray Knob
			x	The Log Cabin
		x		Valley Way Tentsite
			x	Madison Springs Hut
		x		Osgood Tentsite
		x		Pinkham Notch Camp
13			x	Carter Notch Hut
		x		Pinkham Notch Camp
14	x			Rattle River
		x		Imp
			x	AMC Carter Notch Hut
15		x		Trident Col Tentsite
16	x	x		Gentian Pond
17	x			Carlo Col
	x			Full Goose
18	x	x		Speck Pond
19	x	x		Speck Pond
20	x			Baldpate Lean-to
21	x			Hall Mt. Lean-to
22	x			Bemis Mt. Lean-to
23	x			Sabbath Day Pond Lean-to
		x		Little Swift River Pond
24	x			Piazza Rock Lean-to
	x			Poplar Ridge Lean-to
	x			Spaulding Mt. Lean-to
25		x		Crocker Cirque

Hike #	Shelter	Campsite	Lodge/Cabin	Name
26		x		Safford Notch
	x			Little Bigelow Lean-to
27	x			Pierce Pond Lean-to
	x	x		West Carry Pond
28	x			Pleasant Pond Lean-to
29	x	x		Bald Mt.
	x			Moxie Bald Lean-to
	x			Horseshoe Canyon Lean-to
31	x			Leeman Brook Lean-to
	x			Wilson Valley Lean-to
32	x			Long Pond Stream Lean-to
	x			Cloud Pond Lean-to
	x			Chairback Gap Lean-to
33	x			Newhall Lean-to
		x		Tappan
	x			Logan Brook Lean-to
	x			East Branch Lean-to
	x			Cooper Brook Falls Lean-to
34		x		Antlers
	x			Potaywadjo Spring Lean-to
		x		Nahmakanta Stream
35	x			Wadleigh Stream Lean-to
36	x			Rainbow Stream Lean-to
		x		Rainbow Spring
	x			Hurd Brook Lean-to
37		x		Abol Bridge Campground
	x	x	x	Daicey Pond Campground
	x	x		Katahdin Stream Campground
38	x	x	x	Daicey Pond Campground
	x	x		Katahdin Stream Campground

Day Hikes

Depending on your starting time, physical condition, ambition, and the weather, the following hikes can be manageable day hikes. Check "Duration" and "Distance" in the information block at the beginning of the hike before starting. Many of these hikes work well as sections of longer backpacking hikes, and some appear in the "Overnight Hikes" list as well.

- #1, Velvet Rocks
- #2, Moose Mt. and Holts Ledge
- #4, Wachipauka Pond and Webster Slide Mt
- #5, Mt. Moosilauke
- #6, Kinsman Mt.
- #8, Franconia Ridge
- #10, Webster Cliff Trail
- #13, Wildcat Mt.
- #14, Carter Moriah Range
- #15, Androscoggin River to Dream Lake
- #17, Carlo Col and Goose Eye Mt.
- #18, Mahoosuc Notch
- #19, Old Speck
- #20, Baldpate Mt.
- #21, Wyman Mt. to Moody Mt.
- #22, Old Blue, Elephant, and Bemis Mts.
- #23, Sabbath Day Pond
- #24, Saddleback Mt. and Mt. Abraham
- #25, Crocker Mt.
- #26, Little Bigelow
- #28, Pleasant Pond Mt.
- #29, Moxie Bald Mt.
- #30, Buck Hill
- #35, Central Lake Country
- #37, Baxter Ponds
- #38, Mt. Katahdin

Overnight Hikes

These are overnight backpacking trips. Segments of some overnight hikes can also be manageable day hikes.

- #3, Smarts Mt. and Mt. Cube
- #5, Mt. Moosilauke
- #6, Kinsman Mt.
- #8, Franconia Ridge
- #9, The Pemigewasset Wilderness and Zealand Notch
- #10, Webster Cliff Trail
- #11, Mt. Washington and the Southern Presidential Range
- #12, Northern Presidentials
- #14, Carter Moriah Range
- #15, Androscoggin River to Dream Lake
- #16, Dream Lake, Gentian Pond, and Mt. Success
- #17, Carlo Col and Goose Eye Mt.
- #18, Mahoosuc Notch
- #20, Baldpate Mt.
- #21, Wyman Mt. to Moody Mt.
- #22, Old Blue, Elephant, and Bemis Mts.
- #23, Sabbath Day Pond

#24, Saddleback Mt. and Mt. Abraham
#25, Crocker Mt.
#26, Little Bigelow
#27, Carry Ponds
#29, Moxie Bald Mt.
#31, Monson Slate Hills
#32, Barren-Chairback Range
#33, White Cap Mt.
#34, Southern Lake Country
#35, Central Lake Country
#36, Northern Lake Country
#37, Baxter Ponds

OTHER TRAIL SYSTEMS

New Hampshire

The trail network operated by the Appalachian Mountain Club and the U.S. Forest Service in the White Mountains is one of the most extensive in the U.S. A variety of guides, maps, and information about the trails of the White Mountains are available at the AMC's Pinkham Notch Visitor Center, in Pinkham Notch, and Crawford Depot, in Crawford. Write the AMC at 5 Joy St., Boston, MA 02108; 617-523-0636.

The Dartmouth Outing Club maintains another extensive trail system, as well as the AT south of Kinsman Notch in New Hampshire. Visit or write the DOC at Robinson Hall, Box 9, Hanover, NH 03755, or call 603-646-2428.

The Randolph Mountain Club maintains several trails on the north side of Mt. Washington. A map of the area and a guidebook, *Randolph Paths*, are available from the RMC, Randolph, NH 03570.

The Metacomet-Monadnock Trail runs 160 mi. from Mt. Monadnock, in southern New Hampshire, to the Hanging Hills in Meriden, CT. The *Metacomet-Monadnock Trail Guide* is available form the AMC. The 48-mi. Monadnock-Sunapee Greenway runs from Mt. Monadnock north to Mt. Sunapee and is jointly managed by the AMC and the Society for the Protection of New Hampshire Forests. The *Metacomet-Monadnock Trail Guide* is available from the AMC, and from the SPNHF, 54 Portsmouth St., Concord, NH 03301; 603-224-9945.

Maine

Given the remoteness of Maine's mountains and forests, there are few local or regional trail *systems*, other than the Appalachian Trail itself. There are extensive trail systems in Grafton Notch State Park and in the Bigelow Preserve. The most elaborate network of trails is in Baxter State Park. For Baxter information, see the sidebar in Hike #37. The Bibliography lists two titles about hiking in Maine. In the future, the International Appalachian Trail will extend into Canada (see sidebar in Hike #38).

ADDRESS/TELEPHONE

Major Organizations

American Hiking Society, 1422 Fenwick La., Silver Spring, MD 20910; 301-565-6704

Appalachian Mountain Club, 5 Joy St., Boston, MA 02108; 617-523-0636
For their hiking guides: Box 298, Gorham, NH 03581; 800-262-4455

Appalachian Trail Conference, P.O. Box 807, Harpers Ferry, WV 25425-0807; 304-535-6331

Northern New England Hiking and Trail Maintaining Clubs

AMC, Maine Chapter, P.O. Box 1534, Portland, ME 04104; 207-767-2880

Dartmouth Outing Club, Robinson Hall, P.O. Box 9, Hanover, NH 03755; 603-646-2428

Maine Appalachian Trail Club, P.O. Box 283, Augusta, ME 04332

New England Trail Conference, Forrest House, 33 Knollwood Dr., East Longmeadow, MA 01028

Randolph Mountain Club, Randolph, NH 03570

WEB SITES

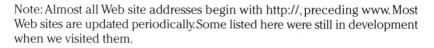

Note: Almost all Web site addresses begin with http://, preceding www. Most Web sites are updated periodically. Some listed here were still in development when we visited them.

Major Organizations

American Hiking Society **www.ahs.simplenet.com**

Dedicated to promoting hiking and to protecting and maintaining America's trails, AHS offers programs, publications (magazine), legislative updates, volunteer vacations, and links to many clubs and resources.

Appalachian Long Distance Hikers Association **www.connix.com/~aldha/**

Savvy advice, networking, forums, volunteering opportunities for long distance hikers.

Appalachian Mountain Club **www.outdoors.org/**

Granddaddy of the eastern hiking clubs, AMC covers not only the northeastern AT but activities and trail reports on many other trails. AMC Books, AMC Outdoors (magazine), adult and kids activities (trips and workshops year-round), conservation initiatives, hiking trip planning, AMC hut reservations, and much more.

Appalachian Trail Conference **www.atconf.org/**

This site is comprehensive, with many lists of and links to regional trail clubs. ATC's "Ultimate Trail Store" has arguably the biggest selection of AT books and maps anywhere (member discounts). Updated trail conditions, permit regulations, and other helpful subjects.

AT Regional Trail Maintaining Clubs

Many regional hiking clubs have their own Web sites, and most of them can be found easily by way of links from the Appalachian Trail Conference Web site listed above. Here are Web sites concerned with the AT in the states covered by this book.

AMC, Maine Chapter **www.gwi.net/amcmaine**

AMC, New Hampshire Chapter **www.amc-nh.org**

Dartmouth Outing Club **www.dartmouth.edu/student/doc/**

Maine Appalachian Trail Club **www.matc.org**

Other AT Web sites

Appalachian Trail Place **www.trailplace.com**

Center for Appalachian Trail Studies. Hosted by Dan "Wingfoot" Bruce, a thru-hiker who maintains a hostel by the trail in Virginia. A spin off from Wingfoot's *The Thru-Hiker's Handbook*. Dozens of searchable databases on AT subjects, many especially helpful to long distance hikers or those with natural history interests. "Mailing lists" of former and would-be thru-hikers, women hikers, teenage hikers, others. Chat rooms. Bibliography. One of the better sites.

The Appalachian Trail Home Page **www.fred.net/kathy/at.html**

The official-sounding name belies the fact that this is a personal home page built by a thru-hiker, Kathy Bilton. Nonetheless, it's one of the better general sites for miscellaneous information about the AT and for connecting with AT people. Links to AT maintaining clubs (also to the AT organizations and to other National Scenic trails), forums for AT issues discussions, advice from thru-hikers, and more.

America's Roof-High Point **www.inch.com/~dipper**

Click on the state map and up comes a home page for the state's highest mountain. This site covers Katahdin (ME) and Mt. Washington (NH). Mountain information is not extensive here however.

The Mountain Zone **www.mountainzone.com/hike/index.html**

Information and resources for mountain hikers, including a section on hiking the AT.

White Mountains Information

A Hiker's Guide to the White Mountains
www3.sympatico.ca/jeff.smith1

Mount Washington Observatory **www.mountwashington.org**

Mountwashington.com **www.mountwashington.com**

New England Hiking Group **www.ultranet.com/~kleonard/hiking**

Old Hutman's Association **www2.ultra.net/~oha**

Society for the Protection of New Hampshire Forests
www.spnhf.org

Views from the Top—Northeast
www.lexicomm.com/whites/index.html

White Mountains Info Server **www.cs.dartmouth.edu/whites**

Commercial and Government Web Sites

General

GORP **www.gorp.com**

Great Outdoor Recreation Pages. From various purveyors of travel and outdoor adventure information, services and supplies. The AT is one small part of this huge, diverse site. Rewarding for those with time to fill.

Magazines

Backpacker **www.bpbasecamp.com**

Extensive, well researched information about hiking worldwide. Many articles on either the AT specifically or on hiking skills and equipment useful to AT trekkers. "Trail Talk Forums" bring hikers together on-line. "Gearfinder" is a searchable database of hiking/camping products. The site is fueled by links to *Backpacker's* advertisers, a convenience or a distraction depending on your disposition.

Outside **outside.starwave.com**

Most of the magazine, on-line. Hiking per se and the AT specifically are only occasionally featured in *Outside* (whose travel beat is worldwide), but the treatment is usually in depth and colorful. Generally aimed at the under 40 crowd. Good articles on fitness and training. Excellent book reviews.

Bookstores

Adventurous Traveler Bookstore **www.AdventurousTraveler.com**

If you are anywhere near Burlington, Vermont, go to this store. Short of that, visit on-line. Over 4000 travel-related titles await you. Extensive AT and other North American hiking book inventory. Maps too. Paper catalogue available.

Amazon **www.amazon.com**

The leader in on-line bookstores. Search the database on the words "Appalachian Trail" for a long list of titles.

Barnes & Noble **www.barnesandnoble.com**

They're everywhere and they carry almost everything. If the local store doesn't have it, search on-line under the subject "Appalachian Trail."

Borders Books & Music **www.borders.com**

Although not as widespread as Barnes & Noble, Borders has an extensive Web site, offering their inventory of books, CDs, and videos on-line.

Maps

Maptech **www.maptech.com/topo**

Maptech has developed a set of high-quality USGS maps on CD-ROM that cover most of the United States. These TopoScout CDs, which are available for purchase, facilitate the close examination of the topography of almost any region in the country, including, of course, the Appalachian Trail. You can reach Maptech at 655 Portsmouth Ave., Greenland, NH 03840; 800-627-7236.

Delorme Map Co. **www.delorme.com**

Detailed atlases for the following AT states: North Carolina, Tennessee, Virginia, Maryland, Pennsylvania, New York, Vermont, New Hampshire, Maine. Delorme, Box 298, Yarmouth, ME 04096; 800-452-5931.

United States Geologic Survey (USGS)
www.usgs.gov/pubprod/products.html

A giant site for both the general public and scientists. This address is for ordering maps. A database facilitates finding the correct map, at the desired scale, for the area you're hiking. 800-USA-MAPS.

Perry-Castaneda Library Map Collection
www.lib.utexas.edu/Libs/PCL/Map-collection/Map-collection.html

An extensive collection of links to on-line map resources around the world. Including not only topographic maps but also historical and weather maps.

Weather

The Weather Underground **www.wunderground.com**

Up to the hour weather reports and forecasts for many cities in the U.S., including numerous smaller cities near the Appalachian Trail.

National Oceanic & Atmospheric Administration
weather.noaa.gov/weather

"NOAA" offers continuously updated weather reports and forecasts all across the country on dedicated radio channels (a lightweight weather-only radio is worth carrying on extended backpacking trips). At home, access NOAA's weather report site at the address above.

Bibliography

Hiking Guides

Appalachian Mountain Club. *AMC Guide to Mount Washington and the Presidential Range.* Appalachian Mountain Club Books, 1992.

Appalachian Mountain Club. *AMC White Mountain Guide.* Appalachian Mountain Club Books, 1992.

Chun Cloe. *50 Hikes in the Maine Mountains.* Backcountry Publications, 1997.

Cilley, Dean, and Susan Cilley, eds. *Appalachian Trail Guide to Maine.* Maine Appalachian Trail Club, 1996.

Clark, Stephen. *Katahdin: A Guide to Baxter State Park and Katahdin.* North Country Press, 1996.

Doan, Daniel. *50 Hikes in the White Mountains.* Backcountry Publications, 1997.

Doan, Daniel. *50 More Hikes in the White Mountains.* Backcountry Publications, 1997.

Hooke, David, ed. *Appalachian Trail Guide to New Hampshire-Vermont.* Appalachian Trail Conference, 1998.

Webster, Ed. *Rock Climbs in the White Mountains of New Hampshire.* Mountain Imagery, 1996.

Maps and Atlases

DeLorme. *Baxter/Katahdin.* DeLorme, 1996.

DeLorme. *Maine Atlas and Gazetteer.* DeLorme, 1998.

DeLorme. *New Hampshire Atlas and Gazetteer.* DeLorme, 1996.

GeoTrek. *TrailMaster.* GeoTrek Corporation, 1996. CD-ROM that includes trail maps and hiking information from AMC and GMC guidebooks. Covers New England states.

North Country Press. *Katahdin Color Map.* North Country Press, 1996. Companion map to Stephen Clark's Katahdin guidebook, referenced above.

U.S. Geological Survey, Topographic maps available in printed versions and on CD-ROM. (To contact USGS, see "Map Sources" under "Maps: Legends, Skills, Sources" in the Introduction and see also "Web sites" in "Useful Information.")

Field Guides and Natural History

Alden, Peter. *Peterson First Guide to Mammals of North America.* Houghton Mifflin, 1987.

Chew, V. Collins. *Underfoot: A Geologic Guide to the Appalachian Trail.* Appalachian Trail Conference, 1993.

Eastman, John. *The Book of Swamp and Bog: Trees, Shrubs, and Wildflowers of Eastern Freshwater Wetlands.* Stackpole Books, 1995.

Foster, Stephen and James A. Duke. *A Field Guide to Medicinal Plants, Eastern and Central North America.* Houghton Mifflin, 1990.

Frost, Ed and Roon. *Mountain Guide: The White Mountains of New Hampshire and Maine.* Glove Compartment Books, 1988.

Johnson, Charles W. *Bogs of the Northeast.* University Press of New England, 1985.

Kricher, John C., and Gordon Morrison. *Ecology of Eastern Forests.* Houghton Mifflin, 1988.

Lawrence, Eleanor, and Cecilia Fitzsimons. *An Instant Guide to Trees.* Longmeadow Press, 1991.

Marchand, Peter J. *North Woods: An Inside Look at the Nature of Forests in the Northeast.* Appalachian Mountain Club Books, 1987.

Newcomb, Lawrence. *Newcomb's Wildflower Guide.* Little, Brown, 1977.

Peterson, Lee Allen. *A Field Guide to Edible Wild Plants of Eastern and Central North America.* Houghton Mifflin, 1977.

Peterson, Roger Tory. *Peterson First Guide to Birds of North America.* Houghton Mifflin, 1986.

Peterson, Roger Tory. *Peterson First Guide to Wildflowers of Northeastern and North-central North America.* Houghton Mifflin, 1986.

Scudder, Brent E. *Scudder's White Mountain Viewing Guide* High Top Press, 1995.

Silverberg, Judith K. *New Hampshire Wildlife Viewing Guide.* Falcon Press, 1997.

Slack, Nancy G., and Allison W. Bell. *AMC Field Guide to the New England Alpine Summits.* Appalachian Mountain Club Books, 1995.

Steele, Frederic L. *At Timberline: A Nature Guide to the Mountains of the Northeast.* Appalachian Mountain Club Books, 1982.

Sutton, Ann, and Myron Sutton. *Eastern Forests* (Audubon Field Guide). Alfred A. Knopf, 1993.

Watts, May Theilgaard. *Tree Finder.* Nature Study Guild, 1986.

General Books: Appalachian Trail

Appalachian Trail Conference. *Walking the Appalachian Trail Step by Step,* Appalachian Trail Conference, 1993.

The Atlanta Journal and Constitution, The News and Observer of Raleigh, The Pittsburgh Post-Gazette, The Hartford Courant, The Maine Sunday Telegram. *Appalachian Adventure.* Longstreet Press, 1995.

Bolgiano, Chris. *The Appalachian Forest: A Search for Roots and Renewal.* Stackpole Books, 1998.

Bruce, Dan "Wingfoot." *The Thru-Hiker's Handbook.* Center for Appalachian Trail Studies, 1997. (Updated annually)

Bryson, Bill. *A Walk in the Woods: Rediscovering America on the Appalachian Trail.* Broadway Books, 1998.

Chase, Jim. *Backpacker Magazine's Guide to the Appalachian Trail.* Stackpole Books, 1989.

Chazin, Daniel D. *Appalachian Trail Data Book 1996.* Appalachian Trail Conference, 1997. (Updated annually)

Emblidge, David. *The Appalachian Trail Reader.* Oxford University Press, 1997.

Fisher, Ronald M. *The Appalachian Trail.* National Geographic Society, 1972.

Fisher, Ronald M. *Mountain Adventure: Exploring the Appalachian Trail.* National Geographic Society, 1988.

Logue, Victoria and Frank. *The Appalachian Trail Backpacker.* Menasha Ridge Press, 1994.

Marshall, Ian. *Story Line: Exploring the Literature of the Appalachian Trail.* University Press of Virginia, 1998.

O'Brien, Bill, ed. *Appalachian Trail Thru-Hikers' Companion.* Appalachian Trail Conference, 1997. (Updated annually)

Stier, Maggie and Ron McAdow. *Into the Mountains: Stories of New England's Most Celebrated Peaks.* Appalachian Mountain Club Books, 1995.

Whalen, Christopher. *The Appalachian Trail Workbook for Planning Thru-Hikes,* Appalachian Trail Conference, 1995.

Practical Advice: Hiking and Camping

Berger, Karen. *Hiking & Backpacking.* W.W. Norton, 1995.

Cary, Alice. *Parents' Guide to Hiking & Camping.* W.W. Norton, 1997.

Fletcher, Colin. *The Complete Walker.* Alfred A. Knopf, 1984.

Hampton, Bruce, and David Cole. *NOLS Soft Paths.* Stackpole Books, 1995.

McManners, Hugh. *The Backpacker's Handbook.* Dorling Kindersley, 1995.

Meyer, Kathleen. *How to Shit in the Woods: An Environmentally Sound Approach to a Lost Art.* Ten Speed Press, 1994.

Waterman, Laura And Guy. *Backwoods Ethics: Environmental Issues for Hikers and Campers.* The Countryman Press, 1993.

Waterman, Laura And Guy. *Wilderness Ethics: Preserving the Spirit of Wildness.* The Countryman Press, 1993.

Viehman, John, ed. *Trailside's Hints & Tips for Outdoor Adventures.* Rodale Press, 1993.

Wood, Robert S. *The 2 Oz. Backpacker.* Ten Speed Press, 1982.

Background Reading

Baxter, Percival. *Greatest Mountain: Katahdin's Wilderness.* Scrimshaw Press, 1972.

Crawford, Lucy *Lucy Crawford's History of the White Mountains.* Appalachian Mountain Club Books, 1978.

Dickerman, Mike. *Along the Beaten Path, Collected Writings from a*

White Mountain Tramper. White Mountain Publishing, 1995.

Doan, Daniel. *Our Last Backpack: A Memoir.* Backcountry Publications, 1993.

Goodman, David. *Classic Backcountry Skiing: A Guide to the Best Ski Tours in New England* Appalachian Mountain Club Books, 1989.

Mudge, John T.B. *The White Mountains: Names, Places & Legends.* Durand Press, 1995.

Muse, Vance. *The Smithsonian Guides to Historic America, Vol. 4: Northern New England.* Stewart, Tabori & Chang, 1998.

Ramsey, Floyd W. *Shrouded Memories: True Stories from the White Mountains of New Hampshire.* Floyd W. Ramsey, 1996.

Schlesinger, Arthur M., Jr., ed. *The Almanac of American History.* Perigee Books, 1983.

Waterman, Laura and Guy. *Forest and Crag: A History of Hiking, Trail Blazing, and Adventure in the Northeast Mountains.* Appalachian Mountain Club Books, 1989.

Index

Page numbers in *italics* refer to topographic maps and itineraries.

HIKING NOTES

ABOUT THE AUTHORS

MICHAEL KODAS wrote the New Hampshire hikes and the Mahoosucs in Maine. He has hiked over 700 AT miles in 9 states. Photojournalist at the *Hartford Courant* (Connecticut), in 1995 Kodas participated in *Appalachian Adventure,* a 5-newspaper relay hike of the entire AT. He has walked in the western U.S., the Pyrenees, and New Zealand, and has circumnavigated Long Island Sound by kayak.

ANDREW WEEGAR is a freelance writer, specializing in natural history and hiking. He lives in North Bridgton, Maine.

GLENN SCHERER wrote the 100 Mile Wilderness hikes in Maine. A Vermont Long Trail thru hiker, he has hiked the AT in Maryland, New Jersey, and New York, and is co-author of *Hikes in the Mid-Atlantic States* in this series. Scherer wrote *Nature Walks in New Jersey* and lives in Highland Lakes, New Jersey.

MARK CONDON, is an outdoor recreation writer who has hiked sections of the AT in New Hampshire, Vermont, and Maine; he has also hiked extensively in the Rockies and the Alps. Condon is editor of *Habitat,* Maine Audubon's magazine. He lives in Bangor, Maine.